CONSERVATIVE
JUDAISM
AND
JEWISH LAW

STUDIES IN
CONSERVATIVE JEWISH THOUGHT

VOLUME I

CONSERVATIVE JUDAISM AND JEWISH LAW

Edited by
SEYMOUR SIEGEL

with
ELLIOT GERTEL

THE RABBINICAL ASSEMBLY
NEW YORK
1977

Library of Congress Cataloging in Publication Data
Main entry under title:

Conservative Judaism and Jewish law.

(Studies in Conservative Jewish thought; v. 1)
Includes index.
1. Conservative Judaism—Addresses, essays, lectures.
2. Jewish law—Philosophy—Addresses, essays, lectures.
3. Responsa—1800-   I. Siegel, Seymour. II. Series.
BM197.5.C67   296.8'342   77-23968
ISBN 0-87068-428-0

DISTRIBUTED BY KTAV PUBLISHING HOUSE, INC.
NEW YORK, NEW YORK 10013

MANUFACTURED IN THE UNITED STATES OF AMERICA

Dedicated to the memory of my father, David ז״ל

TABLE OF CONTENTS

Preface

This volume is the first in a series of readers in Conservative Judaism. A precursor of this book was the anthology *Tradition and Change*, edited by Mordecai Waxman (Burning Bush Press–United Synagogue Book Service). It is hoped that this book will be followed by readers in the Conservative approach to theology, ethics, the Jewish family, ethics and society, and messianism.

The contents of this reader were selected from many journals and books. First, we sifted through the major journals of the Rabbinical Assembly and the Jewish Theological Seminary of America: *Conservative Judaism* and the *Proceedings of the Rabbinical Assembly of America*. When an essay that originally appeared in journal form was later published in a book, we refer to both sources. In the case of the selection from the writings of Professor Abraham J. Heschel, we decided to extract his original article from the *Central Conference of American Rabbis Annual* rather than from his book, *Man's Quest for God*.

We have taken the liberty of deleting all Hebrew characters from the original texts, replacing them with transliterations and appropriate translations and explanations either in the text or in the glossary. When necessary we have deleted complex or specialized allusions from the text, or at least moved them to the footnotes. In some instances we have incorporated into the text stylistic and other corrections sent us by the authors themselves. Certain overly technical footnotes have been deleted.

The guiding principle of our selection was to make it possible for any literate and concerned Jew to gain an appreciation of the diverse and fruitful approaches to Jewish law within Conservative Judaism. Though there are differences of approach and nuance, all the approaches are rooted in the notion expressed by Solomon Schechter that Jewish Law expresses the "collective conscience" of "Catholic Israel." This "conscience" is formed by tradition and yet grows within the world. We hope that the various interpretations expressed in this reader will inspire Jews to begin incorporating more of the regimen of Jewish law into their lives, in order to sanctify existence with the poetry and discipline of a vital heritage.

In order to accentuate the emphases of the selections chosen, each reading has been provided with an introduction calling attention to its main points. The length of the introduction is not necessarily related to the profundity of the ideas expressed in the selection. The sources of each selection, as well as biographical data on the contributors, are provided at the back of this volume. We have not been able to incorporate all the many fine writings produced by thinkers in the Conservative movement. We hope that in the coming volumes of this series we will have an opportunity to bring to the public the thoughts of the leaders of the Conservative movement which have not been included here.

It is our hope that the current volume will introduce the reader to the wealth of ideas that Conservative Judaism has introduced into the contemporary search for a sense of commandment, of the authority of the *halachah*, and a creative encounter with tradition.

It is is our hope also that this text will be especially useful for classes in Judaism as well as adult education classes in synagogues and Jewish centers.

E.G.

Acknowledgments

We are grateful to the publishers and authors listed below for having granted us permission to print excerpts from the following works:

Students, Scholars and Saints, by Louis Ginzberg. Copyright © 1938. Published by The Jewish Publication Society of America. Reprinted by permission of the publisher.

The Future of the American Jew, by Mordecai M. Kaplan. Copyright © 1948. Published by MacMillan Publishing Co. Reprinted by permission of the author.

Conservative Judaism VI:4, pp. 8–26, "Laws as Standards—The Way of Takkanot." Copyright © 1950 by the Rabbinical Assembly. Reprinted by permission.

Proceedings of the Rabbinical Assembly 41–44:64–93, "Authority in Jewish Law." Copyright © 1944 by the Rabbinical Assembly.

Proceedings of the Rabbinical Assembly 39:115–153, "The Shulhan Aruk Today." Copyright © 1939 by the Rabbinical Assembly.

We Have Reason to Believe, by Louis Jacobs. Copyright © 1957. Published by Vallentine, Mitchell and Co., Ltd. Reprinted by permission of the publisher.

Conservative Judaism XXV:3, pp. 33–40, "Ethics and the Halakhah." Copyright © 1971 by the Rabbinical Assembly.

The Yearbook of the Central Conference of American Rabbis, Volume LXIII, pp. 386–409, "Toward an Understanding of Halachah." Copyright © 1953. Published by the Central Conference of American Rabbis. Reprinted by permission of the publisher.

The Meaning of Jewish Law in Conservative Judaism: An Overview and Summary

SEYMOUR SIEGEL

The observance of Jewish law has been the main aim of the Conservative movement since its very beginnings. When Zecharias Frankel founded the Positive-Historical school and when Solomon Schechter proposed the idea of Catholic Israel, the main goal was to defend the importance of *halachah,* Jewish law, against the attacks of the reformers. At the same time, Conservative Judaism recognized that it was not sufficient to refer to the paragraphs of the codified law included in the *Shulchan Aruch.* New times required new ways of observing Jewish law. Many practices which in the course of the centuries had become part of Judaism, attached to the core of Jewish observance, now required modification and change. Therefore, Conservative Judaism had two aims, both of which are discerned in the writings and thought about *halachah* in the literature of the movement: to validate and promote the observance of Jewish law, and to make modification and change possible.

The aims of conservation and progress are part of all living legal systems. Justice Benjamin Cardozo expressed it simply and clearly: "Rest and motion, unrelieved and unchecked, are equally destructive." Professor Louis Finkelstein, one of the great personalities in the history of Conservative Judaism, wrote:

> The truth is that we need law and discipline in life. But this law and discipline must take continual cognizance of the goals they are intended to serve. It is only in bureaucracies, in prisons, and backward schools, that discipline is sometimes regarded as an end in itself. It is one of the great

achievements of Jewish law that it provides in itself the machinery for its interpretations, its expansions, and its applications to changing conditions. The [Jewish Theological] Seminary has accepted the fundamental principle that Jewish law must be preserved but that it is subject to interpretations by those who have mastered it. To effect this plan is not to break with traditional Judaism, but to return to it.

It is the aim of this volume to present the ideologies which have been developed in the Conservative movement to support the twin goals of preservation and change in Jewish law.

The preservative ideology of Conservative Judaism is built on five principles: covenantal theology, the nature of man as a "theological being," a view of the process of Jewish history, a conception of the Jewish people as the bearer of revelation, and an understanding of the nature of change in societies.

I. COVENANTAL THEOLOGY

All modern theologies begin with an analysis of the human condition. Rather than start with an idea of God, we attempt to analyze what it means to be a human being. Theology is an answer to profound and basic human questions. Some of the basic questions asked by Jews aware of their Jewishness are: What is the meaning of being a Jew? What is the essence of Jewish existence? What accounts for the astonishing history of the Jew? Even in modern times, and even among Jews who avowedly deny any divine dimension in life, the questions are still asked. "I have yet to find a Jew," writes Will Herberg, "who does not in some manner or form exhibit this profound sense of difference and special vocation." This "sense of difference" and feeling of a "special vocation" is a reflection of the most basic Jewish perception about Jewishness: that a Jew is a member of a special people; for the religionist, a people of God. This consciousness of "specialness," translated into theological and traditional terms, means that the Jewish people is a covenanted people—a community bound by an agreement, made long ago. This agreement puts upon the Jew the burden and the privilege of being the representative of what is good and precious in human life. Again translated into theological terms, it means that the people of Israel is a "kingdom of priests" and a "holy people." This sense of covenant implies that there is a special law for Jewish existence. Franz Rosenzweig, the great German-Jewish thinker, likened the situation to that of a marriage. First, there is chosenness: one person is chosen from among all the others to be the object of love; then there is a covenant, an agreement, a marriage. Then there is a law governing the relationship between the two partners. For the Jew has been chosen; he has been covenanted; and therefore he observes the law which expresses his relationship to the other partner in the covenant. The Jew lives in the presense of Transcendant Being, and this consciousness is expressed on the level of doing by the observance of the Law. By instituting laws of justice and equity, by regulating his daily life along the contours of Jewish observance, by instituting signs and rituals, *mitzvot* and ordinances which remind the Jew of his holy status, of their sacred history, and their special destiny, the people of Israel expresses its unique character. Covenantal theology, which makes sense of Jewish existence, implies the obligation to observe Jewish law—for there can be no choosing without Law, as there can be no love without some concrete expression.

II. THE NATURE OF MAN

Jewish Law not only expresses the unique character of the Jewish people, it is also an important ingredient of human existence. The fulfillment of the *halachah* makes possible the full development and expression of our humanness. Professor Abraham J. Heschel has eloquently described the human need which Jewish observance expresses:

> Sacred deeds are designed to make living compatible with our sense of the Ineffable. The *mitzvot* are forms of expressing in deed the appreciation of the Ineffable. Religion without *mitzvot* is an experience without the power of expression, a sense of mystery without the power of sanctity, a question without an answer. Without Torah (Jewish observance) we have only deeds that dream of God.

Mitzvot, as Professor Finkelstein expresses it, are propositions in action. They are expressions of our innermost commitments and beliefs. Jewish observance is a means by which we state, more eloquently than in words, what we believe about ourselves and our Jewishness.

Jewish observance not only expresses, it also invokes. It is not only the expression of our feeling for God's presence, it also can raise our consciousness so that we know we are in the presence of the Divine. "As for me," says the psalmist, "I shall behold Thy face in righteous-

ness." Through the practice of righteousness, we are granted the privilege of the sense of God's Presence. Again, in Heschel's striking
phrase, Jewish observance is a "leap of action" through which we are
brought face to face with our Partner in the covenant.

III. THE PROCESS OF JEWISH HISTORY

The hallmark of the modern attitude is a sense of history. This sense of
history means that we realize that all institutions, including religious
institutions, have a *history*. This does not mean merely that they have
endured through time. It means also that the forces of history have
shaped our institutions, modified them and given birth to them. No human institution, including religion, is the same now as it was when it
began. This new outlook implied a certain relativism in the understanding of the structures of society. This, of course, was a blow to the
conceptions which had been the foundation of traditional Judaism.
The implication of historicism is that whatever history has produced,
history can now eliminate. The process of historical change is the only
thing that does not change. It was in this spirit that the early reformers,
especially Geiger and Holdheim, were able to propose a radical over-
haul of Jewish traditions and ideas. Since we have entered a new period of history, they argued, we can now do what our forefathers did—
reform the Judaism we have inherited in order to make it conform to
the new age.

Zecharias Frankel agreed that Jewish faith and practice were the result of history. This, the new *Wissenschaft* was proving every day.
However, Frankel parted company with the reformers on a crucial
point: what should be our attitude toward that which history had bequeathed to us? Were the reformers right in saying that since history
had given, history could now take away? Frankel said, No!

He argued that the contrary was indeed true. Since it was *Jewish* history that had created the institutions we have inherited, it was normative for Jews to adhere to their heritage. Jewish history itself is the
bearer of revelation. He argued: *"Es liegt in dem allgemeinen Bewus-
stein einer Religions gemeinde auch eine Offenbarung, die solange sie
lebensvoll"* ("There inheres in the general consciousness of a religious
community also a Revelation, as long as it is living"). That is why we
cannot abandon the Hebrew language, the structure of the *mitzvot*, and
the love and yearning for Zion. Professor Louis Ginzberg, in a selection included in this volume, summarizes Frankel's view:

Neither for Frankel nor for Graetz was Law identical with the Bible; but in the course of time, whether for weal or for woe, in the development of Jewish history, the former became the specifically Jewish expression of religiousness. The law is active religiousness, and in active religion must lie what is specifically Jewish. One may, for instance, conceive of the origin of the idea of Sabbath rest as the professor of Protestant theology at a German university would conceive it, and yet minutely observe the smallest detail of Sabbath observances . . . For an adherent of this school, the sanctity of the Sabbath reposes not upon the fact that it was proclaimed on Sinai, but on the fact that the Sabbath idea found for thousands of years its expression in Jewish souls.

The origins of the law are really not that crucial, in this view. What is crucial is that the laws have sunk into the consciousness of the Jew and constitute the Jewish way of expressing religiousness. The processes of history have created the values which we hold dear. It is not the *process* itself that is crucial, as it is in the thought of Geiger—but what the process has produced. One of the chief products of Jewish history is the observance of the *mitzvot*. One cannot be religious in a Jewish way without acting in the Jewish way—that is, through the observance of the *halachah*.

IV. THE JEWISH PEOPLE AS BEARER OF REVELATION

No other movement in Judaism has put as much emphasis on the Jewish people as the bearer of revelation as has the Conservative movement. Zecharias Frankel cited the following passage from the Talmud as his watchword:

R. Yochanan said: Our Rabbis investigated the observance of the prohibition against the use of gentile oil, and they found that the observance of the prohibition had not spread amongst the majority of Israel, and our Rabbis relied on the words of R. Shimon b. Gamaliel and on the words of R. Eleazar b. Zadok, who were wont to say, "We do not institute a prohibition on the community unless it is possible for the majority of the community to abide by it."

Solomon Schechter gave the idea of the centrality of the consciousness of the Jewish people in his celebrated statement about the locus of authority in Judaism: (that authority is in) "some living body [which] by reason of its being in touch with the ideal aspirations and the religious needs of the age, is best able to determine the nature of the Secondary meaning (referring to the normative interpretation of Scripture). This living body, however, is not represented by any section of the nation, or any corporate priesthood or rabbinate, but by the collective conscience of Catholic Israel as embodied in the Universal Synagogue."

Rabbi Joshua b. Levi says: "Whenever the *Bet Din* is in doubt as to the interpretation of a law, and you do not know how to comply with it, observe what the people do" (*Yer. Peah* 7:5, cf. *Berachot* 45a). Catholic Israel is the locus of authority, and Catholic Israel has adopted the *halachah* as its mode of religious expression— not its exclusive mode, but its most crucial mode.

The idea of Catholic Israel has been widely criticized as being applicable only in times past, when the preponderant majority of Jews observed the *halachah*. Can it still be utilized in our own day?

Robert Gordis, in an article appearing in this collection, attempted an interesting redefinition of the doctrine of Catholic Israel.

> Catholic Israel is the body of men and women within the Jewish people who accept the authority of Jewish law and are concerned with Jewish observance as a genuine idea. The character of their observance may be rigorous and extend to minutiae, or it may include modifications in detail. Catholic Israel embraces all those, too, who observe Jewish law in general, though they may violate one or another segment, and who are sensitive to the problem of their non-observance because they wish to respect the authority of Jewish law.

Catholic Israel, theologically speaking, is the refractor of the voice of God in matters of Jewish law, because Israel is God's people. When the Jewish community speaks authentically out of its own integrity, it is the medium through which the divine intention for the people is expressed. The idea of Catholic Israel is basic to any understanding of the approach of Conservative Judaism to Jewish Law. It is the collective conscience which endows the Law with sanctity. It is the collective conscience which gives the ultimate judgment about how the law should be changed and modified.

V. A VIEW OF SOCIAL CHANGE

Finally, the preservative aspect of Conservative Judaism is based on a philosophy of social change. Granted that new times require new strategies, new forms, and new visions, change should be gradual and organic—not revolutionary. This view resembles the views of the conservative thinkers like Edmund Burke. Burke believed that tradition was the testing ground for values and habits of doing things.

"Providence," wrote Burke, "acting through the medium of trial and error, has developed hoary habit for some important purpose." It is the tradition of a society which holds it together and which keeps in check the anarchic inclinations often part of the makeup of individuals and groups within society. To do violence to these traditions is to invite disaster, tyranny, and unhappiness.

There must be change, but in the words of Benjamin Disraeli,

> In a progressive society change is constant, and the great question is not whether you should resist change which is inevitable, but whether that change should be carried out in deference to the manners, customs, and the laws and traditions of the people, and not in deference to abstract principles.

Legal systems do change. But they should not change in violent jumps. They change slowly, deliberately, in deference to the customs of the people and in a slow and deliberate manner so as not to destroy the continuity of tradition and the fabric of the community.

These five principles, taken together, establish the validity of the traditional halachic system. They serve as the source of the obligation of Jewish observance. Using these principles and their corollaries, Conservative Judaism strove to preserve the observance of Jewish law in the face of the tremendous pressures of modern life and thought.

II

The second part of the program of Conservative Judaism was to legitimate changes from the accepted practice. The legitimation of modification was established by means of the following principles: a nonfundamentalist view of revelation; discernment of the needs of the time; a recognition of historical development; the need for perspective; the demands of the aggadic and ethical aspects of Judaism; and the acceptance of pluralism in the religious community.

I. DOCTRINE OF REVELATION

The basic question concerning Jewish law involves a doctrine of Revelation. All forms of Judaism accept the notion of God's communicating with man in general and the Jewish people in particular. Most Orthodox thinkers argue that the traditional doctrine of *Torah MiSinai* (the Torah coming from Sinai) posits that God literally commanded everything written in the Torah. This, in their view, makes Jewish law immutable, and change can take place only within the most narrow limits. The Reform thinkers believed that the moral and ethical demands of Judaism were revealed, and that the ritual laws (which means most of the corpus of Jewish law) were the products of human legislation, reflecting various social conditions of the time. This means that *halachah* is not binding today. In recent times, Conservative Judaism has tried to find a third way in which revelation could be taken seriously but not literally. Most thinkers have relied on the thinking of Franz Rosenzweig. Rosenzweig argued that revelation is not the transmittal of concrete directives. Revelation means that man and God have met each other. Revelation means the self-uncovering of the Divine in relation to man. It is the transmission to man of God's love and concern. It is a miracle that God does reveal Himself to man. God could have hidden behind Creation and its iron laws. God is partially hidden so as to make man's acceptance of God the result of free will and not compulsion. But out of the hiding comes the Living God. When God reveals His love and concern, we are called upon to respond with love toward Him and our fellowman. We love with the love with which we are loved. This revelation happens to individuals. It happened to the whole people of Israel, who perceived in their history and destiny the hand of the Living God. Scripture and its interpretation in the rabbinic writings are not *literally* revelation. They are the human recordings of the experience of revelation. Therefore, Scripture is both divine and human. The words contain the divine initiative and the human response to it. In each word the two—the divine and the human—are joined and cannot be separated. Therefore, Scripture and Talmud are infinitely precious—for through them the Divine is revealed. Scripture and Talmud contain the human response—and therefore are not infallible.

As a result of this encounter with the divine, many laws and customs were instituted as expressions of the demands of God as perceived by those who experienced God. Old customs that the Israelites had always observed were infused with new meanings. The Bible is not only the result of revelation. It is also the vehicle of revelation, for by imaginatively confronting the record, we have the chance to come into contact with the Being behind the text. This means that in differing circumstances, new demands will be discerned, and old ones changed. This is the essence of *midrash*, the attempt to relive the revelation and to realize the implications of this event for the here-and-now. The history of Judaism is a history of the interpretation of revelation. In Heschel's striking sentence: "Judaism is a minimum of revelation and a maximum of interpretation." This interpretation is what is included in *midrash* and what is included in whatever a diligent student in the future will discover. The crucible out of which Jewish law is created is the encounter with the record of revelation, by the people of revelation, who attempt ever anew to hear God's voice through the text and attempt to decide what they must do now. This, of course, means that there will be change and modification. It is true, for example, that God countenanced slavery, as is evident in Scripture, when there was no possibility of abolishing the institution. The aim of Jewish law was to humanize the institution until it could be abolished. Though God may have wanted slavery in antiquity, He certainly does not want it now. It is true that God once wanted the law of an "eye for an eye" to be applied literally. He certainly does not want it now. It is possible that God once wanted women to limit themselves to their roles as princesses whose grandeur consisted of being concealed. He probably does not want that now. Total subjectivity is avoided because of the presence of the community and because of the character of Catholic Israel. The concrete laws are not to be viewed as if they were Platonic Ideas eternally residing in the world of Forms. They are dynamic concepts—subject to the dynamic voice of God, which encounters us anew at all times.

II. THE NEEDS OF THE TIME

The need for change in Jewish law is the result of a profound contact with the needs of the Jews in this particular time and place. This contact, born out of a shared destiny and sensitivity to the best that is within our time and place, frequently results in a need to modify existing norms. When the Conservative movement came into being, there was a need to change the synagogue service so that the people coming into the House of God could be moved by the worship and understand it.

The customary way of doing things, especially in the ritual of the synagogue, with its mixture of law and customs, had to be modified so that the whole could stand. The synagogue would have to accommodate families as whole units, not segregate women in special sections or in balconies; the service had to introduce some prayers in the vernacular; the rabbis had to be educated enough to deliver sermons reflecting secular training; and the prayerbook would have to be shortened to remove redundant and un-understandable poems and *piyyutim*. These voices demanding change, so resonant in the Conservative movement, came not out of systematic considerations—but because there was a discernment of the desperate needs of the time. Sometimes these changes were not really needed. It is time to reexamine some of the changes that were instituted. But when one realizes the situation, the desire for change is very demanding.

III. THE HISTORICAL APPROACH

As was stated previously, Conservative Judaism recognizes that which is the basis of scholarship: the historical nature of Jewish tradition. In the previous section we showed that this historical sense validated Jewish observance. However, it is also evident that a historical sense validates necessary change. Though the Laws are the reflection of the divine will, they are influenced by economic, scientific, political, and even textual influences. Even as reluctant a law-changer as the late Professor Boaz Cohen, in the selection included in this volume, writes:

> We conceive of Jewish law as a body of practices and regulations that have undergone a long development since the time of Moses . . . . when we are asked what is the Jewish law on this or that point, we do not answer fully by referring to this or that code, commentary, or *responsum* for no single code is the complete expression of the law. The origin, the transformations of the rule, its archaic features, discarded elements, temporary expedients, idealistic aspirations, as well as its present interpretations are all part of the majestic structure.

With this recognition of the historical character of Jewish law, we find the methodology to affect change today. Thus, for example, if it could be shown that the separation of the sexes in houses of worship was the result of the desire to preserve decorum in the Temple and that this decorum was disturbed when the two sexes were in the place without a separation, it is, then, perfectly obvious that today's society, where the relationships of men and women in society are so much different, and where the family unit is so important, it is a good thing to have mixed seating rather than segregated seating. Of course, it is necessary to avoid the "genetic fallacy," which sees institutions and concepts only as they originated and not in their historical development. However, the historical sense does legitimate changes when such changes are necessary.

IV. THE NEED FOR PERSPECTIVE

One of the basic principles of the Conservative interpretation of Jewish law is the attempt to take into consideration the whole corpus of Jewish law, not just one summary of it—such as the *Shulchan Aruch*. If necessary, it is possible to rely on precedents which are found in other codes or which appear in the Talmud and were not made normative in the later compilations of Jewish law. Professor Boaz Cohen, in the chapter from his writings appearing in this volume, cites the following example of the application of this principle. In the procedure for the conversion of a female proselyte, the author of the *Shulchan Aruch* (*Yoreh Deah*, 268:2) reguires the *tevilah* to take place in the presence of three men. "While the regulation can be traced to Maimonides' code, the *Mishnah Torah*, it is not required by the Talmud where the requirement of witnesses was waived for reasons of delicacy. Apparently Maimonides incorporated the stricter rule from some early source now lost . . . there should be no compunction in reverting to the more ancient practice customary in talmudic times."

V. AGGADAH AND ETHICS

Most important in Conservative Judaism's view of the interpretation of Jewish law is the introduction of the aggadic and ethical component. Since the Law is the expression of the covenant, and a basic aim of the covenantal obligation is the practice of justice and compassion, we cannot sustain the authority of any norm which results in unethical outcomes. When the *halachah* cannot adequately express the *aggadah*, it must be modified. Thus we do not practice the exclusion of *mamzerim* (children born of an incestuous or adulterous relationship) because it is an unfair law. We do not defend the laws of slavery because they are not up to our ethical standards; we accept the marriage of a divorcee and a *kohen* because we feel that the notion of a divorcee being somehow flawed and therefore not worthy of a *kohen* does not square with our notions of what is right and wrong. This does not mean that we are ethically more sensitive than our forebearers. It means that in our situation, certain ethical considerations are present that may not have been present in ancient times. These ethical perceptions come out of our tradition and are applied to the tradition as a whole. Of course, there will be differences of opinion as to the ethical thing to do, and therefore different conceptions about outcomes, but the principle remains.

VI. RELIGIOUS PLURALISM

Because of the above considerations, there will be a variety of practice in the community. Since perceptions of what is needed, what is ethical, etc., will differ, there will be differences in decisions made in different places by different authorities. Thus, if women are not to be given *aliyot* because to do so might offend the congregation (*kevod hatzibbur*), there will be legitimate differences of opinion as to whether this is still true or not. Thus a very traditional congregation, where the worshippers would be outraged by women being called to the Torah, should take this outrage into consideration in determining whether a change should be instituted or not. In other congregations, the *kevod hatzibbur* would be affected by not giving women *aliyot*. As long as the pluralistic practices are born out of serious considerations, and as long as they do not offend the broad consensus of our movement, we are willing to countenance and grant legitimacy to varying practices.

Thus we have outlined the principles by means of which the Conservative movement attempts to fulfill its task—of preserving Jewish law and of modifying it when necessary.

The method of Conservative Judaism when faced with a halachic dilemma is:

1. Seek out the precedent. Unless there is good reason to do otherwise, we are bound to the precedent.
2. In seeking out precedents, we do not necessarily limit ourselves to any specific code.
3. If the precedent is deficient in meeting the needs of the people, if it is clearly foreign to the group of law-observers in the community,

if it is offensive to our ethical sensitivities, or if we do not share its basic scientific, economic, and social assumptions, then the law can be modified either by outright abrogation, or by ignoring it, or by modifying it. Thus, when we are faced with rendering a moral judgment about abortion, we are informed by the tradition, which expresses a bias for the life of the unborn foetus. We find in the tradition, however, that abortion to save the life of the mother is permitted. We find it possible to interpret the meaning of "saving the life of the mother" as involving economic, emotional, and sociological components—thereby legitimating many abortions "for cause."

The Committee on Jewish Law and Standards is frequently mentioned in these pages. This committee, which consists of twenty-five rabbis appointed by the President of the Rabbinical Assembly, is assigned the task of interpreting Jewish law for the Conservative movement. Its decisions are often issued as reflecting both a majority and a minority. According to the regulations of the Rabbinical Assembly, individual rabbis have the privilege of following either the majority or the minority opinion. Since the local rabbi, the *mara d'atra*, is best informed as to the conditions obtaining in his congregation, he has the authority to put the decisions into effect as he sees fit. Only when there is a unanimous opinion, and when this opinion has been raised to the level of a standard of rabbinic practice by a convention of the Rabbinical Assembly, is it incumbent upon the local rabbi to follow the decision of the Committee on Jewish Law and Standards.

In assessing the achievements of Conservative Judaism in the field of Jewish law, we can be proud of the achievements of the law committee in the field of halachah. Though there are colleagues who disagree with several of these decisions, the movement as a whole has shown bold vitality in facing the issues of Jewish law in our time. We have broken down the fences that separated men and women in the synagogue; modernized the liturgy without doing violence to its basic structure; allowed the introduction of instrumental music when it enhances the service and where the congregation is attuned to it; we have clarified the role of electricity on the *Shabbat* and tried to deal constructively with the fact of suburban sprawl, which makes walking to and from the synagogue so difficult. We have contributed very much to the clarification of the problems of *kashrut*. In the field of Jewish family law, we have permitted the marriage of divorcees and *kohanim* and

proselytes and *kohanim*; we have, after many centuries, finally solved
the problem of a woman whose husband refuses to authorize a Jewish
divorce (the *agunah*)—first through the inclusion of a condition in the
marriage contract, formulated by Professor Saul Lieberman, and now
through the invocation of the powers of annulment granted to rabbis.
We have moved into the area of women's rights in the synagogue.
There are many decisions which might be faulted. But there should be
no difference of opinion about the seriousness of our work. We have
tried to remove the embarrassments and impediments which made the
observance of Jewish law so difficult for so many. It is fair to say that
the Conservative movement has done more in the field of *halachah*
than any other body in the twentieth century. As we face the future it is
clear that, if we are to abide by the principles informing the Conservative movement, we must work harder to develop interest in, and commitment to, Jewish law in our communities. We cannot be effective interpreters of the law unless there is a partnership with the people trying to observe it. It is a difficult task that has been undertaken—to re-
new and to retain, to conserve and to progress. We ask divine help in
fulfilling this task.

It is my pleasant task to thank all those who have made the realization of this project possible. It is impossible not to overlook someone—
but first of all, thanks are due to the contributors to this volume, whose
work has shed light on the problem of Jewish law. I wish to thank Elliot Gertel, my collaborator, for his valuable assistance; David Pollock,
for seeing the book through the press; the officials of the Rabbinical
Assembly—especially Rabbi Mordecai Waxman and Rabbi Stanley Rabinowitz for their encouragement during their terms as President of
the Rabbinical Assembly; my dear friends Rabbis Wolfe Kelman and
Jules Harlow for their invaluable encouragement and assistance; and
the members of the Rabbinical Assembly who have entrusted me with
the important task of being Chairman of the Committee on Jewish Law
and Standards.

Part I

THEORIES OF JEWISH LAW

In the following pages we present various expositions of the philosophical foundation of the approach to Jewish law in the Conservative movement. These essays represent the spectrum of opinion existing in Conservative Judaism. They range from the Reconstructionism of Mordecai Kaplan, which emphasizes the civilizational aspect of Jewish law, to Boaz Cohen, who represents a more traditionalist viewpoint. Conventionally, these ideologies are classified as left wing, center, or right wing, depending on their closeness to the traditional statement of Jewish theology.

Notwithstanding the different emphases of the various writers presented in the following pages, a common theme emerges. This theme stresses the authority and necessity for a system of Jewish law. All the writers agree that a Judaism without a system of halachah is inconceivable. Without Jewish law, Jewish faith and life would lack structure, depth, and unity. It is through Jewish law that the Jew normatively expresses his Jewishness and his faith. At the same time, it is necessary to continue the dynamic of Jewish law, which has always responded to new conditions with a readiness to modify and change. The changes are to be made gradually and to conform as much as possible to the normative contours of Judaism.

The assertion of the necessity of both adherence to traditional norms and readiness to modify them when it becomes imperative to do so, is the essence of Conservative Judaism's approach to Jewish law and observance.

ZECHARIAH FRANKEL (1801–1875) was the founder of Positive-Historical Judaism. He dramatically left the Reform Rabbinical Conference held in Frankfurt-on-Main in 1845 articulating his philosophy of Judaism built on the historical foundations of Jewish faith. Positive-Historical Judaism developed into Conservative Judaism in the United States.

In articulating Frankel's view on Jewish law, Professor Louis Ginzberg explains one of the foundations of the viewpoint of Conservative Judaism.

Jewish Law is the "specifically Jewish expression of religiousness." It is the historical means through which the Jewish religious consciousness expresses itself. This means that Jewish law is part of Judaism not because of its origin, but because of its role in the spiritual life of the Jew. We are "not concerned with origins" but "how the institutions" as they have come to be express Jewish feeling and piety.

The Law expresses the moral and religious foundations of the Jewish people. Changes are possible in Jewish law when any particular law ceases to express this religious and ethical thrust.

1

Zechariah Frankel:
Positive-Historical Judaism

LOUIS GINZBERG

Frankel's Theological Standpoint

Let us now pass to a consideration of Frankel's theological standpoint. Although in his communication to the *Hamburg Tempel Verein* he assumed a standpoint which must undoubtedly be styled new, inasmuch as it ran counter to both strict Orthodoxy and Reform, his actual leadership of a new and living school in Judaism must be considered to have begun upon his departure from the celebrated Frankfurt Rabbinical Conference. We are yet too close to that period to give an unbiased judgment concerning that Conference; I, for my part, care not to be designated as a heretic by the one side or as a fanatic by the other. Let us merely examine how far Frankel was justified in warning the reformers of his day that they lacked all scientific principle, lacked all the necessary earnestness, and were wanting in spirituality and perception of the true demands of the times. That these accusations were totally groundless, no one will assert today. As for Frankel's first reproach, that of lack of all guiding principle, it must be remembered that when in the course of the debate he insisted again and again upon some consistent statement of principles which reform was to follow, he was interrupted by cries that in principles his fellow delegates were unanimous. How ill-founded such a statement was will become evident to us when we remember that in that conference the abolition of Sabbath and Holy Days found champions while, at the same time, discussion waxed warm as to the propriety of supplying the ritual bath with "drawn water."

The truth is that even the two most prominent spiritual leaders of the

2

conference, Geiger and Holdheim, were not agreed upon principles. The latter, in his conception of Judaism, was a Polish Pilpulist in modern garb; the former was a historian from the critical school of the German universities. Holdheim desired the reform of Biblical Judaism, which naturally would lead to almost complete negation, seeing that one portion thereof is now no longer specifically Jewish and another not Jewish at all. Geiger, on the other hand, wished to reform Rabbinical Judaism; as a historian he recognized that Rabbinism is itself reform. He desired to retain the spirit while changing the external form. *"Ex lege discere quod nesciebat lex,"* was the formula used eighteen centuries earlier by a great reformer to state his doctrine of a Torahless Judaism.

These facts about the Frankfurt Conference may serve not alone to justify Frankel's charge of a lack of principle in Reform, but also to explain how it came about that he took part in this convention, whose spiritual leaders were Geiger and Holdheim. The very want of unanimity and clarity of purpose in the camp of Reform must have confirmed Frankel in his expectation that if reformers would only come together for an illuminating public discussion of principles, the conservative elements would attain supremacy, even if only because the majority of the reformers at that date had neither the courage nor the steadfastness of conviction to break definitely with Rabbinism and traditional Judaism. Some such intention in Frankel was evidently divined by the leaders of radical Reform, who opposed with all their might the discussion of any question of principle in the conference, and inasmuch as the guidance of the deliberations rested in their hands, they were successful in their opposition.

But Frankel held a trump card in his hand which he very cleverly played, and instead of simply staying away from the conference, which thus determinedly excluded questions of principle, he awaited a fitting and striking opportunity clearly to present his divergent standpoint before the conference, and so bring it to the attention of that large Jewish audience in Germany which was following the deliberations of the Frankfurt Conference with the closest attention. His success was attested by the many enthusiastic addresses he received afterward both from extreme Orthodoxy as represented by Rabbi Solomon Trier, and from the party of moderate progress.

These congratulations were evidence of the gradual growth of a new party of which he was the acknowledged leader, showing that he could have selected no better moment for his public utterance than that in

which all eyes were riveted upon Frankfurt. It was here that he first
gave expression to the designation "Positive-Historic" Judaism as his
religious standpoint, an expression which, for half a century, remained
the shibboleth of the party founded by him.

The Positive-Historical School

As to what is to be understood by this term, or in other words, what was
Frankel's conception of Judaism, it is remarkable to note how little
clearness there exists concerning it. His opponents on both sides
sought to represent him as a man of compromise, as one who would
theoretically permit no barriers against critical investigation but in
practice would make the authority of tradition paramount. But this
conception explains nothing and raises the question, how Frankel
came to assume such an unnatural as well as unscientific position. Psychologically, of course, the case is possible that one in whom religious
sentiment and critical acumen struggled for the mastery might see himself forced arbitrarily to draw the line between theory and practice and
in this way maintain a certain inward equilibrium. But such a psychological explanation would hardly apply to the case of Frankel, who was
a fairly consistent personality. Nor can a creative mind produce a
"creatio ex nihilo," and only when the conditions are present can a
great mind fashion the material at hand.

This "Positive-Historic" school has demonstrated its strength and vi-
ability in the last fifty years especially by its building up "Jewish
science," and no one would care to seek the origin of all it has produced in the psychology of one man. The best and only correct answer
to the question, "What is Positive-Historic Judaism?" was given by
Frankel himself—"Judaism is the religion of the Jews." The best illustration of his conception of Judaism is precisely the instance which induced Frankel to leave the Frankfurt Conference, on which occasion
he, for the first time made use of the expression "Positive-Historic" Judaism. The matter in hand was a discussion of the question whether
and to what extent the Hebrew language should be retained in the synagogue; and when the majority decided that Hebrew must be kept
there only out of consideration for the feelings of the old generation,
Frankel took his departure. It may at first seem somewhat strange that
he calmly sat through all the radical discussions concerning Sabbath
and marriage laws, while he perceived danger to the Jewish religion in

such a matter as the abolition of the Hebrew language. Indeed, the very
lively debate which followed Frankel's address concerning the great
importance of the Hebrew language for synagogue worship serves to
show how few of those present understood him. Of his opponents only
Geiger hit the nail on the head with his remark that language was a national thing, and as such only should it be allowed importance. The
underlying principle at stake is this: does the essence of Judaism lie exclusively in the Jewish religion, that is, in ethical monotheism, or is
Judaism the historical product of the Jewish mind and spirit? The Hebrew language is of course not a religious factor, and even from the
strictest standpoint of the *Shulhan Aruk*, it would be difficult to adduce
any fundamental objection to the use of any other language in prayer.
Still it is true that in the long development of the synagogue service the
Hebrew tongue became that which the sensuous cult of classic nations
or of Catholic Christianity was to those religions, or church music to
Protestantism, an instrument conducive to lofty impressiveness and
edification. The recollection that it was the Hebrew language in which
the Revelation was given, in which the Prophets expressed their high
ideals, in which generations of our fathers breathed forth their suffer-
ings and joys, makes this language a holy one for us, the tones of which
re-echo in our hearts and awaken lofty sentiments. In a word, Hebrew
is the language of the Jewish spirit, and in so far an essential component of our devotional sentiment. It is true that pictorial representations working upon the eye, or musical sounds, may move our sentiment and attune us devotionally; but this is true of mankind in general
and not only specifically of the Jews. The *Jewish* divine service must
therefore specifically influence Jewish minds; hence Frankel considered the Hebrew language as the sole instrument which can give it this
Jewish tinge. In this sense Geiger was consistent in opposing its use as
the expression of Jewish nationalism and in opposing Frankel.

The same conception of Judaism undergirds Frankel's attitude toward the Law, and it is not correct, as is sometimes said, that he
allowed his critical spirit free rein until he came to some point of importance for theology and then refused to allow criticism to carry him
further. I do not propose now to examine Frankel's position regarding
biblical criticism, and am willing to grant the statement (repeatedly
made) that he considered the Bible as a *"noli me tangere"* to be correct.
It must, however, be remarked that Frankel never deduced the authority of the Law from the plenary inspiration of the Bible as the word of
God, and the foremost representative of the Positive-Historic school

next to Frankel was a man who, upon this point, may fairly be styled almost radical. Neither for Frankel nor for Graetz was Law identical with Bible; but in the course of time, whether for weal or for woe, in the development of Jewish history, the former became the specifically Jewish expression of religiousness. The dietary laws are not incumbent upon us because they conduce to moderation, nor the family laws because they further chastity and purity of morals. The Law as a whole is not the means to an end, but the end in itself; the Law is active religiousness, and in active religion must lie what is specifically Jewish. All men need tangible expression to grasp the highest ideas and to keep them clearly before them, to say nothing of the ordinary masses for whom abstract ideas are merely empty words. Our need of sensuous expressions and practical ceremonies brings with it the necessity for the material incorporation of religious conceptions, and various peoples have given them varying forms. The Law is the form in which the Jewish spirit satisfies this need. In the precepts, which are the dramatic representations of the inward feelings, Judaism found a material expression of its religious ideas; through them its abstractions became realities and in them the essential needs themselves, reverence and recognition of the divine will, were expressed. Every form became thus spiritualized and living, bearing within itself a lofty conception.

Theory and Practice

We may now understand the apparent contradiction between the theory and practice of the Positive-Historic school. One may, for instance, conceive of the origin and idea of Sabbath rest as the professor of Protestant theology at a German university would conceive it, and yet minutely observe the smallest detail of the Sabbath observances known to strict Orthodoxy. For an adherent of this school the sanctity of the Sabbath reposes not upon the fact that it was proclaimed on Sinai, but on the fact that the Sabbath idea found for thousands of years its expression in Jewish souls. It is the task of the historian to examine the beginnings and developments of the numerous customs and observances of the Jews; practical Judaism on the other hand is not concerned with origins, but regards the institutions as they have come to be. If we are convinced that Judaism is a religion of deed, expressing itself in observances which are designed to achieve the moral elevation of man and give reality to his religious spirit, we have a principle in obedience to which reforms in Judaism are possible. From this point of view the evaluation of a law is independent of its origin, and thus the line of demarkation between biblical and rabbinical law almost disappears. Characteristic of Frankel's attitude toward this problem is the statement given by him in his *Darke ha-Mishnah* concerning *Sinaitic Traditions*, which caused a great deal of controversy.

In the first section of the *Darke ha-Mishnah* Frankel makes the assertion that the frequently recurring talmudic expression, *Halakah le-Mosheh mi-Sinai*, "a tradition of Moses from Sinai," properly designates those ordinances whose reason and origin were unknown and which, being of remotest antiquity, were looked upon as if they had actually originated on Sinai. Strict Orthodoxy, of course, perceived in this statement a declaration of war against traditional Judaism inasmuch as it denied Sinaitic authority for the "Oral Law." Men like Samson R. Hirsch and Benjamin Auerbach in Germany, Wolf Klein in France, Gottlieb Fischer in Hungary—to mention only a few—attacked Frankel vigorously, accusing him of undermining traditional Judaism. But there were not lacking, on the other side, defenders like Raphael Kirchheim, Saul Kaempf, and to some extent also Solomon L. Rapoport. Curiously enough Frankel took no further notice of these attacks other than to publish an explanation (*Erklarung*) in the *Monatsschrift*, in which, however, the same unclearness of thought and indefiniteness of expression concerning the term "Sinaitic Tradition" prevail as in the *Darke ha-Mishnah*. This was the very cornerstone of offense, and both sides desired a clear statement on the point. To give our opinion today upon this controversy, we can only say that both Frankel and his Orthodox opponents were equally right, each from his own particular standpoint. The Mishnah as well as the Talmud do employ the expression quoted to designate the laws whose origin is acknowledged to be of later date; but it is no less true that they hold that many *Halakot* were imparted orally upon Sinai in addition to the Written Law. Even if we knew nothing of such *Halakot*, the expression "Sinaitic Tradition" used in old sources to describe laws whose origin was no longer known, would imply that there were traditions which were revealed to Moses on Sinai, otherwise this term would never have been used. Strict Orthodoxy, therefore, was correct when its champions insisted upon the recognition of this theory. But it is clear also that Frankel, for whom, as we have seen, the authority of the Bible depended essentially upon the fact that its doctrine had penetrated into the mind and sentiment of the Jewish people, could not make the authority of tradition dependent upon the adoption of such a theory of "Sinaitic Halakot." What distinguishes these Halakot from others is their origin in high antiquity, during the formative period of Jewish history. Just as the character of an individual man is in its essence formed before he attains manhood, though the circumstances of his life modify it, giving prominence to some points and leaving others undeveloped, so in those early centuries were formed that set of ideas and type of mind which took shape in these provisions.

The "Law" is essential to the Jewish religion, but not the laws; though, of course, seeing that the former presumes the latter, if Reform is to be a forward development of Judaism a norm must be maintained, lest Judaism suffer like the bundle of arrows in the fable, and each individual arrow being broken, the whole bundle will be shattered. This norm, according to Frankel, was the Talmudic position that whatever observance is spread through the whole community must not be abrogated by any authority. Frankel, according to his conception of Judaism, could not well arrive at any other conclusion. That which the whole community has adopted and recognized may not be repealed; to do so would be to dissolve Judaism, which is nothing else than the sum of the sentiments and views which dominate Jewish consciousness. In reply to the question as to who must be taken as the representatives of Jewish consciousness, Frankel could only make the reply that only those who saw in Judaism a very definite form of expressing religious thought and feeling, only those who recognized the Law as specifically Jewish, could have the right to decide what portions of it had incorporated themselves into the national consciousness.

Theoretically Frankel's definition of Judaism gives up a large field to Reform; practically, however, Frankel did not follow up the consequences of his doctrine. This must be partially ascribed to the fact that in the proceedings of the radical Reformers he recognized only a species of religious indifferentism totally repugnant to him, and was therefore inclined to side with Orthodoxy, though he differed from it in very essential doctrines. Take, for instance, his belief in the Messiah, which was far from Orthodox as can be seen by his letter to the *Hamburg Tempel Verein*. In view of the present Zionistic movement, it will be of interest to recall the following utterance. "The desire that in a certain corner of the globe—naturally, of course, in the land of our ancestors, so full of the holiest recollections—our nationality should again appear and that we should enjoy the respect which said experience teaches us falls to the lot only of those who possess worldly might, contains in itself nothing wrong; we evidence thereby only that in spite of centuries of suffering and misfortune, we do not despair of ourselves and cherish the idea of a self-dependent and a self-reliant reanimation." The warmth with which Frankel in this letter posits the firm belief in the restoration of the Jewish nation, and his sharp and bitter criticism of the attenuation and the spiritless superficiality which avoided any expression of national character, shows clearly that Frankel realized that Judaism possessed a far broader basis than that of a mere religious community. These words contain a germ of the purely national conception of Judaism which finds expression in many a Zionist tendency of today. For Frankel, it is true, nationalism does not belong to the essence of Judaism, but it is nevertheless necessary for its existence. Breath is not a part of man, it comes to man from without, yet no one can live without breathing. So nationalism is the very air in which Judaism breathes.

Creative Conservatism

The view that only that is Jewish which lives in the consciousness of the Jewish people inclined Frankel, it is true, towards conservatism; but it likewise stimulated him most powerfully to creative thought. His indisputable scientific importance lies undoubtedly in the fact that he is the historian of the Halakah; his efforts in this department constitute a scientific analysis of the national consciousness as expressed in the Halakah, the national mode of life. His researches demonstrated how the individual details of the Halakah came into being and how from small beginnings they poured themselves into that stormy ocean, the "sea of the Talmud." To the landsman the ocean seems one huge immeasurable flood, obeying a single law of ebb and flow and offering a uniform force. Yet in truth we know that the movement of the ocean is the result of many forces; the seeming uniformity covers the energy of a hundred currents and counter-currents. The sea is not one mass but many masses moving along definite lines of their own. It is the same with the "sea of the Talmud." The uniform character of the Talmud exists only for those who merely survey its surface, but not for those who understand how to penetrate its depths. Frankel therefore endeavored to discriminate between those tendencies of the Halakah which were always current, and those which were dictated by the newly-arising needs of the day.

*MORDECAI M. KAPLAN argues that the two most significant contri-
butions of Conservative Judaism are affirmation that the binding
character of halachah need not derive from supernatural revelation and the notion of "Positive-Historical Judaism" which permits only such change "as can be accepted universally throughout
Jewry, and are in harmony with the organic integrity and development of the Jewish people."*

*Kaplan charges that Conservative Judaism has failed to imple-
ment the latter contribution to Jewish thought. While before the
Emancipation halachah reflected the collective will of the Jewish
people interpreted as a divine mandate, the growing participation
of the Jew in the secular state undermined the very status of Jewry
as a people in exile. The Jewish people must therefore be "reconstructed" so that "it may again express its will through the medium of the law." Such reconstruction will occur "only when a sufficient number of affirmative Jews become convinced that there are
need and room in Jewish life for a modern type of democratically
instituted law." What is required in the Diaspora is "Jewish creative effort in the domains of religion and culture." Diaspora Jewry
must reconstruct its domestic relations (i.e., the status of women),
its communal activities, and its ritual practices.*

*Although we can no longer rely on Divine sanctions to enforce
Jewish Law, we can emulate the sanctions of all voluntary organizations in democratic societies. The first step would be to "define
the obligations and privileges of membership in a Jewish community, and to set up the legal basis for the working of its administrative machinery." A Jewish "constitutional law" would
outline the responsibilities of communal leaders and members. In
contributing to the "salvation" of the individual and of human society generally, halachah, as reconstituted, would reflect the will
of God as the Power that makes for salvation. Ritual obligations
must be observed by members of "voluntary associations that
would undertake to abide by them."*

11

The Problem of Jewish Law

MORDECAI M. KAPLAN

Both Orthodoxy and Reform take, each in its own way, a clearly defined attitude toward traditional Jewish law. Orthodoxy regards that law as supernaturally revealed and unalterable, except through some subsequent revelation. Reform regards it as a product of historical evolution and as having lost its function as a result of the Emancipation. It maintains that Jewish religion in our day requires no legal precepts; ethical principles suffice as guides to Jewish behavior. Conservatism rejects both of these assumptions, though it has not arrived as yet at a definite understanding concerning the place of Jewish law in Jewish religion and Jewish life. Among Conservative Jews, great diversity prevails both in the theory and in the practice of Jewish law.

Two Contributions

Thus far the spokesmen of Conservatism have contributed two important principles to the definition of its attitude to Jewish law. The first of these is that the binding character of Jewish law for the Jew does not derive from the belief that it was supernaturally revealed. The law is binding intrinsically, in that it is the expression of the religious spirit of the Jewish people.[1] A Jew who is loyal to his people and its religious aspirations derives from that loyalty sufficient motivation for desiring to strengthen Jewish law as an expression and implementation of Jewish ideals. The mere fact that he regards the law as human and fallible would not interfere with this purpose, any more than an awareness of the inherent limitations of science would weaken a scientist's devotion to his particular scientific interest.

The second contribution of Conservatism to the definition of the attitude which Jews should take to Jewish law is the principle of historical

12

continuity, which was expounded under the term of *Positive Histori-cal Judaism,* by Zechariah Frankel,[2] a century ago, and under the term *Catholic Israel,* by Solomon Schechter,[3] a half century ago. That principle was intended to guide us in accepting or rejecting any proposed changes in Jewish law. Changes in law, according to that principle, must not be made arbitrarily, to accommodate a local or temporary situation. Only such changes are admissible as can be accepted universally throughout Jewry, and are in harmony with the organic integrity and development of the Jewish people. No more influential spokesmen could be sought for any principle than Frankel and Schechter. They carried out the ancient injunction of raising many disciples.[4] Yet nothing whatever has been done by their disciples to implement that principle. That is the case, undoubtedly, because the principle as such is unworkable. It merely illustrates the definition of "Conservative" as one who does not believe in doing a thing for the first time. It is a compromise between wishing to stand still and being afraid to go forward.

Before Emancipation

A realization of what we mean by law in general, and how it functions in human life, will help us to cope with the problem of Jewish law. Law which regulates human conduct expresses the collective will of some organized society, and is such only so long as that society exercises sanctions to enforce it. This implies that law exists as one factor in an organic complex, of which the other factors are: an organized society, a collective will, and sanctions. Not having an independent existence apart from one another, any one of these four factors can be defined only in relation to the remaining three. The concept of law has no meaning except in relation to an organized society which enforces its collective will by means of sanctions. *The differences between various systems of law, or between different stages in the development of the same legal system, correspond to differences in the form of social organization, in the conception of the collective will, and in the nature of the sanctions used to enforce it.*

In every one of these factors, a wide range of variation is possible. Thus the form of organization may vary from a closely knit state, as that of ancient Sparta, to a widely dispersed group like the Jews. The conception of the collective will may vary from one which identifies it with the will of God, so that its principles are supposed to be as inher-

ent in the nature of things as any natural law, to a purely secular covenant. The sanctions may range from an elaborate system of rewards
and punishments at the hands of authorized agencies to a vaguely conceived form of divine retribution in the hereafter. Corresponding to
these variations, the law itself, as the instrument of the collective will,
may vary from a definite, fixed code to customs and conventions which
register the kind of behavior society expects of the individual.

Until modern times Jewish law functioned organically. The Jews always constituted an organic society. They had a collective will, which
they identified with the will of God. The recognition of the societal status of Jewry is evident from the fact that, up to the time of the Emancipation, in such matters as taxation, for example, governments dealt not
with Jews as individuals, but as members of the Jewish community.
Nor did the civil law of the nations among whom Jews lived apply to
the relations between one Jew to another; these were governed entirely
by Jewish law. Moreover, the Jew who excluded himself from participation in Jewish community life, could find asylum in no other community, unless he took the drastic step of apostasy.

The interpretation of the collective will expressed in Jewish law was
that its mandate was of supernatural origin. This gave to the authority
of the law an absolute and infallible character. The law was enforced
both by divine and human sanctions. The divine sanction was princi-
pally the fear of punishment and the hope of reward in the hereafter.
The fact that this sanction was divine added to its efficacy, since, unlike human sanctions, which are dependent on finite powers for their
execution, divine sanctions are imposed by an almighty Power. The
human sanction, in addition to general approval and disapproval of
neighbors, would take the form of the *herem*, or excommunication.

In view of the fact that there was no other community which assumed any responsibility for the welfare of the Jewish individual, the
fear of excommunication was tremendously effective. Thus even the irreligious and heretical person, who might not be deterred from non-
conformity by the divine sanction of the law, was effectively deterred
by the human sanction. Until the Emancipation, therefore, Jewish law,
even though the police power of the Jewish community was limited,
was enforced by sanctions no less effective in their operation than
those of any modern state. That applies to the whole range of Jewish
law—civil, marital and ritual. Before the Emancipation, Jewish law
was everywhere a functioning reality.

Law and Meaning

A cataclysmic change took place, however, with the granting of citizenship to Jews. The first formal recognition of that change was the set of resolutions passed by the Sanhedrin which Napoleon convened in 1806. This was followed by the acceptance of those resolutions by the Brunswick Conference of 1841.[5] These resolutions were in effect a renunciation by the Jewish community of its juridical authority, except in ritual matters and, to a limited extent which involved no conflict with the law of the state, in marital affairs. This undermined the very status of Jewry as a people. To be sure, while governments were so constituted as to make affiliation with the Jewish group or community obligatory, as an alternative to affiliation with the Christian or any other distinctly identifiable group, communal sanctions could still be employed to enforce conformity, at least to a few limited areas of Jewish law. The Jewish community could still define the terms on which the individual would enjoy the benefits of membership in it. The individual Jew, unless he was prepared to join some other religious communion, had to comply with the legal standards on which the community insisted.

But what possibility is there for Jewish law to function in a country such as ours, where church and state are separate, and where the government refuses to interfere in the internal affairs of any religious group? No law can function without sanctions; but sanctions can be applied only by a society from which it is impossible, or extremely disadvantageous, for the individual to withdraw. In American life, Jews and Gentiles do not live in mutually exclusive communities. Theoretically at least, one does not have to become a Christian in order to be accepted in non-Jewish society and to derive the benefits of business, professional and cultural association with Gentiles. It is not even neccessary to relinquish membership in the Jewish community. A Jew may at present disregard every one of the distinctively Jewish ordinances, without fear that his right to membership in any important Jewish agency or organization might be challenged. His financial contribution would never be refused on that account. A Jew who has achieved worldly success is welcome in most congregations, regardless of how he came to be successful.

When we see how non-Jewish it is possible for a Jew to be we are inclined to propound the riddle: when is a Jew not a Jew? But to whom shall we turn for the solution of that riddle? There is today no Jewish body which is authorized to answer that question. Ever since the Jewish community abdicated its autonomous jurisdiction over the civil relations of Jews to one another, Jews have lost the status of a people, and their law has lost the status of law. That is one of the reasons why Jewish law has become defunct.

No Jew who experiences in his own being anything of his people's will to live should accept with equanimity this defunct state of Jewish law. He himself should do something, or persuade others to do something about it. But what he should not do is to resort to self-deluding, compensatory reasoning. Such reasoning is indulged in by those who maintain that the validity of a law has no relation whatever to the number of persons who obey it. According to this view, even if all Jews disregarded their traditional code of law, it would remain just as valid as if every Jew obeyed it, since it derives its authority from God and not from man. This does not square with the general assumption that the law exists for man and not man for the law, an assumption implied in the Rabbinic statement:[6] "The Sabbath is delivered to you, and not you are delivered to the Sabbath."

How absurd it is to maintain that even defunct Jewish law can be valid may be seen from the fact that the application of sanctions is assumed as an integral part of the actual laws as enunciated in the written and in the oral Torah. Even the ancients, from whom we have inherited the conception of our law as divine and independent of human authorship, insisted on its functional relationship to the Jewish people as a societal entity. It is true that they speak of the Torah as having existed before creation and as having been consulted by God when He created the world,[7] thus apparently regarding the Torah as prior to the world. Such hyperboles about the Torah are merely part of their tendency to apotheosize it. But when they spoke of Torah as law, they treated it as existing for Israel. The view that Israel existed for the Torah did not gain much favor among them.[8]

The notion of Jewish law as inherently valid, regardless of the extent to which it is ignored by Jews, is not only untrue but harmful. It obscures the urgent need of reconstituting Jewish society in order that Jewish law may be reinstated. But that is not the only hindrance to the reinstatement of Jewish law. The momentum of the past has for a time, and in certain circles, tended to preserve at least some vestigial remains of the habits which the law enjoins. That fact often obscures the fatal disintegration which is undermining Jewish life. Self-deluding optimism, inertia and lack of imagination prevent us from envisaging the full measure of the upheaval that has overtaken Judaism, in consequence of the loss of its juridical autonomy, and from undertaking the task of reconstructing Jewish law, so that it would resume its function in Jewish life. It is high time that we awake to the fact that the Jewish people has been atomized, and that Jewish law has been nullified. If we still believe in the value of Jewish life and in the importance to it of Jewish law, a difficult but imperative task lies ahead of us. We must reconstitute the Jewish people so that it may again express its will through the medium of law.

The Jewish people, in our day, will be reconstituted as a law-making and law-enforcing body, only when a sufficient number of affirmative Jews become convinced that there are need and room in Jewish life for a modern type of democratically instituted law. Such law would have to be supplementary to the law of the land and recognize its authority. In that respect Jewish law would merely be conforming to one of its own long established principles: "The law of the state is law."[9] To be sure, the original application of that legal maxim was limited in scope whereas now its scope would have to be widened. The reason is that Jews are no longer a "state within a state" but an integral part of the state. This fact would also make it necessary for Jewish law to refrain from interfering with the freedom of economic and social intercourse with the non-Jewish elements of the population. *Whatever Jewish individuality is to be developed in the Diaspora must be the intrinsic product of Jewish creative effort in the domains of religion and culture, and not the result of artificial barriers.*[10]

In rehabilitating Jewish law, it is necessary to take into account the fundamental difference between the opportunities for Jewish living in *Eretz Yisrael* and those in the Diaspora. In *Eretz Yisrael* all human relationships, both those of status and of contract, come within the province of Jewish law. In the Diaspora, Jewish law is necessarily limited by the need for conforming to the law of the land and sharing in the economic, political, social and cultural life of the majority population.

Eretz Yisrael Jewry has not evolved a modern constitution and code of law. Despite the desire to foster a collective Jewish life and to create agencies that make for a maximum of Jewish consciousness, there is no common system of Jewish civil law for the growing population. Whenever those who belong to the old *Yishuv* or to the Orthodox elements in the new *Yishuv* have any disputes that need adjustment, they apply to the rabbinic courts. These courts are notoriously oblivious to the social

ideals and spiritual strivings of modern men, and they have no program for developing the law to meet the complicated conditions of life
in our modern industrial age. In view of the present heterogeneous
character of the population in *Eretz Yisrael* and its preoccupation with
pressing economic, political and defense problems, it is, perhaps, asking too much of the Jews there to work out a civil code that shall adequately express the aspiration for social and ethical idealism of the
modern *Yishuv,* and that shall provide effective means of enforcement.

In the democratic countries where Jewish life is free from besetting
fear and danger, Jewish scholarship would do well to concentrate at
present on the task of evolving a way of living as Jews in our own day.
They should study the general process of social reconstruction and the
part in it played by law-enactment and law-enforcement for the purpose of formulating a constitution and a code both for *Eretz Yisrael*
and for the Diaspora Jewry.

This suggestion will, undoubtedly, be discounted by those who take
the position that law is a natural growth and must be permitted to
emerge spontaneously from its native soil. All attempts deliberately to
formulate law on a rational basis, whether in constitutions or in codes,
are said to be artificial. This is exactly how all the romantic reactionar-
ies among the jurists argued in the early nineteenth century Germany.
Their attitude was one of reaction against rationalism which, presumably, was an invention of the French Revolution.

History, however, has demonstrated where such anti-rationalism
leads. Nazi Germany, with its flouting of reason and justice and its glo-
rification of the folk spirit in law, has proved to what absurdities and
cruelties the assumption that only native law can have validity is liable
to lead. Some of the most successful societies, in point of stability and
successful combination of freedom with social order, owe their success
to so-called artificially formulated constitution and codes of law. Their
experience shows that *Eretz Yisrael* Jewry would do well to call upon
Diaspora Jewry to help it in the upbuilding of Jewish law.

Law in Diaspora

In reconstructing law for Diaspora Jewry, there are but few areas
which have to be considered. First is that of domestic relations. That
would involve reckoning with the change in the status of the woman
from one of inferiority to one of equality. Anyone familiar with tradi-

tional Jewish zeal for keeping domestic relations free from all taint of illegality must realize that this much needed change in the status of woman will not come about without systematic and patient re-education of the Jews. But that change is one of the most crucially necessary because of its social and psychological significance.

There are other areas of Jewish life, however, in which either new law will have to be created or old law changed. The entire range of communal activities presents a field for new Jewish law. If our communal agencies and organizations are not to be merely lengthened shadows of the individuals that control them, but are to contribute toward a sense of Jewish unity and peoplehood, they will have to abide by some over-all set of laws and values which would make for mutual coordination and division of labor, and for internal efficiency and justice. These laws and rules should set forth the duties, the authority, the qualifications for office and the conditions of tenure of all Jewish public servants, and establish codes of right relations between different Jewish corporate agencies, and between them and individuals affected by their operation. But most important of all, the machinery of fund raising for various causes should have its basis in, and be subject to the control of, communal law.

A third area is ritual practice. That is at present where most Jews look for guidance. Ritual practices are the concern of every one who wants to be a Jew, in the fullest sense of the term. However much or little either the observance, or the neglect, of these practices may affect our human relationships, they cannot be ignored. They can serve as a source of immediate good in the life of the individual. In their present state, they are either a nuisance, or an occasion for a sense of guilt. To disregard them in any serious effort at reconstructing Jewish life, on the ground that there are more important problems to cope with, is like disregarding the food and sanitary problems of an army, because the main purpose of an army is not to eat and keep healthy, but to fight and win battles.

How can Jewish society be reconstituted to enable Jewish law to function in these areas? We cannot rely on divine sanctions to enforce the law. That God rewards every act of obedience to Jewish law, and punishes every act of disobedience, is a belief that has long become desiccated, even among those who profess it. There are too many who disregard ritual practice with impunity in this world, and have doubts about any posthumous reward or punishment, particularly for ritual transgressions. We cannot invoke the police power of the state to enforce Jewish law, for that is in violation of the principle of religious freedom, as understood in a democracy. The only sanctions we can apply are those which are applied by all voluntary organizations in democratic countries.

The Jewish community as a whole might constitute itself as an organized body, for the purpose of satisfying the Jewish needs common to all its members. Being organized on a voluntarist, democratic and quasi-contractual basis, the member of that community will be under implied contract to conform to its rules, and to receive the benefits accorded to all members. The part of the law which needs to be elaborated first is what may be called constitutional law. In traditional Jewish law, this was lacking, because Jewry was not a voluntarist society. The Jew had no other community in which he could live. Furthermore, the "divine right" of the interpreters of the law to demand obedience to what they considered the word of God made democratic sanctions of constitutional government superfluous. But, in our day, the first task must be to define the obligations and privileges of membership in a Jewish community, and to set up the legal basis for the workings of its administrative machinery.

Although it is not intended here to present a blue-print of the constitution of the Jewish community (a project for a constitutional convention), certain suggestions may be made, by way of illustration, of the kind of content that would have to be included in such constitutional law. One of the measures it would have to deal with would be requirements for admission to membership. These might include some sort of token payment of dues, by way of registration, agreement to marry within the faith, or to proselytize the non-Jewish partner to a marriage, agreement to provide for such Jewish instruction as the community may deem necessary, willingness to pay such communal taxes for Jewish purposes as the community may require. In turn, the member may then claim such privileges as permission to worship in any of the community's synagogues, religious education for his children, religious services in celebration of *Berith Milah*,[11] *Bar Mitzvah*,[12] marriage, burial in a Jewish cemetery and with Jewish religious rites. All these services would have to be denied to non-members.

Constitutional law would make provision also for instituting a sort of Jewish civil and religious service. It would lay down the qualifications for such public servants as rabbis, cantors, teachers, social-workers, *shohetim*,[13] *mohalim*,[14] et cetera. It would also define the scope of their authority, their duties to the community and their rights in respect to emoluments, tenure of office and promotions. It would define the method by which these detailed regulations could be arrived at and promulgated. Constitutional law would also have to define the necessary institutions through which the services of the community would be extended to the individual. It would have to provide for the orderly functioning of those institutions, so as to avoid jurisdictional disputes and needless duplication. It would have to authorize courts for adjusting violations of its rules and arbitrating conflicts for which no law exists. It would, of course, have to define the legitimate methods of taxation for communal purposes. These taxes would be voluntary, in the sense that they could be evaded by one's resigning from the Jewish community, but would be enforceable by the same method that any organization employs in relation to its own members.

An analogy to the way that such Jewish constitutional law could function is provided by the functioning of the Canon Law of the Anglican Church in England. Although it is the "established Church" of England, its laws are not enforced by the police power of the state. There is as much religious freedom in England as in the United States. Nobody has to belong to the Church. It is assumed, however, that the Church has the right to define, in accordance with its own constitution, the obligations of its members in general, and the special obligations of its functionaries. When one becomes a member of the Church, one assumes the obligation of abiding by its rules. The State, therefore, confirms at one and the same time the Church's right to impose Canon Law on its members, and the right of the member to resign from the Church at will, without being subject to penalty other than deprivation of the privilege of such membership.

The only difference between the functioning of the projected Jewish constitutional community and that of the Anglican Church would be that, in the latter, the secular courts are authorized to inquire into the conformity or non-conformity of the individual with the canons of his Church, whereas, in our case, it would be courts established under the Jewish community's constitution that would conduct the inquiry. These same courts would have jurisdiction only in matters which come within the scope of the over-all constitution of the community. In matters which pertain to any one constituent group affiliated with the community, only that group would be in a position to exercise authority or sanctions. This means that in a democratic environment such as ours, Jewish community life would have to be based on the principle of federation, leaving a large measure of autonomy to each congregation, Jewish center or social service agency.

Only after the Jewish community has established a framework of constitutional law, would it be in a position to define substantive Jewish law in the three main areas open to Jewish life in the Diaspora. In these areas, it would have to reckon with the principles of historic continuity and universal applicability. But it will have to reckon with them, from the standpoint of the modern democratic conception of law. Law can no longer be conceived as unilaterally imposed by a transcendent Deity. We cannot, in our day, hold Mount Sinai over the heads of the Jewish people and say: "Accept this Torah, or else. . . ."[15] We must assume that law is the instrument by which human beings, who feel the need of sharing life, define their common purposes, the mutual relations necessary for their achievement and the sanctions to be employed in enforcing the common will.

Since God is the Power that makes for salvation, and since democratic polity is expected to function as an instrument of a people's quest for salvation, *the law in a democratic polity derives its ultimate validity from the extent to which it conforms with the divine will, by actually contributing to the salvation of the individual and of human society generally.* Government which is based not merely upon the consent, but upon the active participation, of the governed is in a position to verify the deepest insight of religion that every human being is created in the image of God. Consequently any law, which reflects the interests of those who are governed, and who, by obeying it, expect salvation, may be regarded as having divine sanction. When a law is not just or good, it frustrates men's quest for salvation, and therefore, may be viewed as running counter to the will of God.

Any conception of legal authority that denies to the individual, unless he happens to be a rabbi learned in the law, a voice in the determination of the law by which he is to be governed, is undemocratic, unjust and intolerable. Modern man who has tasted of life in a democratic society will not submit to a law to which he is expected to be subject, but in the formulation of which he is denied any share. That share need not take the form of direct referendum or plebiscite. Representative government has proved to be far more democratic than government by plebiscite. The right to choose who shall represent him gives every individual the most effective means of expressing his will in the determination of the law.

Democratic law cannot be developed by interpretation alone; it requires legislation also. Wherever possible, resort should be had to interpretation of existing law rather than to legislation of new law. But when a law has become so obsolete that no reasonable interpretation of it can either remedy some evil or advance some good, it should be superseded by new law in accordance with the vital needs of the people.

Democracy in Ritual?

The attempt to apply the principle of democracy to the area of ritual practice is without precedent, and beset by many difficulties. We must expect much fumbling, before we succeed in beating out a path. On the one hand, as modern-minded men, we cannot conceive of ritual practice as having a theurgic or magical efficacy. At best it can only be a form of religious self-expression. It is unthinkable to resort to sanctions to compel conformity with ritual practices that do not honestly express one's own personal convictions. On the other hand, to treat ritual as if it were a private affair is to fail to appreciate its very significance. A salute to the flag would be meaningless, if every one designed his own flag. Ritual arises from and is directed toward awareness of social unity and communion. Is there a middle course between, on the one hand, unjust and futile effort to impose ritual uniformity and, on the other, complete anarchy, ranging from an excess to the complete abolition of ritual?

The fact that ritual answers an intrinsic need of human nature leads us to believe that it ought to be possible to come upon such a course. Even Jews who are far removed from the traditional way of life are not averse, on principle, to ritual. They would welcome ritual that is endowed with beauty and significance. However, to try to impose on all Jews a regimen of uniform religious observance is out of the question. It should, nevertheless, be possible for like-minded groups to define their own minimum standards of ritual observance, which they would agree to accept, and conformity to which would thus be self-imposed.

The *modus vivendi* here envisaged certainly would not result in that uniformity of Jewish ritual observance which prevailed in the past. But it would do away with the present amorphous and anarchic character of Jewish life. It would make Jews realize that to belong to a Jewish religious organization of any kind imposed more important obligations than merely paying one's dues. It would tend to foster religious self-expression without which religion is starved from inanition.

In the area of ritual observance, psychological as well as legal or rational considerations play an important role. Many people, who have intellectually broken with traditional beliefs or practices, remain under their emotional spell. Although they may long ago have given up all notions of the theurgic efficacy of ritualistic acts, they continue to harbor some vague fear of transgressing a ritual injunction. Even though the utility of some ritual observance may never have been apparent, its arbitrary character may nevertheless have been regarded as essential, so that any attempt to tamper with it is looked upon as destructive of its efficacy.

To the ancients, it did not seem at all unreasonable that the slightest deviation from the dietary laws, or from the laws of the Sabbath should be fraught with unforeseen dangers in this world or the next. That was, in effect, the argument of R. Judah Halevi[16] for the meticulous observance of the *mitzvot;* he compared such observance to the need of following punctiliously a chemical formula as a prerequisite to obtaining some wished-for chemical compound. Those who have acquired this attitude concerning ritual observances cannot shake it off easily. They are inhibited by their irrational sentimentality from contributing to a satisfactory solution of the problem which the ritual practices raise in our life as Jews.

The inertia which is largely responsible for the refusal to recognize any other source of validation for ritual practice than the traditional law places us before the following dilemma: On the one hand, the Jews that we have to count on to evolve the kind of ritual practice needed in our day are necessarily those in whose lives ritual observances play a profoundly religious role. Yet, such is their intransigence that no amount of persuasion will get them to cooperate in behalf of a reasonable and vital approach to this problem. On the other hand, the generation that has never experienced the religious serenity of sincere ritual observance balks at the very idea of bothering with it.

Finally, the fear often expressed by those who oppose all tampering with ritual observances is that, if we permit ourselves to depart in the slightest from the traditionally prescribed routine, we are certain to get farther and farther away from it, until our lives are left entirely void of all religious self-expression, so that Jewish religious life is bound to disintegrate. It cannot be denied that, in our present state of anarchy, and with no sanctions or restraints of any kind to hold us back, leaving the matter of ritual observance to the uncontrolled and unguided will of the individual Jew is certain to undermine the little of Jewish life that still remains. Since religious ritual is essentially a social manifestation, anyone who disregards it embarrasses his neighbor who would like to take it seriously.

Notwithstanding all of these psychological factors which militate against revision of the traditional attitude toward law in the area of ritual practice, we must go through with that revision along the lines here suggested. Social sanctions will have to take the place of the supernatural sanctions assumed by tradition. These sanctions will have to function within the ambit of each religious society or congregation, which shall be expected to set up specific standards of ritual practice for its members.

As previously stated, these standards would vary with the ideological differences among Jews. Sincerely Orthodox Jews would, of course, expect members of their group to conform to all the observances prescribed in the traditional codes. They would have no problems of revaluating Jewish observance, for the traditional ritual laws are in harmony with the ideological premises of their thinking. But that is not true of the other religious groups. Having rejected the notion of laws unilaterally imposed by a transcendent personal Deity, which have to be implicitly obeyed, the other groups must accept the logical consequence of their position, and assume responsibility for developing a regimen of ritual practice that meets their spiritual needs. This means that they must formulate for themselves the criteria by which they will discriminate between observances that should be maintained, or, perhaps, that should be created, and observances that ought to become obsolete.

Thus we are led to conclude that Jewish law cannot function except in a society whose collective will it expresses. That collective will must make itself felt not only through prescriptions, but also through sanctions. The renunciation of Jewish legal autonomy has destroyed the organic character of Jewish society and has rendered Jewish law inoperative. To reinstate Jewish law, it is necessary to reestablish Jewish society. The problem takes on one form in *Eretz Yisrael*, another in the Diaspora. In *Eretz Yisrael* the great need is for a code of civil law to govern all human relationships. In the Diaspora, Jewry must organize voluntary constitutional communities that would regulate Jewish interests, and formulate such laws as would be binding on all Jews. Though ritual regulations cannot be included as part of Jewish constitutional law, they need not be left to individual caprice. Ritual regulations would be observed by members of voluntary associations that would undertake to abide by them.

By such democratic processes Jewish law could again be made to function in Jewish life.

Notes

1. Ginzberg, Louis, *Students, Scholars and Saints,* Phila. 1928, pp. 205-6.
2. Philipson, David, *The Reform Movement in Judaism,* N.Y. 1931, pp. 164-65.
3. A term introduced by Solomon Schechter to designate "All Israel," acting as a spiral unit. *Seminary Addresses,* Cincinatti, 1915, pp. 22-23.
4. *Abot* 1,1.
5. Philipson, David, *op. cit.,* p. 149.
6. *Mehilta* on Exod. 31, 14.
7. *Bereshit Rabbah,* 1,1.
8. *Eliyahu Rabbah,* 16.
9. *Gittin,* 6b.
10. Maimonides, Moses, *Yad ha-Hazakah, Hilkot Avodah Zarah* XI.
11. See Notes, Ch. II, 7, *The Future of the American Jew* (N.Y.: Macmillan, 1948).
12. See Notes, Ch. II. 8, in *ibid.*
13. Those authorized to slaughter animals according to ritual law.
14. Those authorized to perform circumcision.
15. *Shabbat* 88a.
16. Halevi, Judah. *The Kuzari,* translated by Hartwig Hirschfeld, London, 1906, Part III, p. 99.

*JACOB AGUS rejects the reduction of Jewish Law to folkways and to-
kens of nationalism, but also offers a critique of Frankel's notion
of Positive-Historical Judaism. Agus develops the concept of
"philosophical piety" to check Frankel's romanticism as well as
the inflexibility of certain "Orthodox" interpretations. It is not
enough to depend upon "Catholic Israel," since unreasonable
propositions could also be embedded in the psyche of a nation,
and may not merit preservation. Maimonides' philosophical approach can serve as a paradigm for motivating observance of halachah, which is "derived from both the insight of inspired titans
of the spirit and the voluntary acceptance of the people generally." Observances are to be regarded as "disciplines and standards
accepted for the sake of universal, spiritual ends."*

Laws As Standards—
The Way of Takkanot

JACOB B. AGUS

What does Jewish Law, or more accurately, halachah, mean to us? We can scarcely deal with any issue in religious life today, without first wrestling with this question with all the earnestness of which we are capable. To be sure, life is prior to thought, and often enough we may be called upon to act before our thought has been fully crystallized. But, in the realm of the spirit, nothing is ultimately significant and enduring that is not basically and essentially truthful, deriving from the fundamental convictions and dynamic motivations that constitute the permanent core of religion, and that remain eternally valid in the midst of a changing world. From a tactical viewpoint, peripheral considerations are frequently decisive, but we cannot build securely on a solid foundation if we do not envisage clearly the eternal validity and perennially fresh vital essence of Jewish law. What then is this vital essence?

The Orthodox fundamentalist and the classical Reformist are at one in regarding this question as meaningless. The latter disdains a la St. Paul, any "religion of laws", and the former is likely to stare aghast at the audacity of investigating what is obviously so simple. The halachah, in all its ramifications is God-given. Both the Written and the Oral Laws were dictated to Moses at Sinai, and the laws that were subsequently instituted by the properly constituted authorities were also inspired by the *ruach hakodesh.* While areas of indetermination may remain here and there as a task for future generations, the *shulchan aruch* in its entirety, including the commentaries of *Shach* and *Taz,* was generally believed to "have been written with the aid of *ruach hakodesh,* " so that the source of Jewish law was always the Divine Being. Even when a *minhag* attained the force of law it was not because of a high estimate of the will of the *demos,* but simply because

Israel as a whole was conceived to be holy and quasi-prophetic, sensing Divine truth, in its innermost being.

To the literalist, then, Jewish Law, in all its life encompassing scope, was law, in the exact meaning of the term, since it was dictated by the King of the Universe and promulgated through His official channels. The Lord had concluded a covenant with His people, requiring them, as their part of the bargain, to observe His multiple commandments, in order that they might be prosperous in this life and blessed in the hereafter. In this mental world, God is envisioned as the austere King of Kings, promulgating laws for His subjects; as the King Father in heaven teaching His children the proper rules of conduct; as the Judge at the end of days, sitting on His Throne of judgment, with the Torah in His lap; and as a diligent student of the same laws and principles which He has bequeathed to His people. Thus, the Law is either the expression of God's inscrutable Will, or the result of His kindness and solicitude for the best interests of His children, or the reflection of cosmic principles that inhere irrevocably in creation itself. In any event, the Law is superior to all human judgments and must be regarded as absolute in its validity and inexorable in its application.

The full stream of Judaism, through the ages, contained many trends, in addition to the massive current of naive piety. For the sake of clarity in analysis, however, the literalist mentality must be envisaged in all its naivete and inner consistency, in order that the full consequences of its rejection may be realized. Unfortunately, the debates concerning Halachah are all too frequently confounded by ambiguous phrases, which half-conceal and half reveal mental attitudes that are themselves ambivalent, being compounded of both belief and unbelief.

Let us begin our analysis then with a frank and clear rejection of the literalist Orthodox position. We do not believe that God dictated the Torah to Moses, as a scribe to a pupil, and that He had transmitted to Moses all the comments, interpretations and inferences relating to it that were later recorded in the Oral Law. Having taken this step, we find ourselves still profoundly convinced of the importance of the Law and its supreme significance. But if these vague sentiments of reverence are to serve as the enduring foundations for Judaism of the future, they must be envisaged in all clarity as proven true in terms of the contemporary situation and as rooted firmly in the eternal scheme of things. How then shall we think of Halachah?

Beyond Folkways

The Reconstructionists are best acquainted with the conception of "folkways" as the alternative to the Orthodox conception of the Divinely instituted *mitzvoth*. This conception implies that, in the past, the laws were simply the practices of Jewish people, some being derived from pre-Jewish sources and some growing out of their own experience and aspiration; that, in the present, their claim upon the individual is compounded of filial sentiment, national pride, the gregarious instinct and the need of the individual to seek and find his physical and spiritual salvation through the channels of community life; that, in the future, these ceremonies might well be replaced by different social organs that will respond more adequately to the then prevailing folk needs. The term "folkway", evokes the romantic admiration for plain people, who are free from the frequently disturbing and always challenging virus of rationality. It echoes the idealized image of the peasant that was so characteristic a feature of mid-nineteenth century nationalistic literature in Germany and Russia. It is idyllic, almost pastoral in its connotations, redolent of fields and forests, of pre-cityfied, even if not of pre-civilized existence. But, even while it thus echoes the cravings of romantic nationalism, it seems to speak in the scientific accents of the anthropologist, studying primitive societies, and the modern American sociologist, studying the ghettoes of European immigrants in our large metropolitan centers.

Nevertheless, in spite of its romantic undertones and its scientific resonance the term, "folkways," can hardly be regarded as offering an adequate concept for Jewish law in our life. The amazing brilliance and insight with which it was developed assure for it a place in the history of Jewish thought, but, as a contemporary philosophy it is sadly inadequate. Primarily, it lacks the moral quality, which alone evokes a sense of obligation and a feeling of consecration. Why should we strive with might and main to preserve folkways? Their importance is supposed to reside in their inherent appeal and charm, not in any axiomatic claim to loyalty. Is the nostalgic reverence for parental practice to be glorified as an absolute imperative? Such a consummation would indeed offer a strange climax to the great adventure of Judaism, which began with a revolt against established customs and parental mores, as expressed in the command given to Abraham, "go, thou, from thy land, the place where thou wast born and from the house of thy fathers." Nor, does this state of mind in actual practice achieve more than the treasuring of "tallith" and "t'fillin" in public and private museums, the practice of visiting with the old folks on Yom Kippur and the crowding of synagogues for *yizkor,* leading perhaps also to the well-known facetious extreme of eating an extra Kosher dish in celebration of *yahrzeit.*

Certainly, if we pursue the implications of this concept backwards into the past and forward into life,we cannot but repudiate it with vehement finality. For, does it not present to us the image of our people, clinging to its ways and customs, in the face of direst consequences, for no reason save that those were indeed their ways and customs? The motivation of Jewish piety was actually derived from a deep conviction in the truth of Israel's religious heritage, and the consequent common sense preference of eternal reward for temporary bliss.

In this interpretation, however, the glory of Jewish martyrdom for the sake of Divine truth and the soberness of its mentality would be interpreted as the senseless stubbornness of a clannish people, fanatically isolating itself from the ways of the world, forebearing all mundane goods and spiritual values for the sake of mere tribal customs. Is the ardor of tribalism so beautiful a phenomenon, when we observe it among the backward peoples of this globe, that we should be tempted to reinterpret the Jewish past or reconstruct the Jewish present by means of it?—If today, we should see a people tenaciously clinging to its folkways to the point of sacrificing fortune, well-being and even life itself, in an environment where larger horizons, broader loyalties and a fuller life is possible, we should unhesitantingly condemn them as being both monstrously foolish and bitterly reactionary. If, then, the interpretation of Jewish laws as folkways is painfully inadequate to account for their historic function, it cannot serve as a proper vehicle for the momentum of loyalty to transmit its impetus for a creative life in the future. The ideal of clinging tenaciously to folkways, regardless of their intrinsic charm and worth, could only appeal to a transitional generation, that lost the purpose but retained the sentiment of group survival, remaining, for no good reason that it could give, morbidly sensitive to the specter of the melting pot. In a balanced view, the so called "militant" survivalist, who deems group survival per se to be a supreme end of existence is guilty of idolatry, religiously speaking, of vicious abstraction, logically speaking, and of sheer foolishness, practically speaking. Our ancestors were not guilty, in any one of these respects; why should we expect our children, who are likely to outstrip us in worldly wisdom, to fall victims to these delusions?

The Limitations of Nationalism

Conceived in a totally different realm of discourse, the Achad Ha'amist conception of Jewish law as the "exilic garments" of Israel's soul is equally erroneous and misleading. In this view, the vast legal structure of the Jewish faith is interpreted as the product of the subterranean functioning of the national will to live. In the case of an individual, the powerful instincts of self-preservation generate ideas, attitudes and actions that are intended to guard his life, even if, on the rational level, they are "dressed up" in all kinds of rationalizations. The "real reason" for the multifarious actions of people is generally the impulse of self-preservation, though often enough people prefer to explain their actions in terms of "good reasons". In the same manner, the "real reason" for the progressive building up of the high fences of halachah was to assure the survival of the Jewish people, with the entire complex series of religious motivation serving only as the respectable facade for the dynamism of the national instinct. After the Babylonian exile, when the existence of Israel was placed in jeopardy, the national "will to live" began to weave the web of prohibition and interdictions, which had the effect of erecting an impassable barrier between Jew and Gentile and halting the trend of national dissolution. Later, as exile became ever more inexorably the normal state of Jewish existence, this tendency gathered momentum until, even as the turtle, the Jew came to carry his own home with him, wherever he went, permitting but a few chinks in his shell, for outside influences to penetrate.

On this interpretation, Jewish ritual law is indispensable from the standpoint of Jewish survival in the Diaspora. While Achad Ha'am was too inwardly truthful to maintain that religion should serve the ends of nationalism for the people of his generation, many of his followers agreed with Smolenskin and Lilienblum that the *mitzvoth* should continue to be regarded as the national commandments for Israel in exile.

In the United States, this cluster of motivations was a powerful factor among the Conservative-minded laity and rabbinate. One ventures to assert that in the sermons of all wings of American Judaism, the national motif is by far predominant whenever the so called "Jewish way of life," is preached. Implied in this interpretation is the estimation of group survival, not only as a biological instinct but also as a high spiritual obligation, so that the products of the national soul might be regarded as somehow "religious" as well. Echoes of the Halevian conception of Israel as a holy, prophetic people, that will in time be asked by all other nations "what the morrow will bring," were mingled with the sentiments of the Hebraic renaissance and the widespread hysteria of European nationalism, in order to furnish the composite apologia for Jewish ritual, that was actually in vogue in our own time.

Does this conception offer a valid interpretation of the past, adequate motivation in the present or eternal values for the future?—Obviously, it fails in all three domains. In respect of our historic past, a generation of nationalistic historians, led by Simon Dubnow, has not succeeded in hiding the incontrovertible fact that the fundamental motivations of Jewish life, all through the centuries, were derived from their religious convictions and that the survival of the Jewish nationality was an effect rather than a cause. In every generation, Jewish people were willing enough to compromise in regard to all nationalistic values, forsaking their land, language, mores, allegiance to an extra-national authority and accepting foreign national obligations, cultures and even irredentist sentiments with alacrity. But, they were adamant as the Rock of Gibraltar, when the slightest tittle of the Law was involved, remembering the injunction that when a government is suspected of designs against the Jewish faith, resistance to the death must be offered even in so slight a matter as the proper manner of lacing one's shoes.

Nor, can it be maintained that the survival of every branch of a biological or historical group must be regarded as a supreme end in itself. It is of the very essence of the ethical approach, to view all things objectively, to limit the value of every part by the consideration of the welfare of the whole, to think in terms of the unique value of every individual, not the group, and to view with extreme suspicion the tendency to glorify whatever is associated with the first person possessive pronoun. Certainly, if we judge the tree of romantic, biological nationalism by its fruits, we cannot but regard it as a most vicious and most insidiously corrupting aberration of the human mind. With Nazism as the logical culmination of the illogic of total tribalism, it would be the height of folly to regard the miracle of Israel's survival in the past and the rationale of its life in the present as being due to an inversion of the same dark philosophy of blood and folk.

As to the future, can any one seriously claim today that the nationalistic motive can be usefully employed as the foundation for Jewish law? Since the survival of Israel is presumably assured, through the resurgence of the state of Israel, the nationalists in our midst can now afford to forego the aid of religious ceremonies. Those who take their national sentiments seriously will either go to Israel, or else be content to warm themselves by the reflected fire of Israel's reborn, secular life and culture. Those in whom the fervor of nationalism is of a lesser intensity will be prone to regard the establishment of the state of Israel and its gradual fortification as being a sufficient fulfillment of the impulse for group survival. Is not this the attitude of the vast majority of America's immigrant nationalities that are even now commingling to produce the emergent American nation?—To be sure, the sudden resurgence of Israel's strength has moved many people to "accept" their Jewishness, but correspondingly this self-acceptance being a return to a normalcy of feeling is lacking in spiritual content and is quite incapable of opposing the assimilatory trend. On the contrary, it is likely to smooth the path of assimilation, by removing the Jewish feelings of inferiority and allaying the consciousness of Jewish "difference."

Positive-Historical Judaism

Still a different version of the nationalist conception of Jewish law is offered by the so called "historical school", which was begun by Zechariah Frankel and expanded into impressive proportions by Solomon Schechter. To the historians of this school, history is a form of inverted prophecy and is therefore its own vindication. Jewish law, as it developed through the ages, is an organic product of slow gestation reflecting the inner genius and the profundities of the Jewish national character. Accordingly, no merely rational considerations can be allowed to outweigh the massive, historical processes, which echo the depths of the national soul by their very irrationalities. The spiritual history of a people, especially the structure of its laws, represents the gradual unfolding of its inner psyche. Hence, these laws, must not be fundamentally disturbed; they should be allowed to change only in line with their own "positive-historical" grooves—for the law is the incarnation of the people's soul.

It is characteristic of romantic positions, founded as they are on the uncertain haze of emotion and the peculiarly conditioned slant of their adherents that they reveal their weakness the moment they are fully expressed in unsentimental and objective terms. Thus, as here formulated, the historical approach is manifestly the outgrowth of an exaggerated emphasis on a half-truth. It is certain that the legal structure of a people, deprived of a governmental authority is the means whereby its unity is maintained. It is also true that, in its creative period, the no-

blest ideals of a people are translated into the concrete terms of its legislation. But, considered a priori and in the abstract, what is to prevent
historic processes that functioned relatively well in the past to function
poorly in the present, or even to cease functioning altogether?—Historic processes in law, language, literature, politics and every other phase
of culture are, after all, products of multiple factors and relative circumstances. How can they be regarded as sources of absolute value,
sufficient unto themselves?

Actually, the plausibility of the "positive-historical" position is derived not from the intrinsic logic of its argument, but from the combined momentum of an ancient Jewish trend and a resurgent European
reactionary movement. In appearance, at least, Jewish law seemed to
be an independent domain, self-justifying and self-evaluating, regardless of fluctuations in the intellectual climate. Considerations of philosophy and theology appear to have been irrelevant to the unfolding inner logic of halachah. This fact is due, of course, firstly to the civil and
public character of the major part of Jewish law. In such legislation,
cognizance is universally taken of deeds, not opinions. Thus, in Greece
and in Rome, as well as in Judea, charges of "atheism" were concerned
with deeds, not with thoughts. Secondly, it is of the nature of the legal
process for cases to be decided by reference to precedent and accepted
maxims, rather than by a reconsideration of first principles. Thirdly,
halachah was hammered out in its present shape, largely by people
who were entirely consistent in their religious views, but who were not
rationalistic philosophers. Needless to say that it is a far cry from this
statement of a historic fact to the value-proposition that philosophy,
which is systematized common sense, *should* have nothing to do with
halachah. It is a form of self-stultification that Maimonides would not
even allow God to impose upon man. How can practice be permanently separate from its justification in theory? The centuries-long tendency to separate halachah from *aggadah* may have served a useful purpose in the Gaonic times, when it was set in motion, but it is not inherently justifiable. Men like Bialik and Rabbi Kuk, beginning from dia-
metrically opposed starting points, agreed that only through the re-
alignment of *aggadah* with halachah is progress in Judaism made possible.

In addition to reflecting the traditional independence of the domain
of halachah, the "Positive-Historical" school expressed in the field of
Judaism the nineteenth-century philosophy of German reaction. It was
the legal historian Savigny, who first put forward the view that German

law must not be radically modified, inasmuch as it reflects the unfolding soul of the German nation, thereby offering a rationale for the
maintenance of the semi-feudal *ancien regime* against the challenge of
the liberal forces unleashed by the French Revolution. Savigny transferred the Tertullianian reverence for the absurdities of dogma to the
sphere of politics and law, maintaining that the seeming irrationalities
of German law were the more sacred to the nation because of their evident unreason. His interpretation fitted in beautifully with the then
current biological conception of the life of nations, as propounded
especially by Herder and the Schlegel brothers. It was further deepened by the influential and profound works of Fichte, who expounded
the thesis that the Germanic soul has a special affinity with *Vernunft*, a
form of reason that cannot be understood at all by the proponents of
superficial rationalism, such as the French and Jewish liberals. Finally, Hegel climaxed the entire movement by his pedantic portrayal of
the history of culture as being the invariant forms of the universal
mind. The practical import of Hegel's conception was the representa-
tion of the Prussian state and its legal structure as the ultimate revelation of the Divine Being. For history is Divine Judgment, as it were,
and its processes, as outlined in the past, mark out the grooves of
change for the future.

It is in this intellectual atmosphere that it seemed so reasonable to
base the validity of halachah solely on its "positive-historical" character. Stripped of these connotations, it becomes clear that the historical
processes of halachah should be subject to reevaluation in terms of
contemporary ideals, canons of criticism and necessities of circumstance.

Law and Inspiration

The common core of the three interpretations analyzed herein is the
conception of folk, nation or people as accounting not merely for the
external shape and historical character of the halachah, but as constituting the source of the validity and significance of Jewish Law.
Manifestly, this sociological aspect of the law, revealing the massive
group momentum inherent in it, cannot be gainsaid. No man lives
alone, and the bonds of group loyalty, into which we fall by birth, con-
sititute for us the natural matrix of our ideals, determining their external shape and slant. Against those who desert their natural groups to

seek salvation elsewhere, the sociological argument is effective. But, to those who stay within, this phase is the body of the law, as it were, not its soul, and to attempt to base the value of law solely upon the character of the group is both futile and irrational. Only the absolute values of the spiritual life and the happiness of the individual Jew can be regarded as the axiomatic, irreducible foci of Jewish Law. For these are ultimates, in terms of which all group values must be judged.

To discover what halachah should mean for us today, we have to bear in mind firstly that the relationship of the Jew to God is its incontrovertible starting point. Secondly, in Judaism the laws were not only conceived as the word of God, but that they were so conceived because of their inherent worth as instruments of piety. True, they were God-given, but God is not a tyrant, imposing a yoke of obligations out of selfish need or sheer caprice. What does the Lord require of thee?—To fear Him, to love Him, and to walk in His pathways. The *mitzvoth* were given in order that men might be purified through them. Thirdly, the *mitzvoth* were not simply ordained for Jews by the fiat of the Lord; they became obligatory only when the Jewish people accepted them formally in the classic phrase, *na'aseh v'nishma*. Thus, the Torah was offered to the other nations, but it is not for them obligatory since they never accepted it. Fourthly, in addition to the moral-legal basis of halachah, there was always the consciousness of historic necessity, the ever present momentum of the past of which every generation must account anew. The Israelites at Sinai were historically committed already, because of the covenant with their ancestors, and the acceptance of all future generations is only in part voluntary and in part compelled by the realities of history. As the legend put it, the souls of all Israelites down to the end of time were gathered together for the theophany at Sinai. Fifthly, the precepts of halachah consitituted the minimal standards of the community, by no means exhausting the full task and vocation of man. The good man must rise above the general level, *lifnim m'shuras hadin,* and Jerusalem was destroyed because its inhabitants insisted on the strict letter of the law.

Combining all these elements into one formula we arrive at the conception of halachah as the Divinely inspired and self-imposed disciplines of the Jewish people, undertaken for the purpose of elevating the level of individual and group life to the highest rungs of the ideals of Judaism. In this conception, the ideals of Judaism, insofar as they determine the standard images of the perfect individual and the perfect society, are recognized to be the goal and purpose of the entire halachic structure, while the ritual ceremonies are identified as instruments, of relative value and significance. The source of the validity of halachah is thus twofold—deriving in part from the consent of the people and in part from the inherent truth of the ideal embodied in it. If one grants supreme validity to any one ideal of Judaism, to the extent of desiring to share in the Jewish faith and destiny, then he cannot but accord a measure of authority to the legislation of the group as a whole. On the other hand, this allegiance to authority cannot be of an absolute character, since other values and ideals of his may conceivably be in conflict with the precepts of his people's legislation. The relative authority of any law is thus determined jointly by the degree to which it represents the common consent of our people and the measure in which it serves the highest ideals of Judaism.

The expression "divinely inspired and self-imposed" is intended to reflect the fact that the law is derived from both the insight of inspired titans of the spirit and the voluntary acceptance of the people generally. Of especial importance is the insistence on the Divine stamp of the central method of Judaism—the determination to translate abstract ideals into concrete ways of life for the people as a whole. Thus, the vague sentiment of loving God was concretized into the precept to pray three times daily; the recognition of our dependence upon Him, into the requirement to precede every new sensation of enjoyment by a blessing; the idle contemplation of His Nature into firstly the command to study the Torah day and night and secondly the ethically spelled out aspiration to emulate His ways as the infinitely perfect Personality. This method must be regarded as the cornerstone of Judaism, the one ideal which makes all other ideals practically meaningful and which transforms Judaism from a philosophy of monotheism into a monotheistic religion. It is compounded of a profound sense of personal consecration and a healthy regard for the conscience and welfare of the community as a whole.

This conception of the halachah is true to its historical character and development. While it describes the law as being the product of Israel, the two directions of religious love are interpreted as phases of one process. In our view, God is conceived as the Pole of Absolute, Ideal Personality in the back and forth flux of the multiple processes of reality, and the love of Him as the highest peak of the Divine process in the heart of man. For, in the love of God, all moral and esthetic values are fused together into a new and creative unity. If all ideals be conceived as dynamic motivations, deriving from God and leading to Him, then the love of God must be regarded as the parent-ideal, the living focus of the spiritual realm. And the entire halachah, in its manifold stages of growth and regardless of the diverse origins of some of its practices, may be viewed as being motivated by the one sustained attempt to incorporate the love of God as a living reality in every phase of public and private experience. Thus, a Maimonides may speculate on the ideal possibility of worshipping God in wordless silence and rite-less contemplation and recognize at the same time that for most people, such an ideal is all too frequently a snare and a delusion.

Motivations For Observance

No conception of Jewish Law is worthy of consideration if it does not truly capture some of the motivation, which actually functioned in the historic past of our people. For we do not have either the desire or the will to create a new religion. Accordingly, we must inquire whether the interpretation of Law as legislated spiritual disciplines is indeed justified by the testimony of history.

In form, this conception is identical with the major part of halachah, the part that is described as *d'rabonon,* containing the officially authorized interpretations, *takkanoth* and *g'zeroth.* This class of ordinances is thought of as providing an outer area of disciplines intended to safeguard the inner area of Torah-itic *mitzvoth.* The exact boundaries of this area are subject to dispute, Maimonides having provided the widest conception current in rabbinic literature of the extent of the area of laws, that derive their authority from the insight of the rabbis and their collective legislation. Obviously, from the standpoint of historical criticism, there is scarcely a shred of halachah that is not dependent in the last analysis on an authoritative rabbinic interpretation that was duly recorded at one time or another. As Maimonides put it in a different connection, "the gates of interpretation are not closed to us." The words of the Torah are sufficiently tractable to be incorporated into almost any system of legislation. But, the words of the living Torah have been frozen into rigid laws by layer after layer of rabbinic legislation. Thus, in the critical view, the distinction between Torah-itic and rabbinic laws vanishes, so that the final source is rabbinic (*d'rabonon.*)

The realization of this truth need by no means be confined to those who repudiate the literal version of "Torah from Heaven." All who think in historical terms must find it difficult to resist such a conclusion. Hence, the extreme emphasis in halachic literature on the authority of scribes. Consider the implications of utterances such as the following:

"Whoever disputes a word of theirs is as one who opposes God and His Torah, for all their words are of God, and even a Midrash of Moses himself, master of the prophets, could not possibly be set against their words, for their wisdom and *pilpul* is the word which God commanded unto Moses." (*Shaarei Tzedek*—Gaonic Responsa)

"For they are assisted by the Shekinah, and it is not possible that their agreed opinions shall be contrary to the intent of the Torah. . . " (Kusari, III, 41)

Now, the authority of the rabbis was not due to the mere fact of their election, but to their reputed saintliness, capped as it was believed to be by the gift of "Divine Spirit." The authority of the *Shulhan Arukh* was in no small measure due to the mystical visions of its author. Thus, the legislation of the rabbis, designated collectively as *d'rabonon* coincides in form at least with the conception of Jewish law, as outlined herein. It was believed to be "divinely inspired"; the disciplines were "self-imposed," for until and unless the people generally accepted a rabbinic ordinance it was considered as being automatically null and void. The purpose of rabbinic legislation was to maintain the "ideals of Judaism," as they understood them, identifying them on occasion with the ritual of the faith. Our conception of the ideals comprising the essence of Judaism belongs to the tradition of the prophetic-philosophic school of thought, to an analysis of which we shall now turn.

In order to understand the relationship of the substance of our conception, as distinguished from its form, to the basic currents of historical Jewish piety, we must launch upon an inquiry into the motivations that were supposed to underlie the rites and precepts of Judaism. What were the so called *ta-amai ha-mitzvoth,* the motives and purposes which, the Jew felt, supplied sufficient reason for his practice?—There were three categories of explanation, which functioned, sometimes separately, sometimes jointly, as the frames of reference for the reasons of the commandments. There was firstly, the mentality of folk piety, to which God was a quasi-human being, both King and Father. As King, His *mitzvoth* were commands that could not be questioned; as Father, it could be taken for granted that His Commands were somehow intended for the good of mankind, bringing with them life and blessing. A covenant was concluded between Israel and the Lord, requiring the people of Israel, as their part of the agreement to serve Him in ways agreeable to Him. True, a faithful servant will not pester His Master with demands for immediate reward, but the Lord could be trusted "to pay the reward of your work." Whether or not the intent of any particular *mitzvah* be apparent, the ultimate reason is to serve the Lord and to submit to His inscrutable Will.

In the philosophical current of Judaism, all arbitrariness and caprice is removed form the conception of God and the purpose of the *mitzvoth* is conceived to be unequivocally the spiritual perfection of the individual and the ethical perfection of society. The efficacy of the *mitzvoth* consists not in their favorable effect upon the Divine Will, but in their influence upon the human soul, and their reward is supposed to be the automatic, natural rewards of a life dedicated to truth and goodness. The core of Judaism, in this view, is the cluster of universal intellectual and ethical values, and all rites and ceremonies are merely the instruments of its implementation. Thus, Maimonides, after ridiculing those who revel in the occasional irrationalities of the Commandments, offers the classic formulation of the philosophic approach: "But, the matter is without question as we have mentioned—to wit, that every one of the 613 Commandments is motivated either by the purpose of imparting true ideas, or counteracting wrongful opinions, or the establishment of a just order, or the correction of injustice, or the training in good virtues, or the correction of evil practices. Accordingly, the purposes of all the *mitzvoth* fall into the three categories of true ideas, good virtues and the just order of society. . . Thus, these three categories are entirely sufficient to account for every one of the *mitzvoth*." (Moreh, III, 31)

In the philosophy of Maimonides, the highest gift available to man is the attainment of a bond of union with Active Reason and the consequent assurance of immortality. This gift belongs primarily to the faithful devotees of the moral and intellectual life, and only secondarily to the observers of the *mitzvoth,* for the *mitzvoth* are instruments of the life of the spirit, and instruments sometimes fail to achieve their purpose.

The very clarity with which Maimonides presented the viewpoint of philosophical Judaism provoked a violent reaction among the naive believers and their defenders, as is amply demonstrated in the commentaries upon the "Guide" and the polemics that followed upon its publication. But, the sophisticated defenders of fundamentalist Orthodoxy cannot ever be satisfied with the mere reiteration of the *naive* viewpoint. For philosophy compels even its opponents to accept some if not all of its spirit. Thus, the anti-philosophical defense of the *ta-amai ha-mitzvoth* produced in the course of time a quasi-philosophical super-Orthodoxy, which is enshrined in the literature of *Kabbalah.* The logic of *Kabbalah* consists in a polar blend of the personalistic thinking of naive piety and the mechanistic thinking of rationalistic philosophy.

As a result, the Kabbalistic *ta-amai ha-mitzvoth* assume an automatic effect of the commandments upon the soul, but not in universal terms. Also, the commandments are related to cosmic forces, but not with the view of relating them to universal values. Every *mitzvah* is thought of as a chain descending from the spiritual world, bringing down holiness and achieving "unity" and bliss in the world, redeeming it from the power of evil—yes, redeeming even the Divine in the world, so that Israel Baal Shem Tov could even dare to interpret the phrase, "the Lord is your shadow," as meaning that the Deity is affected automatically and made to respond mechanically to our actions and intentions even as a shadow reflects the motion of a body. On the other hand, every sin is compared to a chain linking this world to the manifold worlds of uncleanliness, so that the sinner becomes chained and bound by his sin, even as the Hebrew word *assur,* meaning prohibited, also signified, being "bound"—bound, that is, to the Satanic forces of evil.

The three systems of "reasons for the commandments" were not always kept rigidly apart, for it is a rare thinker who dares to be thoroughly honest and mercilessly self-critical. Jewish pietistic literature is particularly noted for its multifarious eclecticism. Also, the mystical current of piety, motivated by the urge of seeking the "nearness of the Lord", is oftentimes added to all of the three fundamental world-views in Judaism, making the process of analysis that much more difficult. Indeed, one of the deeply rooted errors in Jewish historiography is the bland identification of mysticism with Kabbalah and the consequent failure to recognize the distinction between the several types of mysticism corresponding to the three fundamental patterns of Jewish piety. Nevertheless, upon analysis, the three systems of *ta-amai ha-mitzvoth* become easily distinguishable.

Philosophical Piety

With this analysis in mind, it appears clearly that we today cannot accept either the naive type of philosophy of halachah or the Kabbalistic type. Only the current of philosophical piety, which relates the mitz-voth to the universal ends of the spiritual life, offers an approach adequate to our minds. This current which was by no means confined to the technical literature of Jewish philosophy, always reflected Judaism at its best and at its noblest. The remark attributed to Aristotle that "all Jews are philosophers" does contain a grain of truth, since the impact of Judaism upon the cultural atmosphere of every age was almost always due to the tenacious conviction inherent in it of the supremacy and the ultimate triumph of the values of the spirit—a conviction which is of the essence of the philosophical mood.

To us, then, the laws of Judaism are disciplines and standards accepted for the sake of universal, spiritual ends. To be sure, even the most rarefied expression of philosophical piety was found in the past dogmatic elements. Thus, Maimonides exempted Moses from the general category of inspired thinkers, allowing for him a far greater measure of authority than his philosophy permitted. He also maintained that certain dogmatic beliefs, that were not true, were nevertheless to be accepted in order to avoid shocking the masses and disrupting the unity of the community. While we may readily concur in Maimonides' estimate of the value of dogma and uniform practice for the community of his day, we cannot but assert the obvious truth that in our day insistence on dogma and uniform practice could not possibly serve the cause of unity. In our age, such insistence could serve in fact only as a disruptive force, since only a fraction of our people subscribe to the totality of Jewish law.

If we remove from the philosophical pattern of Jewish piety the dogmatic elements which were never essential to it, we have a conception of Jewish law, which is completely capable of meeting the challenge of our times. The builders of classical Reform sought consciously to build upon the foundations of what they termed "prophetic Judaism", thereby echoing a concept that was derived from the Christian reading of Jewish history. While this concept inspired the magnificent careers of some outstanding personalities, it could not serve as the basis for an enduring faith. The emphasis implicit in it could in fact only contribute to the trend of self-effacement, disintegration and dissolution, thereby making the claim of Christianity to be the rightful heir of prophetic Judaism appear to be incontrovertible. By contrast, philosophical Judaism is not individualistic, sentimental, vague and other worldly; it is sober, well-balanced, thoroughly grounded in the realm of eternal truth and eminently capable of translating the vital essence of Judaism into the realities of our time.

Viewing halachah as a set of standards and disciplines, we conceive of it as a vertical series, a làdder of Jacob, consisting of many rungs that lead from the earthly to the heavenly. There is ample precedent in traditional thought for this conception of multiple rungs in piety. Indeed, a better view still is to think of a threefold ladder, corresponding to the three pillars of the faith: Torah, worship and good deeds. Thus, it is possible to climb high on one ladder, while remaining on the lower rungs of the other ladders. This conception stands in clear contrast to the rigid uniformity of law, in the orthodox sense, that may be compared to a horizontal bridge, in which any breach is fatal. Thus, in halachah conceived as law, one is classed as a heretic if he defies any one precept consistently and consciously, even if he scrupulously observes every other commandment. In this view, compromise and adjustment could only be sponsored by the guile of the opportunist or the despair of the pietist.

On the other hand, our conception of a series of vertical standards permits us to regard all Jewish groups, seeking sincerely to elevate the level of spiritual life, as falling within the pattern of one common endeavor. No longer need the transgressor of one more commandment look upon himself as living outside halachah, so that he no longer has any reason to cling to the rest of the commandments. It becomes possible to recognize the unity of the goal and the relative unity of the pathway, even while taking into account realistically the actual diversity in the standards accepted by different groups and individuals within the several groups. At the same time, this recognition is not a sterile formula intended to smooth the path of practical statesmanship; on the contrary, it is the one conception that makes possible a sustained endeavor in behalf of the continuous and steady raising of standards in Jewish life.

Realizing the vast gulf between halachah and the practices of the people, we may still reject the extremes of desperate Orthodoxy and wholesale repudiation and instead proceed to outline a series of standards that, given maximum effort, could become the accepted practice of our people. Then, we could look forward to a gradual and progressive lifting of standards and their extension to ever wider sections of our people. This could be done without presuming to change the Law save by the implication that the items not included in the program are regarded as non-essential.

The law, taken in its own terms, cannot be changed—leastwise by us. It is possible to speculate on eventual developments in Israel as resulting in sundry modifications, but, we, the writer and the readers of this essay, can no more change the law than we can change anything that belongs to the past. For, in its literal fulness, halachah is not to us a binding Divine imperative. The law could only be changed by people who truly live in it and by it—and it is a moot question, whether or not the inherent logic of being Torah-true permits change. In any event, while we certainly cannot think in terms of altering the law, we can and should reevaluate the law as consisting of standards of piety, of relative contemporary value and urgency. Selecting those of primary importance, we should consider them as the first step on the ladder of Judaism and bend all our efforts for their acceptance by as broad a section of our people as possible. Technically, this policy of setting minimal standards to meet contemporary realities may be expressed in halachic terms as *a ruling required by the time..* As our success grows, it may be possible to set a higher rung as the next immediate goal. In this way, we shall be making fruitful in our day the profound insights which underlie the structure of halachah.

Essentially, the question before us is whether to maintain the steadily disintegrating outer shell of halachah, or to permit its vital seed to produce nourishing fruits for our day. If we think of halachah as legislated standards and then consider the widening gulf between halachah and life, we cannot but be moved to undertake to bridge the gulf by setting standards for our people, which they might accept and which truly contain *ma-or sheba-ya-hadut,* the light which leads steadily upward.

ROBERT GORDIS rejects the Reform, Orthodox, and Kaplanian approaches to halachah, and argues that the mediating philosophy of Conservative Judaism, as articulated in Frankel's view of the "Positive-Historical school" and in Schechter's emphasis on "Catholic Israel," is still the most viable. Despite decline in observance, the Catholic Israel concept needs only to be reformulated in light of what we learn from democratic societies. Catholic Israel is not to be equated with the complacent masses, but with the "body of men and women within the Jewish people, who accept the authority of Jewish law and are concerned with Jewish observance as a genuine issue." Like the guardians of morality on the old American frontier, the constituents of Catholic Israel preserve the sanctions of past generations, providing our ancestors with a vote but not with a veto in the development of Jewish Law. The Word of God is therefore not unlike the Constitution of the United States; Revelation, like lawmaking, is to be regarded as a process and not as an act. While the ultimate authority rests with Catholic Israel, it is the rabbinate's duty to legitimate changes by halachic process, and by educating the people to adopt viable standards of observance.

47

Prefatory Note to
"Authority in Jewish Law"

ROBERT GORDIS

An adequate revision of this paper, written over two decades ago, would require a complete rewriting of the text. This is primarily due to major changes in the status of Jews and Judaism that have taken place in the intervening years.

The emergence of the State of Israel as the single most dynamic influence upon Jewish self-awareness everywhere has had a powerful impact upon Reform Judaism at one end of the spectrum and upon non- (and anti-) Zionist Orthodoxy at the other. Witness the presence of *Agudat Yisrael* members in the Knesset today.

Perhaps equally significant in its impact has been the widespread loss of confidence in man's reason and in his potential for dealing with the massive problems confronting him in the fourth quarter of the twentieth century. As a result, various forms of mysticism, Oriental and Western, genuine and bogus, have proliferated in Europe and America. The same desperate hunger for certainty at all costs has made fundamentalism increasingly attractive in the Western world.

In accordance with the old proverb, *wie es sich christelt, so yudelt es sich.* "As among the Christians, so among the Jews," these trends have produced Jewish counterparts. Adherence by Jews to Jewish mysticism is of course far better than their accession to the various alien cults which appeal to so many. The Orthodox Establishment is increasingly militant and self-confident as a result of its new-found strength. The other groups, including Conservative Judaism, manifest many of the signs of a failure of nerve, such as a sense of inferiority vis-à-vis Orthodoxy, and a loss of self-confidence in their own system of values.

These new trends naturally modify the brief historical survey of the

48

various schools in modern Judaism presented in the opening section of the present paper. Whether, as some observers assert, these new trends are already giving signs of receding cannot now be determined. At all events, the canons here proposed for dealing with the problem of authority in Jewish law seem to me to be relevant and still useful as a stimulus to further thought and action in the movement, so that Jewish law may become truly operative in the life of Judaism and the modern Jew.

Authority in Jewish Law

ROBERT GORDIS

It seems highly probable that the future historian will evaluate the great contribution of our teacher Professor Mordecai M. Kaplan toward the building of a vital Judaism in America not only in terms of his own original achievements, but also in the spirit of the rabbinic dictum: "Even greater than the agent is his achievement." (*Baba Batra* 9b). For over and above the seminal influence of his thought upon our movement from within, Reconstructionism has compelled us to face agonizing problems which we should have preferred to avoid. Only slowly and painfully has a literature on Conservative Judaism been growing up, and it is noteworthy how much of it has arisen as a reaction to the ideas which Doctor Kaplan has presented. Thus both those who accept his point of view in toto, as well as those who are unable to share it in large areas of thought are his disciples, drinking his waters, and being refreshed by his teaching.

This incalculable debt has been augmented by the series of articles "Toward A Guide For Jewish Ritual Usage" recently published as the collective expression of the Reconstructionist Movement.[1] Our own reaction to the series may be summarized by the statement that the problems of Jewish ritual observance today are well set forth, but that the diagnosis is partial and the remedy markedly inadequate. But our concern here is not merely critical. These articles impel the leaders of Conservative Judaism, who are sincerely interested in the progress and intellectual validity of the movement, to grapple with this basic issue of Jewish law in the modern world. This paper is an effort to indicate the character of the problem and perhaps point the way to a solution.

Every student of Jewish life since the period of the Emancipation has noted the parlous state of Jewish observance. The organic pattern of Jewish traditional life has been shattered, and only vestiges are still maintained of such fundamental Jewish institutions as the Sabbath, the holidays, the dietary laws, prayer and the study of the Torah. The fragments that are retained are often as ludicrous in their perverted sense of values as they are tragic in their implications for the future. The mourner who asks the Rabbi whether he may keep his shop open on the Sabbath of *shivah* week since mourning rites do not apply to the Sabbath, is matched by the Jewess who wants to know whether she committed a grave sin by greeting a mourner during the same period, though her conscience does not trouble her about the *terefot* she serves in her home. It is no mere coincidence that these and similar questions are drawn from *Laws of Mourning,* one of the few sections of the *Shulhan Arukh,* that may still be regarded as really alive, in practice as well as in theory!

John Erskine has said, "Nearly every one has religion, at least in the sense that he knows what church he is staying away from." It is only by that definition that most American Jews may be classified as Orthodox, Conservative or Reform, though there are the hosts of the "unaffiliated" for whom even this is too much religion.

Obviously the problem of Jewish observance is the crucial issue facing Judaism in our day. For even if we adopt a secular nationalist attitude toward the Jewish people like Ruppin, or a frankly assimilationist position like Jerome Frank, it is undeniable that the existence of the Jewish group as a recognizable entity, as well as the meaningful survival of Judaism as a spiritual force, is inconceivable without some regimen of ritual. Professor Louis Ginzberg pointed out long ago that *halachah* is far more fundamental in Judaism than *haggadah,* for ideas are volatile, but practices endure. If Jewish practice goes, virtually nothing remains.

Hence it is that the problem of Jewish ritual has been central in all attempts to adjust the Jewish heritage to the modern world. The very complexity of the problem forbids us to dismiss any of the attempted solutions without some consideration, if only to note and avoid their weaknesses.

The Reform Adjustment

Historically, the first attempt at a conscious adjustment of Jewish ritual to the modern world was made by Reform Judaism in Germany and in a more extreme form in the United States. To summarize the development of the entire movement in the broad Hegelian categories so beloved of German thinkers, traditional Judaism was the thesis, the Emancipation and the Enlightenment constituted the antithesis, and Reform Judaism emerged as the synthesis, the resolution of the conflict. Basically, the world-outlook of traditonal Judaism was attacked as incompatible with the rationalism of the modern age. Even more energetically, it was opposed on the ground that it prejudiced the Jews' claim to emancipation, since it presupposed the existence of Israel as a national entity. The practices of traditional Judaism were challenged for both these reasons, as well as on the score of being cumbersome, outlandish and unesthetic by western standards.

Naturally, the degree to which Reform laity and leadership was prepared to scrap Jewish traditional observances varied with the individual, some going only as far as German Reform, which preserved a great deal of Jewish tradition, others as far as American Reform, which retained relatively little. Some leaders did not hesitate to decry circumcision and favored intermarriage. Theoretically, however, Reform in all its wings, had a common platform: it surrendered the binding authority of Jewish law, and then left it free to each individual congregation to preserve such elements of the Jewish ritual as it found convenient or attractive, that is to say, religiously and morally edifying.

The principle underlying this process of selectivity was formulated in the Pittsburgh Platform of 1885.[2] Sections 3 and 4 stated:

"We recognize in the Mosaic legislation a system of training the Jewish people for its mission during its national life in Palestine, and today we accept as binding only its moral laws, and maintain only such ceremonies as elevate and sanctify our lives, but reject all such as are not adapted to the views and habits of modern civilization.

"We hold that all such Mosaic and rabbinical laws as regulate diet, priestly purity, and dress, originated in ages and under the influence of ideas entirely foreign to our present mental and spiritual state. They fail to impress the modern Jew with a spirit of priestly holiness; their observance in our days is apt rather to obstruct than to further modern spiritual elevation."

Actually, the Reform position was not altogether ingenuous. Thus at the Rochester meeting of the C.C.A.R. held in July 1895, a committee specially appointed to consider the question reported that "from the standpoint of Reform Judaism, the whole post-biblical and patristic literature, including the Talmud, casuists, responses, and commentaries, is, and can be considered as, nothing more or less than 'religious literature'. . . . our relations in all religious matters are in no way authoritatively and finally determined by any portion of our post-biblical and patristic literature."[3] Out of deference to the Christian adulation of the Bible, the C.C.A.R. merely denied the authority of the rabbinical codes, saying nothing about the abrogation of Biblical law as well. As Gabriel Riesser had said of German Reform, "The Bible is treated gently (by Reform) because of its notable kinship with Christianity and on account of the august police." Reform was a type of Karaism in reverse—Karaism had begun by challenging the authority of the Talmud, and cleaving to the text of Scripture, but soon found it necessary, in order to make Biblical law function, to create its own Oral Law. Reform began in an anti-Talmudic spirit, and declared itself to be "Mosaic," but it quickly surrendered the binding authority of Biblical law as well. Even if the agitation against circumcision and the sentiment for intermarriage be dismissed as the vagaries of extremists, one has only to recall the virtual nullification of the Biblical laws on the Sabbath rest, fasting on Yom Kippur, divorce, the dietary laws and many others.

The tragic consequences of this consistent Reform policy became obvious in the succeeding fifty years, and in 1937 a new statement of Guiding Principles was finally adopted by the C.C.A.R. The revised statement shows the highest courage and intellectual honesty in modifying what has become "traditional" Reform Judaism. It adopted a considerably more favorable attitude toward the national elements in Judaism, such as Jewish ceremonies, the Hebrew language and the role of Palestine. This development is rich in promise for a deeper Jewish life in Reform circles and is to be greeted with favor.

Yet it is highly significant that the problem of authority in Jewish law is passed in complete silence in the later pronouncement.[4] It merely restates in more sympathetic fashion what had been set forth rather brusquely in 1886, when it declares:

"The Torah, both written and oral, enshrines Israel's evergrowing consciousness of God and of the moral law. . . . Being products of historical processes, certain of its laws have lost their binding force with the passing of the conditions that called them forth."[5] The Platform of 1885 and the statement of 1937 differ in the number of Jewish observances they would like to see preserved, but the basic philosophy is unchanged. Jewish tradition possesses no binding authority; there is no Jewish *law* for the modern Jew.

The drawbacks of the Reform attitude in its older and its newer formulations are self-evident. It makes anarchy ubiquitous and unity impossible of achievement. It destroys the sense of continuity that must link American Israel with the generations of the past and with their brothers throughout the world. Finally it empties Jewish life of so much of its content and warmth as to make it as lifeless and decorous as a corpse. Without binding authority, Judaism is powerless to evoke sacrifice, and without sacrifice, an ideal is doomed. The rewritten Platform of 1937 testifies to the inadequacy of the classic Reform version of Judaism, but in side-stepping the basic issue of the basis for Jewish ritual observance it has failed to solve the heart of the problem. One may doubt whether an attenuated Reform will prove more successful than the most self-confident Reformers of the pioneer ages.

The Orthodox Reaction

A second adjustment of Jewish tradition to the modern world was attempted by Neo-Orthodoxy, whose great spokesman was S. R. Hirsch. This solution possesses the virtue of great simplicity. It meets the impact of the modern world by rejecting *in toto* the contemporary outlook on such religious and philosophic issues as inspiration, the higher criticism of the Bible, miracles, comparative religion, scientific law and the doctrine of evolution. Neo-Orthodoxy admits the difficulties and sacrifices entailed in the maintenance of Jewish law today but demands its scrupulous fulfillment, as being a divine imperative. For Jewish law to its minutest details is literally the command of God. It is true that Jewish law bears the names of legislators, prophets and sages, but, they are passive instruments performing God's will, with personal backgrounds, and historical circumstances playing no decisive part in the process. "Every regulation that an able student is destined to teach throughout time was already proclaimed to Moses at Sinai." (*Yer. Peah* 2,4) Thus Jewish law is the word of God, eternal, immutable, and forever binding upon Israel.

Neo-Orthodoxy, the classsic form of which was expounded in Germany by the Frankfort school, made only two concessions to the modern age. It accepted the Reform theory that Jews now constitute merely a religious communion. The sole difference that sets its attitude apart from Reform is that it believes that in the distant future a supernatural Messiah will miraculously restore the nationhood of Israel. In the second instance, Neo-Orthodoxy brought within the precincts of Judaism the decorum and order characteristic of West-European life.

For certain minds seeking above all things the harbor of certainty, the power and appeal of Neo-orthodoxy is undeniable. But its inability to meet the need of most modern Jews is equally clear. Its practical weakness is that it fails to reckon with the need for change, at least *de jure*. *De facto*, Orthodoxy has been forced to accept modifications which would have been undreamt of a few generations ago.

Perhaps even more important than the practical drawbacks of Neo-Orthodoxy is its weak ideological foundation. Modern historical science has demonstrated the evolutionary character of all human institutions, and Jewish scholarship has revealed the same process at work in Judaism. Orthodox scholars like David Hoffmann, in his critique of the Graf-Wellhausen theory, and Isaac Halevy, the author of *Dorot Harishonim*, in his onslaught on I. H. Weiss' *Dor Dor Vedorshav*, have rendered a superb service in exposing the weaknesses and errors of more radical scholars. Nonetheless they have been powerless to shake the conviction that Judaism has evolved through the ages, and, what is more, been responsive to environmental and even personal factors.

In fine, for a small compact group, Neo-Orthodoxy offers a way of life that is consistent and enduring, though at the cost of spiritual isolation from the modern world. But most modern Jews find it inadequate for their problems and needs.

The Mediating Philosophy

The perils inherent in Reform's nullification of Jewish tradition and Neo-Orthodoxy's petrification of Jewish law, led to the development of a mediating philosophy. This was particularly on the achievement of Jewish scholarship, notably Zunz, Frankel and Graetz in Germany. The movement has never been fortunate in its name. Zechariah Frankel called it by the ponderous German title of *"positiv-historisches Judentum"*; in America, because of its accidental relationship to modern English orthodoxy, it bears the almost equally inadequate name of "Conservative Judaism." There is scant likelihood, however, of any change of nomenclature. Frankel's designation indicated its basic tenet: it accepted as basic the axiom that Judaism had developed historically and then it adopted a positive, favorable attitude toward this historical product. What had been accepted as binding in Judaism could not be abrogated at will by any group.

As Professor Louis Ginzberg summarizes the viewpoint in his paper on Frankel, "for an adherent of this school, the sanctity of the Sabbath reposes not upon the fact that it was proclaimed on Sinai, but on the fact that the Sabbath idea found for thousands of years its expression in Jewish souls. . . . From this point of view, the evaluation of a law is independent of its origin, and thus the line of demarkation between biblical and rabbinical law almost disappears. . . ."[6] Vis-a-vis Orthodoxy, Frankel insisted that Judaism had evolved. In fact he played a great part in revealing the steps of the process. But vis-à-vis Reform, Frankel denied the right to set aside Jewish law and tradition for the sake of personal convenience or political emancipation.

Viewed against the background of the times, Frankel's theory is clearly an effort to create a counterpoise to Reform. Frankel had been revolted at the easy willingness of the delegates to the Brunswick Conference of 1844 to set aside the sancta of Judaism, but he decided to participate the following year in the Frankfort meeting. The break came on the apparently secondary issue of the language in which worship is to be conducted. When the conference voted that prayers could be offered in the vernacular and that Hebrew be retained in the service only in deference to the habits of the older generation, Frankel walked out of the sessions. Thus he bore witness to the national character of Judaism and the binding character of past Jewish practices as norms for the present. Unfortunately, Frankel never dealt fundamentally with the basis of authority, which is the crux of the problem.

It was left for Solomon Schechter to grapple with this issue. As Professor Kaplan has pointed out,[7] the two salient traits in Schechter's attitude were his stress on the primacy of Jewish scholarship and his emphasis on the importance of keeping Jewish life integral and unified. But Schechter did more—he was also aware that the conception of authority was the distinctive element in his outlook, setting it apart from both Orthodoxy and Reform. In his famous introduction to his "Studies in Judaism," he pointed out how modern Jewish historical scholarship had placed authority not in a literal Revelation but in "the conscience of Catholic Israel." "Judaism has distinct precepts and usages and customs, consecrated by the consent of Catholic Israel through thousands of years."[8]

Only through adequate learning would it be possible for Jews and particularly the rabbis, to "know what is vital to Judaism and what may be changed with impunity." He disapproved of continual dropping of various ceremonies which he regarded as essential to religion as well as of unceasing innovations, which must, in the end,—"touch the very vital organism of Judaism."

Schechter had notably deepened the concept of authority for Conservative Judaism, but even in his formulation, which was usually parenthetical and incidental to another theme, the will predominates over the intellect, that is to say, he was primarily concerned with a working formula rather than a logically perfect definition. He, too, had his gaze fixed on Reform against whose inundating tide he sought to erect a dam. Yet it must not be overlooked that this general outlook was sufficiently grounded in reality to serve as the basis for the rapid progress of Conservative Judaism in America and even in pre-war Germany, where Frankel's trend became dominant.

Nevertheless, for all its pragmatic value, the theory of Catholic Israel suffers from self-evident weaknesses. It has the virtue of recognizing the historical and evolving character of Judaism, but then it arbitrarily declares that what traditional Judaism has created until now must henceforth be maintained virtually unchanged. To cite Professor Ginzberg again, the norm according to Frankel was the Talmudic position that whatever observance is spread throughout the whole community must not be abrogated by any authority.[9] It thus creates a dichotomy in Jewish experience between the creative past and the degenerate present. Moreover, had the same doctrine been invoked in past centuries, the development of Judaism, and perhaps its very life, would have been halted. Finally, the practical application of the doctrine offers insuperable obstacles. If by Catholic Israel, whose practice determines what is binding in Judaism, we mean the majority of modern Jews, then we might as well eliminate the Sabbath, the festivals and the dietary laws, since they are violated by most Jews today. If, on the contrary, we subsume under the category of Catholic Israel the observant Jews only, the doctrine means a retention of the status quo, for by definition, an observant Jew is one who observes the Law unchanged.

For these reasons, in spite of the essential soundness of its emphasis upon the evolving nature of Judaism, the binding character of Jewish law and the centrality of Catholic Israel in that development, the theory as set forth by Frankel and Schechter proves unworkable in practice.

Untenable Guidelines

The past few years have therefore witnessed the growth of a new approach to traditional Judaism, Reconstructionism. Within the last years, it has attempted to implement its attitude toward ritual by the publication of a "New Haggadah" and of the series of articles referred to above, entitled "Toward A Guide For Jewish Ritual Usage."

The position there adopted may be summarized as follows: The traditional Jewish code of observance can no longer be maintained in its entirety. For practical and ideological reasons, many, if not most, modern Jews are not prepared to preserve it. The anarchy of Reform, the supernaturalism and reactionary character of Orthodoxy and the indecision and lack of clarity characteristic of Conservatism, render them all inadequate for modern needs.

Hence a new rationale is needed. Every ceremony and rite must be judged in terms of its value as a method of group survival and a means to the personal self-fulfillment and salvation of the individual Jew.[10] We must reckon with the fact that a common pattern of observance is no longer possible. Jews in different lands, even those who vary in their social and educational levels, will diverge in their evaluation of specific rituals. All that may be expected today is a unity of ends; the means will vary sharply among groups and individuals.

Nor does "a stigma attach to those who permit themselves a wide latitude in their departure from traditional norms." For Jewish ritual is no longer to be regarded as law, but as folkways, if only because there can be no law without sanctions and we possess no agencies for enforcing Jewish observance or punishing any infraction of the codes. In fact, Professor Kaplan had urged the substitution of the term *minhagim* or "folk-ways" for "the commandments between man and God," in order to make it clear that "they lack the connotation of being . . . imperative."[11]

The proposed "Guide" then sets up criteria for judging of the value of specific rituals, in terms of the meaningfulness of their form, their content or both. It finally considers in some detail synagogue worship, the sabbath, and "dietary usages," retaining or modifying elements of the traditional codes in the light of the criteria previously developed.

This series has naturally aroused considerable discussion, both written and oral,[12] but here we wish merely to call attention to various details of both the theoretic formulation and the practical applications that are relevant to our purpose. It is not true, for example, that Conservative Judaism makes the survival of the Jewish people the justification of Jewish observance, or that traditional Jews observe the dietary laws "out of fear" and not "out of love." No doubt there are many who maintain Judaism generally out of the "fear of God," but many others are moved by the "love of God" as well.

Moreover, it is grossly insufficient to have unity of purpose with a variety of means, if only because, as John Dewey clearly pointed out, the means you have always with you, while the end belongs to an uncertain future. Given enough variety of means, no unity remains at all.

Dr. Kaplan is undoubtedly correct in stressing the fact that traditional Judaism deprecated the effort to explain the meaning of the *mitzvot*.[13] But this attitude prevailed only during the earlier stages of the
Jewish religion, before the impact of other cultures became more pro-
nounced. When Judaism met Greek thought, whether directly as in
Philo, or through the medium of Arabic civilization, as in medieval
days, the search for the *ta'amay ha-mitzvot* (purpose of the commandments) became a central feature of Jewish religious thought, and the
subject of a considerable literature.

Thus the pioneer of Jewish philosophy, Saadiah, already classifies
the commandments under two headings: *sichliyot* commandments, the
reason for which is clearly evident, and *shimiyot,* those demanding
obedience, though their meaning is not clear. By reinterpreting these
categories in modern terms, we arrive at a sound classification of the
mitzvot, (a) the rational commands, consisting largely of the ethical imperatives wherein Judaism is basically at one with all great religions
and (b) the uniquely traditional forms, the product of historical factors
in Judaism.[14] That the instruments of daily prayer are phylacteries and
not a prayer-carpet cannot be justified on rational grounds, but is the
consequence of a specific Jewish development. Nor need its justification be sought in the area of logic. Every personality, whether that of
an individual or a group, includes rational elements, wherein it will resemble others. But the essence of personality resides in the non-rational elements, which alone are unique and distinctive. To attempt to
build the human spirit purely from rational elements means to create
an automaton, not a living organism.

Beyond "Folkways"

The cardinal weakness, however, of the Reconstructionist approach
lies, we feel, in its denial of the concept of Jewish law. Dr. Kaplan emphatically insists that ritual observances are not law but folk-ways, and
he cites Vinogradoff to prove that law implies sanctions, the employ-
ment of force against the recalcitrant individual. Unless, therefore, we
are prepared to reinstitute flagellation and the other Rabbinic punishments for the violation of the ritual commandments, Jewish ritual observances must be regarded by us merely as folk-ways.

To deal with the practical implications of this attitude before considering its theoretic basis, it seems obvious to us that to declare Jewish observance merely a matter of folk-ways, sounds the death-knell of Judaism as a normative religion. Nowhere is there a deeper "appreciation" of the beauty of Jewish "folk-ways" than among the labor Zionists, for example. The best book thus far written on the Jewish festivals emanates from a member of their circle. But a sympathetic attitude toward these customs, even an emotional relationship, is powerless to effect their observance. Undoubtedly, we prefer the observance of a Third Seder by the Labor Zionists to the Yom Kippur balls of the anarchists forty years ago, but what about the First and Second Seder?

If we abandon the concept of Jewish law, we have unwittingly adopted the principals of Paulinian Christianity. For it must be remembered that Paul was by no means uncompromisingly antinominian at the beginning of his career. On the contrary, his early attitude was one of toleration and even of commendation. In I Cor. 7:19 he declares, "Circumcision is nothing and non-circumcision is nothing, but the keeping of the commandment of the law." In Romans 2:25 he goes further and admits: "Circumcision verily profiteth, if thou keep the law." Yet beginning at that standpoint, it was a series of easy transitions that led him to the complete repudiation of Jewish ritual law and the retention only of the ethical commandments. Ultimately, Paul could insist that keeping the law was a mark of sin.

So much for the practical consequences of this negation of the concept of Jewish law. I confess, however, that I cannot follow the theory of the Reconstructionist approach either. To define law in terms of sanctions seems to me to put the cart before the horse. Not sanctions create law, but law creates sanctions. Vinogradoff, in the quotation cited by Dr. Kaplan does declare:

> "Every legal rule falls into two parts: first, a *command* stating the legal requirement, second, a *sanction* providing that, if the command is not obeyed, force will be employed against the recalcitrant person."

But he is speaking of legal rules regulating human relations and here sanctions are a central feature, for this obvious reason: Legal codes that are concerned with the protection of the individual in society must interpose speedy and effective safeguards against aggression from other individuals. Protection and redress must be *immediate* in order to be effective, since the victim, being human, does not live forever! Hence laws *between man and God* which do not impose human sanctions are dead letters.

But for the religious spirit, the compulsion in law resides elsewhere than in the police power of the state. For the believers in God, every wrong act has its tragic consequence reflected in the universe, and retribution is cosmic:

> the shop is open; and the dealer gives credit; and the ledger lies open; and the hand writes; and whosoever wishes to borrow may come and borrow; and the collectors regularly make their daily round, and exact payment from man whether he is content or not. . . . (Ethics of the Fathers 3:20)

That is the essence of the religious outlook, which therefore regards the world as governed by the Divine law of justice, which is binding upon men even when no human penalties exist or can be enforced. Therein lies the significant contribution which religion makes to morality, its capacity to penetrate to areas beyond the reach of the law. The state punishes me if I hurt my neighbor, but hating him is no less a violation of law, though the courts are powerless to act. Beating one's old father is punishable by sanctions imposed by the police court; disrespect is not punishable by human agency, yet it is none the less binding. These and countless other ethical imperatives are law, not customs, practices or habits, yet no human, external penalty attaches to their violation.

These *a priori* considerations are reinformed by a consideration of Talmudic categories. No one will deny that to the Rabbis, the *mitzvot* were law, of binding power, yet every page of the Talmud refers to such concepts as "Free from penalty but forbidden," "unpunished in human law, but guilty by Divine law," "death at the hand of God." Recently, attention has been called to the phenomenon in Rabbinic law, where legal rules, possessing human sanctions are transferred in the Talmud to the realm of ethics, with no external penalties.[15] In fine, human sanctions cannot serve as the marks of religious law.

But, it will be argued, Rabbinic Judaism regards every enactment of the ritual as well as of the ethical code as literally Divine, and violations of either are believed to entail Divine punishment. But for us today, Revelation rooted in the Divine as is all life, is a never-ending human process, with institutions and ordinances created by men in whom the Divine spirit works. Can we believe that the ritual code is enforceable with penalties? I submit that *in terms of our modern outlook*, it remains true for us today that the violation of Jewish ritual law is attended by Divine sanctions,—*and that no other attitude is possible.* If we declare that the observance of the Sabbath brings deep and abiding rewards to the Jew, that it re-creates his spirit as it regenerates his physical and nervous system, that it brings him into communion with God, links him with the profoundest aspirations of Israel, and draws him into the orbit of Torah, then it follows inescapably that the failure to observe the Sabbath brings its punishment in the impoverishment of the spirit, the denudation of Jewish values and the alienation from the Jewish community, literally "that soul is cut off from its kinsmen."

We naturally picture the manner in which divine sanctions operate as different from the conception of our ancestors, because our conception of God has changed, but we cannot deny that Divine judgment operates in the world. For Conservative Judaism, murder and the infraction of the Sabbath are not on a par (incidentally they are not for Orthodox Judaism either),[16] but they are both violations of Jewish law, differing from each other as crimes, felonies and misdemeanors differ in American law and therefore entailing penalties of varying severity.

Moreover, and this is significant for the outlook of Conservative Judaism, which is based on the historical approach, the content of these categories will differ in time, *pari passu* with changes in conceptions and conditions. The commandment "Thou shalt not kill" was not at the time of its promulgation regarded as prohibiting clan vengeance, but as time went on this was subsumed under the category. First, the Torah limited the activity of the Avenger of the Blood in the case of an unpremeditated killing and established the cities of refuge. By the time of the Second Temple, clan vengeance under any circumstance would have been regarded as murder, pure and simple, had it ever been attempted. The same process of development at work may be observed in the current attitude toward lynching as a crime, concurred in by most, but not yet by all Americans. Some day, God grant it be soon, the mass murder of war will be recognized as part of the prohibition. Not only crimes, but misdemeanors, change with time, but these modifications do not invalidate their status as law.

Therein lies our differentiation from Orthodoxy. We likewise regard ritual observance as part of Jewish law but our attitude toward law differs. We insist upon reckoning with the results of Jewish scholarship which illustrate with myriad of examples the flexible, evolutionary character of Jewish law. For us divine revelation is a never-ending process but we recognize that Moses, Akiba, Maimonides and Karo had a greater meed of revelation than the Brunswick Conference of 1844.

"Catholic Israel" and Authority

Wherein does the authority of Jewish law reside, if revelation did not end at Sinai, or with the Mishnah or the Shulhan Arukh? The answer that Conservative Judaism requires is to be found in the doctrine of Catholic Israel enunciated in general terms by Frankel and Schechter. We need only to explore its implications in terms of our current trends and insights.

Frankel and his colleagues in Germany, and to a lesser degree Schechter in America, were concerned with erecting a dike against the flood-tide of Reform. Hence they evolved the conception of Catholic Israel, which called for the modern loyal Jew to identify himself with the accepted practice of the Jewish people. This concept was fundamentally a static principle, barring the way to change—a historical necessity in their day, when Reform threatened to sweep everything before it. Today, our concern is no longer with preventing extreme innovation but with establishing norms for orderly growth and progress. Yet because of its basic truth, the doctrine of Catholic Israel can prove equally fruitful in our present situation.

The conception of Catholic Israel is basically democratic. It declares that Jewish life is determined by no synod or conference or editorial board, but reflects the aspirations and attitudes of the Jewish people as a whole. Now, theoretically, democracy is, in Lincoln's classic definition, incidentally enunciated centuries earlier in the preface to Wyclif's Bible, "government of the people, by the people, for the people." Practically, however, no democratic government expresses the will of the entire people, but only of those sufficiently interested in it to exercise the franchise and obey the laws. The indifferent citizens who do not exercise the franchise, and the criminals convicted of an offense who forfeit their citizenship, constitute two classes that have no voice in the conduct of the government. At the opposite pole from the criminal are certain extreme idealistic groups, who voluntarily relinquish their rights in the state. H. D. Thoreau, the great New England naturalist, was a philosophical anarchist who wrote on the "Duty of Civil Disobedience." He remains a great American, but he was not consulted in the town meeting at Concord. Similarly, pacifists in the present national crisis are honored for their devotion to principle, and are not expelled from the American people, but they do not ask to decide the military and diplomatic policies of the government. In *posse*, democracy is the government of all the people; *in esse*, it is government by all elements of the people who recognize the authority of the law and actively express their interest, at least by going to the ballot-box. There are times when nearly all eligible voters exercise their franchise. Generally, the percentage is only a fraction, sometimes less than fifty per cent, of the whole. Our government, however, remains a democracy, because potentially every American has a voice in the conduct of its affairs.

Apply this analysis to our problem and it becomes clear that Catholic Israel must be conceived differently from hitherto accepted views. On the one hand, it is not co-extensive with the Jewish people, nor on the other, is it restricted to those who observe the Law unchanged.

Catholic Israel is the body of men and women within the Jewish people, who accept the authority of Jewish law and are concerned with Jewish observance as a genuine issue. It therefore includes all who observe the law, whether formally Orthodox or Conservative or neither. The character of their observance may be rigorous and extend to minutiae, or it may include modifications in detail. Catholic Israel embraces all those, too, who observe Jewish law in general, though they may violate one or another segment, and who are sensitive to the problem of their non-observance because they wish to respect the authority of Jewish law.

Moreover, Catholic Israel is vertical as well as horizontal, that is to say, it includes the generations gone before, whose lives and activities have determined the character of the tradition transmitted to us. Their practice cannot permanently bar the way to growth, but it must necessarily exert influence upon our decisions regarding changes from accepted tradition. They cannot exercise a veto, but they must not be deprived of a vote.

That past generations should play an important role in determining the content of tradition for the present is not astonishing. The sales of "Gone With the Wind" were many thousands of times greater than that of "Hamlet," but the perennial appeal of the latter is more significant of its place in English culture than the "best-seller" qualities of the former. Catholic Israel is universal in time as well as in space.

In spite of widespread impressions to the contrary, Catholic Israel, those within the pale of normative Judaism, was never a monolithic mass, a homogeneous body. The divergences between Hillelites and Shammaites, the distinctions in custom between Palestinian and Babylonian custom, the differences among rationalist, mystic and traditionalist in the Middle Ages down to the *Hasid* and the *Mitnaged* in modern times, all these were often far-reaching, both in theory and in practice. Only the passing of time has blurred the lines and softened the acerbities of controversy.

The character and limits of these differences may be illustrated by two historical instances. Talmudic Judaism had its strict constructionists as well as its liberal interpreters, who greatly extended the scope of the Biblical text. The more liberal exegesis of Akiba generally prevailed over the stricter methods of Ishmael, yet the latter had a by no means inconsiderable influence upon Jewish law. When, however, centuries later, a group of strict constructionists, the Karaites, arose, who denied the entire validity of Talmudic law, they forfeited their right to determine the development of Rabbinic law.

Variations within Catholic Israel always existed. For obvious reasons, they are more marked today than in the past. Catholic Israel is no single, homogeneous group. It has its conservatives and its liberals, as has the American electorate. It is, however, restricted to those who accept the authority of Jewish law.

It need hardly be emphasized that this conception does not read any Jew out of the Jewish fold. It merely declares what should be self-evident, that only those should have a voice in determining the character of Jewish law who recognize its authority. Reform and secularist Jews will continue to select on a purely personal basis certain customs from the pattern of Jewish living that appeal to them. But since they deny the authority of Jewish law, they naturally cannot expect to be consulted in its development. It is true that in recent years, these groups have approved growing numbers of Jewish practices, a tendency eminently to be welcomed and encouraged. But the judgment of the Sages has particular relevancy to our problem.

Change and Development

The conception of Catholic Israel, here proposed, sheds light on the process of change and development and the technique by which these changes are to be legitimized.

Changes in Jewish observance can become part and parcel of Jewish law only if they emanate from Catholic Israel, from those who accept the authority of Jewish law and not from those who for whatever reasons, have broken with it. Thus the Prohibition Amendment was repealed not by the activities of the Capones and the Schultzes, but by the attitudes and behavior of law-abiding American citizens who opposed Prohibition. At the beginning, a small group of dissidents object to a given law, slowly they persuade others to adopt their opinion. When they increase in numbers, the enactment becomes a dead letter, and ultimately disappears from the statute books.

This process of change and development in Jewish law is to be traced, not only during the great creative periods of the Bible and the Talmud, as modern Jewish scholarship has revealed, but even in the abnormal and chaotic history of the modern period. Before our eyes, radical changes are taking place, and this among those who live by Jewish law. The laws of *sha'atnez* and the prohibition of interest are virtually inoperative among traditional Jews, as is the formerly widespread custom of wearing a beard. Shaving, in spite of the five prohibitions involved, is almost universal, even without the shaving powder and the electric razor. The observance of the dietary laws today is generally accompanied by a willingness to eat dairy foods or fish in non-kosher eating houses. Recent inventions have created new problems of observance, and corresponding reactions, on the part of Sabbath observers. The telephone tends to be quite widely used (for social purposes), the radio and television perhaps a little less, and electric lights perhaps a little more. Yet increasingly, these acts are being performed by Sabbath observers. All these and similar modifications have occurred without guidance or even a conscious principle, but the principle does exist. It is Catholic Israel at work, who, if they are not prophets, are the descendants of prophets. (*Pes.* 66b.)

This recognition of Jewish law as the expression of Catholic Israel explains the fact that what was forbidden at one time and properly so, may become permitted at another and with equal justice. For new conditions and attitudes impinge on the lives of men and accordingly modify the outlook and the practices of Catholic Israel. When East-European Jews a century or more ago, objected to the shorter, "German" coats of the *Maskilim,* it was not mere obscurantism, but a recognition that the surrender of the traditional Jewish garb was a symbol of a break with Jewish tradition. But as time went on, the new mode penetrated into traditional circles as well and it now became innocuous.

Without presuming to decide here the Halachic issues involved, it is clear that some warrant for instrumental music in the synagogue may be found in Jewish tradition. Non-Reform circles were adamant in their objection to the innovation in nineteenth century Germany because they recognized that its introduction was directly a *hukat hagoy,* an aping of foreign customs; a conscious effort to pattern the synagogue after the Protestant Church. That factor is by no means negligible even today, but now when a traditional congregation introduces an organ it may be presumed to imitate some contemporary Jewish and not necessarily a Christian model. Of course, the decision with regard to such a step involves many considerations of a non-halakhic character as well.

If Jewish law is a constantly developing organism, wherein does its continuity lie? Precisely in its organic character. It has been pointed out that every living body is constantly engaged in breaking down and replacing its cells, so that within seven years, not a single cell remains unchanged in a human body. If this be true, how can we describe ourselves as identical with the personality we were eight years ago? The answer is obvious: Identity really means continuity, and continuity is preserved because the changes are gradual; we do not rise one morning to discover that every cell in us is new!

The process of growth is slow, it has its stresses and conflicts. By its very nature, every general law will work hardships in exceptional cases that require amelioration. But it remains law, because we believe it to be binding and its observance or violation to entail consequences of good or evil.

From Minority to Masses

Having redefined Catholic Israel as those elements of the Jewish people that recognize the authority of Jewish law and are sensitive to the problem, we cannot overlook the ominous change that has taken place in modern times, in the ratio that Catholic Israel bears to the Jewish people as a whole. That Catholic Israel could be identified by Frankel and Schechter with virtually the entire Jewish people was due to the fact that until recently the two groups were practically coextensive. Today, Catholic Israel in our definition represents only a minority of American Jewry, and with the destruction of the European center, perhaps of world Jewry. A democracy, in which only a fraction of the electorate is interested in the government is in grave danger, and the present status of Jewish religious life in America is equally intolerable.

In fact, a theoretical question may be raised as to the right of a minority to arrogate to itself the title of "Catholic Israel" and then undertake to "legislate" for the majority. If the final authority is vested in the Jewish people and Jews do not observe Jewish ritual, does not their practice or lack of practice become the modern standard of the Jew? Practically and theoretically, then, the concept of Catholic Israel as consisting of a minority is subject to challenge.

The answer lies in the conviction, and in the will behind that conviction, that the present status of Jewish observance is, or must be made, only temporary. To quote an analogy from American experience, we are now at the frontier stage of Jewish life in America. Every American is familiar with the frontier towns that sprang up all over America, particularly in the wake of the Gold Rush and similar mass movements. In these mushroom towns, the basic moral practice of American society was observed by a small and often impotent minority. Drunkenness, murder, gambling and sexual license were often widespread. Had the social behavior of these Western towns been perpetuated, it would have meant the collapse of the accepted moral code of America.

Instead, a contrary process took place. The minority gradually was able to institute law and order and its standards ultimately became dominant. Where did a minority draw the authority to enforce its standards upon the majority? It derived it from the knowledge that its attitudes had the sanction of the entire American people, of whom it constituted an outpost. The weight of that authority ultimately prevailed, even though it was temporarily embodied in a minority. As Lincoln pointed out in his attack on the concept of "popular sovereignty" as expounded by Douglas, Americans would never have admitted the right of Mormons to practice polygamy in the territory they occupied as a majority. It is, of course, undeniable that the frontier spirit, as Professor Turner has stressed, exerted an abiding influence upon the American character and institutions, but the pressure of American life as a whole proved decisive for the frontier towns.

The analogy with the present status of Jewish life in America is striking. "Each man does what is righteous in his own eyes" is as valid a description of our age as of the days of the Judges. Pretending that the present chaos in Jewish life and observance is "the American way," and seeking to justify it or, at least to acquiesce in it, under some high-sounding formula is sheer self-deception, of which true spiritual leaders dare not be guilty. It may be granted that current American-Jewish practice will influence our future code of observance in many ways and must therefore be taken into account. But it is undeniable that there is need of reviving the mass of traditional Jewish rituals by interpreting them in the light of our modern attitudes, and ceaselessly campaigning for their observance.

Therein lies a fundamental challenge of the current crisis to the Jewish spiritual leadership of today, one which has been unconscionably neglected. But the functions of the Rabbinate are not exhausted merely in agitating for Jewish observance. We must not only guide the practice of the people by expounding the values in Jewish ritual observance. We must, when changes are found necessary, create the instruments for bringing the change into the mainstream of Jewish tradition.

The technique for this latter function was evolved by the Rabbis of the Talmud. It resides in the process of interpretation rather than in nullification as a means of development. This contention, however, is frequently denied. It is argued that Akiba could draw fine-spun deductions from the Biblical text which actually were developments beyond it, because he believed it to be literally the Word of God and so both eternal in its application and significant in every syllable, and because the modern sense of historical change was lacking in his day. Since, however, for us, Revelation is no longer literal, but figurative, a process and not an act, and since we possess the modern sense of history, a similar procedure of interpretation is impossible.

This conclusion is, however, open to serious doubt. The Constitution of the United States is not regarded as the literal Word of God even by its most perfervid admirers, and no one believes that its authors foresaw the problems and conditions of our day. Yet the learned Justices of the Supreme Court find it perfectly sensible procedure to declare laws regarding radio chains, trade unions, the closed shop and public utilities "constitutional" or otherwise. By a process of interpretation of the letter of the Constitution, they seek to disclose its spirit and then make it relevant to contemporary needs.

Nor is this all. It is well-known that nine equally honest and reasonably competent judges, will differ as to the constitutionality of a given law, basing their opinions on varying interpretations of the text of the basic document. The inference is clear that, barring an obvious infringement of the Constitution where no difference of opinion is possible, the Justices begin with an attitude on the social utility of a given law and then seek to validate their opinion by a study of the text.

Professor Morris R. Cohen points out that in human affairs, inventing and finding are not antithetical, so that "the process of law making is called finding the law." A judicial decision "decides not so much what the words of a statute ordinarily mean but *what the public, taking all the circumstances of the case into account, should act on.*" He argues forcibly against regarding this process as "spurious interpretation," pointing out that supplementary legislation by judges is not only inevitable but justifiable because *"to make a detailed description of specific human actions and their consequences forbidden or allowed would be an endless and impossible task."* (Italics his) He insists also, that while judges do and must make law, it would be absurd to maintain that "they are in no wise bound and can make any law they please."[17] The analogies with Jewish tradition and our present problem are obvious.

The process in Talmudic law was, as well as one can judge, entirely similar. When two sages differed on a given issue, the Biblical verses they cited were not the reason for their respective positions, only a legal justification. First came a felt need, often embodied in popular practice, then the process of interpretation of Scripture to give it continuity with tradition.

There is nothing in our modern concept of Revelation that makes this process either impossible or outmoded. The survival of the American way depends upon avoiding the Scylla of reaction and the Charybdis of revolution. So, too, the Jewish way of life depends upon our success in avoiding the unbending adherence to the *status quo ante* on the one hand, and wholesale nullification on the other. Our platform must be loyalty to Jewish law, as embodied in the practice and thought of Catholic Israel and subject to the changes adopted by Catholic Israel.

This democratic concept vests the full authority in the people, but that does not imply that the Rabbinate has no part to play in the process. On the contrary, the Rabbinate has a dual function to perform. When a change has already become part of the practice of Catholic Israel, the Rabbi of today, like his predecessors, has the duty of aiding its legitimatization by using the accepted principles of interpretation of the traditional Halachah. But long before this step is reached, the Rabbinate has the duty to guide the path of development of Jewish law by setting up criteria for Jewish observance, evaluating each specific element by those standards and then educating the people to adopt their attitudes.

Criteria for Observance

The establishment of criteria for Jewish observance is no simple matter, as previous efforts in this direction have indicated. All the more reason, therefore for another tentative approach:—

,A. Our attitude toward Jewish observance, as Professor Kaplan has indicated, is not neutral. We are definitely "prejudiced" in favor of Jewish observance. We do not approach Jewish life with a *tabula rasa,* any more than in any department of civilization. "The presumption should always be in favor of traditional procedure."[18]

B. In order that this principle serve as a practical guide, we may suggest, with apologies to Maimonides, a theory of negative attributes. Below we shall adduce four positive norms by which ritual is to be judged. Any Jewish practice *eo ipso* has a claim upon us, unless it can be proved that it does not perform any of these functions, nor can it be reinterpreted to do so.

Thus four criteria may be briefly set forth as follows:—

I. *Cosmic or religious.* These are observances that bind us to the universe and lend a cosmic significance to the events of our ordinary life. Beautiful and meaningful ritual places such occasions as birth, puberty, marriage and death against the background of a vital universe and its Creator. They no longer remain accidents of animal existence. Such activities as eating or enjoying other pleasures are by means of a blessing, invested with a sense of the Divine. The physical and nervous rebuilding of an organism through the Sabbath rest becomes part of the cosmic process. Meaningful ritual invests human life with a sense of holiness. It declares with the unanswerable logic of beauty, that man counts in the universe.

II. *Ethical or Social.* It is of the essence of ideals that they must be taught continually. Unlike the multiplication table, learning them by rote is insufficient, because life which, in the largest sense, depends upon them, is always conspiring through a thousand petty devices to defeat man's aspirations for peace, understanding and justice. As Einstein declared several years ago in an address on education, "With the affairs of human beings, knowledge of truth alone does not suffice. On the contrary, this knowledge must continually be renewed by ceaseless effort, if it is not to be lost. It resembles a statue of marble which stands in the desert and is continuously threatened with burial by the shifting sand. The hands of service must ever be at work, in order that the marble continue lastingly to shine in the sun."[19] To teach ideals perpetually and yet avoid monotony is the special function of ritual. For, being symbolic in character, it lends itself to varying interpretations and avoids the perils of monotony. The *Sukkah,* the *Shofar,* the *Seder,* are rituals symbolizing ideals that can be reinterpreted anew and differently at each season.

III. *Esthetic or play function.* A principal reason for the fact that ritual observance, reverently and meaningfully executed, avoids the pitfalls of monotony is its esthetic character. Rituals constitute a source of poetry in life and offer an avenue of play for adults, who increasingly in our modern civilization find amusement in mechanical, vicarious and commercialized forms only. A religious service offers the adult the opportunity to sing; the Passover *Seder,* a chance to reenact a great drama, the *Habdalah* service, a bit of pageantry, which most grownups find nowhere else. It is symptomatic of the atrophy of the play function that adults who seek to re-introduce a ceremony into their practice after long disuse are self-conscious and uncomfortable about it. It is equally characteristic of the decay of vitality in the Reform synagogue that the congregation is passive and virtually inaudible, spectators rather than participants in a religious service. The esthetic, participating element in Jewish ritual is all the more essential for the psychic well-being of a people.

IV. Finally, Jewish ritual has *national or group-associational values,* linking the individual Jew to his people. While early extreme Reform sought to abolish *Milah,* and decried it as a barbarous custom, the rite of circumcision possessed such strong survival-value that it has remained the universal mark of the covenant of Abraham. Even the dietary laws were never completely abolished by Reform. Until some years ago, the Register of the Hebrew Union College declared that the Dining Hall observed "some dietary laws." American Jewry reflects untold patterns of dietary observance, down to the Jew whose only rule is that he buys his *terefah* meat from a Jewish and not a Gentile butcher! Ludicrous as these variations are from the standpoint of traditional Halachah, they represent the periphery of a circle at the center of which is the full code of *Kashrut.* But all the degrees of observance recognize that the dietary laws draw the Jew close to his people and make him conscious of his Jewish allegiance.

In stressing the national element in Jewish observances, along with the other values inherent in them, we do not hesitate to affirm that whatever strengthens the bond of Jewish loyalty is a good, because we believe profoundly that Jewish survival is a blessing to the world. If that is not our profoundest conviction, we have no business trying to preserve either Judaism or the identity of the Jew.

C. It is obvious that the most valuable elements of Jewish traditional observance perform all these functions, the cosmic, the ethical, the esthetic and the national, and do them well. At times, an observance may perform only one or two of them, but do it to so transcendent a degree as to justify its retention.

By standards such as these the heritage of Jewish ritual must be evaluated. So vital is most of Jewish tradition that by and large, it can be maintained if properly interpreted. Some aspects require modification or reinterpretation or both, and others may need to be discarded. The function of the Rabbi is to foster the appreciation and observance of Jewish ritual, and thus mold the attitude of Catholic Israel.

D. The final authority, however, rests with the Jewish people, though the formal retention, reinterpretation or surrender of Jewish observances should come from accredited rabbinical leadership. So long as some heart-beat of vitality may be detected in a custom, its value should be discussed with an eye to its resuscitation. But death is an unanswerable argument—if it has died utterly and completely, Catholic Israel has spoken and there is no returning.

Action and Standards

It is obvious that the reinterpretation of the concept of Catholic Israel and the concept of the authority of Jewish law, as well as the suggested criteria for evaluating Jewish ritual observances here set forth, do not constitute a solution to the problem of modern Jewish religious life. They are rather the instruments for meeting the challenge which faces Jewish ritual today. There is crying need for a proclamation of the truth that the Jewish people without Judaism is an empty shell, and that Judaism without Jewish observance is a will o' the wisp. That truth must become transmuted into a campaign for Jewish religious life, active, personal, concrete.

Our movement is virtually the only agency on the American scene in position to undertake the effort for the revival and development of Jewish law, because we alone represent the modern interpretation of traditional Judaism. Thus Professor Salo Baron, who bears no official relationship to our movement, out of the fulness of his historical understanding says: "Neo-Orthodoxy, equally with Reform, is a deviation from historical Judaism. No less than Reform, it abandoned Judaism's self-rejuvenating historical dynamism. For this reason we may say that . . . the 'Positive-Historical Judaism' of Zacharias Frankel and Michael Sachs and the Conservative Judaism of America have been much truer to the spirit of traditional Judaism. By maintaining the general validity of traditional Jewish law and combining with it freedom of personal interpretation of the Jewish past and creed, Frankel and his successors hoped to preserve historical continuity."[20] He is clearly aware of the weaknesses of our movement, yet he declares: "It is Conservative Judaism which seems to show the greatest similarities with the method and substance of teaching of the popular leaders during the declining Second Commonwealth, inasmuch as clinging to the traditional mode of life, it nevertheless allows for the adaptation of basic theological concepts to the changing social and cultural needs. Perhaps also like early Pharisaism, it has thus far failed to develop a new comprehensive and uniform philosophy of Judaism."

But if we are to avoid the weaknesses of which Professor Baron speaks, Conservative Judaism, through the Rabbinical Assembly, must begin to grapple energetically with the issues of Jewish law. That we were right on the *agunah* question has been underlined with tragic clarity in the past few years. We are in desperate need of study and action, in the area of family law, in the field of Sabbath observance, the character of our Friday Evening Service and many other phases. Our laymen need a code of Jewish observance, that will reckon with their practice, but not surrender to it.

Authority in Jewish Law

Our Committee on Jewish Law must become the center of our activity. It can do so only if boldly yet reverently it undertakes to formulate Halachah for Conservative Judaism. Its technique must include at least six elements: (a) a careful study of legal tradition with special concern for minority views, (b) a survey of present practices within the various sections of Catholic Israel, (c) an effort to establish optimum standards in terms of contemporary needs, (d) wherever possible, the delimitation of divergent patterns of observance varying from minimum to maximum, and corresponding to the phrases frequent in the traditional codes' "be lenient" or "be stringent." These patterns would clearly point out the varying importance of the details of observance, indicating the basically essential, the optional and the tangential elements in each area of practice, (e) the reinterpretation of traditional Halachah to validate those new practices found acceptable for today, (f) the publication of guides for American Jewry in various areas of Jewish observance, which would indicate the specific values inherent in each rite, as well as the method for observing it. A Guide to Jewish Practice for Conservative Judaism should combine the functions of a *Sefer Ta'amei Hamitzvot,* a rationale for Jewish observance, and a *Shulhan Arukh,* a presentation of Jewish practice, couched in the modern idiom and sensitive to the human condition in our day.

The theoretic formulation of the Halachah for Conservative Judaism is the indispensable prelude to the practical tasks lying before the movement.

With the cooperation of the Jewish Theological Seminary and the participation of the United Synagogue, the Rabbinical Assembly must undertake an active campaign for Jewish living. In each community, some group, however small, would be enlisted in a Fellowship of *Haberim,* who, like the *Haberim* of the Mishnaic period, would undertake to maintain a higher standard of Jewish observance and study in their personal lives than the generality. There might indeed, be several degrees of Haberim, depending on the extent and intensity of the Jewish program undertaken. Such fellowships offer a superb agency for channeling the reborn Jewish spirit for returning service men. Such a movement might well capture the imagination of American Jewry, civilian and veteran alike. The number who would be attracted by its intrinsic appeal and external glamor, might be considerably larger than we dared to anticipate. The synagogue and the Jewish School, now largely impotent, would be reenforced by the most important members of the triad, the Jewish home, and Judaism would cease being a vicarious experience for most Jews, embodied in institutions and expressed almost entirely in financial contributions.

With such a platform and an appeal, Conservative Judaism would fulfill its destiny as the most vital force in American Israel. There will be many who will follow, many more who will listen and many others, who, unpersuaded at the beginning, may be reeducated to the glory and satisfactions inherent in Jewish living.

If we prove worthy, in some slight measure, of our predecessors, it is given us to hope that we may again, as has happened in the past, transform the anarchy and ignorance characteristic of the pioneering stage into a rich, deeply-rooted pattern of Jewish life. Ezra and Nehemiah, who battled against intermarriage and the violation of the Sabbath in Palestine; Rab, who found an open valley in Babylonia which he fenced in (*Hull.* 110a); Moses ben Enoch, who helped lay the foundations of Jewish learning in Spain; all represent the rhythm of Jewish rebirth, which, *mutatis mutandis,* must be recaptured in America as well. Granted that the problems are infinitely more complicated than ever before, as Professor Kaplan has so thoroughly set forth, it too does not follow that our cause gains by inactivity or by surrender to the forces of dissolution.

In contradistinction to the Talmud and the authors of the Reconstructionist "Guide," alike, we feel that "if you have grasped for a little, you have not grasped."

Each rabbi, in isolation, has, for perfectly natural reasons, demanded too little rather than too much from his congregation in regard to ritual observance, and Jewish study. What the individual cannot even hope for may often be achieved by organization—and that is the duty of our movement.

The history of human culture, no less than that of Jewish experience, has shown that ages of indifference and hostility to religion give way to periods of spiritual revival. The skeptical period of the eighteenth century which itself conserved important religious ideals, gave way to the nineteenth century which was, in many respects, a modern age of faith. There are more than a few signs, which the war experience has multiplied ten thousand fold, that modern men are seeking their way to God. I profoundly believe that it is easier, not harder, to win men for the traditional Jewish concept of the Living God as interpreted by our greatest teachers than for a reconstructed concept that denies His existential reality.

Judaism has no room for the anti-rational, for the *credo quia absurdum* attitude, but it does not exclude the emotional, the non-rational, the leap of faith across the abyss of the unknown. A recent radical writer declares: "Religion dissolved into ethicism is no longer religion. What is left to worship after dogmas and mystery have been taken away?"[21] For "dogmas" we may substitute "mitzvot," the obligations of Jewish law, interpreted in the light of our learning and our ideals. Without them, Judaism as a way of life is doomed. There is more than a little truth in the same writer's contention that "the rationalist reform of religion is itself a symptom of religious decay. On the whole, it has done more to accelerate the decay of religion than to prop it up."

Religion is in essence the all-embracing attitude of man toward the universe. It must therefore reckon with the unknown and mysterious in the cosmos as well as with the rational and the known. It dare not minimize the moral imperative to build a just society of just men. Yet to achieve this purpose, it must unfurl the banner of the Living God. To keep that faith ever vivid and real, ritual is essential, as we have seen. Our standpoint must be that ritual is part of Jewish law, possessing a strong sense of continuity with the past and an equally powerful capacity for growth and adaptation to the needs of the present. The crisis is already upon us, and so is the God-given opportunity. The day is short, the work is manifold. Let not the workers be indolent or disheartened, for the reward is very great. It may not be granted us to complete the work, but neither have we the right to desist from it.

Notes

1. *The Reconstructionist,* Vol. VII, no. 13–16, 18. The entire series has been republished under the same title in pamphlet form.

2. For a valuable survey of Reform, see David Philipson, *The Reform Movement in Judaism,* 2nd ed. (New York, 1931). The full text of the Pittsburgh Platform is given in Philipson, op. cit. p. 354 f.

3. Philipson, op. cit. p. 358 f.

4. The details of the adoption of the Statement are extremely illuminating. At the 1936 meeting of the C. C. A. R. a proposed statement of Principles was presented but was laid over to the next conference. This preliminary draft included the following statements:

"For Reform Judaism, Torah represents the whole body of progressive religious values, from the covenant at Sinai to the present day. It is both Haggadah (lore) and Halachah (law). It sounds the eternal imperatives of faith and of duty. Though many of its ancient laws, ceremonial and civil are no longer operative under the changed conditions of the present, "Law" continues to be an abiding element of the Torah of Judaism." . . . "To entrust ourselves voluntarily to the authority of the Torah, as interpreted by sound scholarship and by devoted spiritual leadership, in matters personal and social, is the supreme need of our spiritual life." (*Yearbook, C. C. A. R.* Vol. XLVI, 1936, p. 90 F). This entire material did not reappear in the final draft, nor was any reference made to it in any of the voluminous discussion reported in the Yearbooks of 1936 and 1937.

5. *Yearbook of C. C. A. R.* Vol. XLVII 1937, p. 98.

6. L. Ginzberg *Students, Scholars and Saints* (Phila. 1928), pp. 206–7.

7. In the *Reconstructionist,* Vol. VI, No. 17, Dec. 27, 1940.

8. For these and similar quotations from his writings cited below. See the extremely useful paper by Myer S. Kripke, "Solomon Schechter's Philosophy of Judaism" in the *Reconstructionist,* Vol. III, No. 12 and 13, October 22 and November 5, 1937.

9. Ginzberg, op. cit., p. 209.

10. *The Reconstructionist,* Vol. VII, No. 13, p. 9.

11. M. M. Kaplan, *Judaism As A Civilization,* p. 432.

12. As e.g. B. Z. Bokser, *A Criticism of the Suggested Guide to Jewish Ritual* (Reconstructionist, Vol. VII, 18, Jan. 9, 1942, and Jacob B. Agus, *"The Character of Jewish Piety"* (idem. Vol. VIII, No. 5, April 7, 1942.)

13. Cf. his "Reply" in the *Reconstructionist,* Vol. VII, No. 18, January 9, 1942.

14. Cf. S. W. Baron, *A Social and Religious History of the Jews* (New York 1937) Vol. 1, p. 367.

15. See the suggestive paper by Dr. S. Federbusch *"Mishpat Hahozer Le-Musar"* in *Hadoar,* Vol. XXI No. 39, 40, now republished in his volume *"Hamusar Vehamishpat Beyisrael"* (New York 1943), Chap. 7.

16. Contrast the principle of *pikuach nefesh docheh shabbat.*

(*Shab.* 132a) and the doctrine *Ayn l'cha davar sheomad bifnay pikuach nefesh . . . (Keth. 19a).*

17. M. R. Cohen, *Law and the Social Order* (New York, 1933) pp. 121, 131, 133, 146.

18. M. M. Kaplan, "Reply" cited above.

19. Albert Einstein, "Some Thoughts Concerning Education" in *School and Society,* Nov. 7, 1936, p. 589.

20. S. W. Baron, op. cit., vol. II, pp. 257, 394.

21. Bernard Noskin, "Socialism and Faith," in the *Jewish Frontier,* January 1942, p. 22.

BOAZ COHEN acknowledges that Jewish Law, like all law, is viable only as it is interpreted. He points to several revealing instances where tradition itself has affirmed the necessity of interpretation. With an emphasis on interpretation comes the need for guidelines, for the establishment of authority. The Amoraim *(the later sages) and their successors therefore found it necessary to perpetuate the "myth of the ideal past" (del Vecchio). The Talmud became as sacrosanct to the later masters as the Bible was to the earlier sages. Yet despite the deep reverence that bound each generation to its predecessor, no law code, even the* Shulchan Arukh, *was regarded as beyond the need for interpretation. Cohen devotes the last parts of the essay to principles that can be employed in the interpretation of Jewish Law. Such interpretation must be informed by the important exponents of Historical Judaism—the critical scholars of the nineteenth century Science of Judaism, such as Zechariah Frankel. Cohen suggests that our guidelines for interpretation must reflect the reverence which each generation has had for generations past, and that our aims must be "to preserve as much as possible of the genuine Jewish law and custom as is compatible with modern conditions."*

The Shulhan Aruk
as a Guide
for Religious Practice Today[1]

BOAZ COHEN

I

An ancient Palestinian scholar, R. Levi by name, contrasting the mood of Israel in an earlier and more benign period with that of his own, observed that in times of prosperity the Jews were in a frame of mind to listen to a discourse on Mishnah, Halakah and Talmud, but now, in an epoch of penury and sickening persecution, they prefer to hear sermons of encouragement and consolation.[2]

It is therefore with considerable misgivings that I undertake to address you upon a problem of Halakah, at a time when the existence of a great part of our co-religionists beyond the seas is threatened more seriously than ever before, and entire Jewish communities that once were flourishing, are being pauperized and exterminated in a foul manner by demented hooligans sitting pretty in the seats of the mighty. It is but natural that we should be preoccupied foremost with the salvaging of this human wreckage floating in a cold and unfriendly globe where no one cares or inquires[3] as the prophet neatly puts it. And yet in a time of peril such as this, it is imperative more than ever to turn to our ancestral heritage for aid and comfort. Need I remind you of the splendid advice proffered by R. Akiba shortly before his martyrdom: "Now, when we are occupied with the study of the Torah, we are at such an impasse; how much worse would it be if we desisted from study."[4]

As the secretary of the Committee on Jewish Law for a number of years, it was my honorable and congenial task to study various questions of Jewish law and observance that sprung up in this country. I am now fully persuaded that the time is ripe for us to clarify the nature of those problems and to offer some tentative and provisional suggestions that might prove of assistance in wrestling with uncertainties and perplexities in our time.

It requires little argument to demonstrate that American Jewry is faced with a grave religious dilemma. The number of our people who are influenced in their religious life by Jewish traditions is steadily and rapidly diminishing. Our Jewish legacy is woefully ignored and neglected in this distracted and industrialized society of ours ruled by a materialistic and mechanistic philosophy.

As we can only meet the situation by a candid analysis and a right diagnosis before venturing a prescription, may I state what appear to me to be some of the salient factors that operate in favor of an increasing indifference to Jewish ceremonials.

First, there is the widespread ignorance of the masses both young and old, regarding matters of faith and religious practice. Ignorance breeds not only contempt but fathers feelings of inferiority and self-hate. Judaism, like nature, abhors a vacuum.

Second, the business of providing for the means of subsistence militates against the observance of the Sabbath, the festivals and the dietary laws. We know that these are our last line of defense, and when it is broken through, Judaism has suffered a serious setback.

Third, there are impediments to observance generated by social intercourse. How awkward and inopportune to decline an invitation to dinner at the house of an eminent Gentile or an opulent non-conforming Jew, just because the *Shulhan Aruk* restricts your menu. Furthermore it is more normal to comply with the social etiquette of our friends, than to be finicky in habits of diet, freakish about customs regulated by the calendar, or obstinate in matters settled by the law of the land.

Fourth, there is a manifest maladjustment of Jewish ritual to the contemporary American scene. In the course of the past, minutiae of ritual have multiplied to such a degree that even a sympathetic person, uninitiated in the intricacies of Jewish law, stands flabbergasted at the number of prohibitions, is unable to distinguish between the cardinal and the ephemeral, and is often constrained to forsake altogether what is fundamental in religion while clinging to what is trivial.

Fifth, an imperious challenge to Judaism is offered by the rival teachings of science and philosophy. The younger folks who have received a liberal or professional education in the schools and universities, are asking questions that cannot be answered by mere citation of authorities. There is one particular question which is being asked even more insistently than ever before. Why should I observe this or that ceremony and what is its religious or social significance? There is no simple answer to such a vital query. But I am not called upon here to attempt a response. Suffice it to say that people pay no allegiance to principles they disavow, nor do they observe forms of behavior which evoke no emotional response or intellectual assent in them.

These factors which I have isolated for the sake of analysis do not operate singly, but as in the case of other situations that influence human conduct, are interlaced and interact upon each other. The problem differs considerably in the various communities. In the large cities and in the very small Jewish settlements, religious observance is at a minimum, and ignorance of Judaism at a maximum, and a mere semblance of or pretense to Jewish knowledge is sometimes at a premium. A community fortunate enough to have some wealthy or learned Jews, enthusiastic lay leaders, or a competent rabbi will present a different picture from one where one or several of these circumstances are absent.

No matter what the causes be, observance of Jewish rites is decidedly on the decline, and loyalty to Jewish traditions definitely on the wane. Looking at the scene at close range it is disappointing indeed, especially for those of us who have an abiding faith in the spiritual value of the Jewish religion. However, historical perspective will enable us to estimate the situation in a better light. While it is true that the precepts of Judaism were never set aside with so much abandon and blatancy as now, there are not a few records registering the transgression of Jewish customs even in early times. We know for example that in the Talmudic epoch and even later, the wearing of *tefillin* was not observed by the throng and was esteemed lightly.[5]

Judah Leib Pochawitzer, a native of Pinsk, living in the seventeenth century gives us some interesting glimpses of life in Lithuania of his time.[6] This celebrated preacher whose sermons wielded a great influence upon people of his day, was very much alarmed by the fact that many people were unmindful of Jewish observance and customs. Not only did people indulge in idle chatter during the services in the synagogue, or at home on the Sabbath, or hire *hazzanim* who understood not the meaning of the prayers, but were guilty of much severer offenses, such as lending money on usury without availing themselves of the *heter iska,* and even kept their liquor stores open on the Sabbath.[7] This preacher advocated as a remedy, among other things, that the masses devote themselves more intensely to the study of the *Orah*

Hayyim. He himself had published a commentary upon this part of the *Shulhan Aruk,* drawing heavily upon the *Zohar, Ari, Shelah* and other mystical writings. Judah Ashkenazi, the author of the *Beer Heteb,*[8] has made frequent use of this commentary.

In modern times however, the problem of observance has assumed a much graver aspect. With the advent of emancipation and consequent enlightenment the very foundations of the Jewish religion were subjected to severe criticism. Both the reformers of Germany and the *Maskilim* of Russia[9] looked upon the Talmud and the *Shulhan Aruk* as a barricade obstructing the normal progress of Judaism. The German radicals, overjoyed over the admission of the Jews to Gentile society, felt it their bounden duty to throw off the shackles of the Ghetto, for they considered traditional observances like an inflamed vermiform appendix in the body politic that required surgical treatment. "If thine eye offend thee, pluck it out."

In their opinion Israel would cease to be the suffering servant as soon as its religion was stripped of its nationalistic garb and particularistic tendencies, and became a purely universal religion. After dropping all manners and customs that set him off from his Gentile neighbor, the Jew would remain a passive, if not a quiescent, propagandist of ethical monotheism. One of the leading protagonists of reform went so far as to declare that only the ethical principles of the Torah are binding. In very truth, behold, a belated species of Pauline Judaism!

'Tis strange that from sheer joy of emancipation, the instinct of self-preservation forsook these misguided rabbis. They overlooked with reckless abandon the survival value of age-long traditions and practices.

We now know how premature was their jubilation over emancipation and how feeble a prophylaxis assimilation was against the bacillus of anti-Semitism. By a curious irony of fate, in that self-same country where the Jews attempted to demonstrate most fervently their solidarity with, and their affiliation to the German people, they provoked the fiercest resentment, and Jew-hatred made its most ugly appearance. In some respects the Jews of America are now facing a situation not unlike that which confronted their emancipated co-religionists of Western Europe a century ago.

American Jewry is today divided into three main groups, holding different notions about the principles and precepts of Judaism. The Reform wing deriving its main inspiration from Germany, transcended the founding fathers in their disparagement of Jewish ritual. While

some of the German prototypes were merely decrying the disharmonies and shadows of the *Shulhan Aruk,* their spiritual heirs in a freer
clime abolished not only the rabbinical enactments but repealed the
Law and the Prophets.

It is instructive to recall the interesting debate at the Augsburg
Synod in 1871 provoked by Doctor Wasserman's proposal that the
Shulhan Aruk be thoroughly revised in order to bring Jewish ritual in
unison with the spirit of the time.[10] This suggestion met with little
sympathy at the conference. One rabbi maintained that revision would
imply recognition of the *Shulhan Aruk* as an authority which it was
not, and furthermore, new codification would stifle further development in Judaism. Another held that so much of the *Shulhan Aruk* has
become obsolete that little would remain after a revision, aside from
the Decalogue and what may be derived therefrom. Still another speaker thought revision a futile task because it would not be lasting inasmuch as, in two or three centuries, another revision would be necessary.

The most pointed attack upon the *Shulhan Aruk* was made by the
twenty-eight-year-old Nehemiah Bruell, a disciple of Geiger, and a
scholar of high attainments. "We regret," says Bruell,[11] "that the fluid
word of the Talmud codified in the *Shulhan Aruk* has become petrified,
and we would not like to see a new edition and revision of this book, a
proceeding which could only be injurious to the development of Judaism. Every new revision is a recognition of the book which, as a religious code, has no value for us. I move that we should declare openly
that the *Shulhan Aruk* has no significance for us as a religious code,
since the views written down in the *Shulhan Aruk* never were our
theoretical conviction, and never should be such."

Commenting upon Bruell's remarks, Doctor Philipson writes "Had
the Synod acted upon this suggestion, what a service it would have
rendered! To have declared in open assembly that the *Shulhan Aruk*
has no significance for the Jew as a religious authority would have
been sufficient to have made this Synod ever memorable in the history
of Jewish thought. But the delegates did not rise to the occasion. The
incident closed with Wasserman's withdrawal of the resolution."[12]

Many of the more radical rabbis of those days in blissful ignorance
believed that the Messianic era was fast approaching in view of the impressive progress made by Western civilization in science and letters,
in industry and politics. Was it not said by some ancient Jewish teachers "that the ceremonies will be abrogated in the time to come?"[13] And

very few doubted that they were on the threshold of the time to come. This eschatological belief coupled with a conscious but an unavowed desire to merge their identity in a Christian society, marred their understanding of Jewish law, and made them indifferent to the perpetuation of Judaism in an alien world. With these sentiments and feelings, it would have been a miracle if they could have appreciated the *Shulhan Aruk.*

Orthodoxy, which is represented by groups of different shades of opinion, has, as far as I am aware, formulated no clear and unambiguous point of view. Nominally it stands firm for a literal observance of the *Shulhan Aruk* which it considers as the last word in Jewish law superseding every previous code. Yet there are neo-orthodox rabbis introducing innovations such as preaching in English, conducting late Friday evening services, pursuing secular studies, and making other concessions to popular demands; whereas the vast majority of the laity affiliated with Orthodox congregations are as lax in observance as the non-orthodox. A few enlightened and progressive but inarticulate rabbis of the orthodox school, appreciate that life is playing havoc with traditional practices but recoil from uttering any formula to remedy the situation.

A third group whose origin is coeval with the founding of the Jewish Theological Seminary, has made extraordinary gains in the half century of its existence. It espouses what is commonly known as Conservative Judaism. The exponents of this group have often been charged, I believe unfairly, with being remiss in enunciating their standpoint. In the popular mind Conservative Judaism represents vaguely the middle road between Orthodoxy and Reform. The reformers believe that it is a mild case of Reform Judaism which will become aggravated in the course of time. Thus Professor Philipson writes as follows: "Perhaps the most striking feature in the changing panorama of Jewish religious endeavor, notably in the United States, is the coming of what is now called Conservative Judaism upon the scene. Although its spokesmen are unsympathetic with and even opposed to Reform Judaism, as is evidenced by their occasional public utterances, still paradoxical as it may sound, this neo-conservatism is intimately related to the Reform or Liberal movement. The same causes that led to the arising of the Reform Movement, have also brought forth this latest departure from the Orthodox Judaism of rabbinical tradition. It is largely a question of more or less."[14]

I beg to differ with Doctor Philipson's statement that the disagree-

ment between Reform and Conservative Judaism is a question of more
or less. I wish to quote from the constitution adopted by the Seminary
at its reorganization in 1902 where it was affirmed in limpid language
that the Seminary is dedicated "to the preservation in America of the
knowledge and practice of historical Judaism as ordained in the law of
Moses and expounded by the prophets and sages of Israel in Biblical
and Talmudic writings." I infer from this statement that Historical Judaism sponsors the principle that Scripture and the Talmud are final
authorities in all matters pertaining to belief and observance.

This view, as Professor Louis Ginzberg has observed, is based upon
the historical fact that since the Gaonic period the Jews had accepted
the Talmud as unquestioned authority, as was explicitly stated by Maimonides, Luria and Elijah of Vilna, and was tacitly assumed by all the
legal writers. The purpose of the various codes was utilitarian and not
authoritarian, namely: (1) The systematization of the huge body of
rules in order to facilitate the finding of the law. (2) The determination
of the law in case of conflicting opinions. (3) The incorporation of new
decisions and customs that accumulated in the course of time. Consequently in accordance with this historical conception, the *Shulhan
Aruk* has no more claim to our unquestioned obedience than the Mishneh Torah or the *Semag* or the *Tur,* yet we should accept the *Shulhan
Aruk* as a guide for religious practice which was all that Caro intended
it to be, for the following reasons:

(1) The *Shulhan Aruk* is in the main, a restatement of Talmudic Law
both in form and in spirit, with many elaborations. To reject the *Shulhan Aruk* outright would be tantamount to repudiating the Talmud.

(2) The traditional Jewish way of living as we know it, has been
largely molded after the pattern of the *Shulhan Aruk* since it has been
accepted by the majority of the Jews as an ultimate authority in Jewish
ritual since the seventeenth century. All legal writers in their decisions
have ever since recognized its validity or reckoned with its authority.

(3) The *Shulhan Aruk,* by virtue of the numerous commentaries and
annotations made upon it in connection with practical questions, is
more amenable to adjustment to present conditions than even the
Mishnah, the *Mishneh Torah* or the *Mordecai.*

(4) The continuity of Jewish law can best be preserved by referring
to the *Shulhan Aruk,* as it is with the exception of the *Lebush,* the last
great attempt at codification, and therefore represents the latest phase
in the development of Jewish law.

(5) Finally, since the *Shulhan Aruk* is the best arranged and the most comprehensive code of Jewish practice extant, the task of finding the law is greatly facilitated.

But can the *Shulhan Aruk* guide us today in an industrial and sophisticated environment which is so far away in temper and spirit from the era of its author? As a matter of fact serious doubts arose at the very beginning about the feasibility of adopting the *Shulhan Aruk* as a norm for Jewish life when it appeared. Thus R. Moses Isserles pointed to the grave omission of the Franco-German customs. This defect he himself remedied by his annotations which became an integral part of the *Shulhan Aruk*.

It is my deepest conviction that traditional Jewish law as codified in the *Shulhan Aruk* can be best brought into harmony with contemporary conditions by interpretation, and not by innovation or abrogation. Sohm, a celebrated authority on Roman jurisprudence, writing of the natural conservatism of the ancient Roman lawyers has this to say: "For throughout the long period of one thousand years, extending down to the final stage in the development of Roman law—i.e. down to the Corpus juris civilis of Justinian—the legal force of the Twelve Tables, as the source of all Roman law, was regarded all along as remaining in theory unimpaired, in spite of the fact that when the end came, there was not a stone in the entire structure of the decemviral laws but had long been displaced from its original position. And this was quite in keeping with the conservatism of the Romans and the extreme caution with which they proceeded in all matters of law. Not one letter of the Twelve Tables was to be altered, yet the new spirit was to be infused into the old letter. The decemviral legislation being complete, the time had arrived for an 'interpretatio' which should develop and even alter the law, but should at the same time leave the letter of the law intact."[15]

Similarly the long chain of expounders of Jewish law throughout the trials and tribulations of Jewish history, never declared a Biblical or Talmudical law null and void, but adapted rules that became archaic or obsolete to the changing conditions of the epoch by the time-honored method of interpretation. Neither is the need for interpretation in itself any reproach to the law for no general rule can be so framed as to anticipate every variety of human event. "Indeed law without interpretation," says Pollock, "is like a skeleton without life, and interpretation makes it a living thing."

There can be no valid objection to continuing this process if we un-

derstand aright the nature and scope of interpretation. In its simplest
terms, it signifies the determination of the meaning of the text of the
law when it is obscure or ambiguous or the endeavor to define the
scope of the rule when its formulation is equivocal. Interpretation in
this sense is chiefly found in the commentaries on the Talmud.

Interpretation in the wider sense denotes the process of applying the
law to a particular case. This involves three operations: (1) The finding
of the law which sometimes is the result of a choice among competing
rules or analogies. (2) The determination of the scope and meaning of
the rule when discovered. (3) Application of the rule to the given situation. This type of interpretation can be most profitably studied in the
responsa literature.

In very deed an expostion of the method and principles of interpretation of the mediaeval rabbis will reveal how they came to terms with
the world of events of their time and how Judaism was made effective
and vital by their efforts.

The burden of interpretation today is more onerous than ever before,
for the historical view makes us all too keenly aware of development in
the law, whereas in the past the changes were made unconsciously.
Secondly, a modern philological approach forbids us from reading into
the law that which was not impossible for our predecessors.

To solve the problem that besets us we require a creative interpretation of the law, in oppostion to the mere mechanical process of applying the law. Creative interpretation can only issue from studying the
methods applied by earlier generations combined with experience and
knowledge gained by continuous and open minded observation of life
united with circumspection to exercise proper judicial discretion. The
chief obstacles to such an interpretation would be the failure to comprehend the force and operation of the law, a bleak worship of its letter, an exclusive reverence for precedent, and cold logical ratiocina-
tion, for logic merely helps us to comply with the technicalities of the
law, whereas a certain elasticity is required if we mean to attain the
ends for which the law exists.

Now aphorisms and maxims galore may be culled from the Talmud
which express the motives and principles that guided the rabbis in
their interpretation of the law. These are statements of general policy
and represent tendencies in legal thinking capable of general application. They are useful as far as they go, if we can envisage the situation
to which they referred, but we may be misguided if we attempted to
apply them literally and indiscriminately to the delicate and intricate
problems of today.

II

What are the ideas and principles, the experiences and feelings, the spirit and the attitude that sway us, knowingly or unknowingly, when we render decisions or opinions on questions of law?

The Historical View of the Law

We conceive of Jewish law as a body of practices and regulations that have undergone a long development since the time of Moses, our greatest law-giver, but in their essence and spirit have remained unchanged. The precepts of Scripture and Talmud are uniquely distinguished in that they alone command the unquestioning loyalty and obedience from the Jew. No code subsequent to them has the same sanction, but is valid insofar as it historically and authentically interprets Biblical-Talmudic legislation. When we are asked what is the Jewish law on this or that point we do not answer fully by referring to this or that code, commentary or responsum, for no single code is the complete expression of the law. The origin, the transformations of the rule, its archaic features, discarded elements, temporary expedients,[16] idealistic aspirations as well as its present interpretation are all part of the majestic structure.

The Shulhan Aruk is a Valid Guide

As an inevitable corollary to our first principle follows the view that the *Shulhan Aruk* is a valid guide to Jewish practice but is neither infallible, nor final. Consequently we reserve for ourselves the right in special cases to appeal from the *Shulhan Aruk* to the Talmud or to other legal authorities when in our considered opinion the situation warrants it. We feel at liberty under similar circumstances to review past decisions and to question interpretations presupposed by the *Shulhan Aruk*. I should like to illustrate what I mean by citing the law concerning the proselyte. In the procedure for the admission of proselytes as prescribed in the *Shulhan Aruk*,[17] I find only one rule that offends modern sensibilities, and that is the one requiring the female neophyte to undergo immersion in the presence of three men. While the regulation can be traced to the *Mishneh Torah*,[18] it is not required by the Talmud. According to a *baraita* in *Yebamot*,[19] two learned men were present at the immersion of a male proselyte; but this requirement was waived for reasons of delicacy in the case of a female proselyte as is

clear from the words "they stood outside." Apparently Maimonides incorporated the stricter rule from some early source now lost. Note however that neither the *Halakot Gedolot*[20] nor the *Code of Alfasi* allude to
it. Now it seems to me that with all due respect to Maimonides, our
greatest codifier, that there should be no compunction in reverting to
the more ancient practice customary in Talmudic times, especially
since it is more in accord with modern sentiment.

The Sources of the Shulhan Aruk

We distinguish between the sources of the *Shulhan Aruk*, the Biblical legislation, the Talmudic interpretations, and the post-Talmudic
elaborations giving due weight to each phase in the development of the
law. This was done in each instance by Caro in his epoch-making commentary on the Tur. In this work, Caro exhibits an insight and historical understanding that was uncommon in his time. I shall illustrate
this point from a decision given by R. Isaac ben Sheshet[21] with reference to a man who had no children and wished to marry a very wealthy
woman from Valencia who was over ninety years of age. When the
community issued an injunction against the marriage he appealed to
the Cadi to set it aside on the ground that neither the law of God nor
the rule of the Torah prohibited it. The Ribash replied that there was a
Talmudic law against it, but for many generations previous no Court
ever enforced this rule, nor the rule requiring a couple who were married for ten years without offspring to divorce, nor did it prevent marriage between the daughter of a Kohen or of a scholar and an ig-
noramus. For a strict enforcement of these rules would have wrought
havoc with Jewish family life, he tells us, hence the Courts only compelled obedience to the rules pertaining to consanguinity. Here we see
clearly the Ribash acquiescing in distinctions in Talmudic law made
by public sentiment which he would not have recognized if it referred
to Biblical law.

Laws, Customs and Superstitions

It is necessary to distinguish between law, *halakhah*, customs, *minhag* and superstition[22] in interpretation. The validity of a custom
which is ancient, and has been continuously observed, is interwoven
with the texture of the law and is not repugnant to any fundamental
principle of law or ethics, should be recognized. It would be most im-
prudent for example, to deviate from the practice of covering the head

during religious services, or during the performance of religious acts, although this practice is merely a custom and never received the sanction of law, for the observance of this custom has become the outward symbol of loyalty to traditional Judaism.[23]

To illustrate when it is allowable to differentiate between halakah and *minhag*, I cite the following: "Thus it would be highly improper to solemnize a marriage during *Hol-ha-Moed* since it is expressly proscribed in the Mishnah,[24] whereas under special circumstances it may be permissible during *Sefirah*[25] or on Purim,[26] since it is a post-Talmudic prohibition. In general we are inclined to be more lenient with regard to customs than with strict law."[27]

Many quaint customs[28] and superstitions have arisen in connection with the last rites for the dead and the observance of mourning for the deceased. Although sixty exhaustive chapters in the *Yoreh Deah* are devoted to this topic Caro failed to meet the ravenous demand for more rules. In addition to the *Kaddish,* the custom of visiting the graves of departed relatives,[29] and the ceremony of unveiling[30] have been raised to the dignity of a positive Biblical precept. This unhealthy overemphasis upon, and the mechanical observance of, the rules of mourning, is not due so much to the sentiment of piety as to the feeling of fear and helplessness in the presence of an awful, baffling and discomfiting experience. It betokens that religion is not in a robust state of health, when people claim its comfort and ministrations when they die, while during their life they need not its sanctions.

Our sages tell us "that we should follow the most lenient views with regard to the laws of mourning"[31] but I suppose that a proper reverence for the feelings of the bereaved require a tactful rather than a strictly halakic appraoch to the problem. We should combat however, the importation of non-Jewish customs into the last rites.

The Nature of the Laws

It is useful to bear in mind the distinction between religious and civil law,[32] *issurah* and *marmonah,* the latter being in abeyance now in most countries.[33] The religious law may be further classified as liturgy, ceremonies and family law.[34] It is a fact that the post-Talmudic authorities took more liberty with the liturgy than with the ceremonies. This accounts for the endless diversities of rites that have appeared in the various countries described in a masterly way by Leopold Zunz.

In passing, I wish to touch upon the problem of changing the liturgy which is still being debated. There are two matters to be considered.

(1). The prolixity in the prayers. (2). The allusions in the ritual to obsolete beliefs such as the restoration of the sacrificial cult,[35] the resurrection,[36] or the election of Israel.[37]

There can be no halakic objection to the omission of certain prayers from the service in order to shorten it when the occasion requires it,[38] but it would be dangerous and wanton to tamper with the texts of the prayers with the avowed purpose of bringing them into unison with our present temper. First, we could never reach a general agreement on dismemberment. Secondly, the prayers, based mostly on Scripture, are part of the historical consciousness of Israel, which we dare not lightly disregard. Lastly, in Judaism, prayer is more an expression of the emotions, aspirations, and longing for the Infinite, than a confession of faith. The significance of prayer lies in the depth and the nobility of feeling it can arouse in us, rather than in the intellectual assent it can command. I seriously doubt whether tinkering with the liturgy in itself can bring about this end.

It is interesting to recall the attitude of the halakists anent this question. When Mar Zutra visited R. Ashi while he was in mourning, the Talmud tells us,[39] he inserted in grace after meals the following sentence: "The Good One, Bestower of Good, the True God and Judge, and Righteous Arbiter, takes man away in justice." The *Halakot Gedolot* and *Alfasi* omit the phrase "takes man away in justice" because it implies that man's mortality is part of Divine justice which contradicts the accepted doctrine "that death comes also to the sinless and suffering to the innocent." *Tosafot* and R. Asher object to the innovation and insist upon the retention of Mar Zutra's statement.

There are rules in the *Shulhan Aruk* which today belong to the domain of hygiene.[40] At one time they were considered part of religion. Thus when R. Huna reproached his son Rabbah for failing to attend the brilliant lectures of R. Hisda, his son replied that the lectures dealt not with religion but with worldly affairs such as sanitation and hygiene. His father quickly rejoined "He lectures upon the vital problems of health and you term them mundane matters. That is all the more reason you should attend."[41] Most of these regulations, insofar as they are antiquated, may be safely ignored.

The Need for Perspective

In evaluating the various rules and customs it is imperative to maintain a sense of proportion. According to the traditional conception, all the laws are equally of divine origin, yet the rabbis divided the precepts into lighter and weightier commands indicating that some are relatively more important than others. The gauge used to estimate the scale of values varied. The severity of punishment attending the infraction of the law determined the relative gravity of the command.[42] The ease of difficulty with which the law could be perfected was occasionally taken as a standard for comparison. The ceremony of *Sukkah*[43] and the duty of sending the mother bird away when the fledglings are taken,[44] were considered as light commands *mitzvot kalot*. From various sources we learn that our forebears sacrificed their lives rather than desecrate the Sabbath, the dietary laws and circumcision.[45] This speaks volumes for the high regard they attached to these ceremonies. Observe that before the proselyte was admitted to the Jewish fold he was to be instructed according to the Talmud,[46] in the weighty commands *mitzvot chamurot* such as the Sabbath and the dietary laws,[47] and the lighter commands, such as the poor laws: *leket, shichah, u'peah*. The statement that the ceremony of *tzitzit* (wearing of fringe) is equal to all the ceremonies,[48] is perhaps an effort to strengthen a generally neglected law.

The verse "thou shalt not seethe a kid in its mother's milk" thrice repeated in the Torah, inspired the later casuists to extensive elaborations and subtleties collected in the section on meat and milk (*basar vichalav*). A true perspective, not an easy attainment, is necessary if we are going to realize the relative significance of all these details. There are other judgments and adjustments that must be made on the basis of an extra-legal approach, such as feeling and intuition. Thus keeping one's business open on the Sabbath[49] and carrying a handkerchief[50] in one's pocket, are both prohibited by the law, but the rule does not coincide with our feeling. We will not consider one who carries a watch, a handkerchief, a key, or a cane as a Sabbath breaker. Zechariah Frankel, the chief exponent of Positive-Historical Judaism in Germany, permitted the carrying of an umbrella on the Sabbath.

A true perspective is not purely subjective but develops from an interrelated knowledge of Jewish life, from a synoptic and well-balanced view of Jewish law, from an apprehension of the essence and not merely the casual details of religion. To avoid the mistake of taking distorted images or optical illusions as true perspectives, we must know something of the various aspects of religion.

"In religion, so long as it is alive," says Julian Huxley, "four aspects are blended. There is immediate emotional experience; there is ritual

expression; there is a connection with morality; and there is an intellectual scaffolding of ideas and beliefs. These can never be wholly dis-
entangled. Even in the most personal of mystical experiences there is a
setting of mind and body which is itself a ritual act; there is a background of consciously or unconsciously held beliefs which influence
the form of experience; there is an experience of rightness which over-
flows on to abstract views of morality and conduct. Ritual again, if it be
fulfilling its true mission will itself be a source of religious feeling, but
a ritual which is moving and significant to a mind imbued with one set
of intellectual ideas will appear meaningless against another background of belief, and a degraded mumbo-jumbo against yet another."[51]

Importance of Public Opinion

It goes without saying that we must reckon with the sentiment of the
people if we wish to interpret a living law, for no system of rules can be
imposed upon a group that does not meet with their approval. Many
statements can be cited from the Talmud and later authorities to show
how keenly aware they were of this fact. Thus R. Joshua ben Levi says:
"Whenever the Beth Din is in doubt as to the interpretation of a law,
and you do not know how to comply with it, observe what the people
do."[52] Well enough to say "observe what the people do" but what people do we mean? Shall it be the ever dwindling minority who declare:
"Till heaven and earth pass, one jot or tittle shall in no wise pass from
the law, till all be fulfilled," or shall we consider the large sect that is
apathetic to, if not disdainful of Jewish ceremonials and say: "It is vain
to serve God; and what profit is it that we have kept His charge, and
that we have walked mournfully because of the Lord of Hosts?" Or
should we rather not think of that group that is loyal to Judaism and
would fain observe the Jewish way of life, but recoil from the mounds
and mounds of rules, the *tilin tilin shel halakot.*

There are, for example, an increasing number of observant Jews who
rationalize the practice of kindling electric lights on the Sabbath, especially if a "Shabbos Goy" is not available. Others who feel reluctant to
disregard this time-honored prohibition, will answer a telephone. Still
others will shrink from performing this act, but will press an electric
button, whereas the Ultra-Orthodox will abstain from ringing the bell
or using a house elevator.[53] While these subtle distinctions represent a
casuistry of common sense, they are lay fallacies in the law.

Spirit of the Times

The spirit of our age (Zeitgeist) differs greatly from that of Caro's epoch. The *Shulhan Aruk*, like all Jewish codes of law, presupposes a deep spirit of piety and exhales a fragrance of religious idealism. Indeed the opening paragraph of the *Shulhan Aruk* bids the Jew to be cognizant at all times of the presence of God, and to motivate his conduct in accordance with this belief. The real *Shulhan Aruk* Jew of bygone times, was one who regarded every command be it ritual, legal or ethical as ordinances of Divine origin. To practice the precepts of Judaism was a joy to him no matter what the difficulties were, even at the risk of martyrdom.[54] His character was transformed by its precepts because its doctrines were sincerely held and vitally apprehended. It was natural that a passion for exacting rules *chamurot* existed.[55] There were of course, some variations from the main theme including undertones and disharmonies, but they were not impressive enough to be disturbing.

Today we are living in an essentially irreligious and irreverent age. One cannot escape the feeling that the rise of the totalitarian states demanding and getting the exclusive worship from the individual is the result of the decay of modern religion which set in long before the World War. The decline of religion brought in its train the Fall of Man in the Garden of a cunning and crafty civilization. But even the small sect that wishes to perpetuate religion puts a different assessment upon its nature and function. With John Stuart Mill, the modernist views religion as a social process originating in the complex life of man's desires and emotions directed toward ideal ends. Its purpose is to foster the growth of human personality. It is no mean task for religion to be the champion of personality in a seemingly impersonal world, for science and invention have created a type of civilization in which human personality is debased. Yet the element of piety should not be absent from a well-balanced personality, nor is it incompatible with a critical faculty. 'Tis true that so far as piety is an inward feeling and illumination, it cannot be taught, but in so far as it is a response to religious and social ideals of one's group it can be elicited by implanting a sympathy for the ideals and aspirations of Judaism through a religious education with an idealistic motivation and approval, rather than through pure factual instruction.

It is when traditional piety is believed to come into conflict with the development of human character and its needs that the problem is posed. Thus according to the strict law it is interdicted not only to turn on a radio on the Sabbath but also to instruct a Gentile on Friday to do it on the Sabbath.[56] A person imbued with profound piety would scarcely rebel against this far-reaching ordinance but a modern person would view this rule as needlessly harsh inasmuch as it would deprive him of the pleasure of listening to exalted music.

Piety can of course, be carried to excess when it is not tempered with wisdom as the rabbis already observed. A young scholar[57] was reciting in the presence of Raba bar Rab Huna the rule that killing serpents and scorpions on the Sabbath was considered improper by the pious. Whereupon Raba exclaimed that the sages are displeased with such pious folk.

The Ends We Seek
Influence Our Attitude

In interpretation we must not indiscriminately adopt the consistent policy to be either strict and severe, or liberal and lenient. We must be guided by the ends we are seeking, namely the preservation of traditional practices in their typically Jewish form. In our days when the people have taken so many liberties with the ritual, we should insist upon their performance and adopt a stringent attitude just as Rab did when he noticed violations of the law due to ignorance in his day.[58] On the other hand when justice to individuals is involved as in various aspects of domestic relations, I believe that we cannot conscientiously decline to take a human and humane view and bend all our efforts to interpret the law as liberally as is consistent with the spirit and intent of the law. In such cases there is no question but that the courage to be mild is more meritorious.[59] In general, it would be safe to say that our attitude must vary depending upon the case or situation at hand, because no unbreakable rule can be laid down.

Continuity of Jewish Law

One of the most fundamental principles in our approach to Jewish law must be the preservation of the continuity of Jewish tradition which was maintained in unbroken succession from remote antiquity. The first paragraph in *Abot* enumerates the links in the chain of tradition from Moses to the men of the Great Synagogue, and Maimonides in his introduction to the *Mishneh Torah* enumerates the links in the chain down to the time of R. Ashi. Now when we maintained before that the Talmud is our final authority, we did not contemplate a reversion to the laws and customs of that period. We would not advocate a *heter* for eating chicken with milk because it was customary to do so in the locality of R. Jose the Galilean.[60] That would be impossible and absurd as for the English to relapse into Elizabethan manners and speech. The principle of continuity was well expressed by the Gaonim in the legal maxim "the practice is in accordance with the latest authorities", *hilkatah kibatra'i*. Accordingly, the decisions of the *Aharonim*, the *Shak*, the *Taz*, the *Magen Abraham*, and the *Beer-Heteb* are valid for us in so far as they represent persistent and characteristic trends in the continuity of the Jewish tradition.

Thus I have endeavored to sum up in a general way the notions and ideas that regulate our interpretation of the law of today. These are in the main the same principles that guided the rabbis of the Talmud[61] and of the Middle Ages. The problems are different today because the social life and the political conditions and the *Weltanschauung,* as well as the economic circumstances of the Jews of those times have been basically transformed.

III

What is the nature of the difficulties that confront us now?

(1) There are cases where the law is clear but it is out of harmony with economic conditions, and is accordingly impossible of observance by many of those who are inclined religiously, e.g. the closing of shops on the Sabbath; others living in small communities where there is no *shohet,* or those whose business requires them to travel find it well nigh impracticable to observe the dietary laws, not to speak of the regulations concerning food prepared by Gentiles.[62] With regard to these infractions our attitude can only be that the Merciful One pardon the unavoidable transgression.[63]

(2) Other religious precepts for social reasons are very difficult or inconvenient to perform. In little villages, where the members of a congregation are scattered over wider areas, and live far from the synagogue, they find it compulsory to travel on Friday night if they wish to attend services. I doubt whether a halakic remedy can be found.[64] Our position must be that it is better that they err unwittingly than presumptuously.[65]

Other rules are at variance with the manners of Western civilization such as the prohibition of shaving. There is even a reference as early as the Yerushalmi indicating that among the Palestinian Jews this law was disregarded.[66] From the responsa of the eighteenth century we learn that shaving was quite common among the Jews of Italy. The violation of this law provoked some halakic complications such as the question whether a person who shaved was competent as a witness inasmuch as he transgressed a Biblical law. There is an interesting responsum in the *Pahad Yizhak*[67] which vividly portrays conditions very analogous to those of our own day, which I cite at length. "A" before he died made out a will, in which he bequeathed all of his property to his mother, and left nothing to his four sisters. After A's death, his mother entered into possession of the estate which she bestowed as a gift while still living, on her two sons-in-law. After a year and a half she died, and the sons-in-law assumed title to the property. Then the four sisters of A instituted a suit against the two sons-in-law on the ground that they were unjustly disinherited by their mother, for according to the civil and natural law they were entitled to their legitim,[68] i.e. the portion of the estate to which upon the death of the parents, the children are entitled and which cannot be affected by any testamentary provision made by the decedent without cause. Furthermore they claimed that the mother's title to the property was invalid because one of the witnesses to the will was disqualified inasmuch as he used to drink Gentile wine, and being a barber, shaved himself and others.

The defendants claimed first that legitim is not recognized by Jewish law and that they were unaware of the fact that the witness was incompetent, since he was upright in business and was the keeper of the royal seal. Heretofore witnesses were never barred for drinking Gentile wine or shaving and were allowed to attest wills, marriage certificates and writs of divorce.

The rabbi decided that the plaintiffs were not entitled to redress on the ground of legitim as Jewish law does not recognize the jus naturalis *dat ha-tevah* and the Mishnah[69] states explicitly that if one disinherits his children, the act is valid but the sages disapprove of the action.

This rule has been accepted by all the codifiers. With regard to the impeachment of the witness, the following must be considered. He could not be barred on the first charge preferred against him on the grounds of drinking Gentile wine because that is only a rabbinical prohibition, and the rule is that persons who have violated rabbinical ordinances do not become disqualified to testify until it has been announced in the synagogue.[70]

The second charge preferred against the witness was more serious, since shaving is prohibited in the Bible. But even in the case of the violation of a Biblical law, a person is barred from acting as a witness only if he realizes the gravity of his crime, as Maimonides pointed out,[71] and is aware that it disqualifies him from testifying. But this is not the case here since shaving has become so common that even the rabbis refrain from rebuking the people for it, in accordance with the maxim "Just as it is proper to admonish a person who will obey, so it is improper to admonish one who will disobey"[72] and consequently he could not have perceived the seriousness of the offense. Furthermore since the sisters did not begin their suit during their mother's lifetime they indicated by this silence their abandonment of the claim, and whereas the will was made in anticipation of death, no witnesses were necessary, as the testament was undisputed. Lastly it would be against the general welfare to disqualify this person, because ever so many marriage certificates and other documents were signed by persons who committed the same offense. I have quoted in extenso to show how a rabbi dealt with problems not merely in a legal manner but considered also the public good.

(3) There are cases where the law inflicts hardships and injustice on innocent parties. I am referring to the inadequacies of the Jewish law of divorce in the present social and economic setup. This is a matter which no rationalization can gloss over. We cannot consistently be deaf to the pleas of the suffering *agunah* and profess belief in the sublime utterance of Jeremiah:[73] "I am the Lord who exercises mercy, justice and righteousness in the earth; for in these I delight, saith the Lord."

Furthermore, as Professor Ellwood has well said: "Judaism got its lofty moral tone from the projection, idealization, and spiritualization of the values found in the ancient Jewish family. The concepts and phraseology of Judaism can indeed be understood only through understanding the ancient Jewish family."[74] This lofty moral tone must also be extended to those cases of unavoidable frustrations in family life, especially since Judaism permits the marriage bonds to be torn asunder. It is a historical fact that the main objective of the rabbis in their rulings on divorce was to shear the husband of the plenary powers granted to him by Scripture by introducing technicalities with regard to the writ of divorce in order to protect the woman. Hence they required a *get* to be written specifically for the woman herself; that the husband order the scribe in person to write the *get* without being able to delegate this authority to another. They recognized grounds which entitled the wife to sue for divorce. In cases when the husband met with foul play, they dispensed with the usual requirement of two witnesses to certify the fact of death in order to permit the wife to remarry. How does the problem arise? The iron clad rule which permits a *get* to be written only by the express command of the husband, leaves the woman without redress when he has disappeared, or refuses to grant her a *get* although he may have obtained a civil divorce and remarried. The situation is aggravated in our time because the Beth Din cannot even exercise a persuasive influence over a refractory husband.

This problem, to be sure, has been agitating the rabbis for a long time, and it is the oriental rabbis who have been more alert. A variety of solutions have been offered to the public.[75] A rabbi of Egypt has proposed the conditional marriage to be set aside at the discretion of the court.[76] Aside from the possible halakic uncertainties, it robs matrimony of the stability and the equilibrium such a fundamental human institution requires. My friend Doctor Epstein has earned the profound gratitude of every one for the tireless and unselfish manner in which he has devoted himself to the task of finding a solution for the *agunah.* In his proposal[77] he tries to circumvent the law by arranging for the husband at the time of marriage, to appoint a *sheliah* to order a scribe to write a *get* to be delivered in case of certain contingencies. He can cite good authorities and precedent for his novel assumptions and daring combinations. My friend Doctor Drob insists that there are flies in the ointment. To me it seems that the greatest objection is a spiritual one. It is totally out of harmony with the spirit of halo and consecration that attends the marriage ceremony, when human feelings run very high, to ask the husband to dictate in cold calculation, arrangements for a possible future rupture of the matrimonial relationship. There is, it is true, precedent for such a procedure in Babylonian Law.[78] Of course, I may be quite wrong as to how other people feel about it.

I have been thinking for quite some time whether we should seek relief for the *agunah* by exploring the possibility and advisability of liberalizing the law of annulment.[79] The Mishnah[80] for example recognizes the principle of *kidushe ta'ut,* whereby the marriage is null and void if one of the parties to the marriage was a victim of fraudulent misrepresentation. The theory underlying this rule is as follows: If the mistake induced by fraud or misrepresentation was fundamental enough, then there never was real consent, and the marriage being a contract, requiring the consent of both parties, is void. R. Simon ben Zemah Duran[81] and other authorities follow this line of reasoning in cases where one of the parties to the marriage was impotent at the time of nuptials. 'Tis true that the medieval authorities[82] departed far from the view of the Mishnah and annulled the marriage only when there was a double stipulation, *t'nai kaful,* and other technicalities.

What I am thinking of is the possibility of an application of the principle found in the Talmud, namely, that a woman would not have given her consent to marriage if it ultimately led to very disagreeable circumstances.[83] Since marriage is a contract requiring consent of both parties, I raise the following question: Would a woman have given her consent to marriage if she knew at the time of marriage that her husband would leave her permanently through no fault of hers, some time after marriage and that he would refuse to give her a *get,* although he remarried subsequently to a civil divorce? I wonder. I grant that this is not positive or actual fraud, since it is not due to any deceit practiced at the time of marriage, but is it not what is known in common law, as constructive fraud? Were there not some dishonest tendencies and blemishes in the character of such a man at the time of marriage which did not blossom out until after the springtime of matrimony? Is it true today that every woman is so intent upon marriage that she yields her consent on any terms? I am not putting forth any proposal, but I believe this suggestion deserves more thought than I have given to it so far, and more research in Jewish law is required for its legal sanction.

As for the problem of a recalcitrant *yabam*[84] who declines for purposes of extortion to undergo the ceremony of *halizah,* I see no remedy.[85] As in a machine, some parts of the machinery of the law are inert.

(4) There are many points of law which are uncertain and are the subject of controversy. Numerous instances may be cited from the codes and commentaries.[86] I shall make mention of two cases which are of current interest.

First is the question concerning the validity of civil marriage.[87] Already in the last century sore disagreement existed among the authorities as to whether such a marriage necessitated a *get.* In more recent times the late Professor Hoffmann[88] as well as Rabbi Joseph Rosin[89] decided that it did. The Committee on Jewish Law and Standards took the same stand on the question because it accorded with the general practice of the Orthodox rabbis of this country, as well as for logical rather than for purely legal reasons. For it would have been unwise to deny the status of marriage to a couple who dwelt together as man and wife and were so reputed by all their friends, although a stamp of quasi approval is given to matrimony without religious ceremony. Civil marriage followed by connubial relations, has the same status that a common law marriage would have in Jewish law, for cohabitation without proper intent is not recognized as a way of establishing the matrimonial relationship. On the other hand this decision is not inconsistent with the refusal to recognize civil divorce, because in Jewish law, the termination of marriage is affected only through the instrumentality of a duly executed writ.

Secondly and much less momentous, is the question whether the sturgeon is kosher or not, which hinges upon a correct and valid definition of scales, a moot point among the legal commentators. According to Nahmanides,[90] scales are round and horny plates like nails, removable from the skin by hand or knife, like the skin of fruit or bark of a tree, but if it is not removable at all, then they are no scales. This interpretation is based on the Aramaic rendering . Ezekiel Landau[91] is supposed to have permitted fish whose scales were removable only after having been soaked in lye water for three hours. Aaron Chorin,[92] disciple of Ezekiel Landau and one of the earliest Reform rabbis in Hungary also allowed it. A storm of controversy followed his decision and among the Orthodox rabbis, it became a battle-cry against reform.

The question is still unsettled as to what is the accepted legal definition of scales, and whether the sturgeon has scales in the ritual sense of the term.[93]

Finally there are problems, many of a congregational character,[94] for which there are no precedents in the *Shulhan Aruk,* and which actually do not involve a question of law, such as the following: May a Jew who has married an unconverted Gentile woman enroll as a member in the congregation, or may women sit on the *bimah* during Divine services? And many others. In answering such questions we are to be guided by a sense of propriety and expediency as well as by an intuitive feeling as to what is the Jewish way of dealing with those situations. I have been able here only to touch upon a few of the most striking maladjustments in our midst, but I hope I have succeeded in indicating an acceptable approach to their solution.

Before concluding I wish to make a plea and a proposal. Historians have argued interminably over the question whether the leaders of a generation mold the ideas and influence the conduct of their age or merely voice the inarticulate aspirations and sentiments of their fellow-men. In truth both views represent the two sides of a medal. Now it is our duty as trustees of the legacy of Judaism[95] to direct our people in the right use thereof. This we can do if we are acquainted with the terms of the legacy.

We have good reasons to be exceedingly proud of our magnificent achievements in the manifold fields of community organization, relief work, Jewish education, Zionist leadership, youth activities and good will. But we have seriously neglected to cultivate the vineyard of Jewish law. I wish to make a plea for a renaissance of the study of Jewish law among our alumni. No matter how adequately or inadequately we may have been equipped when we entered the rabbinate, continuous application to its study is necessary if we wish to remain or become versed in the law. I am not referring now to the critical study thereof, such as would eventuate in a D.H.L. thesis and degree. I am thinking of the study of that part of the law that was traditionally considered as prerequisite for rendering authoritative decisions on ritual law. Personally I should like to see the revival of the Kallah convention under the leadership of Professor Ginzberg such as the Rabbinical Assembly sponsored several years ago.

An intensification of the study of Jewish law will (1) dissolve the feeling of inadequacy and inferiority many entertain in the presence of the superior halakic learning of the old-style rabbis, and lead to a reconstruction of faith in ourselves; (2) enable us to use the *Shulhan Aruk* more intelligently as a guide for religious practice and to render more authentic decisions, and (3) remove thereby the reproach of our Orthodox opponents and raise the prestige of the Rabbinical Assembly to a point where it will command the authority and the respect of Catholic Israel in America in matters of law. I propose that the Rabbinical Assembly authorize the Committee on Jewish Law to prepare for publication a *Handbook on Jewish Law* in order that the discord and the confusion that is rife in our midst anent many customs and ceremonies be abated, and that uncertainties and perplexities occasioned by the rise of new problems be terminated.

In conclusion, I shall paraphrase a Midrash[96] on the merits of the study of the law. When Jeremiah exclaimed: "'Who is the wise man, that he may understand this? And who is he to whom the mouth of the Lord hath spoken, that he may declare it? Wherefore is the land perished and laid waste like a wilderness, so that none passeth through?' Neither sage nor seer nor seraph could venture a reply. The Lord saith: Because they have forsaken my law. Would that they had rather forsaken Me but pursued the study of the Torah, for the powerful illumination emanating from the Torah would have led them back to the right way and brought them nigh unto Me."

Notes

1. It is a pleasure to record my indebtedness to Professor Ginzberg for the stimulating suggestions I received from him in connection with this paper. He is the first in modern times to have recognized the importance of the principle of authority in Jewish tradition and to have clarified this conception which is basic to an understanding of the entire problem of Jewish law today.

2. *Canticles Rabbah* II. 14 (ed. Horeb, f. 27b).

3. Ezekiel 34–6, cf. also *Sotah* 49a.

4. *Berakot* 61b.

5. Boaz Cohen, *Konteros ha-Teshubot,* p. 4, note 2.

6. Cf. *Dibre Hakamim,* Hamburg 1692, f. 3a of the introduction.

7. For the Arenkama, as he terms it, cf. Gessen in the *Russian Jewish Encyclopedia,* s.v. Arenda III, 74–87, for traffic in wine, cf. Voltke, s.v. Vinniye Promisle l.c. V. 609–14, and for the violation of Shabbat see Dubnow, *Pinkas Ha-Medinah,* Berlin 1925, Index s.v. *Hillul Shabbat.*

8. It is noteworthy that four scholars have written commentaries on the *Shulhan Aruk* entitled *Beer Heteb.* The first is R. Isaiah ben Abraham (a grandson of David ha-Levi, author of the *Taz*), who wrote a commentary on *Orah Hayyim,* printed in Amsterdam 1708. The second is Judah Ashkenazi who wrote a commentary upon the first three parts of the *Shulhan Aruk.* R. Isaiah's commentary is cited by Judah Ashkenazi as the *Beer Hatav* in my possession. Cf. e.g. *Orah Hayyim* 196, 1 and 3; 202, 6; 235, 2; 266. 13; 289, 1; 298, 11. The third is R. Zechariah Mendel ben Aryeh Lob of Cracow who wrote on the *Yoreh Deah* and *Hoshen Mishpat.* The fourth is R. Moses Frankfurter of Amsterdam who commented upon the *Hoshen Mishpat.*

9. In order to wean the Jews away from the Talmud the Russian government commanded Leo Mandelstamm to translate the *Mishneh Torah* into German and ordered that it be studied in the Jewish schools, cf. P. Kon in *Iwo Blaetter,* XIII, 1938, p. 579.

10. *Verhandlungen der zweiten israelitischen Synode zu Augsburg* 1871, Berlin 1873, p. 159–170.

11. l. c., p. 166.

12. D. Philipson, *Reform Movement in Judaism,* p. 324.

13. Niddah 61b. On the attitude of Reform cf. Schechter's article on Geiger in his *Studies in Judaism,* 3rd Series, especially pp. 71–83.

14. Preface to *Reform Movement in Judaism,* cf. also p. 380–381.

15. *Institutes of Roman Law,* Oxford 1926, 2nd edition, pp. 55–56.

16. For example when the Jewish people were being decimated by dire persecution, the authorities sought morally and legally to encourage the growth of population. Thus Maimonides writes, "He who increases the Jewish population by one person, is considered as if he built the world" (*Ishut* XV. 15). R. Asher (*Yeb.* VI. 15) and R. Joseph ibn Habib laid down the rule that if a man

was not married before he reached the age of twenty, the Beth Din could compel him to do so (for the age limit of 20, cf. *Kid.* 29b, and *Ishut* XV, 2). This rule was incorporated in the *Tur* and *Shulhan Aruk Eben ha-Ezer* I. 3. At a subsequent period it was found highly impracticable to enforce this emergency measure and we find R. Solomon Luria writing that it was best not to attempt to carry out this rule. There were many bachelors in his time who neither devoted themselves to the study of the Torah, nor led a sinless life, he tells us, yet inasmuch as they found it difficult to earn a livelihood due to the hard times, and large dowries were expected of them, marriage could not be forced upon them. *Yam Shel Shelomah* to Yeb. VII. 40. R. Moses Isserles incorporated Luria's opinion in his glosses to the *Shulhan Aruk.*

17. *Yoreh Deah* 268, 2.

18. *Issure Biah* XIV. 6.

19. 47b.

20. In *Hilkot Milah,* ed. Warsaw 1874, f. 48b, it is stated that when the Gentile female slave goes to the *mikvah,* she is accompanied by a woman.

21. Responsa no. 15.

22. Cf. D. Joel, *Der Aberglaube und die Stellung des Judenthums zu demselben* I–II, Breslau 1881–83; J. Finkelscherer, *Mose Maimunis Stellung zum Aberglauben und zur Mystik,* Breslau 1894; J. Trachtenberg, *Jewish Magic and Superstition,* N.Y. 1939.

23. Cf. *Ned.* 30b, T. *Erubin* XI. 16, p. 153, as well as the passages in *Jewish Encyclopedia,* s.v. Bareheadedness, *Artsot ha-Hayyim,* 1860, p. 14, and Goldziher, Die Entblossung des Hauptes, *Der Islam* Vi. 301–316, Lauterbach in the *Year Book of the C.C.A.R.* 38, 1938 Medini in *sdei hemed Warsaw* 1896 pp. 159–160 an Kasher in *Horeb* IV, pp. 195–206.

24. *Moed Katan* I. 7.

25. The custom not to marry during the *Sefirah* can be traced only to Geonic times, cf. *Shaare Teshubah,* no. 278, and Ibn Ghayyat, *Hilkot Pesahim,* Berlin 1864, p. 51, and *Beth Joseph* to *Orah Hayyim* 493.

26. This prohibition originated in post-Geonic times, cf. the full citation of authorities in *Darke Mosheh* to *Tur Orah Hayyim* 696.

27. For the differentiation between law and custom cf. for example *Yeb.* 13b, *Nid.* 66a and *Yer. Shebiit* V. 1.

28. The custom for example of not using the shoes of the deceased goes back to the *Sefer Hasidim,* ed. Wistinetzki, p. 379, no. 1544, as Professor Ginzberg has observed. Cf. also Nacht, "Symbolism of the Shoe," *J.Q.R., N.S.* VI, 1915, p. 14, and Levy, "Die Schuhsymbolik," *M.G.W.J.* 62. 1918, p. 178–185. Many customs in the *Shulhan Aruk* can be traced to the *Zohar,* cf. *Beer Heteb* passim, Reifmann in *Bet Talmud* II, 1882, p. 87 and *Jewish Encyclopedia,* IV, 519.

29. The custom of visiting the graves is mentioned already in *Taanit* 16a with reference to public fast days. In the days of the *Tosafot* it was customary to do so on the ninth of Ab, and since the time of Jacob ben Moses Mollen, also on the day before the New Year, and the day before Yom Kippur (Maharil, ed. Warsaw 1874, p. 33b, and *Darke Mosheh* to *Tur Orah Hayyim* 581). In connection with this practice it became customary to give charity while visiting the grave; (Kol Bo, quoted by Isserles to *Orah Hayyim* 581 and *Shelah,* ed. Lemberg 1860, p. 144a), cf. also I. Levi, *R. E. J.* 47 (1903), 214–220; not to visit the

same grave twice in one day. (View of Issac Luria quoted by *Beer Heteb* to *Orah Hayyim* l.c.), to visit graves of Gentiles provided there were no idolatrous images, in the absence of Jewish cemeteries; (*Beer Heteb* l.c. 559), not to visit the cemetery in a state of impurity since one was susceptible to attack by the demons (View of Isaac Luria quoted by the Beer Heteb l.c.), not to walk on the graves proper, but to keep at a safe distance of four cubits, lest one be exposed to the evil spirits, (Danzig, *Hayye Adam*, 135.25). R. Elijah of Lublin was pondering over the question whether it was necessary in a town which had two cemeteries, to visit both (*Yad Eliyah*, Amsterdam 1712 no. 31). In the Talmud two reasons are given for the custom (1) that the dead interceded in behalf of the living, (2) that the atmosphere of the graveyard put the worshipper in a proper mood for praying. The first reason seems to be the oldest. Thus the primitives, would go to the grave, pour water over it, and pray for rain when the land suffered from unseasonable drought (Frazer, *Golden Bough* I, 286). Caleb prayed upon the graves of the patriarchs, *Sotah* 34b, *Sefer Hasidim* ed. Wistinetzki, p. 377 no. 1537; In the Middle Ages the question was discussed whether a Kohen was permitted to visit the graves of the righteous, cf. Israel of Shklov, *Peat ha-Shulhan*, Jerusalem 1911, I, p. 11b and Toledano, *Yam ha-Gadol*, Cairo 1932, no. 65. For the custom of throwing grass or pebbles on the tombstone when visiting cemeteries, cf. *Beer Heteb* to *Orah Hayyim* 224.11. An edition of *Tehinot* to be read while visiting graves on the eve of Rosh Hashanah and the eve of Yom Kippur was published in Salonika 1651, cf. Yaari, *Kiryat Sefer* XVI, 381. Simon Levy, *La Viste aux Morts in Les Loisirs d'un rabbin*, Paris 1892, p. 129 ff. and Trachtenberg, *Jewish Magic and Superstition*, N.Y. 1939, pp. 64–65.

30. The elaborate ceremony in connection with the unveiling of a tombstone is of recent origin, cf. I. L. Leucht; Order of Services . . . at the setting of Tombstones. New Orleans 1880 and Mordecai Winkler: *Lebushe Mordecai*, 2d Series, Miskolez 1939, *Yoreh Deah* 140.

31. *Erubin* 46a and parallels.

32. For the profound influence of religion upon civil law cf. Fustel de Coulanges, *The Ancient City*, N.Y. 1916, p. 49 ff.

33. Until recent times it was deemed highly improper to go to Gentile courts for civil actions. Thus one who was guilty of such an offense was considered unfit to act as a *Hazzan* on the New Year or Day of Atonement (Aaron Sason, *Torat Emet*, no. 157, quoted by the *Beer Heteb* to *Orah Hayyim*, 53–25). For the medieval ordinances on this subject, cf. Finkelstein, *Jewish Self Government in the Middle Ages*, pp. 42, 43, 156.

34. The nearest equivalent to the term "family law" is found in *Shab.* 130a where it is stated that Israel complained bitterly over the restrictions in Jewish law concerning the family.

35. The practice to commemorate the destruction of the temple by midnight prayers reaches back to Geonic times, (cf. Lewin, *Ozar ha-Geonim, Berakot*, p. 3) and was especially recommended by R. Asher (*Berakot* I.3). This custom was rooted deeply in the strong feeling over the loss of the national shrine. In later times due to mystic influence, many uninspiring meditations were introduced known as *Tikkun Hazot*, and special societies were organized to recite them, cf. *Jewish Encyclopedia*, IV. 550 and Elbogen, *Der judische Gottesdienst*, Berlin 1924, p. 387, 389.

36. Maimonides interpreted the doctrine of resurrection of the body which he realized was so deeply rooted in rabbinic thought (cf. Lowinger, "Die Auferstehung in der judischen Tradition," in *Jahrbuch fur judische Volkskunde,* ed. Grunwald, Berlin 1923, pp. 23–122), to refer to the Messianic era, (cf. his "Treatise on Resurrection" ed. Joshua Finkel in the *Proceedings of the American Academy for Jewish Research,* Vol. IX, N.Y. 1939) but in the world to come the soul will survive everlastingly only in a disembodied form, (*Hilkot Teshubah* VIII.2). The later rabbis discussed the question whether a woman who died and was resurrected miraculously was allowed to remarry during the lifetime of her husband, cf. *Beer Heteb* and *Pithe Teshubah* to *Eben ha-Ezer* 17. 1.

37. The doctrine of election is by no means antiquated and as Professor H. Wheeler Robinson well says "it is the mandate to a minority to persist in their purpose as being the purpose of God. The particularism it involves belongs to every high mission, and is no mark of provincialism in religion," *Record and Revelation,* Oxford 1938, p. 327.

38. For the rules concerning one who came late to the services, cf. *Orah Hayyim* 52. An abridged form of grace was composed by R. Naphtali, cf. *Beer Heteb* to *Orah Hayyim* 192, 1.

39. *Berakot* 46b.

40. M. S. Bamberger, "Die Hygiene des Shulhan Aruk," in Max Grunwald, *Die Hygiene der Juden,* Dresden 1911, pp. 231–243.

41. *Shabbat* 82a.

42. *Yoma* 85b, *Shebuot* 39a. Although the punishment for homicide was not as severe as that for other sins, yet Maimonides considered it by far the greatest crime, (*Rotseah* IV. 9), whereas he instances the rule about *shaatnez* and cutting around the corners of the head as examples of light sins (*Teshubah* III, 9) see also *Sanh.* 74b. For the eight grievous sins, cf. Ginzberg, *Legends of the Jews,* VI. 364.

43. *Abodah Zarah* 3a.

44. *Mishnah Hullin* end, and *Yerushalmi Kid.* 61b. cf. also *Taanit* 11a. The command given to Adam was considered easy, whereas Joseph is commended for having refrained from yielding to the temptation of committing a most serious offense, *Gen. R.* 87.5, (ed. Theodore Albeck, p. 1066–7,) and *Sfire Numbers* 115, ed. Horowitz, p. 128.

45. Cf. e.g. I. Maccabees I. 41–53, and Greenstone in *Jewish Encyclopedia* s.v. Martyrdom.

46. *Yebamot* 46b.

47. Cf. also *Tosefta Ketubot* IV. 11.

48. Cf. *Ned.* 25a. The same remark is made about other precepts, e.g. for the Sabbath, cf. *Tanhuma, Ki Tissa* 33, and for circumcision cf. *Ned.* 32a. In *Menahot* 44a, the law of fringes is considered a light precept. Cf. *Rashi* to *Sanh.* 110b s.v. *Mitsva* and Strack and Billerbeck, *Commentary on Matthew* I:900–905.

49. The rabbis do not include buying and selling in the thirty-nine prohibited works but Philo says that Moses ordained "abstaining from work and profitmaking crafts and professions and business to get a livelihood," (*Moses* II. 211, ed. F. H. Colson; Vol. VI. 533). Abraham Danzig writes that a person is disqualified to act as a *shohet* if he desecrates the Sabbath, provided the act is biblically prohibited, if it were a violation of a rabbinical enactment such as

engaging in commercial transactions on the Sabbath, then he is not debarred, cf. *Chochmat Adam*, I.8.

50. Cf. *Orah Hayyim* 301.23 and *Pahad Yitshak* s.v. Fazzoletto. p. 2b. The Yiddish word for handkerchief "fachelke" is derived from the Italian, cf. also Cecil Roth, *The Jewish Contribution to Civilization*, p. 54. Rashi in *Shab.* 120b explains "Sudar" as handkerchief.

51. *What Dare I Think*, N.Y. 1931, pp. 221–22.

52. *Yer. Peah* VII. 5 cf. also *Ber.* 45a.

53. For the latest responsum on this subject, cf. Toledano, *Yam ha-Gadol*, no. 26.

54. *Yoreh Deah* 157. Cf. also Schechter's article: "Joy of the Law," in *Aspects of Rabbinic Theology*, pp. 148–169.

55. Protests against an excess of *humrot* were uttered by R. David ibn Zimra, cf. his Responsa I, 163, and II. 637. It was natural for folk who believed in the divine source of every command to observe them punctiliously and err on the side of caution. Professor Marx is of the opinion that many severities were introduced during the persecutions in Germany for which Jews blamed their sinfulness. Numerous *humrot* from the twelfth century can be traced to that feeling.

56. This rule goes back to Saadia Gaon, quoted by R. Asher (B.M. VII. 6). Cf. also Maimonides, Hilkot Shabbot VI. 1 and the commentaries, *Orah Hayyim* 307.2; Rabiah (ed. Aptowitzer) I.434–5; R. Eliezer of Metz, *Sefer Yereim ha-Shalem* no. 148 f. 142a and Responsa of R. Meir of Rothenburg, Budapest 1895 no. 202.

57. *Shabbat* 121b.

58. *Hullin* 110a, similarly R. Manshia was strict in his decisions to questions put to him by the people of Cascara (for the name cf. *J. Q. R., N. S.* 27, 1936, p. 71 note 11) because they were lax in observance.

59. *Berakot* 60a.

60. *Shabbat* 130a.

61. The rabbis realized too that times had changed, cf. D. Stossel, "Von den Abanderungsmoglichkeiten in rabbinischen Schriften unter besonderer Berucksichtigung des Prinzips," in *Kroner-Festschrift*, Breslau 1917, pp. 27–66; and *Proceedings of the Rabbinical Assembly*, Vol. V, p. 187 note 53.

62. *Yoreh Deah* 113.

63. *Baba Kamma* 28b.

64. Cf. Responsum by Toledano l. c. no. 28.

65. Cf. *Tosefta Sotah* XV. 10 and parallels.

66. Professor Ginzberg has given an excellent historical survey of this subject in the *Jewish Encyclopedia* s.v. Beard.

67. s.v. *Pesulin min ha-Torah*, p. 35–36 cf. also *Pithe Teshubah* to Eben ha-Ezer 42.5, Isaac Handel, Edut le-Yisroel, Vienna 1866.

68. For legitim in Roman law, cf. F. Mancaleone, "Le donazioni tra virie la legittima del patrono nel diritto romano classico" in *Studi di diritto romano in onore di Vittorio Scialoia*, Milan 1905, Vol. II. 609–25, and for Italian law, cf. M. C. Zanzucchi, *Le Successioni Legitime*, Milan s.a.

69. *Baba Batra* VIII. 5.

70. Cf. *Hoshen Mishpat* 34, 23.

71. *Hilkot Edut* XII. 1.

72. *Yebamot* 65b, *Yer. Terumot* V end and parallels.

73. IX. 23.

74. *Reconstruction of Religion, a Sociological Study*, N.Y. 1922, p. 193.

75. Cf. Margulies, *"Kiddushin al Tenai"* in *Rivista Israelitica* IV (1907), 87–91; Shapotnik, *Herut Olam*, London 1928; Lubetzki, *En Tenai be-Nisuin*, Vilna 1930; Henkin, *Perusha Ibra*, N.Y.

76. Hayyim Moses Rigrano, *Kiddushin al-Tenai*, 1925. Toledano in *Yam ha-Gadol*. no. 74. His plan was opposed by Ben Zion Uziel in *Mishpete Uziel*. Tel Aviv 1935, Vol. II, nos. 45–46. Uziel wrote against the *Mahberet Kiddushin al-Tenai*, issued by the Turkish rabbis, l. c. no. 44.

77. *Hazaah le-maan Takkanot Agunot*, N.Y. 1930. In a recent volume entitled *"Li-sheelot ha-Agunah"* Doctor Epstein reprints his *Hazaah*, publishes the proposal of Ben Zion Alkalai and discusses the various halakic objections that have been lodged against his *Takkanah*.

78. Cf. Barton, A *Sketch of Semitic Origins*, N.Y. 1902, p. 46, note 2.

79. Cf. Epstein, "Marriage Annulment" in the *Proceedings of the Rabbinical Assembly*, 1928, p. 71–83. A Portuguese rabbi, Samuel ben Halat of the 15th century tried to solve the *Agunah* problem by annulment, cf. Toledano in *Ozar ha-Hayyim*, 1930, p. 210–224 and his *Yam ha-Gadol* no. 74.

80. *Kiddushin* III. 5, cf. *Tosefta* II. 5.

81. Responsa no. 1. cf. E. Goldberg, *Koha de-Hetera*, N.Y. 1922, where the entire question is fully dealt with.

82. Thus Rashi explains *Kidushe Ta'ut* in *Ketubot* 51b as referring to *Tenai Kaful*. It is interesting to note that while *M. Kiddushin* III. 5 is literally repeated in the *Mishneh Torah, Ishut* VIII. 6, it is omitted entirely in *Eben ha-Ezer* 38.24. Cf. *Tosafot Kid.* 49b s.v. who felt that there were cases where fraud was a ground for invalidating a contract.

83. *Baba Kamma* 110b.

84. There are many responsa which deal with such instances. Of particular interest is the case of David Bindigo of Avignon discussed at length in the Responsa of Moses Galante no. 77. For the rarer case of a stubborn *Yebamah*, cf. *Responsa of R. Nissim* no. 61.

85. Lampronti officiated once at a wedding where the *Kiddushin* were given on condition that the marriage would be void if the husband died without issue, in order to obviate the *Halizah* ceremony. This he did with the approval of Mordecai Bassano, cf. *Pahad Yitshak* s.v. *Ah* ed. Lyck 1864, f. 102b.

86. Already in early times there are references to uncertainties in the law that awaited decisions. Thus in I. Maccabees IV. 46 we read "Until the prophet should come and decide," cf. Ginzberg, *Eine unbekannte judische Sekte*, pp. 303–317, where this matter is thoroughly discussed.

87. The literature on the subject is fairly extensive.

88. *Melamed le-Hoil* III, 20.

89. *Zaphenat Pa-aneah*, I, 26. Rabbi Rosin requires a special kind of a *get* but I do not know the source for this, inasmuch as there is no mention of it either in the Talmud or in the later authorities.

90. Commentary on Leviticus XI. 9.

91. *Noda be-Yehudah*, 2nd series, *Yoreh Deah* 28.

92. Cf. *Jewish Encyclopedia* IV. 43 where the controversial literature is cited.

93. Cf. *Pithe Teshubah* to *Yoreh Deah* 83 and Hoffmann, *Melamed le-Hoil* II, 21, and *Pahad Yizhak* s.v. *Dagim*.

94. Cf. *Shab.* 139a *Hilkot Zibbur*, the *Halakot Gedolot*, too, has a section entitled *Hilkot Zarke Zibbur* (ed. Warsaw 1876, p. 90–92).

95. Cf. Deut. XXIII. 4 where the Torah is spoken of as an inheritance.

96. Cf. *Ekah Rabbah* Intro. I, 1., *Yer. Hagigah* 1:76c, *Nedarim* 81a and ps. Rashi, ad locum.

LOUIS JACOBS argues that Biblical criticism (and, for that matter, scrutiny of the entire Jewish tradition with historical-critical tools) need not undermine the cardinal Jewish affirmation that halachah is divine because its Biblical origin is divine. The modern Jew must make one of three choices: to accept the full critical position, to reject the critical approach altogether, or to abide in the Positive-Historical tradition as originally conceived by Zechariah Frankel. Jacobs summarizes the positions of some modern Jewish theologians who adhere to the Historical school, and cites ten revealing Rabbinic sources to demonstrate that "long before the rise of modern criticism some of the Jewish teachers had a conception of revelation which leaves room for the idea of human cooperation with the divine." Jacobs finds wisdom in the thought of Emil Brunner (1889-1975), the Protestant theologian, who compared revelation to a phonograph record. The voice of the artist who delights us is the voice of God; the distortions are due to the necessary agency of man, who is summoned to be God's partner in the work of revelation no less than in the continuing process of creation.

111

A Synthesis of the Traditional and Critical Views

LOUIS JACOBS

Three distinct attitudes are possible with regard to the challenge of Bible criticism and its implications for Jewish observance, and each of these has found protagonists among Jews in this century. There is the school which accepts the critical position more or less *in toto* to the detriment not alone of the doctrine of "Torah from Heaven" but also of the practical observances of Judaism. Another school feels obliged to reject entirely, and to combat positively in the name of Orthodoxy, any untraditional views. And there is the third view according to which a synthesis between the traditional and critical theories is possible and that, in any event, the attitude of respect, reverence and obedience *vis-a-vis* Jewish observance is not radically affected by an "untraditional" outlook on questions of Biblical authorship and composition.

Most thinkers of the Reform school, nowadays, adopt, more or less, the full critical position and draw from it what appears to them to be the logical conclusion that the ritual precepts of the Pentateuch are no longer binding upon Jews, not having been given by God to Moses. The lofty ethical standards of the Bible and the principles of justice, righteousness and holiness are binding because of their basic truth and their appeal to man's higher nature.

Opponents of the Critical School

The second view is that of such Orthodox scholars as David Hoffmann (1843-1921), the author of the brilliant *Die wichtigsten Instanzen gegen die Graf-Wellhausensche Hypothese*. Hoffmann attacks the critics with great acumen and tremendous erudition on their own ground and with their own methods. But it is not without significance that Hoffman

112

himself was the originator of what has been called 'The Higher Criticism of the Mishnah', in which the great Code of Jewish law is subjected to exactly the same kind of literary analysis—various 'strata', redactors and all—which the critics use in their investigations into the Biblical literature. As Hoffman in fact declares, his opposition to the Higher Criticism is on grounds of *faith*. As an Orthodox Jew he feels compelled to reject the critical position as erroneous and he then uses his considerable skill in demolishing the edifice the critics have so laboriously erected.

Dr. J. H. Hertz, the late Chief Rabbi of the British Empire, was one of the most determined opponents of the critical theory, calling the Graf-Wellhausen hypothesis a perversion of history and a desecration of religion. Dr. Hertz devotes a large portion of his famous commentary to the *Pentateuch* to attacking the Higher Criticism. Typical of his remarks in this connection is the following: "The procedure of the critics in connection with the Creation and Deluge chapters is typical of their method throughout. It justifies the protest of the late Lord Chancellor of England, the Earl of Halsbury—an excellent judge of evidence—who in 1915 found himself impelled to declare: 'For my own part I consider the assignment of different fragments of Genesis to a number of wholly imaginary authors, great rubbish. I do not understand the attitude of those men who base a whole theory of this kind on hypotheses for which there is no evidence whatsoever.' A generation before the Earl of Halsbury, the historian Lecky gave expression to a similar judgment, in the following words: 'I may be pardoned for expressing my belief that this kind of investigation is often pursued with an exaggerated confidence. Plausible conjecture is too easily mistaken for positive proof. Undue significance is attached to what may be mere casual coincidence, and a minuteness of accuracy is professed in discriminating between different elements in a narrative which cannot be attained by mere internal evidence'."[1]

Another View

Many modern scholars without any theological bias reject the hypothesis on purely scientific grounds. The Uppsala School, Umberto Cassutto, Ezekiel Kaufmann and others have all suggested alternative theories, though none of these is in complete accord with the traditional view. Professor Cassutto,[2] for example, takes each of the five pillars on which the Documentary Hypothesis stands—the different divine names, the differences in style and language, contradictions between two passages, repetitions in two passages, and the combination of two accounts—and demonstrates that they have been set up by scholars incapable of appreciating the niceties of ancient Hebrew style and linguistic distinctions. To give but one example, the expressions 'going out of Egypt' and 'going *up* out of Egypt' are not at all due to different sources, each with its own idiom, but they represent the expressions of the same 'source' for two different things—the one refers to the Exodus alone, the other to the whole journey of the Israelites from Egypt to the Promised Land. But Cassutto recognises—and here we arrive at the third point of view—that unfounded though the Documentary Hypothesis is, the question is a *literary* one, not a religious question. 'We must approach this task', writes Cassutto, 'with complete objectivity, without any sort of preconception in favour of one school or another. We must be ready from the beginning of our investigation to accept its results wherever they may lead. And there is no need for us to be alarmed for the honour of our Torah and its holiness. The honour of our Torah and its holiness are above the realm of literary criticism, they depend on the inner content of the books of the Torah and are in no way dependent on the solution of literary problems which have to do merely with the external form, with the 'language of men' in which, as the Rabbis say, the Torah speaks. . . .'[3] *This, in fact, is the fundamental question—not whether this or that theory is correct, but whether the appeal to tradition is valid in matters to which the normal canons of historical and literary method apply, and whether the authority of Jewish Law is weakened as a result of scientific investigation.* The third view holds that we can afford to be objective in examining the literary problems of the Bible and that it does not at all follow that because, as a result of more highly developed methods of investigation, including the use of archaeological evidence, we are compelled to adopt different views from the ancients, we must automatically give up the rich and spiritually satisfying tradition that has been built up with devotion and self-sacrifice by the wisest and best of Jews.

The Third View

This third view is finding an increasing number of adherents. This historical school argues that literary problems can only be solved by the use of those methods which have been applied so successfully in the examination of other documents of antiquity—the Greek and Latin classics, for example. Its members will keep an open mind on many of the problems, realizing that after so many centuries many of the difficulties never will be solved. But this approach in no way invalidates the observance of Jewish practices. These derive their authority from the undeniable fact that they have provided Jews with 'ladders to heaven' and still have the power of sanctifying Jewish life in accordance with the Jewish ideal; because of this we recognise that it was God who gave them and it is His will that we obey when we submit to the Torah discipline. As Franz Rosenzweig has so finely put it: "Where we differ from orthodoxy is in our reluctance to draw from our belief in the holiness or uniqueness of the Torah, and in its character of revelation, any conclusions as to its literary genesis and the philological value of the text as it has come down to us. If all of Wellhausen's theories were correct and the Samaritans really had the better text, our faith would not be shaken in the least."[4]

A Fascinating Responsum

One of the most original thinkers among the Rabbis of the older school, Rabbi Hayyim Hirschenson, wrote some years ago a fascinating Responsum on the Jewish attitude to Bible criticism. Hirschenson, who was asked if Bible criticism may be taught at the Hebrew University, endeavoured to apply Halachic method to the problem. The Halachah knows of three categories with regard to liability—these are, *hayyabh*, 'obligation', i.e. the incurment of a penalty; *patur* 'exemption' but *assur* 'forbidden', i.e. though there is no penalty for the offence there is prohibition; and *patur* and *muttar*, 'exempt and permitted', i.e. not only is there no penalty but there is no prohibition. With regard to Sabbath law, for instance, work prohibited in the Bible involves the full penalty of Sabbath desecration; work forbidden by rabbinic law is prohibited but there is no penalty attached to the prohibition; and there are certain forms of work involving no prohibition whatsoever. Hirschenson suggests[5] that the main objection in the Talmudic sources to the rejection of the doctrine of 'Torah from Heaven' is that such a rejection impugns the honesty of Moses by suggesting that he wrote something he had not received from God. The *hayyabh* offence in this field, for which the penalty of exclusion from the World

to Come is incurred, is the denigration of Moses' character in maintaining that he wilfully forged the Biblical documents. On the other hand,
the study of textual criticism is both *patur* and *muttar*, for, as we have
seen, such criticism was at times resorted to in the Talmudic age. Modern Bible Criticism does not suggest that Moses forged the documents
but they are not the work of Moses at all. This, because it is in opposition to the established traditions of our people, is *assur* 'forbidden,' but
not *hayyabh*. Hence, Hirschenson concludes it would not be necessary
for the Orthodox Jew to boycott the Hebrew University because some
of its professors espouse the cause of Higher Criticism.

Reinterpretation

Hirschenson's view as it stands is hardly historical. It is, to say the
least, unlikely that the chief purpose of those who so zealously fought
on behalf of the doctrine of 'Torah from Heaven' was to safeguard the
reputation of Moses. But accepting his adoption of Halachic categories
we can say much for the view that present-day criticism would not fall
under the complete *hayyabh* ban of the Rabbis. The chief concern of
the Rabbis was not with questions of authorship but of inspiration. Is
the Torah the word of God? This was the concern of the ancient teachers. In Talmudic times, no one, not even the heretic, doubted that the
Torah was written by Moses. Hence, in those days the fundamental
question was did Moses write it of his own accord or under divine inspiration? Even if the most radical theories of the critics are accepted
this means no more than that the base of the problem has been shifted,
but the question of the divine origin of the Torah is not radically affected. An excellent illustration of this is the Talmudic debates on whether
the book of Ecclesiastes is to be admitted into the Canon of Holy Writ.
Those who would admit it argue that Solomon wrote it under the influence of the divine spirit. Those who oppose its admission argue that it
is the product of 'Solomon's wisdom', i.e. the fruit of his own, unin-
spired thinking.[6] In other words the Solomonic authorship of the book
was accepted by everyone; the only question to be considered was, is
the book so inspired as to merit inclusion in the Canon? Now that all
scholars are unanimous in rejecting the Solomonic authorship of the
book, there is still no reason for rejecting the opinion that it is worthy
of inclusion in the Canon on account of its inspiration.

There is much, too, in the suggestion that the Rabbis had a sound polemical motive in emphasizing that the whole of the Torah was given 'at once' to Moses. They were chiefly concerned with a rebuttal of the Christian view that the Torah was a temporary institution, that there had been a 'progressive revelation' and that, therefore, the 'New Testament' could be looked upon as a culmination of the 'Old'.[7] Students of the Talmudic and Midrashic literature will recall many such examples of religious polemic, consciously erring on the side of anachronism, in order to make its point clear. A good example of this is the oft-repeated Rabbinic teaching that Abraham kept the whole of the Torah before it was given—in contradistinction to the Christian view that it was not necessary to keep the Torah in order to lead the good life.[8]

Dr. J. Abelson has thus stated the third view of which we have spoken. "The correct perspective of the matter seems to be as follows: the modern criticism of the Bible on the one hand, and faith in Judaism on the other hand, can be regarded as two distinct compartments. For criticism, even at its best, is speculative and tentative, something always liable to be modified or proved wrong and having to be replaced by something else. It is an intellectual exercise, subject to all the doubts and guesses which are inseparable from such exercises. But our accredited truths of Judaism have their foundations more deeply and strongly laid than all this. And our faith in them not only need be uninjured by our faith in criticism, but need not be affected by the latter at all. The two are quite consistent and can be held simultaneously. I can quite understand any one talking as follows: I like the Higher Criticism, I study it, I appreciate much of its teaching and its general sentiment, I fancy that much in Judaism can be brought into line with it, I think that it may be in accordance with truth and it may not be in accordance with truth, and therefore I sit on the hedge; as to my notions of the basic truths of Judaism, my reading in criticism has not changed them one bit. The one is airy, floating intellectualism, the other is consolidated religion. They lie in different spheres and have no necessary bearing one on the other."[9]

Another Version of the Third View

A somewhat different, but similarly helpful, view is expounded by Will Herberg,[10] claiming to follow Rosenzweig, Buber, Niebuhr and Brunner. In this view, both modernism and fundamentalism are wrong in insisting that our concept of revelation must be either one or the other. The third way is not 'between' modernism and fundamentalism but beyond and distinct from both, so that those who tread this way may take Scripture with the utmost seriousness as the record of revelation while avoiding the pitfalls of fundamentalism. As Herberg puts it: "In this view, a shift in the very meaning of the term 'revelation' is involved. Revelation is not the communication of infallible information, as the fundamentalists claim, nor is it the outpouring of 'inspired' sages and poets, as the modernists conceive it. Revelation is the *self-disclosure of God in his dealings with the world.* Scripture is thus not itself revelation but a humanly mediated record of revelation. It is a story composed of many strands and fragments, each arising in its own time, place and circumstances, yet it is essentially one, for it is throughout the story of the encounter of God and man in the history of Israel. Scripture as revelation is not a compendium of recondite information or metaphysical propositions; it is quite literally *Heilsgeschichte,* redemptive history."

It goes without saying that these or similar views which see no incompatibility between the idea of Scripture as the Word of God and the use of critical *methods* in its investigation, can only be entertained if the doctrine of 'verbal' inspiration is rejected. It is true that in the vast range of Jewish teaching on revelation there are numerous passages in which 'verbal' inspiration is accepted or, at least, hinted at. But this is not the whole story. It can be demonstrated that long before the rise of modern criticism some of the Jewish teachers had a conception of revelation which leaves room for the idea of human cooperation with the divine. It will be helpful if a few of the passages containing these ideas are quoted.

(1) The Talmud[11] tells of an oven, the ritual purity of which is debated by R. Eliezer (2nd Cent. C.E.) and the Sages. R. Eliezer said to the Sages: 'If the ruling is as I hold let this carob-tree prove it.' Thereupon the carob-tree was torn out of its place but the Sages retorted: 'No proof can be brought from a carob-tree.' R. Eliezer then said: 'If the ruling accords with me, let the stream of water prove it.' Whereupon the stream flowed backwards but the Sages said: 'No proof can be brought from a stream of water.' Again R. Eliezer urged: Let the walls of the House of Learning prove it. Whereupon the walls of the House of Learning began to totter but the Sages remained unconvinced. Finally, R. Eliezer said: 'If I am right let it be proved from Heaven,' and a Heavenly voice cried out: 'Why do you dispute with R. Eliezer, seeing that in all matters the law is in accord with his ruling?' But R. Joshua

said: 'It is not in Heaven[12]—the Torah states 'After the majority must one incline[13] and this means that the law must be decided by a majority of human judges and no appeal to a heavenly voice is valid.' " The story concludes that when R. Nathan met Elijah, the Prophet, he asked him: What did the Holy One blessed be He do in that hour? And the answer was that He laughed with joy, saying, "My sons have defeated Me, My sons have defeated Me!"

(2) They were disputing in the Heavenly Academy: If the bright spot preceded the white hair,[14] he is unclean; if the reverse he is clean. If in doubt—the Holy One, blessed be He, ruled, clean; the entire Heavenly Academy ruled, *He* is unclean. They asked: Who shall decide it? Rabbah bar Nahmani, for he is a great authority on these matters. Rabbah died and as he died he exclaimed, 'Clean, clean!'[15]

(3) R. Isaac said: The same watchword (communication) is revealed to many prophets, yet no two prophets prophecy in the identical phraseology, if they are true prophets.[16] An anticipation of the recognition by modern scholars that the prophetic inspiration is mediated through the personality of the prophet; Amos speaking in the language of a herdsman, Isaiah in the language of a prince.

(4) Isaiah and Ezekiel both saw the King, say the Rabbis,[17] but Isaiah as a city-dweller, familiar with the sight of the king and his court, hence his description is brief, Ezekiel as a rustic who is filled with wonder at the unfamiliar sight, hence his description is lengthy.

(5) Rab Judah said in the name of Rab: when Moses ascended on high he found the Holy One, blessed be He, engaged in fixing crowns to the letters of the Torah. Moses asked after the meaning of these crowns and God told him that there will arise a man, at the end of many generations, Akiba ben Joseph by name, who will expound upon each tittle heaps and heaps of laws. 'Lord of the Universe', said Moses, 'permit me to see him'. God replied: 'Turn thee round'. Moses went and sat behind eight rows of Akiba's disciples. Not being able to follow their discussions he was ill at ease, but when they came to a certain subject and the disciples said to the master: 'Whence do you know it?' and the latter replied: 'It is a law given to Moses on Sinai,' he was comforted. Thereupon he returned to the Holy One, blessed be He, and said: 'Lord of the Universe, Thou hast such a man and Thou givest the Torah by me!'[18] He replied, 'Be silent, for so it has come to My mind'. In other words the Torah that Akiba was teaching was so different from the Torah given to Moses—because the social, economic, political and religious conditions were so different in Akiba's day—that, at first,

Moses could not recognize his Torah in the Torah taught by Akiba. But he was reassured when he realized that Akiba's Torah was *implicit* in his Torah, was, indeed, an attempt to make his Torah relevant to the spiritual needs of Jews in the age of Akiba.

(6) R. Ishmael b. Elisha (1st-2nd Cent. C.E.) disagreed with those of his contemporaries who derived rules and teachings from a pleonastic word or syllable, e.g. the use of the infinite absolute form of the verb. For instance, the verse concerning idolators in which it is said that they 'will *surely* be cut off'—*hikkareth tikkareth*[19] is interpreted by Akiba to convey the thought that they will be cut off in both this world and the next. To this Ishmael replied that no teachings can be derived from such expressions for this is how Hebrew was spoken and 'the Torah speaks in the language of men'![20]

Maimonides used this principle to explain the Biblical anthropomorphisms.[21]

(7) When a Rabbinic precept is carried out, e.g. the kindling of the Hannukah lights, the blessing to be recited runs: 'Who hast sanctified us with His commandments and *hast commanded* us to . . .[22] In other words, not only did the Rabbis recognise a human element in the Bible, they perceived the divine in post-Biblical developments of Judaism.

(8) Azariah Figo (1579–1647) gives this interpretation to the Rabbinic distinction between Moses and other prophets: that he saw God through a polished glass while they saw Him through a dim glass. Moses saw God Himself, as if through a window pane; the other prophets saw only His image as reflected in a mirror, i.e. through their own personalities,[23] as we would say. Figo's view goes further than the Rabbinic views mentioned above (3 and 4). The Rabbis speak of the prophets seeing God and *expressing* what they had seen through their personalities; Figo speaks of the prophets *seeing* God through their own personalities!

(9) Isaac of Vorka (a famous Hasidic Rabbi) said: It is told in the Midrash: The ministering angels once said to God: 'you have permitted Moses to write whatever he wants to, so there is nothing to prevent him from saying to Israel: I have given you the Torah'. God replied: 'This he would not do, but if he did he would still be keeping faith with me'. The Rabbi interpreted this with a parable. A merchant wanted to go on a journey. He took an assistant and let him work in his shop. He himself spent most of his time in the adjoining room from where he could

hear what was going on next door. During the first few weeks he sometimes heard his assistant tell a customer 'The master cannot let this go
for so low a price'. The merchant did not go on his journey. During the
next few weeks he occasionally heard the voice next door say: 'We cannot let it go for so low a price'. He still postponed his journey. But in
the next few weeks he heard the assistant say: 'I cannot let it go for so
low a price'. It was then that he started on his journey.[24]

(10) The rival schools of Hillel and Shammai debated, we are told,
for a number of years, whose ruling should be accepted. Eventually a
Heavenly voice proclaimed: 'The words of both are the words of the
living God, but the rule is in accordance with the school of Hillel'[25]—
another example of Rabbinic recognition of the divine in post-Biblical
developments.

Allowing for the legendary nature of some of the above passages, it
must be obvious that many Jewish teachers conceived of revelation in
more dynamic terms than the doctrine of 'verbal' inspiration would imply. For them, revelation is an encounter between the divine and the
human, so that there is a human as well as a divine factor in revelation,
God revealing His Will not alone to men but *through* men. No doubt
our new attitude to the Biblical record, in which, as the result of historical, literary and archaeological investigations, the Bible is seen
against the background of the times in which its various books were
written, ascribes more to the human element than the ancients would
have done, but this is a difference in degree, not in kind. The new
knowledge need not in any way affect our reverence for the Bible and
our loyalty to its teachings. God's Power is not lessened because He
preferred to co-operate with His creatures in producing the Book of
Books. Applying his words to our problem, we can fittingly quote the
penetrating observation of the ancient Talmudic sage, that in every
passage in the Bible where the greatness of God is mentioned, there
you find also His humility.[26]

This chapter might suitably be concluded with the splendid illustration of the point of view we have been trying to sketch, given by Emil
Brunner. Brunner asks us to think of a gramophone record. The voice
we hear on the record is the voice we want to hear, it is the actual voice
of the artist who delights us, but we hear it through the inevitable distortions of the record. We hear the authentic voice of God speaking to
us through the pages of the Bible—we know that it is the voice of God
because of the uniqueness of its message and the response it awakens

in our higher nature—and its truth is in no way affected in that we can only hear that voice through the medium of human beings who, hearing it for the first time, endeavoured to record it for us.

Notes

1. By far the best and most effective critique of the Documentary Hypothesis in English is that of Solomon Goldman in his *In the Beginning,* to which the reader is referred. N.Y., 1941, p. 77f. Cf. the same author's *The Book of Books, An Introduction,* Phil., 1948.

2. *The Documentary Hypothesis* (Hebrew), Sec. Ed., Jer. 1953.

3. *Ibid.,* pp. 16–17.

4. *Franz Rosenzweig—His Life and Thought,* N.Y., 1953, p. 158.

5. *Malki Ba-Kodesh,* Vols. I and II, St. Louis, 1919–1921.

6. *Tos. Yad.* II:14; *Meg.* 7a.

7. See Bernard J. Bamberger: "Revelations of the Torah After Sinai," in *Hebrew Union College Annual,* Vol. XVI, 1941, p. 97f.

8. See Ginzberg's *Legends of the Jews,* Vol. V,p. 259, n. 275.

9. 'Bible Problems and Modern Knowledge', in *The Jewish Review,* March, 1913, p. 483. The whole article is well worth careful study.

10. *Judaism and Modern Man,* p. 243f.

11. *B.M.* 59b.

12. Deut. xxx. 12.

13. Ex. xxiii. 2.

14. See Lev. xiii. 1–3.

15. *B.M.* 86a.

16. *Sanh.* 89a.

17. *Hag.* 13b.

18. *Men.* 29b.

19. Num. xv. 31.

20. *Sifre Num.* 15. 31; *Yer. Yeb.* viii, 8d; *Yer. Ned.* i. 36c; *B.M.* 31b and freq. see *J.E.* Vol. VI, p. 649.

21. *Guide,* Part I, Chapter xxvi. Cf. Bahya: 'Duties of the Heart,' *Sha'ar Ha-Yihud,* Chapter 10.

22. See *Sabb.* 23a.

23. *Binnah Le-'Ittim,* P. II, Ser. 44, quoted by Israel Bettan, *Studies in Jewish Preaching,* Cincinatti, 1939, pl 255–256.

24. Buber: *Tales of the Hasidim, The Later Masters,* N.Y., 1948, p. 295–296.

25. *Erub.* 13b.

26. *Meg.* 31a.

SEYMOUR SIEGEL argues in this paper that Jewish Law is the embodiment of Jewish Ethics. Therefore, if some specific Jewish norm conflicts with our ethical sensitivity, it should be ignored or abolished. This approach represents the factor of aggada (Jewish ideas and theology) as being the controlling factor in the evaluation of halachah (Jewish law).

It is recommended that such halachot as prohibiting the mamzer (the product of an incestuous or adulterous relationship) to marry into the congregaton of Israel; the prohibition of a divorcee to marry a kohen (a descendant of the tribe of Aaron), or the discrimination against women in synagogue ritual be modified or ignored.

123

Ethics and the Halakhah

SEYMOUR SIEGEL

A religious community, it is said, is a group of people who tell the same stories to one another. In regard to the Jewish community, it is necessary to add—and who practice the same things with one another. But what we practice as Jews is challenged today on many fronts.

We must make decisions about the relationship of our ethical outlook to the revolutionary movements in the world; face problems relating to the Jewish communities around the world and the interests of the state of Israel; confront ethical issues raised by the fact that we have moved from a position of complete powerlessness (a condition which is not without its ethical advantages) into a position of relative power (a condition which results in ethical dilemmas). I would like to discuss one phase of our general problem to which our movement can make a definite contribution. This is, the problem of the relation between ethical values and the *halakhah.*

A recent article by Amnon Rubenstein, the distinguished dean of the Law School at Tel Aviv University, speaks directly to this issue.[1] Dr. Rubenstein tells of a case where a man sued his wife for divorce in the Israeli courts. When the judges were reluctant to grant the divorce, he produced a document (which he had kept undisclosed for twenty years) proving that he was a *kohen* and therefore was not allowed to marry his wife in the first place, since she had been a divorcee and thus was forbidden to a *kohen* according to the Levitical law. The court, following Jewish law, ordered a *get,* and absolved the husband from assuming the wife's support, since the marriage had been invalid *ab initio.*

This sad story, related by Dr. Rubenstein in anger, is painful not only because the unfortunate lady had to suffer, but, most of all, because this suffering was the result of the application of Jewish law, a law which is said to be "perfect and restores the soul."[2] It is my thesis that according to our interpretation of Judaism, the ethical values of our tradition should have the power to judge the particulars of Jewish law. If any law in our tradition does not fulfill our ethical values, then the law should be abolished or revised. This point of view can be supported historically and theologically

Theological Foundation

The theological foundation of Jewish ethics is the duty to imitate God—to "go in His ways."[3] This duty is rooted in the character of man as created in the image of God. Since we are created in His image, we have both the responsibility and the capacity to follow Him. But we are bidden to follow God, not to impersonate Him. That is to say, we are to imitate the Almighty in His qualities of mercy, kindness, justice, and love. We must not pretend to be God—that is, to generate our own law and to pretend to Omnipotence. We *follow* God by doing deeds of lovingkindness and justice. We dare not (though often we do) pretend that we *are* God.

The ethical demand to imitate God is the foundation of the specific laws of the Torah. The laws are expressions of the ethical demand in concrete terms. The laws have other functions, too. The rituals and the "laws of holiness" are means by which we approach the Almighty. They make it possible to relive the sacred history of the Jews; they are signs and reminders of the divine relationship to Israel. However, the main point of contact between the divine and the human is through the ethical demand.

Yehezkel Kaufmann, analyzing the prophetic view of the divine-human relationship, explains this approach:

> It was the prophets who expressed for the first time the idea that the cult of the nation as a whole . . . has no intrinsic value. . . . The prophets . . . declared that its [the election] object was to publish the knowledge of God and realize His moral will . . . the purpose [of the cult] is to serve as a symbol and expression of knowledge of God, a memorial to His covenant. . . . Morality is an absolute value, for it is divine in essence. The God who demands righteousness, justice, kindness, and compassion is Himself just, gracious, kind, and compassionate. Moral goodness makes man share, as it were, in the divine nature. Classical prophecy established a hierarchy of value; both cult and morality are God's command and part of His covenant, and both are expressions of knowledge of God. But while

the cult is sacred only as a symbol, morality is essentially godlike, being a reflection of the qualities of God.[4]

Extending this analysis we affirm that what is primary in Jewish faith is God's turning to us and offering His covenant to the people of Israel. His turning to us makes it imperative that we attempt to share in the divine essence by pursuing a life of justice and kindness. This demand gave birth to the specific laws which are embodiments and concretizations of these responsibilities. We do not share the fundamentalist belief that the specific laws in their precise formulation are God's revelation. God's revelation is His turning to us, His making a covenant with us, and His demand upon us to imitate Him. The specific laws are *responses* to revelation; they are not the *content* of the revelation. The demands of morality are absolute. The specific laws are relative. Thus, if because of changing conditions the specific laws no longer express the ethical values which Tradition teaches (these ethical values, it must be stressed, are rooted in the Tradition), we have the responsibility to revise the laws, rather than allow them to fall into desuetude.

Historic Flexibility

The process of revision in the light of ethical values is characteristic of the creative period of Jewish law, especially during talmudic times. Let me cite two striking examples of this tendency: [5]

1) In Mishna *Keritut,* end of chapter 1, we read: "If a woman has five births [and was therefore obligated to bring five offerings], she may bring one and thereby be permitted to eat from the sacrifices, but she must later bring the remainder of the sacrifices. . . . Once [as a result of this ruling] pigeons [used for sacrifices] rose in price until they were one golden dinar. Rabban Simeon ben Gamaliel said: 'By the Temple, I will not rest this night until the pigeons will be purchased for silver dinarii.' He went into the *Bet Midrash* and taught: 'A woman who has five births may bring one sacrifice and this is sufficient' . . . and the pigeons then sold for a quarter of a silver dinar."

2) In *Pesahim* 30a, Samuel maintained: "They [*hametz* pots] need not be broken, but can be kept until after its period and [then] used." The Talmud explains that Samuel is consistent with his view. ". . . For Samuel said to the hardware merchants: Charge an equita-

ble price for your pots, for if not I will publicly lecture that the law is in accordance with R. Simeon." (The explanation: People did break their pots before Passover, and the merchants took advantage of the increased demand after Passover to raise prices. Thereupon Samuel threatened that he would publicly lecture that leaven kept over Passover is not forbidden, so that people need not break their pots.)

From these and many other examples it is clear that the sages modified the law when they saw that following another norm would result in unfavorable results. Ethical considerations and public policy were sufficient to change the decision. In this connection it is interesting to read a comment by Yehoshua Walk Katz in his commentary, *Derisha*, to the *Tur Hoshen Mishpat* 1:1:

> When the rabbis spoke of a true judgment which conforms to the truth, they meant to say that the judge should judge according to the place and the time, so that the judgment may be truly true. A judge should not always rule according to the letter of the law . . . if he does not do this then he may be a true judge, but his judgments are not true.[6]

It is possible to formulate the approach in terms of the relationship between the *aggadah* and the *halakhah*. If we loosely define the *aggadah* as the expression of the ethical and theological values of Judaism, and the *halakhah* as their embodiment, then our thesis is that the *aggadah* should control the *halakhah*—not vice versa.

In the literature of Judaism various opinions have been formulated concerning the relationship of *aggadah* and *halakhah*. Rab Hai Gaon states: "The words of the *aggadah* are not authorative, since each one [of the Sages] said what was in his heart . . . therefore we do not rely on them [the words of the *aggadah*]."[7] A modern expression of this view can be found in the words of Isaiah Leibowitz of the Hebrew University: "Judaism is nothing more than the embodiment of the *halakhah*."[8]

For us, the *aggadah* is all important, for it is the expression of Jewish values and world-outlook. The *halakhah* is its embodiment. We do not intend, of course, to diminish the value of the *halakhah* in pressing this formulation. Indeed, it is our view that there is no better way to preserve the integrity and the authority of Jewish law than by revising it when it needs revision. Edmund Burke, perhaps the greatest of all conservative (politics, of course) thinkers, said: A state without the means of changing its laws is without the means of preserving its laws. Mena-

chem Mendel of Kotzk put the idea in a striking saying: Do not make a
pesel [an idol] of the *asher tsivkha hashem elokekha* [what God has
commanded you].[9]

Theory Into Practice

I would like to cite several concrete examples where, I believe, the law
must be revised in the light of the ethical values and goals of Judaism.
I am proud of the fact that the Law Committee of the Rabbinical Assembly has taken action in most of these areas.

The first area is that which was touched upon by Dr. Rubenstein in
the article alluded to above—the prohibitions surrounding the marriage of a *kohen* to a divorcee or proselyte. The inherited norm which
forbids such unions is based on two assumptions which we find hard
to accept. One is that a *kohen* may not marry a divorcee because he
"brings to the altar the bread of god."[10] That is, the *kohen* is to be considered a special individual because of his service in the Temple. The
other assumption underlying this norm is that there is something tainted in a divorcee or a convert. The two assumptions are not acceptable
today. Whatever deference is paid to the *kohen* flows from historical
memory and historical anticipation. But this is only of symbolic value,
and should not touch upon the lives of private individuals. Nor do we
accept the notion that a divorcee or a convert is so tainted that she is
not worthy of marrying a *kohen*.

Therefore, we urge all halakhic bodies to follow the action of our
movement—to dissolve the norm and permit the marriage of a *kohen* to
any Jewish woman. This action expresses our respect for the *halakhah*,
and our view of the subordination of the halakhic norms to the demands of our ethical and moral tradition.

It is basic to our understanding of the nature of religion that marriage—the establishment of a common life and destiny—should be
sanctified by a religious rite. From this it flows naturally that when
such a union is dissolved, it should also be marked by a religious ceremony of some sort. But this does not mean that the specific means of
dissolution inherited from the tradition have an absolute claim upon
us. We have a responsibility toward the historic norms which we have
inherited, but this responsibility does not extend so far that we must
accept them when they result in unethical situations.

For example, not long ago a woman appeared before the *Bet Din* of

the Rabbinical Assembly. She had been divorced from her husband for
some time and had been granted custody of their child. The husband
subsequently married a non-Jew. Now the woman wished to remarry
and petitioned her husband for a *get*. He said that he would comply—if
he received custody of the child. The woman cried to the rabbis: How
can my ex-husband use Jewish law, which he defies (by marrying out
of the faith), to deprive me of my child? The rabbis decided to invoke
the principle of *afkanihu rabbanan kidushin miney*, the ancient power
which the ecclesiastical court has to annul a marriage retroactively;
they freed the woman to remarry.[11]

   This does not mean that we are more compassionate than our forefathers or the judges of the Israeli courts. They, of course, know this
principle too. But they do not invoke it because of technical reasons,
and because they are bound by their fundamentalist faith to accept the
idea that not only did God command us to order marriage and divorce
according to religious norms, but that He also specified the technical
ways in which this should be done, and that no other forms are possible.

   In our view, family life has been placed within a religious framework in response to the divine will. But the specifics of this religious
framework reflect particular conditions and assumptions—in the case
of divorce, a patriarchal structure of society in which women are under
the protection of the man. This framework must now be revised to accord with today's conditions and assumptions.

   There has been considerable discussion of the notion of *mamzerut*
(illegitimacy) in the Israeli press recently. According to this notion, a
sin committed by parents causes the child to be so flawed that he cannot enter into the Jewish community through marriage. The imposition
of this norm causes untold difficulties, especially in the absorption of
groups of Jews who have been removed from the main body of Israel—e.g. the Bene Israel and the Falashas. As these groups have not
been instructed in the specifics of religious divorce laws, they are presumed to include *mamzerim* within their numbers. The problem of
mamzerut is bound to be exacerbated when large scale immigration occurs from the communist-bloc countries. Many women, it is to be assumed, married without religious divorces and therefore technically
gave birth to *mamzerim*.

   The *Midrash* (*Vayikra Rabba*, end of *Parshat Emor*, and in the parallels) expresses the injustice which flows from the notion of *mamzerut*.
Daniel Hayata commented that the verse in *Kohelet* 4:1: "I considered

all the oppressions that are done under the sun; and behold the tears of such as were oppressed, and they had no comforter; and on the side of their oppressors there was power, but they had no comforter," referred to *mamzerim.* *"Behold the tears of such as are oppressed*—the fathers of these [the *mamzerim*] sinned, and these are humiliated . . . what sin have they committed? *They have no comforter; and on the side of their oppressors there was power*—their oppressors refers to the Sanhedrin of Israel which comes upon them with the authority of the Torah. . . . The Holy One blessed be He says, I will have to comfort them."

It seems timely for us to rule now that the whole notion of *mamzerut* has lost its force and should be ignored. Let us do now what the *Kadosh barukh Hu* is to do in the future.

It is, of course, possible to add many more examples of norms which should be revised in the light of our ethical values. These revisions which flow from our conception of Jewish law and its origin will serve to strengthen the authority of Jewish law in our lives. But it is not sufficient merely to revise *halakhah* in the light of our ethical conceptions. It is also necessary to broaden *halakhah* so that it will *incorporate* ethics. We must convert *aggadah* into *halakhah,* make *din* what is now *lifnim mishurat hadin,* make that which is exhortatory, mandatory.

Let me cite a few examples, based on articles that have recently appeared in the Israeli press.

An ethical, as well as practical, problem which troubles many concerns the cost of some of our religious ceremonies—weddings, bar mitzvahs and funerals. It would be advisable to limit, by *halakhah,* the amount of money permitted to be spent on such occasions. (There are precedents for this dating back to the Middle Ages.) The Israeli press has reported that several parents in Bene Berak rebelled against their children (reversing the usual procedure) when the latter demanded expensive weddings. The parents felt that *pikuah nefesh dokheh luksus,* the demands of life take precedence over luxury. In the broad sense, this norm refers to the moral health of our community. Many sensitive people, especially among the young (though not limited to them), are repelled by the conspicuous consumption visible in Jewish ceremonies. If we could find the will to limit the costs of weddings, bar mitzvahs and funerals, this would be a powerful force in making our community more sensitive to the enormous needs of the world.

Let us turn now to the Sabbath, Israel's greatest treasure. We who love the Sabbath know its delights. But it is also true that in a country such as Israel, where there is no *shabbat sheni shel galuyot*, the Sunday, those who observe the law are under great hardship when they cannot travel or refresh themselves on the beaches or in the countryside. From an economic standpoint, Israel cannot afford the luxury of a five-day working week. But several months ago, Rabbi Norman Lamm made a suggestion which, I believe, should be enthusiastically endorsed. He urged a *takkanah* (legislation) making *Rosh Hodesh* a working holiday. This would provide an opportunity for a day of recreation, and would also add meaning to *Rosh Hodesh*.

We are not the first to see in Judaism a command toward the ethical life. The Jewish reformers in the nineteenth century, Ahad Ha'am and the founders of socialist Zionism, were also aware that the essence of Judaism resided in its moral demands. They erred, however, in feeling that the moral demand could be sundered from *halakhah*. We have learned, since then, that partial Judaism is ineffectual Judaism. It is a mistaken belief that morality is the whole of Judaism.

Our conception of Judaism is organic; it encompasses ethics and ritual, *aggadah* and *halakhah*, commandments between man and man and commandments between man and God. There is no such thing as a Judaism of ethics alone, just as there is no such thing as a Judaism of *halakhah* alone.

Our challenge is to find within our tradition the strength and the wisdom to confront the agonizing problems of our time: the problems of the individual—his loneliness, his anxiety and his fears; the problems of the society—how to promote peace without also promoting tyranny, how to abolish poverty, how to create a compassionate society. The problems of Jewish ritual discussed above may seem trivial in the light of the world shaking issues which call us to decision. But we have an important principle to guide us: *ayn biklal elah mah she-biprat;* the inner life of a community must be strengthened before it can effectively confront the outer world.

A tree flourishes when its roots are strong. If we apply our ethical values to the structure of Jewish law, if we incorporate our ethical values into Jewish law—only then do we remain true to the tradition of Judaism, a tradition which sees the whole of life as its province, and seeks to create a way of life in response to *derekh haShem*, the way of God, a life of righteousness and justice.

Notes

1. *HaAretz,* February 19, 1971.
2. Psalms 19:7.
3. Deuteronomy 28:9.
4. *The Religion of Israel,* pp. 366-367.
5. For a further discussion of these examples, see S. Siegel, "Religion and Social Action," *Proceedings of the Rabbinical Assembly,* 1961, p. 160, n. 41.
6. It is, of course, true that in *diney mamonot,* the latitude given to the judge is extremely wide. Yet the comment is certainly pertinent to our subject.
7. These remarks by Rab Hai Gaon are found in the *Otsar HaGeonim* to *Hagiga,* p. 59. For an elaboration of the whole issue concerning the relationship between the *halakhah* and the *aggadah,* see A.J. Heschel, *Torah Min Hashamayim,* vol. I, p. xxv.
8. For a characteristic expression of Professor Leibowitz' views, see *Hazzut,* vol. IV, 5718, p. 70.
9. See *Emet V'Emuna,* p. 13.
10. Leviticus 21:7.
11. See the excellent discussion by Professor Simon Greenberg in *Conservative Judaism,* vol. XXIV, no. 3 (Spring 1970).

*Many thinkers who have described Jewish law as a system of symbols
have nevertheless affirmed that halachah is more than the principles that we take various observances to symbolize: it somehow
integrates Divine will with the collective will of the Jewish people.
ABRAHAM JOSHUA HESCHEL goes even further, declaring
that observance of the commandments because of what we believe
them to symbolize is the supreme danger to religion. "Symbolic
knowledge" would reduce religion to well-acted fiction, but "the
order of Jewish living is meant to be, not a set of rituals, but an order of all of man's existence, shaping all his traits, interests, and
dispositions. . . . " The problem is not how much halachah to observe, but how to observe. There is no sense in arguing over how
much of the Torah was revealed at Sinai; in order to live Torah,
we must regard it as "a vision of man from the point of view of
God." If we consider God from the point of view of man, we cannot pray, let alone stake our personal integrity on a law held to be
revealed. One must approach halachah with a "spiritual" logic;
the Jew must take a "leap of action" to "surpass his needs, to do
more than he understands in order to understand more than he
does." Unless we rise to the spiritual order of the Jewish people,
the avenue to holiness will be closed.*

Toward an Understanding of Halachah

ABRAHAM J. HESCHEL

Beyond Symbols

I came with great hunger to the University of Berlin to study philosophy. I looked for a system of thought, for the depth of the spirit, for the meaning of existence. Erudite and profound scholars gave courses in logic, epistemology, esthetics, ethics and metaphysics. They opened the gates of the history of philosophy. I was exposed to the austere discipline of unremitting inquiry and self-criticism. I communed with the thinkers of the past who knew how to meet intellectual adversity with fortitude, and learned to dedicate myself to the examination of basic premises at the risk of failure.

What were the trends of thought to which I was exposed at the university?

Kant, who held dominion over many minds had demonstrated that it is utterly impossible to attain knowledge of the world . . . because knowledge is always in the form of categories and these, in the last analysis, are only representational constructions for the purpose of apperceiving what is given. Objects possessing attributes, causes that work, are all mythical. We can only say that objective phenomena are regarded *as if* they behaved in such and such a way, and there is absolutely no justification for assuming any dogmatic attitude and changing the "as if" into a "that." Salomon Maimon was probably the first to sum up Kantian philosophy by saying that only *symbolic knowledge* is possible.

In the light of such a theory, what is the status of religious knowledge? We must, of course, give up hope of ever attaining a valid concept of the supernatural in an objective sense, yet since for practical reasons it is useful to cherish the idea of God, let us retain that idea and claim that while our knowledge of God is not objectively true, it is still *symbolically* true.

Thus, symbolism became the supreme category in understanding religious truth. It has become a truism that religion is largely an affair of symbols. Translated into simpler terms this view regards religion as a *fiction,* useful to society or to man's personal well-being. Religion is not a relationship of man to God but a relationship of man to the symbol of his highest ideals. There is no God, but we must go on worshipping his symbol.

The idea of symbolism is, of course, not a modern invention. New is the role it has now assumed. In earlier times, symbolism was regarded as a form of *religious thinking;* in modern times religion is regarded as a form of *symbolic thinking.*

It was at an early phase of my studies at the university that I came to realize: *If God is a symbol, He is a fiction.* But if God is *real,* then He is able to express His will unambiguously. Symbols are makeshifts, necessary to those who cannot express themselves unambiguously.

There is darkness in the world and horror in the soul. What is it that the world needs most? Harsh and bitter are the problems which religion comes to solve: ignorance, evil, malice, power, agony, despair. These problems cannot be solved through generalities, through philosophical symbols. Our problem is: Do we believe what we confess? Do we mean what we say?

We do not suffer symbolically. We suffer literally, truly, deeply. Symbolic remedies are quackery. The will of God is either real or a delusion.

This was the most important challenge to me: "We have eyes to see but see not; we have ears to hear but hear not." Any other issue was relevant only in so far as it helped me to answer that challenge.

I became increasingly aware of the gulf that separated my views from those held at the university. I had come with a sense of anxiety: how can I rationally find a way where ultimate meaning lies, a way of living where one would never miss a reference to supreme significance? Why am I here at all, and what is my purpose? I did not even know how to phrase my concern. But to my teachers that was a question unworthy of philosophical analysis.

I realized: my teachers were prisoners of a Greek-German way of thinking. They were fettered in categories which presupposed certain metaphysical assumptions which could never be proved. The questions I was moved by could not even be adequately phrased in categories of their thinking.

My assumption was: man's dignity consists in his having been created in the likeness of God. My question was: how must man, a being who is in essence the image of God, think, feel and act? To them, religion was a feeling. To me, religion included the insights of the Torah which is a vision of man from the point of view of God. They spoke of God from the point of view of man. To them God was an idea, a postulate of reason. They granted Him the status of being a logical possibility. But to assume that He had existence would have been a crime against epistemology.

The problem to my professors was how to be good. In my ears the question rang: how to be holy. At the time I realized: There is much that philosophy could learn from Jewish life. To the philosophers: the idea of the good was the most exalted idea, the ultimate idea. To Judaism the idea of the good is pen-ultimate. It cannot exist without the holy. The good is the base, the holy is the summit. Man cannot be good unless he strives to be holy.

To have an idea of the good is not the same as living by the insight, "Blessed is the man who does not forget Thee."

I did not come to the university because I did not know the idea of the good, but to learn why the idea of the good is valid, why and whether values had meaning. Yet I discovered that values sweet to taste proved sour in analysis; the prototypes were firm, the models flabby. Must speculation and existence remain like two infinite parallel lines that never meet? Or perhaps this impossibility of juncture is the result of the fact that our speculation suffers from what is called in astronomy a parallax, from the apparent displacement of the object, caused by the actual change of point of observation?

The Urge to Pray

In those months in Berlin I went through moments of profound bitterness. I felt very much alone with my own problems and anxieties. I walked alone in the evenings through the magnificent streets of Berlin. I admired the solidity of its architecture, the overwhelming drive and power of a dynamic civilization. There were concerts, theatres, and lectures by famous scholars about the latest theories and inventions, and I was pondering whether to go to the new Max Reinhardt play or to a lecture about the theory of relativity.

Suddenly I noticed the sun had gone down, evening had arrived.

"When should the Shema be read in the evenings . . . "

(Berachot 2a)

I had forgotten God—I had forgotten Sinai—I had forgotten that sunset is my business—that my task is "to perfect the world under the kingdom of the Almighty."

So I began to utter the words "who by His word brings forth the evening twilight."

And Goethe's famous poem rang in my ear:

Ueber allen Gipfeln ist Ruh
O'er all the hilltops is quiet now.

No, that was pagan thinking. To the pagan eye the mystery of life is *Ruh'*, death, oblivion.

To us Jews, there is meaning beyond the mystery. We would say

Uber allen Gipfeln ist Gottes Wort.
O'er all the hilltops is the word of God.

The meaning of life is to do His will . . .

By His word cometh evening twilight

And His love is manifested in His teaching us Torah, precepts, laws.

Ueber allen Gipfeln is God's love for man—
"With everlasting love hast Thou loved thy people Israel
Torah, commandments, ordinances and judgments hast Thou taught us."

How much guidance, how many ultimate insights are found in the *Siddur.*

How grateful I am to God that there is a duty to worship, a law to remind my distraught mind that it is time to think of God, time to disregard my ego for at least a moment! It is such happiness to belong to an order of the divine will.

I am not always in a mood to pray. I do not always have the vision and the strength to say a word in the presence of God. But when I am weak, it is the law that gives me strength; when my vision is dim, it is duty that gives me insight.

Indeed, there is something which is far greater than my desire to pray. Namely, God's desire that I pray. There is something which is far greater than my will to believe. Namely, God's will that I believe. How insignificant is my praying in the midst of a cosmic process! Unless it is the will of God that I pray, how ludicrous it is to pray.

On that evening, in the streets of Berlin, I was not in a mood to pray. My heart was heavy, my soul was sad. It was difficult for the lofty words of prayer to break through the dark clouds of my inner life.

But how would I dare not to *davn*? How would I dare to miss an evening prayer? *Me-ematay korin et Shma.* "Out of *emah,* out of fear of God do we read the *Shma.*"

The following morning I awoke in my student garret. Now, the magnificent achievements in the field of physiology and psychology have, of course, not diminished, but rather increased my sense of wonder for the human body and soul. And so I prayed

"Thou has fashioned man in wisdom."
"Lord, the soul which thou hast given me is pure."

Yet how am I going to keep my soul clean?

The most important problem which a human being must face daily is: How to maintain one's integrity in a world where power, success and money are valued above all else? How to remain clean amidst the mud of falsehood and malice that soil our society?

The soul is clean, but within it resides a power for evil, "a strange god,"[1] that seeks constantly to get the upper hand over man and to kill him; and if God did not help him he could not resist it, as it is said, 'the wicked watches the righteous, and seeks to slay him.'"[2]

Every morning I take a piece of cloth—neither elegant nor solemn, of no particular esthetic beauty, a *talit,* wrap myself in it and say:

"How precious is Thy kindness, O God! The children of man take refuge in the shadow of Thy wings. They have their fill of the choice food of Thy house, and Thou givest them drink of Thy stream of delights. For with Thee is the fountain of life; by Thy light do we see light. Continue Thy kindness to those who know Thee, and Thy righteousness to the upright in heart."

But, then, I ask myself: Have I got a right to take my refuge in Him? to drink of the stream of His delights? to expect Him to continue His kindness? But God wants me to be close to Him, even to bind every morning His word as a sign on my hand, and between my eyes, winding the strap three times round the middle finger. I would remind myself the word that God spoke to *me* through His prophet Hosea:

"I will betroth you to myself forever; I will betroth you to myself in righteousness and in justice, in kindness and in mercy. I will betroth you to myself in faithfulness; and you shall know the Lord." It is an act of betrothal, a promise to marry . . . It is an act of God, falling in love with His people. But the engagement depends on righteousness, justice, kindness, mercy.

The Dangers

Why did I decide to take *halachah* seriously in spite of the numerous perplexities in which I became enmeshed?

Why did I pray, although I was not in a mood to pray? And why was I able to pray in spite of being unprepared to pray? What was my situation after the reminder to pray *Maariv* struck my mind? The duty to worship stood as a thought of ineffable meaning; doubt, the voice of disbelief, was ready to challenge it. But where should the engagement take place? In an act of reflection the duty to worship is a mere thought, timid, frail, a mere shadow of reality, while the voice of disbelief is a power, well-armed with the weight of inertia and the preference for abstention. In such an engagement prayer would be fought *in absentia,* and the issue would be decided without actually joining the battle. It was fair, therefore, to give the weaker rival a chance: to pray first, to fight later.

I realized that just as you cannot study philosophy through praying, you cannot study prayer through philosophizing. And what applies to prayer is true in regard to the essentials of Jewish observance.

What I wanted to avoid was not only the failure to pray to God during a whole evening of my life but *the loss of the whole,* the loss of belonging to the spiritual order of Jewish living. It is true that some people are so busy with collecting shreds and patches of the law, that they hardly think of weaving the pattern of the whole. But there is also the danger of being so enchanted by the whole as to lose sight of the detail. It became increasingly clear to me that the order of Jewish living is meant to be, not a set of rituals, but an order of all of man's existence, shaping all his traits, interests and dispositions; "not so much the performance of single acts, the taking of a step now and then, as the pursuit of a way, being on the way; not so much the acts of fulfilling as the state of being committed to the task, the belonging to an order in which single deeds, aggregates of religious feeling, sporadic sentiments, moral episodes become a part of a complete pattern" (270).[3]

The ineffable Name, we have forgotten how to pronounce it. We have almost forgotten how to spell it. We may totally forget how to recognize it.

There are a number of ideas concerning Jewish law which have proved most inimical to its survival, and I would like to refer to two. First is the assumption that either you observe all or nothing; all of its rules are of equal importance; and if one brick is removed, the whole edifice must collapse. Such intransigence, laudable as it may be as an expression of devoutness, is neither historically nor theologically justified. There were ages in Jewish history when some aspects of Jewish ritual observance were not adhered to by people who had otherwise lived according to the law. And where is the man who could claim that he has been able to fulfill literally the *mitzvah* of "Love your neighbor as yourself"?

Where is the worry about the spiritual inadequacy of that which admittedly should not be abandoned? Where is our anxiety about the barrenness of our praying, the conventionality of our ceremonialism?

The problem, then, that cries for a solution is not: everything or nothing, total or partial obedience to the law; the problem is authentic or forged, genuine or artificial observance. The problem is not *how much* but *how to* observe. The problem is whether we *obey* or whether we merely *play* with the word of God.

Second is the assumption that every iota of the law was revealed to Moses at Sinai. This is an unwarranted extension of the rabbinic concept of revelation. "Could Moses have learned the whole Torah? Of the Torah it says, *The measure thereof is longer than the earth, and broader than the sea* (Job 11:9); could then Moses have learned it in forty days? No, it was only the principles thereof which God taught Moses."[4]

The role of the sages in interpreting the word of the Bible and their power to issue new ordinances is a basic element of Jewish belief and something for which our sages found sanction in Deuteronomy 17:11. The awareness of the expanding nature of Jewish law was expressed by such a great saint and authority as Rabbi Isaiah Horovitz in his *Shenai Luhot Ha-b'rit.*

"And now I will explain the phenomenon that in every generation the number of restrictions [in the *halachah*] is increased. In the time of Moses, only what he had explicitly received at Sinai (the written law) was binding, plus several ordinances which he added for whatever reasons he saw fit. [However] the prophets, the Tannaim, and the rabbis of every generation [have continued to multiply these restrictions]. The reason is, that as the venom of the serpent spreads, greater protection is needed. The Holy One provided for us three hundred and sixty-five prohibitions in order to prevent the venom from becoming too active. Therefore, whenever the venom of a generation grows virulent, more restrictions must be imposed. Had this [the spread of venom] been the situation at the time of the giving of the Torah, [those interdictions] would have been specifically included in it. However instead, the later ordinances derive their authority from God's command—'make a protection for the law'—which means 'make necessary ordinances according to the state of each generation' and these have the same authority as the Torah itself."[5]

There are times in Jewish history when the main issue is not what parts of the *halachah* cannot be fulfilled but what parts of the *halachah* can be and ought to be fulfilled, fulfilled as *halachah*, as an expression and interpretation of the will of God.

There are many problems which we encounter in our reflections on the issue of Jewish observance. I wish to discuss briefly several of these problems, namely: the relation of observance to our understanding of the will of God; the meaning of observance to man; the regularity of worship; inwardness and the essence of religion; the relevance of the external deeds.

The Meaning of Observance

From a rationalist's point of view it does not seem plausible to assume that the infinite, ultimate supreme Being is concerned with my putting on *tefillin* every day. It is, indeed, strange to believe that God should care whether a particular individual will eat leavened or unleavened bread during a particular season of the year. However, it is that paradox, namely that the infinite God is intimately concerned with finite man and his finite deeds; that nothing is trite or irrelevant in the eyes of God, which is the very essence of the prophetic faith.

There are people who are hesitant to take seriously the possibility of our knowing what the will of God demands of us. Yet we all whole-heartedly accept Micah's words: "He has showed you, O man, what is good, and what does the Lord require of you, but to do justice, and to love kindness and to walk humbly with your God." If we believe that there is something which God requires of man, then what is our belief if not *faith in the will of God, certainly of knowing what His will demands of us?* If we are ready to believe that God requires of me "to do justice," is it more difficult for us to believe that God requires of us to be holy? If we are ready to believe that it is God who requires us "to love kindness," is it more difficult to believe that God requires us to hallow the Sabbath and not to violate its sanctity?

If it is the word of Micah uttering the will of God that we believe in, and not a peg on which to hang views we derived from rationalist philosophies, then "to love justice" is just as much *halachah* as the prohibition of making a fire on the Seventh Day. If, however, all we can hear in these words are echoes of Western philosophy rather than the voice of Micah, does that not mean that the prophet has nothing to say to any of us?

A serious difficulty is the problem of *the meaning of Jewish observance*. The modern Jew cannot accept the way of static obedience as a short-cut to the mystery of the divine will. His religious situation is not conducive to an attitude of intellectual or spiritual surrender. He is not ready to sacrifice his liberty on the altar of loyalty to the spirit of his ancestors. He will only respond to a demonstration that there is meaning to be found in what we expect him to do. His primary difficulty is not in his inability to comprehend the *Divine origin* of the law; his essential difficulty is in his inability to sense *the presence of Divine meaning* in the fulfillment of the law.

Let us never forget that some of the basic theological presuppositions of Judaism cannot be justified in terms of human reason. Its conception of the nature of man as having been created in the likeness of God, its conception of God and history, of prayer and even of morality, defy some of the realizations at which we have honestly arrived at the end of our analysis and scrutiny. The demands of piety are a mystery before which man is reduced to reverence and silence. In a technological society, when religion becomes a function, piety, too, is an instrument to satisfy his needs. We must, therefore, be particularly careful not to fall into the habit of looking at religion as if it were a machine which can be worked, an organization which can be run according to one's calculations.

The problem of how to live as a Jew cannot be solved in terms of common sense and common experience. The order of Jewish living is a spiritual one; it has a spiritual logic of its own which cannot be apprehended unless its basic terms are lived and appreciated.

It is in regard to this problem that we must keep in mind three things. a) Divine meaning is *spiritual* meaning; b) the apprehension of Divine meaning is contingent upon *spiritual preparedness;* c) it is experienced *in acts,* rather than in speculation.

a) The problem of ethics is: what is the ideal or principle of conduct that is *rationally* justifiable? While to religion the problem of living is: what is the ideal or principle of living that is *spiritually* justifiable? The legitimate question concerning the forms of Jewish observance is, therefore, the question: Are they spiritually meaningful?

We should, consequently, not evaluate the *mitzvoth* by the amount of rational meaning we may discover at their basis. Religion is not within but beyond the limits of mere reason. Its task is not to compete with reason, to be a source of speculative ideas, but to aid us where reason gives us only partial aid. Its meaning must be understood in terms *compatible with the sense of the ineffable.* Frequently where concepts fail, where rational understanding ends, the meaning of observance begins. Its purpose is not essentially to serve hygiene, happiness or the vitality of man; its purpose is to add holiness to hygiene, grandeur to happiness, spirit to vitality.

Spiritual meaning is not always limpid; transparency is the quality of glass, while diamonds are distinguished by refractive power and the play of prismatic colors.

Indeed, any reason we may advance for our loyalty to the Jewish order of living merely points to one of its many facets. To say that the *mitzvoth* have meaning is less accurate than saying that they lead us to wells of emergent meaning, to experiences which are full of hidden brilliance of the holy, suddenly blazing in our thoughts.

Those who, out of their commendable desire to save the Jewish way of life, bring its meaning under the hammer, tend to sell it at the end to the lowest bidder. The highest values are not in demand and are not saleable on the market-place. In spiritual life some experiences are like a *camera obscura,* through which light has to enter in order to form an image upon the mind, the image of ineffable intelligibility. Insistence upon explaining and relating the holy to the relative and functional is like lighting a candle in the camera.

Works of piety are like works of art. They are functional, they serve a purpose, but their essence is intrinsic; their value is in what they are in themselves.

b) Sensitivity to spiritual meaning is not easily won; it is the fruit of hard, constant devotion, of insistence upon remaining true to a vision. It is "an endless pilgrimage . . . a drive towards serving Him who rings our hearts like a bell, as if He were waiting to enter our lives . . . Its essence is not revealed in the way we utter it, but in the soul's being in accord with what is relevant to God; in the extension of our love to what God may approve, our being carried away by the tide of His thoughts, rising beyond the desolate ken of man's despair." (174).

"God's grace resounds in our lives like a staccato. Only by retaining the seemingly disconnected notes comes the ability to grasp the theme." (88).

c) What is the Jewish way to God? It is not a way of ascending the ladder of speculation. Our understanding of God is not the triumphant outcome of an assault upon the riddles of the universe nor a donation we receive in return for intellectual surrender. Our understanding comes by the way of *mitzvah*. By living as Jews we attain our faith as Jews. We do not have faith in deeds; we attain faith through deeds.

When Moses recounted to the people the laws of the covenant with God, the people responded: "We will do and we will hear." This statement was interpreted to mean: *In doing we perceive.*

A Jew is asked to take *a leap of action* rather than *a leap of thought:* to surpass his needs, to do more than he understands in order to understand more than he does. In carrying out the word of the Torah he is ushered into the presence of spiritual meaning. Through the ecstasy of deeds he learns to be certain of the presence of God.

Jewish law is a sacred prosody. The Divine sings in our deeds, the Divine is disclosed in our deeds. Our effort is but a counterpoint in the music of His will. In exposing our lives to God we discover the Divine within ourselves and its accord with the Divine beyond ourselves.

If at the moment of doing a *mitzvah* once perceived to be thus sublime, thus Divine, you are in it with all your heart and with all your soul, there is no great distance between you and God. For acts of holiness uttered by the soul disclose the holiness of God hidden in every moment of time. And His holiness and He are one.

Why Routine?

Why should worship be bound to regular occasions? Why impose a calendar on the soul? Is not regularity of observance a menace to the freedom of the heart?

Strict observance of a way of life at fixed times and in identical forms tend to become a matter of routine, of outward compliance. How to prevent observance from becoming stereotyped, mechanical, was, indeed, a perennial worry in the history of Judaism. The cry of the prophet: "Their heart is far from me" was a signal of alarm.

Should I reject the regularity of prayer and rely on the inspiration of the heart and only worship when I am touched by the spirit? Should I resolve: unless the spirit comes, I shall abstain from praying? The deeper truth is that routine breeds attention, calling forth a response where the soul would otherwise remain dormant. One is committed to being affected by the holy, if he abides at the threshold of its realm. Should it be left to every individual to find his own forms of worship whenever the spirit would move him? Yet who is able to extemporize a prayer without falling into the trap of cliches? Moreover, spiritual substance grows in clinging to a source of spirit richer than one's own.

Inspirations are brief, sporadic and rare. In the long interims the mind is often dull, bare and vapid. There is hardly a soul that can radiate more light than it receives. To perform a *mitzvah* is to meet the spirit. But the spirit is not something we can acquire once and for all but something we must constantly live with and pray for. For this reason the Jewish way of life is to reiterate the ritual, to meet the spirit again and again, the spirit in oneself and the spirit that hovers over all beings.

At the root of our difficulties in appreciating the role of *halachah* in religious living is, I believe, our conception of the very essence of religion. "We are often inclined to define the essence of religion as a state of the soul, as inwardness, as an absolute feeling, and expect a person who is religious to be endowed with a kind of sentiment too deep to rise to the surface of common deeds, as if religion were a plant that can only thrive at the bottom of the ocean. Now to Judaism religion is not a feeling for something that is, but *an answer* to Him who is asking us to live in a certain way. *It is in its very origin a consciousness of duty, of being committed to higher ends;* a realization that life is not only man's but also God's sphere of interest" (175).

"God asks for the heart." Yet does he ask for the heart only? Is the right intention enough? Some doctrines insist that love is the sole condition for salvation (the Sufis, *Bhakti-mārga*), stressing the importance of inwardness, of love or faith, to the exclusion of good works.

Paul waged a passionate battle against the power of law and proclaimed instead the religion of grace. Law, he claimed, cannot conquer sin, nor can righteousness be attained through works of law. A man is justified "by faith without the deeds of the law."[5]

That salvation is attained by faith alone was Luther's central thesis. The antinomian tendency resulted in the overemphasis on love and faith to the exclusion of good works.

The Formula of Concord of 1580 condemns the statement that good works are necessary to salvation and rejects the doctrine that they are harmful to salvation. According to *Ritschl,* the doctrine of the merit of good deeds is an intruder in the domain of Christian theology; the only way of salvation is justification by faith. Barth, following Kierkegaard, voices Lutheran thoughts, when he claims that man's deeds are too sinful to be good. There are fundamentally no human deeds, which, because of their significance in this world, find favor in God's eyes. God can be approached through God alone.

Paraphrasing the Paulinian doctrine that man is saved by faith alone, Kant and his diciples taught that the essence of religion or morality would consist in an absolute quality of the soul or the will, regardless of the actions that may come out of it or the ends that may be attained. Accordingly, the value of a religious act would be determined wholly by the intensity of one's faith or by the rectitude of one's inner disposition. The intention, not the deed, the *how,* not the *what* of one's conduct, would be essential, and no motive other than the sense of duty would be of any moral value. Thus acts of kindness, when not dictated by the sense of duty, would not be better than cruelty; while compassion or regard for human happiness as such is looked upon as an ulterior motive. "I would not break my word even to save mankind," exclaimed Fichte. As if his own salvation and righteousness were more important to him than the fate of all men. Does not such an attitude illustrate the truth of the proverb: "The road to hell is paved with good intentions"? Should we not say that a concern with one's own salvation and righteousness, that outweighs the regard for the welfare of one other human being cannot be qualified as a good intention?

The crisis of ethics has its root in formalism, in the view that the essence of the good is in the good intention. Seeing how difficult it is to attain it, modern man despaired. In the name of good intentions, evil was fostered.

To us this doctrine is the essential heresy. Judaism stands and falls

with the idea of the absolute relevance of human deeds. Even to God
we ascribe the deed. *Imitatio dei* is in deeds. The deed is the source of
holiness.

"Faith does not come to an end with attaining certainty of God's existence. Faith is the beginning of intense craving to enter an active relationship with Him who is beyond the mystery, to bring together all
the might that is within us with all that is spiritual beyond us. At the
root of our yearning for integrity is a stir of the inexpressible within us
to commune with the ineffable beyond us. But what is the language of
that communication, without which our impulse remains inartiuclate?

"We are taught that what God asks of man is more than an inner attitude, that He gives man not only *life* but also *a law*, that His will is to
be served not only adored, *obeyed* not only *worshipped*. Faith comes
over us like a force urging to action. We respond by pledging ourselves
to constancy of devotion, committing us to the presence of God. This
remains a life allegiance involving restraint, submission, self-control
and courage.

"Judaism insists upon establishing a unity of *faith* and *creed,* of
piety and *halachah*, of *devotion* and *deed*. Faith is but a seed, while the
deed is its growth or decay. Faith disembodied, faith that tries to grow
in splendid isolation, is but a ghost, for which there is no place in our
psychophysical world.

"What *creed* is in relation to *faith,* the *halachah* is in relation to
piety. As faith cannot exist without a creed, piety cannot subsist without a pattern of deeds; as intelligence cannot be separated from training, religion cannot be divorced from conduct. Judaism is lived in
deeds, not only in thoughts.

"A pattern for living—the object of our most urgent quest—which
would correspond to man's ultimate dignity, must take into consideration not only his ability to exploit the forces of nature and to appreciate
the loveliness of its forms, but also his unique sense of the ineffable. It
must be a design, not only for the satisfaction of needs, but also for the
attainment of an end," the end of being *a holy people* (175-76).

Beyond the Heart

The integrity of life is not exclusively a thing of the heart, and Jewish piety is therefore more than consciousness of the moral law. The innermost chamber must be guarded at the uttermost outposts. Religion
is not the same as spiritualism; what man does in his concrete physical

existence is directly relevant to the divine. Spirituality is the goal, not the way of man. In this world music is played on physical instruments, and to the Jew the *mitzvoth* are the instruments by which the holy is performed. If man were only mind, worship in thought would be the form in which to commune with God. But man is body and soul, and his goal is to live so that both "his heart and his flesh should sing to the living God."

Moreover, worship is not one thing, and living, another. Does Judaism consist of sporadic landmarks in the realm of living, of temples in splendid isolation, of festive celebrations on extraordinary days? The synagogue is not a retreat, and that which is decisive is not the performance of rituals at distinguished occasions, but how they affect the climate of the entire life.

The highest peak of spiritual living is not necessarily reached in rare moments of ecstasy; the highest peak lies wherever we are and may be ascended in a common deed. There can be as sublime a holiness in fulfilling friendship, in observing dietary laws, day by day, as in uttering a prayer on the Day of Atonement.

Jewish tradition maintains that there is no exterritoriality in the realm of the spirit. Economics, politics, dietetics are just as much as ethics within its sphere. It is in man's intimate rather than public life, in the way he fulfills his physiological functions that character is formed. It is immensely significant that, according to the Book of Genesis, the first prohibition given to man concerned the enjoyment of the forbidden fruit.

"The fate of a people . . . is decided according to whether they begin culture at the right place—not at the soul. The right place is the body, demeanor, diet, physiology; the rest follows . . . contempt of the body is the greatest mishap." Judaism begins at the bottom, taking very seriously the forms of one's behavior in relation to the external, even conventional functions, and amenities of life, teaching us how to eat, how to rest, how to act. The discipline of feelings and thoughts comes second. The body must be persuaded first. "Thou shalt not covet" is the last of the Ten Commandments, even though it may be the first in the case history of the aforementioned transgressions. While not prescribing a diet—vegetarian or otherwise—demanding abstinence from narcotics or stimulants, Judaism is very much concerned with what and how a person ought to eat. A sacred discipline for the body is as important as bodily strength.

In order to attain an adequate appreciation of the preciousness that the Jewish way of living is capable of bestowing upon us, we should initiate a thorough cleaning of the minds. Every one of us should be asked to make one major sacrifice: to sacrifice his prejudice against our heritage. We should strive to cultivate an atmosphere in which the values of Jewish faith and piety could be cherished, an atmosphere in which the Jewish form of living is the heartily approved or at least respected pattern, in which sensitivity to *kashruth* is not regarded as treason against the American constitution and reverence for the Sabbath is not considered conspiracy against progress.

Without solidarity with our forebears, the solidarity with our brothers will remain feeble. The vertical unity of Israel is essential to the horizontal unity of *kelal yisrael*. Identification with what is undying in Israel, the appreciation of what was supremely significant throughout the ages, the endeavor to integrate the abiding teachings and aspirations of the past into our own thinking will enable us to be creative, to expand, not to imitate or to repeat. Survival of Israel means that we carry on our independent dialogue with the past. Our way of life must remain such as would be, to some degree, intelligible to Isaiah and Rabbi Yochanan ben Zakkai, to Maimonides and the Baal Shem.

Let us be under no illusion. The task is hard. However, if it is true that the good cannot exist without the holy, what are we doing for the purpose of securing holiness in the world? Can we afford to be indifferent, to forget the responsibility which the position of leadership bestows upon us?

A wide stream of human callousness separates us from the realm of holiness. Neither an individual man nor a single generation can by its own power erect a bridge that would reach that realm. For ages our fathers have labored in building a sacred bridge. *We who have not crossed the stream, must beware lest we burn the bridge.*

More Than Manners

Prompted by an intuition that we cannot live by a disembodied faith, many people today speak of the advisability of introducing "rituals, customs, and ceremonies."[6]

Is it symbolism that God desires? Is it ceremonialism that the prophets called for? Are *"customs and ceremonies"* the central issue of Jewish observance? *"Customs and ceremonies"* are an external affair, an esthetic delight; something cherished in academic fraternities or at graduation exercises at American universities.

But since when has esthetics become supreme authority in matters of

religion? Customs, ceremonies are fine, enchanting, playful. But is
Judaism a religion of play? What is the authentic origin of these
terms—*customs and ceremonies?* I must confess that I have difficulty
translating "ceremonies" into Hebrew. Customs—*minhagim*—have
given us a lot of trouble in the past. *Minhagim* have often stultified
Jewish life. According to Rabbenu Tam, the word *minhag*, custom,
consists of the same four letters as the word *gehinom.*[7]

Let us beware lest we reduce Bible to literature, Jewish observance
to good manners, the Talmud to Emily Post.

There are spiritual reasons which compel me to feel alarmed when
hearing the terms *customs and ceremonies.* What is the worth of cele-
brating the Seder on Passover eve, if it is nothing but a ceremony? An
annual reenactment of quaint antiquities? Ceremonies end in routine,
and routine is the great enemy of the spirit.

A religious act is something in which the soul must be able to participate; out of which inner devotion, *kavanah*, must evolve. But what *kavanah* should I entertain if entering the *sukkah* is a mere ceremony?

Let us be frank. Too often a ceremony is the homage which disbelief
pays to faith. Do we want such homage?

Judaism does not stand on ceremonies . . . Jewish piety is an answer to God, expressed in the language of *mitzvoth* rather than in the
language of *ceremonies.* The *mitzvah* rather than the ceremony is our
fundamental category. What is the difference between the two categories?

Ceremonies whether in the form of things or in the form of actions
are required by custom and convention; *mitzvoth* are required by Torah. Ceremonies are relevant to man; *mitzvoth* are relevant to God.
Ceremonies are folkways; *mitzvoth* are ways to God. Ceremonies are
expressions of the human mind; what they express and their power to
express depend on a mental act of man; their significance is gone when
man ceases to be responsive to them. Ceremonies are like the moon,
they have no light of their own. *Mitzvoth*, on the other hand, are expressions or interpretations of the will of God. While they are meaningful to man, the source of their meaning is not in the understanding
of man but in the love of God. Ceremonies are created for the purpose
of *signifying: mitzvoth* were given for the purpose of *sanctifying.* This
is their function: to refine, to ennoble, to sanctify man. They confer holiness upon us, whether or not we know exactly what they signify.

A *mitzvah* is more than *man's reference to God;* it is also *God's reference to man.* In carrying out a *mitzvah* we acknowledge the fact of God
being concerned with our fulfillment of His will.

Is this religion of human will prophetic Judaism? Is this the spirit of "we will do and we will obey"?

Remember the words of Deuteronomy: "Beware, lest there be among you a man or woman, or family, or tribe, whose heart turns away this day from the Lord, our God . . . one who, when he hears the words of this sworn covenant, blesses himself in his heart, saying: I shall be safe (I shall have peace of mind), though I walk according to the dictates of my heart." (29:18 f.)

"Do not follow your own hearts" (Numbers 15:39). How can one pray "Help us, O God, to banish from our hearts . . . self-sufficient leaning upon our own reason" (The Union Prayer Book, p. 101), and proclaim at the same time that Judaism is basically a religion of man's will and choice?

Is it not our duty to insist that man is not the measure of all things? To deny that man is all and there is none else beside him? Don't we believe that God, too, has a voice in human life? Is it not the essence of prophetic Judaism to say: It is God who spoke to me, therefore I want to fulfill His will?

Notes

1. *Shabbath* 105b. *Begufo* does not mean the body but the self or the essence of man; it is used by R. Abin as a paraphrase of *bach*, "in thee", Psalms 81:10. Compare the expression *Gufei Tora, Mishnah Hagigah* 1, 8, which means "the essentials of Torah"; see also *Aboth* 3, 18, *Guffei Halachot*.

2. *Sukkah* 52b.

3. Numbers in parentheses in this essay refer to pages of the author's *Man Is Not Alone.*

4. *Exodus Rabba* 41,6.

5. Romans 3:28. "By the deeds of the law there shall no flesh be justified in his sight; for by the law is knowledge of sin".

6. Morton M. Berman, *The Survey of Current Reform Practice by Laymen,* delivered at the 42nd general assembly of the Union of American Hebrew Congregations, April 22, 1953.

7. See *Shiltey Giborim* on the Mordecai, *Gittin* 85a; also *Teshuvot* Maharan Mints, no. 67.

*WILL HERBERG outlines the "process of existential identification"
by which the Jew becomes a "Jew-in-faith." To be an authentic
Jew is to affirm the "true" redemptive history, as opposed to the
"false" or idolatrous redemptive histories of totalistic nationalism, communism, and fascism. The Torah is received as we "actually" stand at the foot of Mount Sinai through existential "repetition." We receive the same Torah as our fathers, yet "we who receive it are different and we hear it in a different way." We accept
the Torah as our Teaching when we realize that it is our task to
perceive it as we read it, as we discover God's word in the written
words.*

*Because Herberg's approach is existential, he does not ap-
proach the problem of observance by urging reverence for authority or participation in "Catholic Israel." To achieve the authentic
life of Jew qua Jew, one's convictions must be "truly existential
and involve the entire being": thinking, feeling, and doing—the
three dimensions of personality. Herberg argues that halachah itself suggests an existential approach, for no commandment is conceived as "absolute in the sense of being automatically applicable
without regard to circumstances."*

Torah: Teaching, Law and Way

WILL HERBERG

No word in Jewish religion is so indefinable and yet so indispensable as the word *Torah*. It is Law, yet more than Law, for it is also Teaching and Way. It is a book, an idea, a quality of life. It is the Pentateuch; the Bible in all its parts; the Bible and the rabbinical writings; all writings dealing with revelation; all reflection and tradition dealing with God, man and the world.[1] It is represented as a bride, the daughter of God, as a crown, a jewel, a sword; as fire and water; as life, but to those who are unworthy, as poison and death.[2] It is the pre-existent Wisdom or Word of God, present at creation and acting as the "architect" of the creative work. It preserves the world from destruction; without it all creation would lapse into chaos: it is the harmony and law of the universe. It is all this and much more, for the exaltation of the Torah in Jewish tradition is a theme which no words can exhaust. But what, after all, is Torah, and what does it mean to the living Jew, here and now?

Perhaps it would be well to approach this problem from the point of view of *Heilsgeschichte* or redemptive history. What is the meaning of Torah in terms of the redemptive history which is Jewish religion?

True Redemptive History

Redemptive history is not merely history of redemption; it is also redeeming history, history with the power to save. The Jew achieves salvation not through purely individual, mystical exercises which somehow bring him into union with God. The Jew becomes a "true Jew" and makes available to himself the resources of divine grace under the covenant by making Israel's past his own, its sacred history the "background" of his own life.[3] It is by this process of *existential identifica-*

tion that the Jew becomes a Jew-in-faith, that his existence becomes authentically Jewish existence and he is enabled to encounter God as a Son of the Covenant, within the framework of the divine election. This existential self-integration into the sacred history of Israel gives the individual Jew a grounding in the past, a place of standing in the present, a hope for the future. It gives a context of ultimate significance to life, and that is itself redemption from the blank meaninglessness of self-contained existence. The authentic I-Thou relation between man and God, which we saw to be the existential content of salvation, emerges for the Jew within the framework of his personally appropriated redemptive history.

From this point of view, and this is the point of view most congenial to biblical thought, Jewish faith is the affirmation of the sacred history of Israel as one's own particular history, as one's own "true past." It is the way by which the power of redemptive history becomes effectual *for us* . Idolatry is false redemptive history and therefore false faith. It is easy to see this if we think of the demonic idolatries rampant in the modern world. Totalistic nationalism, communism, fascism, each has its own special *Heilsgeschichte,* cutting across and challenging those of Judaism and Christianity. Each has its own redemptive pattern of history, its own sacred calendar of holy days, in which this redemptive history is proclaimed and enacted; each has its own great redeeming event in the past which gives promise of still greater redemption to come. Each offers the believer a significant context of life, a significant past, in terms of which his existence is given larger meaning and his future made to yield the promise of salvation. Each, in short, parodies the authentic redemptive history of mankind as expressed in Hebraic religion. In this sense, our idolatries are spurious, man-created redemptive histories, just as the gods of idolatry are spurious, man-created idols. Each of us has many contexts of life which strive to serve, partially at least, as redemptive histories—the family, the nation, the labor movement, social and political causes, etc. These all tend to give some fragmentary meaning to certain aspects of life. They become idolatrous only when they claim to provide the full and ultimate meaning of existence. It is then that they must be broken by repentance—that is, by return to one's true *Heilsgeschichte* in which is encountered the Living God in his "mighty deeds" of judgment and mercy.

The true redemptive history for the Jew—and in a rather different sense for the Christian as well—is the sacred history of Israel. One becomes a Jew-in-faith by becoming an "Israelite," by *re-enacting* in *his own life* the redemptive career of Israel. Hebraic religion is historical religion, above all in the sense that the believer must himself appropriate it in his own life as his own history. Every believing Jew in his own life stands in the place of Abraham our father and in his own life re-enacts the historical encounter between Israel and God. The three great festivals of Judaism—*Pesah* (Passover), *Shabuot* (Pentecost) and *Sukkot* (Tabernacles)—whatever may be their original roots in "nature," gain their religious significance through the fact that they are *history festivals.*[4] They are the liturgical pattern in which the crucial event in the redemptive history of Israel—Exodus-Sinai—is re-enacted and through which the individual Jew integrates himself into that redemptive history. These festivals are not mere commemorations. They are decisive moments in which eternity enters time, in which the temporal takes on the dimensions of the eternal. They are moments when sacred history is repeated in our own lives. In the Passover ritual, every Jew, insofar as he participates in it existentially, becomes an Israelite contemporary with Moses, whom God is drawing out of Egypt, the house of bondage, to bring to the foot of Sinai to receive the Torah. "All this I do," the Passover *Haggadah* represents the Jew as saying in explanation of the order of service, "all this I do because of what God did for *me* in bringing me forth from Egypt."[5] For *me,* not for my ancestors or for someone else, but for me in exactly the same way as He did for Moses and the Israelite slaves of the time. *Shabuot* is the reception of the Torah at Sinai, and he for whom this festival has its authentic existential significance, *himself* goes to Sinai in fear and trembling to receive the Torah. He knows that what Moses told the Israelites "when they had come out of Egypt beyond the Jordan, in the valley opposite Beth-Peor" applies to him just as truly, for he, too, is one of the children of Israel whom God has delivered: "Hear, O Israel. . . the Lord our God made not his covenant with our fathers, but with *us,* even *us,* who are all of us here alive this day" (Deut. 5:5). And what is true of *Pesah* and *Shabuot* is also true of *Sukkot,* which relates to the wandering in the Wilderness. These three festivals are for us the living re-enactment of the formative events in the redemptive history of Israel. Just as Israel became Israel through the events to which they refer, so the individual Jew becomes a Jew-in-faith by "repeating" these events in his own life. It is neither past time nor timeless eternity in which we live in faith, but *contemporaneity.*[6] "He who does not *himself* remember that God led him out of Egypt," says Martin Buber, "he who does not *himself* await the Messiah, is no longer a true Jew."[7]

Torah as Teaching

To be a Jew means not only to stand in Abraham's place and answer "Here am I" to God's call when and where it comes; it means also to stand at the foot of Sinai and receive the Torah, not figuratively, but actually, through existential "repetition." "On this day, Israel came to Mount Sinai," we read in Scripture (Exod. 19:1). "Why on *this* day rather than on *that* day?" ask the rabbis. "So that you may regard it," they answer, "as though the Torah were given *this* day,[8]. . . as a new proclamation which all run to read."[9] Yet, although each of us stands at the foot of Sinai and receives the Torah as did the children of Israel in days of old, we stand *now*, not then. It is not so much that we stand at a different time; rather it is that we stand in a different context of life. It is the same Torah, yet different, because we who receive it are different and we hear it in a different way.

What is this Torah which each of us receives at Sinai as God's truth and yet which each of us must "make true" for himself?

Torah, in the first place, is *Teaching,* and its acquisition, in the familiar term, is "learning." In this sense, we may take Torah to represent the entire biblical-rabbinic tradition of "religious" wisdom, remembering, however, that for the rabbis, "if religion is anything, it is everything."[10] Torah starts with the Bible. From the very beginning, however, it is not the Bible simply as written, but the Bible as read and understood. And yet what is thus "added" to the Bible is not really added, for can the Bible have any living significance except as read and understood and therefore as "added to"? This is the truth in the Orthodox contention that the Oral Torah (tradition) was given to Moses along with the Written Torah (Bible) on Sinai and is therefore just as truly revelation. Here, too, I think Franz Rosenzweig has put the matter in a more striking and existentially truer way than Orthodox fundamentalism is willing to do. "[To the Orthodox]." he writes, "the Oral Torah is a stream parallel to the Written Torah and sprung from the same source. For us, it is the completion of the unity of the Book-as-written through the unity of the Book-as-read. Both unities are equally wonderful. The historical view discovers multiplicity in the Book-as-written as well as in the Book-as-read: multiplicity of centuries, multiplicity of writers and readers. The eye that sees the Book not from the outside but in its inner coherence sees it not merely as written but as read. In the former, it sees the unity of teaching; in the latter, it finds the unity of learning, one's own learning together with the learning of centuries. Tradition, halakic and haggadic, itself becomes an element in [understanding and] translation."[11] Thus, the Torah is "from Sinai," and yet the "Torah from Sinai" includes, as the Talmud assures us, everything that the earnest and sincere spirit propounds in trying to understand it and make it vital for life.[12] All is Torah as Teaching.

The Rosenzweigian distinction between the Book-as-written and the Book-as-read applies not only to the Bible but to all the "religious" literature of Israel as soon as that is given the permanence and authority of writing. Once, the Mishnah and Talmud were Oral Torah, "completing" the unity of the Bible as Written Torah. But soon the Mishnah and Talmud themselves became Written Torah and were themselves "completed" in a continuing tradition of Oral Torah. That is why he who wants to appropriate for himself the Torah in its fulness must appropriate it as total living tradition. We cannot start with any external criterion of value, whether it be the distinction between the biblical and the extra-biblical, the "essential" and the "nonessential," the religiously "inspiring" and the religiously "uninspiring." Whatever distinctions and discriminations have to be made must come from *within* the total living tradition of Torah as distinctions and discriminations of parts in terms of the whole; but it is the whole that is the Teaching and must be acquired as "learning." The continuity of Torah, as written and as read, was well understood by the rabbis, who affirmed, to use Schechter's words, that "prophecy [is] the 'word of God' and the continuation of his voice heard on Mount Sinai, a voice which will cease only with the Messianic times—perhaps because the earth will be full of the knowledge of God and all the people of the Lord will be prophets."[13] Let us remember, however, that this "voice," like the word of God at Sinai, reaches us only as mediated through the minds and hearts of men and therefore in a relativized and fallible form. To discover the world of God in the words of the writings is the effort of all "learning," and is a task never done.

Since Torah is Teaching and its acquisition "learning," the study of Torah has from early time been the great and absorbing concern of the believing Jew. It is equivalent to the Temple sacrifices, we are told;[14] indeed, it is that for which man is created.[15] It would be utterly wrong to conclude from this emphasis on study that Jewish spirituality runs dry in the sands of intellectualism and scholasticism. Study of the Torah is something very different in Jewish reality: it is a genuine spiritual exercise, the characteristic and authentic Jewish equivalent of mystical communion with God. Indeed, it is rather more likely to run over into mysticism than into intellectualism, although neither excess is intrinsic to it. Certainly, the coachmen of Warsaw who—as reported by the scholar mentioned by Dr. Heschel[16]—were wont to seize a few moments from their work to gather in a group to con a page of the Talmud, were no intellectuals concerned only with the intricacies of scholastic dialectics. They were deeply earnest mean thirsting for spiritual refreshment, for communion with the Living God, and they found it, as countless generations of Jews before them had found it, in the study of Torah. "Oh, how I love thy Torah; it is my meditation all day long" (Ps. 119:97): with Torah understood in its fullest, this may be taken as the authentic attitude of the believing Jew to Torah as Teaching.

Torah as Law

Yet the study of Torah is as nothing or worse than nothing if it is not associated with doing. Indeed, it is held to be of such transcendent value precisely because it is relevant to life and action.[17] This leads us to a consideration of Torah as Law.

Torah is not in itself identical with law, as the usual translation would make it.[18] But it is Law, or halakah, in one of its aspects. Torah as Law reflects the fact that the Jew, in his covenant-existence, lives "under the Law," which is the consititution, so to speak, of the elect community, the "holiness-code" of the covenant-folk. That this conviction of living "under the Law" need not entail a graceless legalism or the notion of self-salvation through good works the slightest acquaintance with genuine Jewish spirituality or the most cursory reference to the Prayer Book—which, as Schechter points out,[19] is the best witness to authentic Jewish belief—is enough to prove. Certainly the countless generations of Jews who have prayed daily, "Our Father, our King, be gracious unto us, for we have no merits. . . Our Father, our King, if thou shouldst take account of iniquities, who could stand? . . . We know we have no merits, so deal with us graciously for thy Name's sake. As a father has compassion on his children, so, O Lord, have compassion upon us. . . Righteousness is thine, O Lord, and confusion is ours. How can we complain? What can we say? How can we justify ourselves?. . . Save us because of thy grace, O Lord"—the people who uttered these prayers were under no illusion that they could save themselves through the accumulation of merit. Nor can the rabbis—who, for all their circumstantial enumeration of commandments, taught that all were ultimately "compressed" or reduced to one, "The righteous shall live by his faith"[20]—be charged with the fragmentation and trivialization of the divine imperative. Yet, though it does not succumb to legalism, normative Jewish faith is halakic through and through in the sense that it is oriented to the Torah as Law as well as to the Torah as Teaching.

Torah as Law, like Torah as Teaching, is not merely the Pentateuch, not merely the Bible, not merely these plus the Talmud. It is the entire living body of tradition that confronts us with its claim, and its claim is to the totality of life.

Torah as Law is the divine imperative in all its unity and absolute demand. It "derives its authority from the Kingdom [of God]," as Schechter points out.[21] It is not merely an aggregation of particular commandments; it is in the first place, the affirmation of the total kingship of God, and to this everything else is subordinated. "Why," asks R. Joshua b. Karha, "does the section [of the *Shema*] *Hear, O Israel* precede *And it shall come to pass if ye shall hearken?* So that a man may first take upon him the yoke of the Kingdom of Heaven and afterward take upon him the yoke of the commandments."[22] *First,* the yoke of the Kingdom; *then,* the yoke of the commandments. Just as sin, rebellion against God and his kingship, is the source and origin of particular sins, so the acknowledgment of the divine kingship is the source, basis and sanction of the particular commandments. But just as, on the other hand, no man can be merely sinful in the abstract without engaging in particular sinful activities, so no man can truly acknowledge the kingship of God without subjecting himself to his Law in its particularity as commandments.

The commandments *(mitzvot)* that follow upon the acknowledgment of the divine sovereignty are in themselves neither absolute nor unchangeable, however much they may appear to be so in the conventional formulation. They are, in fact, generally recognized, though not always explicitly, to be changing and relative to the human situation. No commandment is conceived as absolute in the sense of being automatically applicable without regard to circumstances. Even the Sabbath, the rabbis teach, "is delivered into the hand of man (to break it when necessary), and not man into the power of the Sabbath."[23] "Danger to life annuls the Sabbath. . . ,[24] and one Sabbath may be violated to save many.[25] And what is true of the Sabbath is, of course, equally or even more true of other commandments. The general principle is, "that a man shall *live* by them—live, not die."[26] This principle provides not only a criterion for the application, suspension and, where necessary, the violation of particular commandments, but also a rule, though by no means the only one, by which orderly change and development are made possible. To take a famous example, biblical law requires the cancellation of all debts in the sabbatical year (Deut. 15:1-3). However this law of *shemittah* may have worked in very ancient days, by the time of Hillel, circumstances had so changed as to make it a serious threat to economic and social life. In the Mishnah, we are told that when Hillel saw that people were refusing to make loans for fear that they would be canceled on the seventh year and were thus offending against a commandment (to help those in need), he devised a procedure *(prosbul)* by which the biblical requirement could be avoided and lenders could grant loans without fear of cancellation.[27] Thus was a solemn Scriptural injunction annulled on the grounds of economic necessity (the need for an extensive credit system). The fact that the annulment was not explicitly recognized as such but was presented under cover of a legal fiction as an interpretation of the Scriptural provision casts important light on the methods and devices by which change was effected; it does not alter the fact that change there was and radical change at that. Interpretation, reinterpretation, enactments both positive and negative, emergence of the new and obsolescence of what has become meaningless: all of these processes find plentiful illustration in the development of the halakah through the centuries.[28] Torah as Law is very far indeed from being a fixed and rigid legalistic system without concern for human needs and changing requirements. It recognizes, by implication and act and sometimes even in so many words, the essential relativity of the commandments and their susceptibility to change in response to changing conditions. The lifeless rigidity that characterizes a certain type of contemporary Orthodoxy is very far indeed from the classical conception and practice.

Interpretation and Conviction

Jewish thought has made a variety of distinctions among the *mitzvot*—"heavy" and light," moral and ceremonial, rational and nonrational, those relating to God and those relating to one's neighbor. While under Torah as Law, all commandments are the same in nature and sanction, there are purposes for which such distinctions, properly qualified, can be of use.

For most Jews today, the existential significance of the various kinds of commandments is by no means the same. A good many—those dealing with political, criminal and civil law, for example—have lost all practical meaning since they have been superseded by the law of the state, and, according to the ancient rabbinical maxim, "The law of the state is the law."[29] Others, such as those relating to the Temple sacrifices, are obviously of no contemporary relevance. There are, in fact, left but two kinds of commandments that are of direct concern: the moral prescriptions, on the one side, and the "ritual" or "ceremonial" observances, on the other.

Most people today, as did some of the rabbis of former times, consider the moral commandments to be essentially grounded in reason or natural law, so that "these things, if they had not been written [by God] would have had to be written [by man]."[30] We have seen that there is good reason to doubt this notion. But however that may be, it is obviously not the ethical laws included in halakah that perplex the modern Jew; it is the so-called "ritual observances"—*kashrut*, Sabbath, circumcision—that perplex him. Not that he usually insists on being supplied with a "reason" for each particular observance.[31] What he is concerned with is something more serious and more basic. What are observances *as such* for? What is their religious meaning? What part do they play in religious life?

These questions, in the acute practical form in which they are put, are essentially new, for rarely before modern times did such a problem arise for masses of Jews. The necessity and binding power of the *mitzvot* were always taken for granted, and while there were always plenty of "sinners in Israel," the principle itself was never seriously challenged. This, of course, is no longer the case today. The principle *is* challenged, both in theory and in practice. And so the contemporary Jew requires an answer in essentially new terms; the conventional formulas, however much truth they may contain, will no longer do.

But conventional formulas are all that the spokesmen of Orthodoxy, even of its modern branches, seem able to supply. The ritual observances are the direct command of God and therefore must be obeyed: that is virtually all they have to say. If it is pointed out that these ritual observances have changed in many important respects through the centuries, so that they cannot possibly be the eternal and unchanging word of God, we are assured that such change, emergence and obsolescence are only apparent. All the *mitzvot* comprising the Oral Law were given to Moses on Sinai along with the written Torah; subsequent generations have simply "uncovered" the *mitzvot* through the use of certain canonical rules of interpretation. This type of fundamentalism runs counter to the plain evidence of the facts[32] and can obviously have but little appeal to the contemporary Jew who is existentially concerned with making the special observances of his faith religiously available to himself.

At the opposite pole is the position of "classical" or old-line Reform Judaism. In this view, the traditional ritual observances are written off as largely obsolete, religiously peripheral and unnecessary to Judaism in its "pure" creedal form. Recently there has been some shift within American Reform toward a greater measure of observance, but this has been due, in part at least, to a growing cultural nationalism with only a remote religious reference. In any case, no new conception has been developed in Reform circles to replace the obviously untenable position of old-line Reform.

Under the influence of secular Jewish nationalism, a new regard for certain traditional holidays and observances has emerged. These are approved because they seem to be the most significant and enduring aspect of "Jewish culture" and thus very useful to stimulate folk solidarity and promote folk survival. Often these secular survivalist arguments are presented under religious guise, but sometimes their non-religious character is frankly avowed. In any case, this approach is not one that is likely to appeal to those who take Jewish faith seriously. It involves not only the idolatrous exaltation of folk or national values, but also a deliberate exploitation of sacred things that must appear very close to sacrilege to the religious mind. It bears an uncomfortable resemblance to the postion once adopted by Charles Maurras, leader of the ultranationalist L'Action Française, in relation to the Catholic Church. Himself an unbelieving positivist of the Comtean school, Maurras strongly urged support of the Church and its ceremonies. "Differing on the truth," he explained, "we have come to agree on the useful. Divergencies of speculation persist but we have reached a practical accord on the value of Catholicism to the nation."[33] Sincere Catholics were outraged at this overture, and I do not think its Jewish counterpart is likely to commend itself any more favorably to the believing Jew.

Reconstructionism has attempted to develop a philosophy of ritual observance which would avoid the pitfalls of all of these positions. It

regards observances not as halakah (binding law) but simply as traditional Jewish folkways which should be pruned, modified, but on the
whole preserved for their functional utility. This is defined as the twofold purpose of contributing simultaneously to "Jewish survival" and
the "enrichment of Jewish spiritual life." But "Jewish survival," without the conviction of Israel's election and vocation—and this teaching
Reconstructionism rejects—is simply a narrow ethnocentrism indistin-
guishable from secular "folkism," while "enrichment of spiritual life,"
in the context of Reconstructionist thinking, easily falls into subject-
ivism and a kind of religio-aesthetic sentimentality which searches for
psychological devices to make one "feel spiritual." In the end, the observances lose all compelling religious power and become mere "folkish" trimmings of a subjective "religious experience."[34]

Yet although fundamentalism, modernism, secularism and Reconstructionism must all be rejected insofar as they attempt to provide an
adequate answer to the problem of religious observance, they all have
something significant to say. Orthodoxy contains the crucial emphasis
on the centrality and unique importance to Jewish faith of ritual observance as halakah, while modernism places a valid stress on free inquiry and historical criticism. Reconstructionism deserves recognition
for its insistence on the interplay of historical continuity and change in
the tradition. Even secular "folkism" is in order when it points to the
undeniable socio-cultural role of religious observances. There is some
degree of partial truth, greater or less, in each of these positions but
none of them is adequate. It is necessary to find a new approach that
will preserve the valid emphasis of tradition and yet make that emphasis intelligible to the contemporary believing Jew.

Let us note, in the first place, that all religious observance, existentially considered, is the *acting-out* of one's religious convictions. Our
convictions if they are truly existential and involve the entire being,
operate along all three dimensions of the personality: thinking, feeling
and doing. Of these, the aspect of doing is perhaps as important in religion as either of the others. Not only early religion, but religion in general, seems to be in a basic sense a dromenon, a pattern of *doing*,[35] at
least as much as a way of thinking and feeling. We need not agree entirely with Rosenzweig, who commends "the Pharisees and the saints
of the Church" for knowing that "man's understanding extends only as
far as his doing"[36]—this probably goes too far—to appreciate the fact
that a man's understanding *involves* his doing. Man being the unitary
creature he is, no one can be said really to hold any conviction if it does

not somehow find expression in a pattern of doing. Jewish religious thought is particularly sensitive to this truth, for, as Dr. Finkelstein points out, "the ultimate expression of Jewish doctrine remains to this day that of 'propositions in action.' "[37]

Religious observance is, then, in effect the *doing* of one's religious convictions. Now, among Jewish observances, there are two kinds: those that are of a *general-religious* type, more or less common to all religions (prayer, communal worship, consecration of birth, marriage and death), and those of the *special-Jewish* type, that are held to apply to Jews and to Jews only (circumcision, *kashrut,* Sabbath, etc.). A believing Jew will feel that his Christian neighbor ought to pray, attend church and give his children a religious training, but no Jew, not even the most orthodox, will feel that a Christian ought to observe *kashrut* or light the Sabbath candles. These things are somehow meant for Jews alone. It is with observances of this latter kind that we are here primarily concerned.

What is the religious significance of these observances? Is it not obvious that they are, in effect, the *acting-out* of the Jew's affirmation of the election of Israel and its "separation" as "priest-people?" "You shall be holy unto me, for I have separated you from among the nations that you should be mine" (Lev. 20:26): in this proclamation lies the meaning of Israel's existence and the ultimate grounding of the halakic code of ritual observance. The Jew, who, in existential "repetition," stands at the foot of Sinai and receives the Torah, receives it not only as a teaching about the election of Israel but also as a code, a "holiness-code," in terms of which he is to enact that teaching into the pattern of his life.[38] "Law, lived and experienced, is expression and justification of the divine election of Israel. Both belong together."[39]

In this view, Jewish ritual observance is halakah, for the Jew lives "under the Law," and the special discipline to which the halakah subjects him is the commandment of God involved in the election of Israel. But this is a far cry from asserting, as do the fundamentalists, that the particular, detailed observances confronting the Jew at any time are the eternal prescriptions of God, communicated to Moses on Mount Sinai. Nor, on the other hand, are they "mere" human inventions. As with Scripture, so with halakah, it is fruitless, even meaningless, to attempt a simple and definitive differentiation between the "human" and the "divine." One cannot accept the "general principle" as divine but relegate the particular commandments to the rank of the peripheral and "merely human." The "general principle" cannot be really *understood*

unless particular commandments are *observed.* "The truth of the theological connection between Chosenness and Law becomes evident
when we actually fulfill the command. Only the 'living reality,' the un-
mediated experience of the single law, leads to a conception of the objective theological act."[40] Observances have their history; they have
arisen, changed and many of them lost their effectiveness with the passage of time. The commandments, like the Bible, are immediately the
products of human life, as the modernists claim. But they are not therefore any the less the commandments of God. God operates in and
through history, and the history of Israel certainly cannot be dissociated from the divine intent for Israel. It is the historical belief and practice of the community of Israel—*kelal Yisrael*[41]—that provides us with
the contents of halakah. In the tradition of Israel, we find the unique
and inseparable combination of the divine and the human that constitutes the Torah as Teaching and Law.

Buber has objected to the "ritualistic" emphasis of the halakic tradition on the ground that it "hampers the striving for realization." "The
will to the covenant with God through the perfected reality of life in
true community," he explains, "can only emerge in power where one
does not believe that the covenant with God is already fulfilled in essence through the observance of prescribed forms."[42] This is a basic argument against the halakic concept, and it cannot be denied that it has
its force. Were the "observance of prescribed forms" held to be in itself
sufficient for the fulfilment of the covenant, then it would deserve all
the denunciation that the prophets heaped upon "burnt-offerings" and
"sacrifices," and insofar as halakic observance is sometimes so conceived, it deserves such condemnation. But the halakic concept is in itself very far from legalistic ritualism. The election and vocation of Israel mean more, much more, than fixed ritual observance; they include
the entire moral law, and no area of life is unaffected by their trans-
forming power. Buber, moreover, himself speaks of the "mysteries
whose meaning no one learns who does not himself join in the
dance."[43] The halakic pattern is the "dance" in which the Jew learns
the "mystery" of the election of Israel.

But in order to have this significance, the ritual observances performed must be not just halakah, but halakah-*for-me.* Rosenzweig
deals with this problem—which is a problem particularly, though not
exclusively, for those Jews of our time who "return" to Judaism and
have to begin "acquiring" the halakah—in a profound essay, *"Die
Bauleute."*[44] He stresses the necessity of an existential appropriation of

the Torah as Law by each individual Jew standing face to face with God. Unless a *mitzvah* is really made one's own, unless it can be and is performed with true inwardness, it has no effective power. The entire body of halakic tradition, ever changing in its historical conditionedness, yet ever the same, confronts the individual Jew as *Gesetz* ("law" in the external sense, mere "substance"). To become operative, it must be turned into *Gebot* ("commandment" in the inner sense, an inward compulsion to deed). "In the realm of Law, as in the realm of Teaching, contents and material must cease to be mere substance and must be transformed into inner power. *Gesetz* [must]. . . become *Gebot*, which, in the very moment it is heard, turns into deed. The living reality *(Heutigkeit)* is the purpose of the law. This aim, however, is not to be achieved by obedience to the paragraphs of a code. Only personal ability to fulfill the precept can decide. We choose; but it is a choice based on high responsibility."[45] Thus, through responsible personal appropriation, halakah-as-such is transformed into halakah-for-me and becomes operative as the way in which I as a Jew *live out* in ritual pattern my existential affirmation of faith. No man can decide for another what he can or cannot make his own; each must decide for himself, in responsible recognition of the claim that the tradition of the Law has upon him, but for himself nevertheless. In the end, the appropriation of Torah as Law is an existential decision made in divine-human encounter as at Sinai. In the end, too, everyone who has taken upon himself the yoke of the Kingdom and the commandments is vindicated before God for what he does in the full consciousness of responsibility, according to the saying of R. Zedekiah b. Abraham: "Every man receives reward from God for what he is convinced is right, if this conviction has no other motive but the love of God."[46]

Torah as Way

Torah as Law is the active side of Torah as Teaching. It embraces not merely ritual observance, but in a sense everything the Jew does, for it recognizes no ultimate distinctions in the totality of life, which is all subject to God and his Law. Law and Teaching constitute two aspects of the same reality, and that reality, in unity and synthesis, is Torah as Way.

The conception of Torah as Way has exercised the imagination of Jewish mystics through the ages. In their visions, it has become virtually the Way, or *Tao,* of the universe—the premundane Word and Wisdom of God operative as the L'ogos in the creation and maintenance of the cosmos. But if we desire to avoid such theosophical speculation, so alien to the "reverential agnosticism"[47] that characterizes the prophetic faith, we will think of Torah as the Way for the Jew in his life under the covenant.

Here, too, everything depends on decision. Every Jew is under the covenant, whether by birth or adoption; and once under the covenant, his covenant-existence is an objective fact independent of his will. He can no more help it than he can help being a man of the twentieth century or the son of his father. The son is indeed confronted with a crucial decision: to be a good son or a bad son, to live up to or to repudiate the responsibilities of sonship, but no matter what he does or desires to do, he cannot make himself not the son of his father. So too the Jew. He is confronted with a crucial, life-determining choice: to acknowledge and try to live up to or to repudiate the responsibilities of his Jewish covenant-existence, but no matter what he does, he cannot remove himself from under the covenant and its obligations.[48] The fateful decision confronting every Jew is therefore not: Shall I or shall I not come under the covenant? but: Shall I affirm my covenant-existence and live an *authentic* life or shall I deny it and as a consequence live an *inauthentic* one? Judaism is the living out of the affirmative decision. It is the decision to take the Way of the Torah.

The consequences of this decision, both in its individual and collective aspects, are vast and far-reaching. Covenant-existence for the Jew is not a mere figure of speech; it is an objective though supernatural fact. It enters into the Jew's very being, and the attempt to deny it or to repudiate its responsibilities must lead to deep inner division which may manifest itself disastrously in various psychological, social and cultural forms. Ezekiel's thunderous words against the faithless community of his time apply with equal force to the Jewish individual and Jewish community of all times: "And that which comes into your minds shall not be at all, in that you say, We will be as the nations, the races of the lands, to serve wood and stone. As I live, says the Lord God, with a mighty hand, with an outstretched arm and an outpoured fury, will I be king over you" (Ezek. 20:32-33). This is the same "mighty hand and outstretched arm" that delivered Israel from Egypt;[49] but now it no longer delivers, it destroys. Against those who repudiate it in word or deed, the divine election under the covenant turns into the wrath of God. For what they are doing is to deny their true redemptive history and seek salvation elsewhere, by worshiping other gods, which are mere "wood and stone" even though they be compounded of the best that science and philosophy can provide.

But if the repudiation of his true redemptive history is so destructive to the Jew, his wholehearted affirmation of the covenant brings with it the divine blessing of authenticity. Authentic Jewish covenant-existence made operative in life: that is the Torah in its totality as Way.

Because of this ambivalence, the Torah is decision and judgment. It is decision, for it confronts every Jew with the demand for recognition and appropriation, not only once for all but at every moment of existence: "Choose you this day whom you will serve" (Jos. 24:15). It is judgment because, upon this decision, depends the Jew's existence as Jew: "It is not a trifling thing for you; it is your life" (Deut. 32:47). Or, as the rabbis put it, Torah may be either balm or poison. "For him who deals rightly with it, it is a drug for life; but for him who deals wrongly with it, it is a drug for death."[50] Torah is for the Jew the permanent *crisis* of his life, for it is demand, decision and judgment. But it is also *joy*, for it is the testimony of the election, the abiding expression of God's mighty act of redemption in the past and the promise of the greater and final redemption to come. It is at once the symbol and the embodiment of Israel's redemptive history.

Torah as Way is the totality of everything that has meaning for the Jew in his religious existence. To live a Torah-true life is, for him, to live a life that is true to his inmost being because it is true to the God who is the source and law of that being.

Notes

1. "The comprehensive name for the divine revelation, written and oral, in which the Jews possessed the sole standard and norm of their religion, is *Torah*. It is a source of manifold misconception that the word is customarily translated 'law,' though it is not easy to suggest any one English word by which it would be rendered. 'Law' must, however, not be understood in the restricted sense of legislation, but it must be taken to include the whole of revelation—all that God has made known of his nature, character and purpose, of what he would have man be and do. . . . In a word, Torah in one aspect is the vehicle; in another and deeper view, it is the whole content of revelation." G.F. Moore, *Judaism* (Harvard University: Cambridge, Mass., 1927), I, 263.

2. See C. G. Montefiore and H. Loewe, *A Rabbinic Anthology* (Macmillan:

London, 1938), chap. v, "The Law"; also Solomon Schechter, *Some Aspects of Rabbinic Theology* (Macmillan: New York, 1909), chaps. viii, "The 'Law,' " and ix, "The Law as Personified in the Literature."

3. "[In the history of Israel] we see the prehistory of our own life, each of us the prehistory of his own life." Martin Buber, *Drei Reden uber das Judentum* (Literarische Anstalt Rutten & Loening: Frankfort, 1920), p. 28.

4. The transformation in rabbinic tradition of these "nature" festivals into history festivals expresses better than anything else the true genius of the Jewish religion. Those who today are trying to convert them back into "nature" festivals are, wittingly or unwittingly, trying to undo the work of the rabbis and to paganize Jewish observance.—"It is well known that the ancient Israelitic festivals were taken over from the previous oriental cultures of Canaan and Babylonia. But in each case, ancient Judaism changed the fundamental meaning of the festival first by adding to it, then by substituting for its natural a historical interpretation. Thus, the *shalosh regalim,* the three great holidays of the year, originally natural holidays of agricultural production, became, for the Jews, holidays commemorating great historical events. Passover, the ancient spring festival, became and remained the festival of the Exodus from Egypt, or of the origin of the Jewish nation. Pentecost, still 'the day of the first fruits' in the Old Testament, was transformed by the early Pharisees into a memorial chiefly of the giving of the Torah, i.e., of the foundation of the Jewish religion. The Feast of Tabernacles celebrates chiefly the migration through the desert. . . ." S. W. Baron, *A Social and Religious History of the Jews* (Columbia University: New York), I, 5.

5. "In every generation, one should regard himself as personally having come out of Egypt." M. Pesahim 10.5.

6. Cf. Will Herberg, " *Beyond Time and Eternity:* Reflections on Passover and Easter," *Christianity and Crisis,* Vol. IX (April 18, 1949), No. 6.

7. Buber, "Der Preis," *Der Jude,* Vol. II (October, 1917), No. 8; *Die judische Bewegung,* ((Judischer Verlag: Berlin, 1916), II, 123-24.

8. *Tanh. B. Yitro,* 38b.

9. *Pesik. K.* 102a. "To the Rabbis and their followers, the Revelation at Sinai and all that it implies was not a mere reminiscence or tradition. . . . Through their intense faith, they rewitnessed it in their own souls, so that it became to them a personal experience." Schechter, *Some Aspects of Rabbinic Theology,* p. 24.

10. Schechter, *op. cit.,* p. 142.

11. Franz Rosenzweig, *Briefe* (Schocken: Berlin, 1935), pp. 582-83.

12. "Whatever a discerning disciple will one day proclaim before his teacher was already said by Moses on Sinai." *J.* Peah 9b.

"Rabbi Isaac said: The Prophets drew from Sinai all their future utterances. . . . Not only to the Prophets alone does this apply but to all the sages that are destined to arise in after days." Tanh. Yitro, 11, 124. Note, however, that Sinai is taken as the criterion of all that is valid as future Torah.

13. Schechter, op. cit., p. 123.

14. *M. Abot* 2.9.

15 *Tanh. B., Ahare Mot,* 35a.

16. A.J. Heschel, *The Earth is the Lord's* (Schuman: New York, 1950), p. 46.

17. The question was discussed: Is study the greater thing or doing? R. Tarfon said doing, but Rabbi Akiba insisted on study on the ground that "study leads to doing." *B. Kidd.* 40b. To this all agreed. See also Sifre, Deut. 48:84b. "One who studies with an intent other than to act, it were better for him had he never been created." *J. Shabbat* 3b.

18. "It must be stated that the term *Law or Nomos* is not a correct rendering of the Hebrew word *Torah.* The legalist element, which might rightly be called the Law, represents only one side of the Torah. To the Jew, the word Torah means a teaching or instruction of any kind. It may be either a general principle or a specific injunction, whether it be found in the Pentateuch or in other parts of Scripture, or even outside the canon. The juxtaposition in which *Torah* and *Mitzvot,* Teaching and Commandments, are to be found in the Rabbinic literature, implies already that the former means something more than merely the Law." Schechter, *op. cit.,* p. 117.

19. Schechter, *op. cit.,* pp. 9-11.

20. *B. Makkot* 23b-24a. The biblical quotation is from Hab. 2:4.

21. Schechter, *op. cit.,* p. 116.

The total claim of God upon Israel is, as we have seen, related to the divine act of deliverance from Egypt: "We were Pharaoh's slaves in Egypt, and the Lord brought us out of Egypt with a mighty hand. . . . And the Lord commanded us to observe all these statutes and fear the Lord our God, for our good always. . . . " Deut. 6:20-24.

22. *M. Ber.* 2.2.

23. Schechter, *op. cit.,* p. 152. See *Mekilta* on Exod. 31:13.

24. *Tanh. B., Massee,* 81a.

25. *Mekilta, Shabb.* 1.

26. Sifra 86b. Three commandments, however—the prohibition of idolatry, murder and sexual "impurity"—are to be observed even at the risk of death. *B. Sanh.* 74a.

27. *M. Shebiit* 10.3-7.

28. See the extremely informative and illuminating article by Robert Gordis. "The Nature of Jewish Tradition," *Jewish Frontier,* Vol. XIV (November, 1947), No. 11.

29. *B. Gittin* 10b and parallels.

30. *B. Yoma* 67b.

31. Maimonides has some interesting remarks, cast in a rather modern anthropological vein, on the origins of some of the biblical prohibitions. See Leon Roth, *The Guide for the Perplexed: Moses Maimonides* (Hutchinson's University Library: London, 1948), pp. 75-76. In general, however, the rabbis discourage speculation on these matters as vain and confusing.

32. See the study by Robert Gordis referred to above.

33. Quoted by Carlton J. H. Hayes, *The Historical Evolution of Modern Nationalism* (Smith: New York, 1931), p. 209.

34. "Toward a Guide for Jewish Ritual Usage," Reconstructionist Pamphlet No. 4, pp. 7 and 8. Particularly revealing is this passage: "A satisfactory rationale for Jewish [ritual] usage is one that would recognize in it both a method of group survival and a means to the personal self-fulfilment or salvation of the individual Jew. Through it, the individual Jew will know the exhilaration of

fully identifying himself with his people and thereby saving his own life from dullness, drabness, and triviality." Thus, even the "personal" aspect is reduced to the "folkish."

35. Jane Harrison, *Ancient Art and Ritual* (Oxford: New York, 1948), pp. 35-38.

"The ritual is a symbolic expression of thoughts and feelings by action." Erich Fromm, *Psychoanalysis and Religion* (Yale University: New Haven, Conn., 1950), p. 109.

36. Rosenzweig, "Das neue Denken, "Kleinere Schriften (Schocken: Berlin, 1937), p. 374.

37. Louis Finkelstein, "The Role of Dogma in Judaism," *The Thomist: Maritain Volume* (Sheed & Ward: New York, 1943), Vol. V, January, 1943.

38. It is not without significance that, according to some scholars, most of the biblical "purity" regulations were originally binding upon the priestly group alone. As all Israel became a "kingdom of priests," these observances were extended to the entire people.

39. So N. N. Glatzer ("Franz Rosenzweig," *Yivo Annual of Jewish Social Science:* I, p. 125) summarizes the position taken by Franz Rosenzweig in his essay "Gottlich und Menschlich" (*Briefe,* , pp. 518-21).

40. Glatzer, op. cit., p. 124: Rosenzweig, *op. cit.,* p. 519.

41. Schechter uses the term, "Catholic Israel." *Studies in Judaism* (Jewish Publication Society: Philadelphia, 1945), First Series, pp. xviii-xix.

42. Buber, *Der heilige Weg* (Literarische Anstalt Rutten & Loening: Frankfort, 1920), p. 53. A somewhat more *heilsgeschichtliche* formulation of the same argument is to be found in Buber's "The Two Foci of the Jewish Soul," *Israel and the World* (Schocken: New York, 1948), pp. 28-29: "My point of view with regard to this subject [Law] diverges from the traditional. It is not a-nomistic, but neither is it entirely nomistic.. . . The teaching of Judaism comes from Sinai; it is Moses' teaching. But the soul of Judaism is pre-Sinaitic; it is the soul which approached Sinai and there received what it did receive; it is older than Moses; it is patriarchal, Abraham's soul, or more truly, since it concerns the product of a primordial age, it is Jacob's soul. The Law put on the soul, and the soul can never again be understood outside of the Law; yet the soul itself is not of the Law." This is to be associated with Buber's denial that Exodus-Sinai constitutes the "center" of Israel's redemptive history: "The Bible does not set a past event as midpoint between origin and goal. It interposes a movable, circling midpoint which cannot be pinned to any set time, for it is the moment when I . . . catch through the words of the Bible the voice which from the earliest beginnings has been speaking in the direction of the goal. . . . The revelation at Sinai is not this midpoint itself, but the perceiving of it, and such perception is possible at any time." "The Man of Today and the Jewish Bible," *Israel and the World,* p. 94.

43. Buber, "What is Man," *Between Man and Man* (Kegan Paul: London, 1947), p. 192. Cf. Finkelstein: "Vivid enough for those who are sensitive to them, such propositions expressed in action or commandments have little or no meaning for anyone outside the group which practices them." "The Role of Dogma in Judaism," *op. cit.,* p. 106. Also Rosenzweig: "No single command-

ment can be made intelligible as a 'religious' demand to anyone who stands outside." *Briefe*, p. 519.

44. Rosenzweig, *Kleinere Schriften*, pp. 106-21.

45. Glatzer, *op. cit.*, p. 124; Rosenzweig, *op. cit.*, pp. 116, 120.

46. Schechter, *Studies*, First Series, p. 325.

47. See above, chap. 17, note 7.

48. "The Israelites have been chosen by God to be his sons and servants. There is no escape. God will use them for his purpose, whether they will or no." Thus do Montefiore and Loewe formulate the normative rabbinical view. *A Rabbinic Anthology*, p. 123.

49. "And brought forth Israel from the midst of them [the Egyptians] . . . with a mighty hand and outstretched arm." Ps. 136:11-12.

50. *B. Shab.* 88b; *B. Yoma* 72b.

SIMON GREENBERG provides a viable approach to the classical Rabbinic doctrine of "Torah Min Ha-sha-mayim," the Divine Origin of Torah (lit., "The Teaching from Heaven"). In his creative excursus on Boaz Cohen's paper on "Canons of Interpretation of Jewish Law," Greenberg affirms the supreme importance of the concept of K'nesset Yisrael (the Hebrew equivalent for Schechter's phrase," "Catholic Israel"), "by which we mean that the Jewish people must be regarded as one community with respect to the essential principles of Jewish Law and observance." Otherwise, we undermine the very notion of an all-embracing, unique Divine Revelation to be tended by a united Jewish people.

The problem is that there is no agency to affirm any common standard of observance or to legislate new laws or abrogate old ones. Halachah has always staked its supreme authority on Divine communication, although "those who stressed the revelatory origin of the Law did not thereby deny its intrinsic goodness and rationality. . . . " Greenberg argues that the concept of a revealed law is indispensable to the meaningful continuity of Judaism as a philosophy and pattern of life, to the existence of the Jewish people, and to the moral life of man. Rationalizations of halachah, however valuable, will never prove fully satisfying to the committed or convincing to the non-observant. What makes Jewish Law inspiring and worth-while is its cosmic significance, its affirmation that man is God's partner in the universe, and is therefore capable of transcending his "biologically felt and rationally comprehended wants."

175

A Revealed Law

SIMON GREENBERG[1]

A Master's Legacy

For more than three decades, Dr. Boaz Cohen served on the faculty of the Jewish Theological Seminary, and as the recognized authority on Rabbinic law among the members of the Law Committee. In both capacities he was called upon to apply his encyclopedic knowledge of Jewish law to the practical exigencies of life, probably more often than any other member of the Rabbinical Assembly. The activities of these two bodies, their deliberations and decisions, reflect the basic principles that characterize the Conservative approach to Jewish law more tangibly and relevantly than do those of any other constituted agency of the Rabbinical Assembly. In papers prepared for various occasions, Rabbi Cohen formulated his understanding of these principles and how they are to be applied. These papers have been gathered into one volume under the title, *Law and Tradition in Judaism.*[2]

The reader of these papers cannot but be impressed by their author's vast erudition. Rabbi Cohen is a master not only of Rabbinic law and literature. He is also one of the most learned students of the law in general and of Roman law in particular. Hence, he is able to illuminate his subject matter with light from many another source.

The reader's second impression is one of intellectual honesty, struggling boldly if not at all times successfully (at least from this reader's point of view), with the logically intractable problems of change and continuity within a tradition.

Each essay is a complete unit unto itself. Yet such is the breadth of Rabbi Cohen's knowledge and the essential consistency of his philosophic outlook that though these essays were written over a period of three decades there is little repetition or contradiction. Each essay is a fresh approach to the central theme. Rabbi Cohen formulates that

176

theme as follows: Though " . . . traditional Judaism can be fully grasped only in the light of its five-fold tradition" (*i.e.*, Halakhic, Ethical, Theological, Philosophical, Mystical), " . . . the Halakhic tradition is primary and takes precedence over the other traditions, when they come in conflict with it" (pp. viii–x). Basic to this Halakhic tradition is the proposition that, "Biblical law is not subject to abrogation, but can only be amended through the traditional method of interpretation" (p. 26). It is to a manifold exposition of "the methods of interpretation" that these essays are devoted.

Rabbi Cohen's erudition serves him gloriously in expounding the methods of interpretation developed by the Rabbis. His paper on "Sabbath Prohibitions Known as *Shebut*" may well serve as a model for the presentation of the history of the scores of legal concepts created by the Rabbis whereby Jewish law was enabled to grow and change while preserving its essential character. Most of these concepts have yet to be studied and presented with such thoroughness, at least in English.

In an extended essay, "Law and Ethics in the Light of the Jewish Tradition," Rabbi Cohen amply demonstrates that "Many interpretations of the rabbis which apparently are a deviation from the letter of the Biblical law, were undoubtedly animated by ethical considerations" (p. 216). It is to be regretted that he does not discuss those instances in which the Rabbis did not deviate from "the letter of the Law" when it would appear that ethical considerations would justify such a step. This, after all, is the crux of the dilemma for many of us.

Similarly, his essay, "The Responsum of Maimonides Concerning Music," includes the remark that "Law cannot arrest the operation of human instincts" (p. 173). Dr. Cohen arrives at this conclusion after pointing out that the Rabbis failed in their efforts to limit music in Jewish life to religious purposes only. Surely music is not the only instance in which "human instincts" proved mightier than Rabbinic or even Biblical injunctions. There must be much that we can learn from a careful, comprehensive study of such instances. It should be made.

Rabbi Cohen does not limit himself to scholarly studies of the past. He also attempts to formulate "Canons of Interpretations of Jewish Law" for our guidance. Ten such principles are presented in one of the essays. Listed among these principles is the proposition that "We should aim to interpret merely for American Jewry, and not for 'Catholic Israel' . . . " (p. 61). This seems to be in direct contradiction with an opinion formulated in an earlier essay to the effect that "There must not be, e.g. a Conservative law on *kashrut,* the Sabbath, or *gittin,* in contrast to the Orthodox law on the same subject. . . . What we must never let come to pass is the origin of a new faction in Judaism" (p. 29). In that same essay Dr. Cohen declares that, "Fundamental to our thinking is the doctrine of *K'nesset Yisrael,* by which we mean that the Jewish people must be regarded as one community with respect to the essential principles of Jewish Law and observance" (pp. 27–28). Perhaps this contradiction is but a reflection of Rabbi Cohen's wise warning to us that in interpreting our tradition, " . . . we must consider whether we should dedicate ourselves to the implacable ideal of consistency . . . " (p. 61).

Rabbi Cohen believes that "The introduction of the historical point of view . . . has revolutionized the whole structure of Jewish learning including the study of the Halakhah, with far-reaching effects" (p. 27). He identifies these far-reaching effects with "expending more time and energy on the original sources of the Talmud rather than on the pilpulistic commentaries" (p. 30); distinguishing the sources of the Shulhan Arukh and giving due weight to each (p. 76); discovering the reasoning processes, the rationalizations and motivations that are concealed in the Rabbis' seemingly peculiar and artificial exegesis (p. 12); distinguishing between law, custom and superstituion (p. 77); giving due consideration to economic and social conditions (p. 90); and to our sense of propriety and expediency (p. 95).

Dr. Cohen offers three criteria for the interpretation of Jewish law. In order to be valid, an interpretation must be "right, proper, and acceptable. By right, we mean what is deemed valid in Jewish law by a body of scholars that is competent to pass judgment on them" (p. 116). Rabbi Cohen does not indicate how that "body of scholars" is to be organized, though at one point he seems to have felt that "the Palestinian rabbinate" might become that body (p. 35). Unfortunately, the rabbinate as presently organized in the State of Israel does not, by and large, share the historical point of view in its interpretation of Jewish law, nor does it enjoy the confidence of the whole of *Kenesset Yisrael.*

" . . . the remedy [interpretation] must be proper so as not to offend our moral sense" (p. 117). But again, Rabbi Cohen does not indicate whose "moral sense" he has in mind. Certainly, we do not all have the same "moral sense." Finally, Rabbi Cohen suggests that an interpretation must be "acceptable to *Kenesset Yisrael,* to the learned as well as to the laity, to the pious as well as to the religiously indifferent" (p. 117). Obviously, few interepretations could meet all three qualifications.

The Problem of Enforcement

Many of the difficulties which we face in our efforts at adjusting Jewish law to new circumstances while preserving its essential continuity, are faced by all peoples with a long and cherished tradition. However, two factors distinguish the problems faced by Jewish law today from those faced by other systems of law. (1) There is no agency which can exercise effective authority to enforce it. (2) No agency is endowed with the right to legislate new laws or to interpret or abrogate the old ones.

This essay will focus attention upon the problem raised by the first factor, namely, the absence of an agency exercising effective power to enforce the law. This has raised the question whether the concept of law applies at all to the injunctions and admonitions of the Jewish religion. We shall not dwell upon the semantic difficulties which this question raises. For us, the concept "Jewish law" refers to the existence of a well-organized, carefully articulated set of principles and precepts whose purpose it is to direct human behavior in almost every area of human concern. Moreover there are men and women who voluntarily subject themselves to the demands of these principles and precepts and hope that their descendants will do likewise. Jewish law is today a relevant reality because there are such people in goodly number.

The fact that the concept of law is generally understood to imply the existence of an enforcement agency indicates one of the basic characteristics of laws, namely, that obedience to them usually involves the individual in some measure of unpleasantness. The degree of unpleasantness involved is of little moment; once a habit of obedience is established and its compensations experienced, the inconvenience involved in observing the law may be reduced to a minimum or entirely eliminated. In every instance, the very fact that a law had to be enacted and sanctions imposed indicates that even the best-intentioned people are inclined to avoid what is enjoined by the law. Rabbi Judah the Prince probably had this in mind when he admonished, "Reckon the loss incurred by the fulfillment of a *mitzvah* against the reward secured by its observance, and the gain derived from a transgression against the loss it involves" (Avot 2:1). Note that in the case of a *mitzvah* one becomes conscious first of the loss incurred; in the case of a transgression, of the gain. It must be so of necessity. How else could one explain the constant need to exhort people to perform *mitzvot* and to avoid transgressions?

Because obedience to the law so often involves some measure of unpleasantness, effective enforcement agencies are required even in the case of the most obviously beneficial laws, such as those regulating traffic, and even in the most civilized societies. The character of Jewish law and the circumstances of Jewish life made the problem of enforcing the law particularly difficult. Jewish law contains many provisions which, by their very nature, cannot be enforced by any human agency. The code which commands us not to steal and not to deal falsely also enjoins us not to "hate thy brother in thy heart" and "to love thy neighbor as thyself" (Leviticus 19). Moreover, even when there was an effective Jewish government in Jerusalem, some Jewish communities were beyond the reach of its powers of enforcement. Within those dispersed communities a substantial number of people voluntarily subjected themselves to the authority of Jewish law. Since Jewish law calls for the performance of acts involving considerable difficulty and since it contains provisions which under the most favorable political circumstances were beyond the power of the civil authority to enforce, the question of the ultimate sanction of Jewish law was always high on the agenda of Jewish life.

Until comparatively recent times, authoritative expounders of Jewish law agreed that it should be obeyed because it is the revealed will of God. To be sure, Rabbinic literature and particularly medieval Jewish philosophic literature abound in statements pointing to the intrinsic moral goodness and rationality of the Law. However, not even the most zealous rationalist attributed the *authority* of the Law to its moral excellence and inherent rationality. And just as those who stressed the revelatory origin of the Law did not thereby deny its instrinsic goodness and rationality, so those who preferred to stress its rationality in no way desired to imply that its authority rested on any basis other than *revelation*.

It is the Law which has established the pattern of Jewish life, with its religious, educational and philanthropic institutions, dietary laws, family relations and ethical obligations. Hence, the question facing those who are committed to the preservation and enhancement of this Jewish pattern of life is whether it can be done without the concept not merely of Law but of a *revealed* Law.

 Those who today are thus committed are divided into three camps. The first camp rejects not only the concept of a revealed Law but even of Law *per se* as applicable to the Jewish pattern of life. Since the concept of Law inherently involves the performance of acts which one may find unpleasant, those who would eliminate the concept completely from Jewish religious life tend to take the position that only those aspects of the traditional pattern of Jewish life which people readily delight to observe should be preserved. As for the rest, it not only may be, but it will and should be discarded.

Those in this camp who do not reject the concept of Law, but only that of a revealed Law, argue that every custom, practice, or precept must stand or fall on the basis of its intrinsic rationality. Hence, those practices which are not amenable to satisfactory rationalization not only may, but should, be discarded. Since proponents of this attitude have no generally accepted standards for "satisfactory rationalization," the violence that this approach has done to the historic pattern of Jewish life is too well known to require elaboration.

The second camp is made up of those who retain the concept of a revealed Law, but insist upon interpreting it in the narrowest possible sense as to time and place and in the broadest possible sense as to its provisions. They maintain for all practical purposes that "In the third month after the children of Israel were gone forth out of the land of Egypt" (Exodus 19:1), the Law, as embodied in the latest edition of the traditional code, was revealed at Sinai.

The third camp consists of those who are equally insistent upon retaining the concept of a revealed Law, but would interpret the concept in the widest possible sense as to time and place, and in the narrowest possible sense as to its provisions. They would apply to the legal codes those methods of discriminatory study referred to by Dr. Cohen. They would scrutinize the provisions of the codes in the light of modern historical, psychological and philological studies. But, however broad their interpretation of revelation might be, they would neverthelss insist upon its indispensability to any system of Jewish thought which would lay claim to authenticity and meaningful continuity. No matter how niggardly they might be in applying this concept to the specific contents of the codes, or how widely they might differ in regard to the specific content to which it should be applied, they nevertheless would insist that it is significantly applicable to a substantial core of those codes. This, it seems to me, is the position of Dr. Cohen, a position which in essence I, and I believe the main body of the Rabbinical Assembly, share with him.

Revelation as Necessity

One who presumes to speak of a revealed Law cannot avoid questions
regarding the time and place of the revelation. Did it occur as a "per-
ceptible event in the external world" or was it, as Dr. Cohen seems to
feel, "the internal experience of the prophet permeated by the divine
spirit" (pp. 23–24)? Elsewhere I have struggled with that question and
shall not now return to it.[3] I wanted here to indicate why I believe that
the concept of a revealed Law must be maintained not as the empty
shell of a once firmly held conviction, but as the expression of a conviction indispensable (a) to the meaningful continuity of Judaism as a
philosophy and pattern of life, (b) to the existence of the Jewish people
and (c) to the moral life of man.

It will help us understand why the concept of a revealed Law is indispensable to us today if we understand why the concept came to occupy so central a position in Jewish thought. Note that we are not in-
quiring how the concept came into being. If we reject *in toto* the tradition that at Sinai the Israelites experienced an overwhelming event at
which time a Law was revealed to them, then we have no way of establishing with any degree of certainty why the Israelites alone among all
the known people of history, attributed direct divine origin to both
their civil and religious law.[4] The most that we can hope to do is to try
to explain how the concept functioned, that is, to what need it responded. The exposition of how a concept functioned is not equivalent to an
explanation of how and why it came into being. Nor does the manner
of its functioning validate its cognitive content. It indicates merely
what psychological, intellectual and emotional needs of the individual
or of the group the concept served. Those needs were undoubtedly
very real and urgent or else the concept would never have assumed so
central a position in Jewish thought. If those needs still exist today, we
must ask whether they are being served or can be served by a concept
more acceptable to us.

Among the most deeply-felt needs of our ancestors was that of appro-
priately expressing their sense of overwhelming awe when they con-
templated the grandeur and the majesty of the contents of the Law.
"See, I have imparted to you laws and norms. . . . Observe them
faithfully, for that will be proof of your wisdom and discernment to
other peoples, who on hearing of all these laws will say: 'Surely that is
a great nation of wise and discerning people.' . . . What great nation
has laws and norms as perfect as all this teaching that I set before you

this day?" (Deuteronomy 4:5–8). The ecstasy and admiration and hence the love and loyalty which the Law called forth in the hearts of our fathers is mirrored in Psalm 119 and in hundreds of other passages in Biblical and Rabbinic literature. Our fathers could rationally attribute the perfection which they found in it only to its divine origin. Our ancestors' frame of mind is movingly reflected in a comment made to me by Professor Ernst Simon as we left a synagogue in Jerusalem on the Sabbath. "When I read some of the stirring passages in Deuteronomy," he said, "I cannot understand how anyone can believe that they were written by a human being."

But far more universally experienced and more deeply felt was the need for a logically and emotionally compelling rationale to buttress a pattern of life which included socially "offensive" institutions such as the Sabbath and the dietary laws, personally demanding injunctions such as those regulating the most intimate relations between the sexes, and intellectually and spiritually burdensome chores, such as the study of an unspoken language and attachment to a land one often neither lived in nor saw. The concept that the Law which established this physically burdensome and spiritually taxing pattern of life was revealed, has proved over the centuries to be more effective than any other in offering a rationale equal to the task of making this pattern of life acceptable even under the most trying circumstances, not to all Jews, to be sure, but to a number large enough to assure the preservation of the pattern and with it of the Jewish people itself. For it can hardly be gainsaid that before the modern era in Jewish history only those Jews remained Jews for whom the concept of revealed Law had vital relevance and significance.

There are two reasons for this. In the first place, no one could possibly produce a fully comprehensible and acceptable rationalization for all elements in the traditional pattern of Jewish life. Ingenious thinkers have rationalized the Sabbath, the dietary laws and the civil and ethical laws of the Torah, but it is beyond the power of the most ardent apologist to formulate a satisfactory rationale for the *hukim*—laws of the red heifer, of cloth made from a mixture of wool and linen, of the sacrificial system and similar laws. Secondly, it was obvious from earliest times that while rationalizations in completely comprehensible human terms were undoubtedly of great importance in sustaining one's determination to observe the Law, *in themselves* they rarely, if ever, were able to move the nonobservant to observe, or the observant to persist in his observance in the face of long and burdensome hardships. Moralists and psychologists have wrestled with only indifferent success in their search for an answer to the question why Reason, when appealing only to those factors which are completely within the scope of its comprehension, is rarely adequate to the task of moving men consistently to observe even precepts which involve only a modicum of discomfort in comparison to the obvious beneficial results their observance entails. We shall not presume to be able to do what they have failed to do. We shall point only to those aspects of the question which are relevant to our purposes.

One of these aspects is reflected in the Rabbinic discussion of the cause that led to King Solomon's defections from the Law. Among the laws rationalized in the Torah, two refer to the conduct of the king. He was not to keep great numbers of horses, because that might lead to traffic with Egypt and the Lord had warned that "You must not go back that way again." Nor was the king to have many wives, "lest his heart go astray" after foreign gods (Deuteronomy 17:16–17). Since the purpose to be served by both these laws is thus clearly indicated, Solomon—the Rabbis say—decided that he could fulfill the purposes without obeying the laws.

A rationale implies that the law is subsidiary to the purpose it is intended to serve. This inevitably leads to the conclusion that it should be permissible to disregard the law if there appears to be an equally effective but less burdensome way to serve the indicated purpose. Very few human beings, from the very young to the very old, are so utterly bereft of ingenuity that they cannot envision achieving a desirable goal in a manner that appears less burdensome than the one suggested by teachers, elders or group experience. And very few people will refrain from choosing the easier path if there is nothing to prevent them from so doing.

Moreover, our most eleborate rationalizations of a law limit its significance to consequences already experienced or anticipated. But the consequences of any act are potentially infinite in number, and the nonforeseeable consequences of any act far outnumber the experienced and foreseeable ones. One of the fundamental components of the religious life is the faith that the beneficial but nonforeseeable results of an act which religion enjoins are far greater than any foreseeable results. Hence, when even the most ardent rationalist of the past insisted that the authority of the law rested not upon its humanly comprehended rationality but upon its divine origin, he was in effect saying that the authority of the law rested not upon our reason but upon divine Reason, that the rationality which we are able to attribute to the law is too narrow in scope to contain the divine Reason.

Our collective experience, in many crucial instances, has vindicated this position. All the beneficial consequences which resulted from the institution of the Sabbath for both Jews and mankind at large could not possibly have been foreseen two thousand years ago, when Jews were mocked for maintaining so "obviously foolish" an institution. The practice of circumcision, now almost universally adopted, was declared to be a relic of barbarism even by some of the founders of Reform Judaism. Jewish laws concerning relations between husband and wife are only now being rationized as physically and psychologically sound. The overtones of infinite meaning which our observant fathers subconsciously and intuitively experienced and which everyone who faithfully observes the Law experiences in a measure, can never be fully and cogently verbalized. The concept of revealed Law expresses an awareness of the reality of these intuitively experienced, but nonverbalized meanings, and transmutes them into a conscious source of inner strength indispensable to the observance of the Law over a long period of time and in the face of ever-present obstacles.

I repeatedly refer to the presence of obstacles, of immediate unpleasantnesses involved in the observance of the Law and to the need for each Jew to face up to them throughout his lifetime, because I believe this to be basic not only to the problem of Jewish existence, but also to that of living the good life. To be sure, one should, when expounding the Law, stress primarily its inherent rationality as reflected in the readily comprehensible beneficent consequences following upon its observance. However, an exposition of the Law which does not take into account the sacrifices which its observance often entails, reflects neither honest thinking nor sound pedagogy. The greatest harm we can do to anyone—child or adult—is to give him the impression that being an ethical person and a good Jew is easy, that it will involve him only in pleasant experiences. It is simply not true, and no one matures ethically and religiously until the unplesant experience is faced triumphantly.

Unpleasant experiences are inherent in the demands of the logically most acceptable laws, whether they be the laws requiring us to deal honestly in business transactions or those enjoining upon us abstention from work on the Sabbath. One must be naive indeed to imagine that resisting temptation of any kind is always a pleasant experience for anyone but the tried and tested saint.

Nor can all of our rationalizations of the traditional Sabbath as an invaluable boon to one's physical and spiritual welfare convince one that he ought not to harvest his fields or keep his place of business open on that day. These rationalizations undoubtedly help those who for other conscious or subconscious reasons are committed Sabbath observers, to persist in their observance. However, after more than four decades of rather intimate contact with thousands of Jewish laymen I cannot name a half-dozen who were moved by these rationalizations to become traditional Sabbath observers.

The intelligent, intellectually honest observer of the traditional pattern of Jewish life was always conscious of the sacrifice, the immediate hardships which it involved. He was always equally conscious of the fact that he could avoid them by rejecting the Law. Moreover, as Dr. Cohen points out, there is no acceptable "remedy within the Law" for some of the unpleasantnesses which at times are inevitably involved in its observance, even as there is no morally acceptable "remedy" for the unpleasantness involved in returning found money when the owner is known and the finder can be discovered only by his own admission.

The Law was not intended to be either the lackey of our mundane physical needs and passions—though it is in no way their enemy—nor even of our nobler impulses and aspirations, though it unquestionably buttresses and sustains them. Its purpose is to make us servants of the Lord. This attitude which is repeatedly expressed by the Rabbis is perhaps most pointedly refected in the injunction that "he who says 'have pity upon us even as Thou dost pity the bird' (Deuteronomy 22:6–7) is to be silenced" (*Berakhot* 33b). No one has been more consistent than the Rabbis in teaching that God is a merciful and loving Father. Why, then, did they reject so appealing a rationalization of the Deuteronomic law? Because, as one of the Rabbis in the Talmud there puts it, "This would rouse jealousy among God's creatures" since God seemed to have favored one creature, the mother bird, above others. If the laws of the Torah are to be understood in terms of God's mercy, how explain the fact that the Torah permits us to slaughter animals for food? (see Maimonides, *Commentary on the Mishnah, ad loc.*). Did God's mercy fail Him when He permitted us the flesh of sheep? Above all, was it merciful of God to demand that Jews choose to live lives of poverty and persecution, rather than to violate the Sabbath or accept baptism?

The historic experiences of the Jewish people have always compelled them to grapple with the paradox that the God of mercy commanded them to perform acts which, from the human point of view, all too often proved not to be merciful either to the actor or those acted upon. The concept of revealed Law enabled our fathers not only to live with this paradox but also to accept both terms of it as valid. It matured them as men and sustained them spiritually in their heroic efforts to live ethically as Jews, even though being Jews and living ethically often involved great sacrifices.

This, then, is the second vital need which the concept of a revealed Law served in the life of our fathers. It was the ultimate rationale for the hardships which being a Jew and living a moral life inevitably and under the best of circumstances entail.

The third, universal human need profoundly experienced by our fathers which the concept of revealed Law helped to satisfy was the need to feel that human life had ultimate significance, that man was not created to "labor in vain nor to bring forth confusion" (Isaiah 65:23), that their mundane concerns as well as their noble aspirations had cosmic significance. The quality of one's life depends not merely upon his recognition that he is not God, but equally upon his conviction that he is, as the Rabbis put it, God's partner in the universe, and that God looks to him for aid in completing His creation. In obeying a natural law discovered by science, we avoid physical pain and frustration. In obeying the revealed Law of Judaism, our fathers undoubtedly experienced the *simhah shel mitzvah,* the joy in the performance of *mitzvot.* But when obedience involved pain, they were sustained by the conviction that they were acting as the partners of the Creator of the Universe.

Man cannot possibly feel that his actions are of cosmic significance if he can relate them all to a purpose satisfying his immediate, mundane, completely comprehensible needs. Man cannot escape a sense of futility and menainglessness unless he transcends his biologically felt and rationally comprehended wants. This inevitably involves the subjection of oneself to demands that contradict one's immediate, biologically rooted personal satisfactions. Subjugation to such demands makes sense only when those demands are given cosmic significance. It was the concept of the revealed Law which alone was capable of transmuting the mundane suffering involved in living as a Jew in the here and now into transcendent spiritual joy not only in contemplation of future rewards but in the actual here and now.

These, then, were the psychological and emotional needs of the individual Jew to which the concept of a revealed Law proved heretofore to be intellectually the most adequate, and emotionally the most effective response. But, in meeting these needs of the individual Jew, the concept simultaneously performed an indispensable service to the Jewish people. *By bestowing finality and irrevocability upon the basic pattern of Jewish life, it became the most important single factor in the preservation of the Jewish people.*

A Pattern of Life

Every people which becomes conscious of its identity as a group associates its self-identity primarily with one or all of three factors: (a) the territory it occupies, (b) the language it speaks and (c) the pattern of life which distinguishes it from other groups. These three factors are not of equal importance in the life of any one group; nor does any one of the three factors play an equally important role in the lives of all groups. By and large, territory has been the strongest single factor bestowing self-consciousness upon a group as long as it occupies that territory and is determined to defend it. Severance of a whole people or of significant segments of it from the native soil, whether voluntary or compulsory, usually has been followed by disintegration of the exiled groups's self-identity. If a significant portion of the group continued to live on its native soil, nostalgic attachment to the land of origin would continue to bind the dispersed segments to that group. But such nostalgic attachment usually has never persisted beyond the second or third generation, after which the dispersed segments either were completely assimilated within the larger community of which they were a part, or, like the French Canadians and South African Dutchmen, began to think of themselves as a distinct entity having no particular allegiance to any other large group. Immigrant groups in America maintain only the most tenuous ties with their country of origin beyond the second generation.

In comparatively recent times, language has become an unprecedentedly important factor for conscious group identity. Attachment to language today rivals attachment to soil in intensity. Many leaders consider it to be the most significant factor maintaining the self-identity of their groups. Hence, the desperate attempts of the Irish to revive the knowledge and use of Gaelic among the Irish everywhere, and of Jews to revive the knowledge and use of Hebrew among Jews everywhere. But no people thus far has succeeded in maintaining a widespread knowledge and use of its language among those of its members living as a minority in societies where they are free to mingle with the majority group.

The factor bestowing self-consciousness upon a group that seems to have the greatest vitality and the greatest power of adaptability is the group's pattern of life. Though the pattern as a whole is usually discarded, some aspects of it linger long after attachment to land or language has disappeared. Scotsmen who never have visited Scotland and no longer speak Scottish will, on set occasions, sport their bagpipes and kilts. Dutchmen who do not know their language and have never visited Holland will adorn their communities and their homes with miniature models of windmills, with wooden shoes and with tulips. Irishmen who have no knowledge of Gaelic and no particular attachment to Ireland will continue to delight in the green on St. Patrick's Day.

This attachment to a distinctive group pattern of life or some aspect of it, universally tenacious as it is, was never as pervasive and determinative of the group's destiny as it proved to be in the case of the Jewish people. Moreover, the Jewish pattern of life was so marvelously constructed that both land and language were an integral part of it and continued through it to function as vital factors in the life of the people. Thus the Hebrew language was preserved because it was an indispensable element in the pattern of life established by the revealed Law. The Torah had to be read publicly in Hebrew. Public prayer had to be recited in Hebrew. The earliest Jewish Diaspora communities retained their attachment to the land only insofar as it played a significant role in the pattern of life they continued to live, that is, only insofar as it was the goal of a religious pilgrimage or played a part in the celebration of a festival or in the prayers of the Synagogue. When they lost interest in that pattern of life, their interest in the land also inevitably ceased. Hence, while the land and language continued to play an important role in the life and thought of the Jews, they did so until recent times only because they were part of a pattern of life believed to have been established by a revealed Law and therefore possessing ultimate, irrevocable significance. When, in the past, faith in the ultimate significance of that pattern of life died, concern for the language and the land withered and died with it.

The concept of a revealed Law has fallen into disrepute among Jews in our day, resulting in widespread disaffection from the Jewish pattern of life and ultimately from the Jewish people. This fact has caused a widespread search for a substitute. A number of substitutes have been offered; chief among them are: (a) Jewish nationhood or the more innocuous concept of Jewish peoplehood,[5] (b) the Hebrew language and (c) concern for the State of Israel. Undoubtedly these have been the most powerful antidotes to Jewish group disintegration within the last three generations. Nor have they yet run their beneficent course. Fortunately they still have, and for a long time may continue to have, considerable vigor and vitality.

Each of these three factors has inherent virtue which everyone concerned with the preservation of the Jewish people is in duty bound to cherish and to nurture. But neither history nor contemporary experience offers cogent reasons leading us to believe that any one or all of them can displace the authentic pattern of Jewish life as established by the Law, as the bond of meaningful Jewish self-identity either for the individual or for the community. Each one of these factors—significant as it unquestionably is—will, when separated from the authentic pattern of Jewish life as established by the Law, at best flourish but briefly like a flower separated from its roots. I believe, therefore, that the preservation of the Jewish people anywhere in the world depends upon the preservation of the basic pattern of Jewish life as established by the Law. I believe, moreover, that it was the concept of the revealed Law which sustained our fathers in their allegiance to the pattern of life established by the Law, and that neither we nor our descendants will remain loyal to it unless we set at the heart of our philosophy of life either the concept of the revealed Law as conceived by our fathers or some acceptable but equally cogent, modern version of it. Whether such an "equally cogent, modern version" can be formulated is the question which should be at the very heart of the concern of all those who are interested in the future of the Jews and the Jewish religion. I believe that it can be done.

To those who look to the State of Israel and to the Hebrew language as the future substitutes for the traditional Jewish pattern of life as established by the Law, and who not only reject the traditional version of the concept of a revealed Law but also do not believe that a modern, cogent version of it can be formulated, I venture to offer an analogy which, though imperfect as all analogies of necessity are, I find helpful and suggestive. I hope they, too, will find it helpful.

The relationship of the Jewish people to the pattern of life established by the Law is analogous in four essential aspects to the relationship of the Jewish people to the Hebrew language and the land of Israel. The relationship in each case (a) is final and irrevocable; (b) its origin is beyond the reach of reason; (c) it *can* be tampered with but only to a limited extent, without dangerously impairing the vitality of Judaism and the Jewish people; (d) its maintenance involved repeated and serious sacrifices.

The Zionist Movement, against all considerations of "common sense" determined early in its career that the relationship between the Jewish people and the Hebrew language and *Eretz Yisrael* is final and irrevocable. There was no rationally compelling argument against the position of the Territorialists in 1900, or against that of the Yiddishists when more than three-quarters of the Jewish people spoke Yiddish, or against those who advocated the use of a European language for the Technion in Haifa in 1913. But Zionists based their contention upon the logically unprovable conviction that there can be no significant sense of continuity and self-identity for the Jewish people except as it is related to the Land of Israel and the Hebrew language. The relationship of a people to its language is not, in its origin, a matter of conscious choice. It belongs to the eternal mysteries which surround all of human life. Nor does the Tradition envision the origin of the relationship of the Jewish people with the Land of Israel as having been a matter of the people's conscious choice. The Tradition attributes the establishment of that relationship to a Divine act of grace. There are Zionists who prefer another explanation for the origin of the relationship between the people of Israel and the Land of Israel. They agree, however, with those Zionists who do accept the Tradition in this—that this relationship once having been established assumes a finality and an irrevocability whose validity can not be successfully challenged by an appeal to reason. It is a relationship whose essential quality is beyond the reach of reason. Reason plays only a secondary role in determining whether one accepts or rejects the irrevocability of that relationship.

But the finality and irrevocability of the relationship do not imply fixity and rigidity in the related factors. The related factors undergo constant change. The Jewish people is, as a biological entity, certainly not the same today as it was two thousand years ago. No one at all acquainted with the vicissitudes of Jewish history can deny the obvious fact that the Jewish people has over the centuries received large admixtures of so-called non-Jewish blood, through proselytization, intermarriage, and the ravages of pogroms and wars. And yet those admixtures were never at any time so great as to destroy the sense of ethnic kinship among the people. This biological admixture is continuing today for the same reasons and with the same effects as in the past. The new elements made their impress but did not destroy the people's sense of essential biological continuity. There are those who like to believe that the Jewish people represent a "racially pure" group and who look askance at the acceptance of any non-Jew into the fellowship of the Jewish people. And there are those who would open the doors wide to admit anyone at all into that fellowship without requiring any more of the newcomer than a statement that he would want to be counted as one of us. And there are those who are ready to accept non-Jews into the fellowship of the Jewish people but only on condition that it would not lead to the destruction of the essential character of that fellowship. They, I believe, represent the mainstream of Jewish historic continuity.

Nor is the Hebrew language the same today as it was two thousand or even a hundred years ago or as it will be a generation from now. The prevalent differences of opinion regarding changes in the Hebrew language are substantially the same as those regarding changes in the Jewish pattern of life. There are purists who would preserve the vocabulary and grammatical structure intact as it came to us from the past, using only old Hebrew roots and combinations of them to express new terms. Others would introduce foreign elements with almost reckless thoughtlessness. Some would even change the script. There are those who would have the people at large, rather than the Hebrew Language Academy determine the proper grammatical structure and vocabulary. However, the overwhelming majority seem to acknowledge the inevitability of linguistic change and want merely to control its frequency and character so that there will be no radical break with the inner genius of the language. They differ only in what would constitute a radical break.

The land, too, is undergoing change. The State of Israel today is neither the country of David nor of the Maccabees. New "holy places" are appearing. The country is being industrialized and mechanized. One can no longer experience there the very sights, smells and sounds that our ancestors experienced in the days of King David or of the Maccabees or even in the days before the rise of the State of Israel. Some people refuse to be reconciled to the changes in the land's borders. Some bemoan its complete modernization. But even those who welcome some or all of the changes agree that Jerusalem as capital could not be replaced by any other city, even as Uganda never could have become a new *Eretz Yisrael.*

Similarly, the pattern of Jewish life will undergo change, as it has in the past. But its essential character must be preserved. What that essential character consists of will remain subject to discussion among those interested in its preservation. To me it seems certain that the Synagogue, the Hebrew language, the Sabbath, holy days and festivals, the dietary laws, the laws of Jewish marriage and divorce, and vital concern for the Jewish autonomous community in *Eretz Yisrael* are among its indispensable elements. There may be variations of emphasis in regard to each one of these elements. But whoever would set a pattern of Jewish life which completely omits any of these is, in my opinion, striking a blow at the vital center of the whole pattern.

Can this pattern be maintained without some version of the concept of revealed Law? At one time I blithely might have answered, "Yes," though intuitively I always had very grave doubts. Today I am as convinced as it is possible for a human being to be in such matters, that it cannot. And since I am equally convinced that with the disintegration of the Jewish pattern of life the Jewish people will disintegrate, I believe that every thinking Jew—if he is to remain a *profoundly committed* Jew regardless of where he lives—must come to terms intellectually and emotionally with the concept of a revealed Law, either as formulated by the Tradition or with some version of it which is more acceptable to him and serves his intellectual and emotional needs as effectively as the traditional concept served our fathers. The fundamental task of Jewish spiritual and intellectual leaders of every generation is to help their generation to come to terms with this concept in a constructive, positive manner.[6] Dr. Boaz Cohen's volume, *Law and Tradition in Judaism,* is a very important contribution to the all-too-meager literature on this subject.

Notes

1. This chapter originally appeared as an article in *Conservative Judaism,* vol. xix, No. 1 (Fall 1964), pp. 36–50

2. New York: The Jewish Theological Seminary of America, 1959.

3. See "God, Man, Torah, and Israel." in *Foundation of a Faith* (NY: Burning Bush Press, 1967).

4. *Sefer Ha-Yovel Li-Yehezhel Kaufmann* (Jerusalem: The Magnes Press-Hebrew University, 1960), pp. 9 ff.

5. See the chapter on "The Concept of K'lal Yisrael" in *Foundations of a Faith.*

6. See note 3 above.

LOUIS FINKELSTEIN suggests that Hillel's concept of Torah as a commentary to the commandment to love one's neighbor, is to perceive Torah as a symbolic way of expressing the commandment or imperative of love of humanity and of God. Even the Biblical proposition that all men were created in God's image is an "efficient" symbol, for it does not only symbolize love but also leads one to love; not connoting merely an abstract idea of worth or equality, but imbues us with love of man. The principle effect of Torah is "preoccupation with learning how to love man"; through study of the Law for the sake of observance, the Jew engenders love of fellowman in preparation for the rare occasions when one can express it. We show our love of God by loving His children. Within halachah, the approach of Hillel has been the dominant trend of thought. Finkelstein observes that study of the Torah not only teaches men to love one another, but enables them to perceive that "love for men reaches its climax" in bringing them near to the study of Torah. While the Shammaite approach to halachah stressed fear of God over love of Him and obedience over understanding, the anthropocentricism of Hillelite theology and the theocentricism of Shammaite theology both seek to raise the standards of human conduct in order that the glory of God become "most clearly manifest on earth."

195

Judaism as a System of Symbols

LOUIS FINKELSTEIN

The purpose of this paper is to analyze the system of symbolic actions and conduct, which is basic to Judaism. I hope that in this way new light may be shed both on the role of symbols in the communication of ideas, and on the nature of the Jewish faith.

About two thousand years ago, a pagan approached the most learned Jewish sage of his day, Hillel, with a strange proposal. "Teach me the whole of the Torah* in as short a time as I can stand on one leg," he said, "and I will become a proselyte." "The whole of the Torah," replied Hillel, "consists of the commandment, 'Do to no one what is distasteful to thee.' All the rest is commentary. Proceed to study it."

From the point of view of his status as a man and the perfection of his soul, the pagan who addressed Hillel, and became a proselyte, gained no advantage whatever. He accepted new obligations as a Jew, to fol-

*In this paper, I use the term, *Torah*, in its traditional sense, as encompassing the whole of the Jewish religious tradition—Scripture, Talmud, commentaries on both, discussions of learned problems in both, Rabbinical responsa, and indeed anything relating to the religious life. In a sense, as will be seen below, the term might be even more comprehensive, for science, social science, and any other pursuit become *Torah*, if studied in order to understand religious truth. However, I should add that in Judaism the study and practice of Torah expected from a member of the faith involve all the ritual and legal, as well as moral commandments, whereas those which constitute Torah for the rest of the world involve in effect only the moral law. A pagan who studies the Torah stands higher than a high priest, according to a famous maxim of the Talmud; but obviously the Torah which elevates the non-Jew to this high status, does not include the ritual commandments, which have no relevance for him. Hence all the advantages which the study of Torah (including its ritual) bestows on Jews are bestowed also on Gentiles, who are concerned with the study and application of the moral law. In the discussion below, therefore, whenever the word, *Torah,* is used, the reader must bear in mind that it has one meaning when relating to Jews (who are under obligation to observe the ritual), and another, when relating to the rest of the world, which need not concern itself with Jewish ritual.

The summary of the Torah was given by Hillel to the pagan in the Palestinian vernacu-

196

low the ritual commandments. But, presumably, he was among the "pious of the peoples of the world" or he would not have approached Hillel with his curious request, in the first place. In that event, his contribution as servant of God was not less than it became after his proselytization and acceptance of all the commandments. In effect, from this point of view, generally but not universally held in early Rabbinic sources, the relation of humanity to the Jews (so far as religion and Torah are concerned) may be compared to that of the Jews themselves to the Aaronid priests among them. The latter have some special commandments to observe, and therefore a status of their own. But their piety, if they fulfil all their commandments, is not greater than that of the rest of the Jews, who fulfil those obligatory for themselves. Only in so far as one may consider the "multiplication of commandments" a form of sanctification or special dedication, can the Aaronid priest be said to occupy a privileged position among men. He is, as it were, in a position of special peril, charged with particularly laborious service, and he may rightly regard this as an advantage and sanctification for which to be grateful. So the Jews, generally, charged with many commandments and exposed to many perils, may feel that this is an opportunity for service to God, for which they should be particularly grateful. But in viewing the human scene as a whole, it is obvious that, provided each person performs the duties assigned him, there is in reality no difference of status among men before God. All acquire the same immortality on the same *relative* terms—that is, the study and fulfilment of the commandments which they are obligated to perform.

---

lar of the day, Aramaic. In fact, Hillel was simply quoting one of the standard Aramaic versions of the commandment, "Thou shalt love thy neighbor as thyself." The ancient Aramaic translator had paraphrased the Hebrew original, so as to make its generalizations precise and concrete. Thus Hillel was actually saying that the commandment, "Thou shalt love thy neighbor as thyself," was the all inclusive principle of the Torah. This view was made explicit by a later disciple of Hillel's School, the foremost sage of his own time, Rabbi Akiba.

The expression, "All the rest is commentary," requires analysis. Hillel, obviously a meticulously observant Jew, did not mean to depreciate the rest of the commandments. For him, a scholar of first rank, a commentary was not a matter of slight importance—without it the text would be unintelligible. The point he was making, apparently, was that the whole Torah derived its meaning from the light it shed on the principle of universal human love. To fast on the Day of Atonement, to pray, to believe in God, to observe the Sabbath and the dietary laws, are not ends in themselves; they are means of bringing human beings to greater love of one another. This is, of course, what the Prophet had said many centuries earlier, when he declared that the fast which God desires is one which leads to breaking the bonds of wickedness, to helping the needy, to freeing the crushed.

Symbols as Commentary

Hillel's concept of the Torah as commentary to the commandment to love one's neighbor implies, I believe, the belief that all of Judaism is either a symbolic way of expressing that commandment, or a validation of it. The commandment itself, as Bertrand Russell remarks, is simply a proposition in the imperative form. It is an assertion that all men are deservant of love. This proposition can be stated in words; it can also be enacted in life. It can be made more meaningful, through analysis of its basic premises. All this, according to Hillel, is the real function of the rest of the Torah. The ritual and moral commandments, and the legal system of the Torah are dramatizations of the belief in human dignity; and the narrative portions offer a validation of the belief. This validation, important in itself, is, from the viewpoint of Torah, merely a symbolic way of expressing its central idea.

From his experience as student and teacher, Hillel knew that a very important way of communicating value-judgments was to demonstrate their validity. An ethical norm becomes immensely more significant, when one understands why one is asked to follow it. The belief that all men are deservant of respect or affection is an abstraction, appealing to the mind, but it achieves powerful influence over the whole person, when associated with the emotionally satisfying concept that all men are children of God. Thus, while the belief that man is made "in the image of God" has its own validity, and philosophically speaking is significant in its own right, from the point of view of ethical conduct, it is a symbol, a means of communicating the duty of love for human kind, and at the same time inculcating that love, and making it easier to accept. It is therefore what might be called an "efficient" symbol, in that it not merely connotes the idea, it also is capable of imbuing one with it.

Accordingly, even that part of the Torah which merely validates the idea of universal human love, also symbolizes it.

Preoccupation with Love

The love for man which Hillel regarded as the most comprehensive principle in Judaism is not sentimental sympathy with weakness or mere pity. To love man, we learn from other sayings of Hillel, is to elicit from him that which is noblest in him. " Be of the disciples of Aaron," he taught, "loving peace, pursuing peace, loving man, and *bring-*

ing them nearer to the Torah." Obviously, the greatest kindness we can offer our fellows is what we should seek for ourselves. We have to love our fellows as we love ourselves, not in some other way—for true love for ourselves is not self-pity nor self-indulgence, but understanding the meaning of life, and fulfilling our potentialities. Love for our fellows also means bringing them nearer to that understanding and that fulfilment.

The Torah to which men are "brought near" by those who love them is not merely the observance of the commandments, but more especially study of them. The ritual and moral systems of the Torah derive their importance for mankind particularly through the opportunity they afford for devotion to the analysis of the good life and of just behavior. In this concern for the good life and just behavior, man attains his real perfection, which is only incidentally, though quite inevitably, expressed in the application of his discoveries to the daily business of life. Just as true love of parent for child can find positive expression in action only on occasion, and is usually limited either to negative non-interference, or to contemplation of the child, planning for it, thinking about it—all intellectual efforts—so love for man, generally, can find concrete expression in positive behavior only from time to time; while during the rest of life, this love is expressed either negatively, by refraining from injury to one's neighbor, or in the positive study of how to help him.

The obligation to love one's neighbor and bring him near the Torah is clarified by the fact that in the study of Torah, one not only fulfils one's duty, but also one's self. The student of Torah discovers in the process not merely how to help others, but a supreme delight, which, in his affection for mankind, he desires to be shared by the rest of it. The situation might resemble that of a man who, deeply in love, is preoccupied with the desire to please his beloved, but also wants her to share the delight which being-in-love gives him; and who therefore seeks to elicit from her an ability to love, even if he should not be the object of it.

Because preoccupation with learning how to love man is the principal theme of the Torah, occasional differences of judgment about the application of that love to particular situations are not too significant. As we shall see, these differences are in part related to differences in situation. What may be love in one age may not be in another; what may be helpful in certain regions, and to people with one cultural background may be harmful to others. Even disagreements arising in abstract judgment reflect the fact that rational men of goodwill may differ regarding the application to a specific situation of the general principles of Torah. Such disagreement may be the result of the finitude of the human mind, and should be accepted with the resignation with which one accepts man's mortality and his other limitations.

The belief that study of Torah is man's preeminent duty and his supreme fulfilment, implied in the various sayings of Hillel, is explicitly and emphatically stated by Rabbi Akiba. According to him, study of the Torah is more important than obedience to it. Although in time of persecution, one may find oneself unable to observe the Torah, one must never desist from the duty of studying or teaching it. Hence, Rabbi Akiba died a martyr to his desire to teach the Law, not in an effort publicly to observe it.

Hillel's principle thus becomes paradoxical. He regards the commandments of the Torah as symbols, expressing love for man; but the study and teaching of those symbols, while themselves commandments and therefore means for expressing love for man, are also the fulfilment of universal human love.

Conceived in these terms, love for man cannot be distinguished from love for God. At the moment of his martyrdom, Rabbi Akiba declared that he accepted his fate gladly, because in his death he was vindicating his love for God. The commandment, "And thou shalt love the Lord, thy God, with all thy heart, and with all thy soul, and with all thy might," was for him identical with the commandment, "Thou shalt love thy neighbor as thyself."

We frequently symbolize affection to our friends by expressing affection for their children; and we can indicate our love for God in no more effective manner than by developing love for His children. On the other hand, the kindest contribution we can make to the lives of our friends' children may be the development of better relationships between them and their parents; and the foremost love we can show men is to help them find in themselves love for their Father Who is in Heaven.

Study of the Torah teaches men how to love one another; love for men reaches its climax in bringing them near to the study of Torah. In the process of study, man cannot but come to love God; yet the purpose of study is to develop an understanding of the love of man.

Fear of God

Because Hillel believed that the observance of the commandments is not an aim in itself, but an intricate symbolism, inculcating love for man, he felt that fear of God was not enough. Fear of God may lead to the observance of His commandments; it cannot make them the means for developing love of one's fellowmen. To have the effect of communicating the feeling of love for one's fellowmen, the symbols have to be carried out, not in fear, but in love—love of God. Fostered by the study and teaching of Torah, this love inevitably stimulates them. The commandment, "and thou shalt love the Lord, thy God," is followed at once by the commandment, "And thou shalt teach them (the commandments) diligently unto your children, talking of them, when thou sittest in thy house, and when thou walkest by the way, and when thou liest down, and when thou risest up."

The approach to Judaism thus far described, was maintained by the School of Hillel, but vehemently opposed, in virtually every one of its implications, by the School of Shammai. It is probable that had Shammai been asked to name a single commandment, in which all the others were included, and had he consented to do so, he would have selected not, "And thou shalt love thy neighbor as thyself," but "And thou shalt love the Lord, thy God." However, for Shammai, this commandment itself meant something very different from what it meant for Hillel. For Shammai and his following, God, not man, gives meaning to existence; and it is in terms of God alone that man can formulate his duty. Whereas for Hillel and his disciples, the world is essentially a school in which man can attain perfection and our duty is to help him attain that perfection; for Shammai the world is a temple or palace, in which everything depends on how the Master is served. For Hillel obedience to God's will is important, because in that way man develops devotion to Him; and in the study of the ways in which God's will is to be performed in the world, man achieves self-perfection, and through instruction can bestow perfection also on his neighbor. For Shammai, devotion to God derives its meaning from the fact that it leads to obedience to His commandments, and this obedience is the aim of human existence.

The School of Shammai therefore held that love of God was not enough; it was necessary also to fear Him, so that one obeyed Him implicitly and under all cirumstances. Study of the Torah was important only in so far as it was necessary to know how to perform the com-

mandments; it had no virtue in itself. Therefore, according to this
School, it was unnecessary to instruct everyone in the Torah. Study of
the Torah could be reserved for priests and other privileged groups. In
fact, it was unwise and unjust to encourage the poor to study, for the
time they devoted to study was necessarily taken from their daily work,
and meant increased suffering for them and their families.

To the School of Shammai the repeated commandment of the Torah
to love God meant simply to be devoted to Him, as a loyal slave is devoted to his master. Such devotion is not easily distinguished from
"fear" or "awe." The slave trained to obey can scarcely distinguish his
unwillingness to anger his master from the desire to please him.

Just as for Hillel the Torah is a symbolic system, expressing in various ways the basic principle that all men must be loved, for Shammai
the Torah is a symbolic system, expressing the idea that God must be
obeyed. For Hillel and his School, a commandment to be performed
properly must be understood and appreciated; obedience, without
such understanding is not helpful. Shammai insisted that even babies
had to observe the ritual commandments, because it is the formal obedience to the commandment which counts and in which God's power
to compel obedience to His will is made manifest. Hence, when Shammai's grandson was born during the *Sukkot* festival, the happy grandfather removed the ceiling of the room in which the child lay and covered it with boughs and leaves, so that he might dwell in a booth, in accordance with the Law. (The Law does not require women to dwell in
booths during the festival; so that Shammai did not insist on performing the ritual for the mother.) It is said that the School of Shammai
would make babies of two and three fast on the Day of Atonement.

For both Schools, Judaism or the Torah is a symbolic system, expressing basic ideas, primarily in the form of commanded behavior. Whatever its basic theme, Judaism expresses it most naturally not in propositions, but in gesture; its ideas are formulated in a series of forms
which must be acted out as in a pageant, not articulated as verbal assertions.

The dominant principle of the Torah, whether love for man or obedience to God, obviously expresses itself in every commandment—ritual,
moral, or legal. But perhaps we may take it that from the viewpoint of
the School of Hillel, the legal and moral law reflects the ideas of the
Torah directly, and the ritual system only indirectly. From the viewpoint of the School of Shammai, the contrary is true. The ritual system

of sacrifice and observance reflects the principle of fear of God most directly. The legal and moral systems suggest that fear, indirectly,
through the just relations they impose on the children of God.

Poetry and Prose

Ritual observance may be positive or negative, and both types have
their role in the human pageant. The positive commandments (such as
eating unleavened bread on the first night of Passover, or dwelling in
booths during the Feast of Tabernacles, or reciting the prayers, or the
ancient offering of sacrifices in the Temple) have the great virtue of em-
phatic declaration of the truths inculcated in the whole Torah. Holy
days, holy places, holy vessels, holy rituals, derive their sacredness
from the fact that they make men especially mindful of the meaning of
life and the Torah. The negative ritual commandments (such as refraining from forbidden food, forbidden marriages, and forbidden actions of various kinds) have the merit of continuity. Their symbolism is
not vivid, but it is uninterrupted. They are the prose of the Torah; the
positive commandments are its poetry. In the observance of the negative commandments, whether ritualistic or ethical, one is always re-
minded of one's relationship to God; in the observance of the positive
ritual and ethical commandments, one is permeated with the deepest
meanings of the Torah.

From the time of Ben Sira, it has been customary to express this idea
in somewhat different phraseology. To observe the negative commandments, he suggests, is to express fear of God, whereas to observe the
positive ones is to express love for Him. I believe that this "fear"
signifies constant awareness of God, and that "love" means especially
profound emotional attachment, which can come only at rare seasons,
and which as a constant state would be beyond virtually any human
being. The relation of man to God in this respect is analogous to human relationships. A faithful husband, wife, friend, or citizen will never violate his loyalty through any act which might betray the trust
placed in him. But it is only at special times that an opportunity arises
to exhibit positively and fully one's devotion to one's spouse, friend, or
country.

The moral commandments differ from the ritualistic ones in being,
so to speak, onomatopoeic, at least for men of Western culture. Thus

the prohibition of murder suggests the sanctity of life, with a clarity and directness which the ritual of the Day of Atonement, for example, may lack. The former needs no verbal commentary to explain its meaning; the latter does. Of the former, the Rabbinic sages consider that they are "commandments, which if they were not written down, could have been arrived at through reason"; the latter are commandments which "the nations of the world and the evil impulse are continually challenging" as arbitrary and meaningless. The language of the former is universal, that of the latter particular.

The legal commandments or institutions have the same general purpose as the moral and ritualistic ones. They are propositions in action, and are thus symbols, expressing basic ideas of the Torah. In a way, they should be the most easily understood part of the Torah, for they belong to the general realm of law and jurisprudence. As Justice Cardozo points out, every judge is in effect a philosopher (though he may not know it), for in his effort to apply the law to particular cases, he is inevitably giving effect to a special outlook on life. (We have seen in fact that to a certain degree this is true of every human being, because everyone is constantly making decisions with regard to conduct, and these decisions, dealing with moral, ritualistic, or simply polite relations of life, express in their own way basic ideas regarding life and existence.)

The principles underlying the Torah as a whole, and opposing philosophies of the different Pharisaic Schools, are perhaps better expressed in the legal decisions than in any other part of the Torah. Thus the view of Shammai that a principal who asks an agent to violate the law is responsible for the crime, is opposed by the School of Hillel, as an invasion of the rule of individual human responsibility, and therefore individual human dignity. The perpetrator of a wrong is penalized in the Hillelite view in order to bring him to repentance or as a deterrent from crime. Punishment is justified as a means of education. Therefore, the agent, if a rational person, through appropriate punishment should either himself be taught, or be made an example for others to learn the principle that God's commandments must be given preference over those of any individual.

Again, the School of Shammai holds that if a person steals material for a building and uses it in construction, he does not fulfil his duty of repentance unless he returns the actual material to the original owner, even though in the process he must destroy his own building. The School of Hillel, sympathizing with the repentant wrongdoer, permits him to repay the costs of the stolen material. Here again, the School of Shammai vigorously asserts the right of a person to his property, wherever it may be; and that it is the duty of one who has taken wrongful posession to return the property regardless of cost. The School of Hillel is more concerned with repentance than with the return of property; and, in order to make repentance feasible, permits payment in money, rather than the return of the stolen goods.

From the point of view of the School of Shammai, man's great limitations are a fatal misfortune. In the nature of things, man is never, or rarely, the perfect servant. The consciousness of failure, or, to use the theological expression, of sinfulness, should accordingly weigh heavily on all of us. Our only hope even for partial escape from sinfulness lies in this consciousness. A great part of the world, if I interpret the views of the School of Shammai correctly, will, according to it, suffer severe punishment in afterlife for its many derelictions in this life. Only the few whose merits outweigh their sins will receive reward in a resurrected world. Because the chances of man to escape sinfulness and failure are so few, because he is so likely to court everlasting penalties in the future, because he can scarcely hope to please his Maker, it would, according to the School of Shammai, have been better for him not to have been created. But, as man's existence is not really significant in itself, that fact was not a reasonable argument against his creation. The question was whether his creation served a purpose beyond himself; and apparently it did, or it would not have occurred.

This emphasis on man's sin and inadequacy is foreign to the thought of the School of Hillel. From its point of view, man's imperfection is his opportunity. Had he been perfect, there would be no need for study and for teaching the Torah, and the human process would have ended before it began. The Torah was not given to the angels, because they do not need it; their very perfection prevents them from enjoying the supreme bliss of life, which is the study of how to achieve perfection. No matter how inadequate man's performance may be, his striving for adequacy, and his desire to understand how to live, makes his journey through the world a useful and rewarding enterprise. In the school of life, prizes are awarded not for proficiency, which depends on external circumstances, but for effort. Like a child in a kindergarten, man need not be ashamed of his errors or his ignorance. Youth, inexperience, and impediments are his challenges; without them, life would not be an education at all, but a state. Hence, the School of Hillel taught that it was good for man to have been created. No matter how much he may

suffer, no matter how sadly he may fail, he has the opportunity of striving and learning: and that is what counts.

Man's striving to perfection is itself perfection; for perfection, so far
as the temporal world is concerned, consists of progress toward fulfilment, not of fulfilment. But, the School of Hillel maintained, the man
who has striven, studied, and performed the commandments to the
best of his ability, in the course of temporal life will also have achieved
more than fulfilment in this world—he will also gain immortality of
the soul. The effort to attain a just life, through study, is thus not only
an end in itself, in that it makes the temporal life significant, it also
leads to an endless existence in a future, spiritual realm.

Nature and History

The belief that the good life symbolizes basic ideas is associated with
the belief that existence, as a whole, has a theme and is essentially a
symbol. This approach to existence is fundamental to the Hebraic tradition, and is responsible for the unique interpretation put on the
world, life, and history, by the Prophets, and the Pharisaic and Talmudic scholars.

One of the most effective expressions of this conviction is to be
found in the Nineteenth Psalm:

The heavens declare the glory of God,
And the firmament showeth His handiwork;
Day unto day uttereth speech,
And night unto night revealeth knowledge;
There is no speech, there are no words,
Neither is their voice heard.
Their line is gone out through all the earth,
And their words to the end of the world.
In them hath He set a tent for the sun,
Which is as a bridegroom coming out of his chamber,
And rejoiceth as a strong man to run his course.
His going forth is from the end of the heaven,
And his circuit unto the ends of it;
And there is nothing hid from the heat thereof.

The law of the Lord is perfect, restoring the soul;
The testimony of the Lord is sure, making wise the simple.

The precepts of the Lord are right, rejoicing the heart;
The commandment of the Lord is pure, enlightening the eyes.

Whether the juxtaposition of the hymn in praise of Torah and that in praise of Nature was the work of the original author of this Psalm or a later editor (as held by many modern students), is irrelevant. In its present form, the Psalm asserts that the theme, symbolized by Nature, as a whole, and that symbolized by the Torah, as a way of life, are identical. The identity of purpose between existence as a whole, and the Torah as a series of commandments, is one of the favorite themes of the Rabbinic homily or *midrash*. The midrash expresses this idea allegorically when it maintains that before creating the world God consulted the Torah. In fact, one of God's daily concerns, like that of a pious Jew, is study of Torah, and instruction in it for the righteous who are in Paradise!

The Divine process and the human process have the same theme; in the study and pursuit of Torah, man is simply carrying out in his own life the purposes which God had in mind in the creation of the world.

Rightly understood, nature and human history are thus each a revelation of God's will and a commentary on each other. The effort to interpret history as a revelation of the Divine process fills a large part of Scripture, and is one of the main themes of the Rabbinic *aggadah* or legend. The Torah is not limited to the commandments, because it involves more than a system of human behavior. It also involves a philosophy of existence itself.

The history of the world and particulary of Israel, as given in Scripture, and elaborated in the Talmudic writings, is not therefore a mere chronicle, composed for man's amusement or to satisfy his curiosity. It is an effort to give man a point of view. Thus the sacred writers are more interested in the philosophy of history than in history; their theme is frankly the lesson of existence, rather than existence. From this point of view, Philo, Maimonides, and all the foremost interpreters of Scripture are right in asserting that the narratives of the Torah are allegorical, or perhaps it would be more nearly precise to say, didactic. Presumably nothing is included which will not stir men's emotions and minds to an understanding of the basic theme of Scripture. And when a story is foreshortened, that is done because the foreshortening will not prevent an understanding of what has really occurred, and may indeed promote it.

The manner in which the Rabbinic sages, and some later writers of

Scripture itself (like the author of the Book of Chronicles), take liberties with the older narrative amply demonstrates their conviction that it is not the precision, but the implication, of the account which matters. Thus the story of the Exodus, as given in the various Rabbinic midrashim, is not only a vast elaboration of that found in Scripture, but differs from it in some basic details. For example, one midrash maintains that only a small fraction of the Israelites in Egypt left that country, whereas a literal interpretation of the Scriptures would certainly give the impression that all the Israelites, and many others, participated in the miracle. The Rabbinic author must have had very good reason for the expression of this view. He was, presumably, projecting to the situation in Egypt the conditions of his own day, when a large proportion of the Jews were tending to leave their faith, and assumed that despite such dereliction, the future of the faith and the people was secure. Thus, his denial that all the Israelites left Egypt had the same purpose as the original assertion that all of them were redeemed—namely, to strengthen the faith and fortitude of the people in an hour of crisis, and to assure them that despite such defections as might occur, the faith—maintained by a saving remnant—would endure.

The didactic , rather than simply informational, purpose of Scriptural narrative is clearly indicated in the Bible itself, in its double accounts of various incidents. Thus the two stories of Creation are apparently intended to convey in the first chapters of Genesis two supplementary series of lessons, each significant in its own way. The first chapter of Genesis stresses the importance of the individual, the equality of men, the equality of the sexes, the role of man as having dominion over nature, and the worth of man as bearing the Divine image. The second chapter stresses the unity of the family, the relation of husband and wife as superseding that of child to parent, the dignity and purity of the human body in itself, and the origin of embarrassment for it in sinfulness and concupiscence.

The Book of Judges, Samuel, Kings, and Chronicles, as well as the historical sections of the literary Prophets, all are concerned very largely with what may be called the moral and spiritual interpretation of history. This narrative is intimately associated with the form of behavior enjoined by Scripture; and the message of the Prophets is essentially that the world process makes for the fulfilment of Torah as a way of life, just as the Torah as a way of life is in itself a fulfilment of the world process.

Relativism of Symbols

Because the theme is of transcending importance in Judaism, and the symbol obviously secondary to it, there is little hesitation either in Scripture or in Talmud, in substituting new conceptual symbolism when that becomes necessary for the articulation of the theme. Thus, in the early chapters of Genesis and virtually throughout the Pentateuch, God speaks to Moses face to face; He descends to earth to investigate the sins of man; He closes the door of the Ark to protect Noah; He smells the odor of the burnt offerings, sacrificed to Him. This is not mere primitivism. Long before the appearance of the Hebrew Scriptures, men had recognized the distinction between mountains, rivers, the sun, the moon, the stars, and artifacts, on the one hand, and the spirits inhabiting them, on the other. Everywhere men distinguished man's spirit or shade from his body. However, the Prophets ignore this distinction—precisely because it might seem to provide a rational basis for idol worship. The Prophets decline to argue the existence of a shade, independent of the human body, or a god, independent of the idol bearing its name. They generally speak and write as though there were only one realm of existence, that which is spatial, tangible, and visible. They refuse to speculate on the difference between man's spirit and his body.

All this was changed as the danger of idol worship receded, and was replaced with the peril of monolatry, or syncretistic identification of the God of the Torah with one of the deities of polytheism. In the later Prophets, and in the Talmudic works, as well as the great Bible versions, there is continued emphasis on the transcendence and spirituality of God, and resistance to anthropomorphism. This is because there was no longer any real danger that the masses of the Jews would become idol worshipers, but great danger that they would conceive their Deity as simply one of two gods (as did the Persians), or one among many gods, as did the Greeks. Once the anthropomorphic conception of God was replaced by an emphasis on His spirituality, man's likeness and kinship to God were associated, at least in some circles, not with similarity in form, but in the kinship between man's spirit and the Deity. The contrast between man's spirit, which is immortal, and man's body, which is temporal, was stressed, because that difference emphasized precisely what Scripture sought to convey in its own symbolism, namely, man's likeness to God. This view, as we have ob-

served, was predominant for the School of Hillel, as for their predecessors in somewhat earlier ages, in the generations between the end of
Prophecy and the rise of Pharisaism. For the School of Shammai,
man's worth consisted in the fact that he was permitted to be the servant of God, a priest in the immense Divine Temple, which is the temporal world. There is no need for similarity between priest and Deity,
in order that the priest may share the holiness of the Deity. And the
Shammaites apparently saw no reason to stress any common element
in the nature of man and God, in order to indicate the true quality of
human worth.

The change of emphasis between Scriptural attitude toward God and
man, and that common in the Pharisaic Schools of Hillel and Shammai, reminds us that whereas basic ideas are permanent and objective,
the symbolism in which they are expressed must necessarily be relative
to the people who employ it. The Talmudic sages were well aware of
this necessary relativism of symbolic expression, and they maintain
that "although the pillar (on the *ad hoc* altar, consisting of a single
rock) was beloved as a means of worship by the Patriarchs, it was ob-
jectionable in the time of their descendants."

This relativism of symbols is illustrated by many differences between the Schools of Shammai and Hillel in regard to legal and ritual,
and even moral issues. The same idea was necessarily expressed by
varying symbolisms in different social groups. It would take us too far
afield and require far more space than is here available, to demonstrate
the point, but I am convinced that the Shammaitic symbolism was
largely derived from a cultural tradition which was priestly, rural, aris-
tocratic, and provincial; while that of Hillel and his School was based
on a tradition and environment which were essentially lay, urban, democratic, and native to the marketplace of Jerusalem. This relativism
of symbols must not, however, be interpreted as implying a relativism
also with regard to the truths they symbolize. There are basic truths, regarding existence and the moral and spirtual realms, which are eternally valid. But the manner in which these are expressed or symbolized,
whether in ritual, legal, or moral maxims, or in the description of
events past or present, is necessarily as relative to the life of the community as any other means of communicating ideas, including language itself.

The divergence between the Schools of Shammai and Hillel with regard to such ideas as the primacy of fear of God or love for Him, was

symbolic. The anthropocentrism of Hillelite theology, and the theocentrism of Shammaitic theology, both have the same purpose—the raising of the standards of human conduct, in which the glory of God becomes most clearly manifest on earth. In Scripture the two ideas are not separate; and many Rabbinic scholars regarded the disagreements between the Schools in their interpretation of tradition as a misfortune. However, misfortune or not, it was inevitable that the readers of Scripture in the marketplace of Jerusalem should see in it something other than did readers in the villages of Galilee.

The fact that formulated ideas themselves can be symbols, and are dependent on the human background of the individuals in whose minds they are conceived, naturally raises the questions: What are objective ideas which transcend cultural and social differences? How can ideas, of any kind, be distinguished from the symbols in which they are expressed, and what effect does the symbolic expression have on the nature of the idea? Is there any approach to ideas so universal that the relativism of their symbolic expression can be transcended?

From the viewpoint of the Jewish tradition, the truly basic ideas of life or existence cannot be expressed in verbal propositions of language as it has thus far developed. Verbal propositions are too nearly precise, and therefore too narrow, to express the complexity, depth, and breadth of actualities. We sometimes escape the difficulty involved in the precision of verbal propositions (which is of course one of their main advantages, as well as a serious disadvantage) by resort to deliberate ambiguities, using words, which have several meanings, each precise, but different, to cover a variety of ideas. However, this ambiguity enables us only to escape from the confinement to a single interpretation of ideas. It does not permit expression of ideas as wholes. Thus the assertion that God is anthropomorphic or non-anthropomorphic, or that man is essentially a body, and only secondarily a shade, or essentially a soul, and only secondarily a body, despite all the ambiguities and vagueness involved in such terms as "spiritual," "shade," "soul," "essentially," "anthropomorphic," and "non-anthropomorphic," fails to express the basic concept of man's relation to God, which the Torah, according to both the Schools of Shammai and of Hillel, seeks to convey. Man's dignity is effectively articulated by associating with him, recognizing him as a brother, treating him with respect, particularly when his outward appearance, his difference, his poverty, or his background, suggest lesser dignity. God's relation to man, as father, king, overwhelming benefactor, source of all good, and of all meaning, is expressed more effectively through an effort to discover or fulfil His will (so far as possible) than in any verbal assertion.

Obviously, assertion through symbols of behavior has its own limitations. Behavior assertions are imprecise, and easily become, so to speak, nonsense syllables. It is possible to observe all the forms of the law, without feeling any of the emotions associated with them, or having any consciousness of the ideas inculcated in them. (Indeed, as we have seen, the School of Shammai does not regard such unawareness as making for inevitable futility. According to them, apparently, to be effective, the articulation of ideas need not involve more than behavior. This concept, though on the surface strange, is not really different from that widely held in our day, namely, that articulation of ideas *in words alone* has significance.)

Presumably, neither the expression of ideas in words alone nor in behavior alone is adequate. Perhaps the articulation of ideas in both words and behavior, and the recognition of the relation of the two forms, is needed to identify the kind of concept which is eternally valid. Thus the difference between the anthropocentric and theocentric approaches to life, which appears not only in the differences between the ancient Rabbinic Schools, but also in differences among philosophers of all ages, conceals a basic agreement on common respect for the spiritual, as opposed to the material; for the universal as contrasted with the particularistic; for the permanent, as contrasted with the transient; for the creative, as contrasted with the possessive; for the cooperative, as contrasted with the competitive; for conscious direction, as contrasted with easy drifting; for an awareness of goals, as contrasted with refusal to recognize them. These attitudes can be expressed in behavior forms which both supplement and break through the rigidities and limitations of verbal formulation; but also require verbal formulation, so that men may know what it is they are acting out.

Life as a Pageant

The disagreements between the Schools of Shammai and Hillel, both as to forms and the meaning of forms, are (as seen from the perspective of another age, and another civilization) infinitely less important than their common approach to life as a pageant, in which the basic theme of existence—no matter how that was precisely formulated—had to be enacted. This meant that every action of life could, and in the life of a saint, did become a meaningful gesture; and that life as a whole could become a liturgical drama, as it were, conveying ideas and thus serving a purpose beyond itself. While existence and human behavior have a common theme, man cannot derive the laws controlling his actions from a study of Nature alone; but he can understand Nature better, if he understands the laws governing his behavior and his relations to his fellowmen. Studies in science and history, which regarded by themselves merely satisfy human curiosity or increase human power (which might be evil), are invaluable as commentaries on Torah and as means for its validation and better understanding and appreciation.

Without being aware of the vastness and complexity of material existence as revealed by modern science, the ancient Rabbis knew enough about Nature to realize the disproportion in size between its physical immensity and man's physical tininess. This contrast gave them no concern whatever. It is strange, indeed, that it should give so much concern to many modern thinkers. The Rabbinic scholars did not consider their time wasted in giving instruction to a thousand pupils, though only one hundred might show promise, and only one attain real fulfilment; any more than we consider as sheer waste the establishment of a thousand universities because they are necessary to the development of a small number who will contribute effectively to human culture, or the maintenance of hundreds of thousands of printing presses and the publication of millions of books, in order that one view which has significance may not be suppressed. It is of the essence of the liberal tradition that even false and misleading views should be permitted to circulate, because the effort to suppress them will involve necessarily the suppression of possible truth. If man, despite his limited resources and energies, must allow himself the luxury of intellectual and spiritual wastage, in order that he may salvage what is worthwhile, why should not Nature indulge in vast creation, in order that there may emerge here and there, in its enormous recesses, beings capable of conscious dramatization of ideas, which are ultimately the goal of both their existence and that of Nature itself?

The concept of existence and life as having meaning and purpose, bestows on both a particular grandeur; and if the meaning of existence is most clearly exhibited in the emergence of conscious beings who, able to follow justice or injustice, prefer justice, and deliberately fashion their lives as a fulfilment of the Divine drama, the enormous stage erected for their activity is not by any means wasted.

A curious fate has, however, befallen the concept of life as meaningful. It has permeated all of Western civilization, and has moved warri-
ors like Napoleon, as much as it did saints like Rabbi Akiba and Maimonides. In the modified form, in which many children of Western
culture accept the concept, it becomes not a means for drawing men
together, but for setting them apart; it ceases to be a theme, capable of
offsetting man's hunger for individual or group primacy, but on the
contrary becomes rationalization for that hunger. Frequently, consciousness of a role in history is dissociated from mankind and existence as a whole, and is associated rather with the fate and ambition of
persons, institutions, and groups.

A vivid conception of history when regarded as a drama, involving
all mankind or all existence, tends to make the role of the individual or
his group creative and constructive. This is especially the case if one
recognizes also the fact that the meaning of the drama is expressed not
only in its final act (which may be infinitely or indefinitely distant in
time), but in every scene. An equally vivid conception of history and
its significance can, however, be destructive, if one's view of it is limited to one's own role or that of one's special group, or if one overlooks
the significance of each scene, and is wholly preoccupied with the final
one.

It is the fatal inadequacy of the Apocalyptist, perhaps of the Shammaite generally, that his preoccupation with the final act of the world
drama makes him callous to the evils of the intermediate ones; and
conceiving of the pageant of human existence as deriving its full meaning from the final scene (perhaps endless, yet far off), he may indulge
either in the vision or even in the practice of horrible cruelties for the
moment. It is a no less fatal inadequacy on the part of individuals and
groups to regard the world as deriving its meaning from themselves,
instead of their deriving their meaning from service to mankind or love
for God.

The Shammaitic conception that the world exists for the glory of
God, and that He is the Hero as well as the Author of the drama of existence, thus lent itself to neglect of the interests of individual men and
of delight in the ultimate vindication of God, in the final destruction of
wickedness and the wicked. The Hillelite concept of life as a school
inures one to the pains one has to undergo in the process of learning,
and yet does not harden one to cruelties, which one may tend to inflict
on others. It was perhaps also natural that the School of Shammai, concerned only with the vindication of God, should have regarded His tri-

umph as sufficient, if the people of Israel alone recognized Him, and remained His loyal servants, in whom His victory over His enemies would be made manifest. Opposing the Shammaities, the Hillelites could not accept so complacent a view with regard to the vast majority of mankind, and held that the world process, while perhaps especially manifest in the history of Israel, was one in which all human beings had a part.

While formally the School of Hillel triumphed when a decision had to be taken regarding the respective positions of the Schools some time early in the Second Century of the Common Era, the views associated with the School of Shammai have by no means disappeared either in Judaism or among the religions and systems of ideas affected by it. The issue whether the drama of human existence is to be regarded primarily as anthropocentric or theocentric has by no means been resolved; nor is it clear whether Judaism finds its fulfilment in the study of Torah in the temporal world (which only incidentally leads to an immortal future), or in the Kingdom of God in the afterworld, which can be obtained only through obedience to His commandments in the present one. One may wonder whether any of the frightful calamities which have occurred to Judaism and the Jews in these many generations have more greatly impeded its service to civilization and to mankind, than its inability to resolve this basic dilemma, and to achieve, in the expression of the Talmud, "the study of Torah as it was given to Moses," without conflict as to its meaning. In an age which more than any other requires for its very safety and for the endurance of civilization itself, a clear concept of purpose, whether dedication to God or love for man, the analysis and solution of the ancient perplexity may have a special purpose to serve.

MAX KADUSHIN *notes that in Rabbinic society, there was no radical difference between sage and folk. The Sages were "representatives of the folk, albeit at its best." Thus they immersed themselves in aggadah (homiletical lore) as well as in halachah (law), for scholar as well as artisan had to concretize the value-concepts embedded in the psyche of the people of Torah.*

Halachah, which "prescribed ways for the concretizations of the concepts in day-to-day living," is more precise than aggadic homily, because of the "internal nexus between the laws themselves which . . . allows them to be classified and organized in accordance with their content." The Rabbis investigated, with hermeneutic principles, the "nexus" between the laws. Yet halachah, "nexus and all," does leave room for divergence in law, and thus reflects what Kadushin calls the "organismic, non-rigid nature of the value-complex." Both the law and sermons of the Rabbis were informed by the value-concepts of the whole people, evoking the concepts' drive toward concretization in everyday life. The value-concepts act "steadily in concert"; they do so "as a category of thought, speech and action" which Kadushin describes as the "category of significance." Halachot (specific laws), like aggadot (specific sermons) reflect the "organismic character of the value-concepts."

217

Halakah and Haggadah

MAX KADUSHIN

It is only partly true that the value-concepts, being represented by terms, were transmitted from generation to generation in the same way as the other words of the language. Ordinary social interaction suffices for the maintenance and transmission of the terms constituting the bulk of the usual vocabulary. These terms are cognitive concepts. They refer to things, qualities, relationships, and are rooted in everyday objective, perceptual experience. But value-concepts are not rooted in perceptual experience. For the maintenance and transmission of value-concepts, concepts which do not refer to objective things and qualities, ordinary social interaction is not enough. There must be a supplementary form of communication that will help make the value-concepts as vivid as the objective cognitive concepts, and their use as frequent. That supplement to the speech of ordinary social interaction was the *Haggadah.* Arising primarily as sermons to the masses, it approximated the actual manner in which the value-concepts were imbedded in daily situations and in ordinary conversation. *Haggadah* was, therefore, a kind of extension of the use of value-concepts in ordinary social intercourse, and that accounts for its effectiveness as a means of instruction.

In order to produce this literature, the Rabbis had, apparently, to meet three requirements. Obviously, to teach they had first to learn, and the Rabbis remained students throughout their lives. The great academies not only handed down the learning of the past, they promoted interchange of views and opinions among the mature scholars; and these creative discussions served to train the younger disciples, who were allowed to put questions and even to venture opinions.[1] And yet, despite the fact that the Rabbis "spent more time in the *Bet ha-Midrash* (the academy) than beyond its walls,"[2] they were not a cloistered group and not a professional class. Thus they met the second requirement, namely, that there be no gap between the authors or teachers and the folk. They taught the adult members of their communities but received therefor neither salaries nor gifts.[3] Instead of forming a separate professional class, the Rabbis were bound up with the life of the people as a whole, and members of every economic group were to be found among them. Louis Ginzberg has noticed that "more than one hundred scholars mentioned in the Talmud were artisans, a considerable number were tradesmen, and others were physicians or followed various professions."[4] Some of the greatest of the Rabbis made their living with their hands—Hillel was a carpenter, Joshua b. Hananiah a smith, Johanan a shoemaker.[5] Such men were representative of the folk, albeit of the folk at its best. By the same token, the value-concepts embodied in their teachings were the value-concepts of the folk. That is why *Haggadah* was an extension of the use of the value-concepts in ordinary social intercourse. Finally, for their teaching to be effective, they had themselves to embody the ideals which they preached. "It was not the learning of the *Talmid Ḥakam*," says Ginzberg, "that gave him his position but his ideal life."[6] The high regard for the *Ḥakam* or the *Talmid Ḥakam*[7] was not something fleeting or fluctuating but has permanently affected the character of the concept itself. We may recall that *Ḥakam* and *Zaddik* are overlapping concepts, that *the learned* is a term used interchangeably, on occasion, with *the righteous*.[8] And if the Rabbi was effective as an example, it was, again, because the circumstances of his life were the same as those of the folk in general. The people could not help but feel that, under the very circumstances in which they lived their lives, the teachings of the Rabbis could be carried out into practice.

The Rabbis took every possible opportunity to instruct and to train the folk. They spoke at betrothals and weddings; they delivered eulogies at funerals, and on returning gave talks of comfort to the mourners; they combined the amenities of social life with instruction or edification, as when they were guests anywhere, or at leave-taking.[9] Their main occasions for instruction were, however, on the Sabbath and the Festivals, when they interpreted the day's lection from the Pentateuch or the Prophets to the members of the community at large, both men and women.[10] It is the content of these sermons, which included things of such popular appeal as parables, folk-tales, fables and the like,[11] that has come down to us in the great compilations forming the bulk of *Haggadah*.

Characteristic of the Rabbis' relation to the folk, of the identity of their interests with those of the folk, is the Rabbis' own attitude toward *Haggadah*. They did not view it as something fit only for the masses, but to which they themselves were superior; on the contrary, they felt themselves deeply in need of *Haggadah*, regarding it as one of the great divisions of Torah, and the study of which was incumbent upon them. "Thou shalt not say, 'I have studied *Halakot*—that is sufficient for me,'" warns a statement in a Tannaitic *Midrash*, and it goes on to interpret "for by everything that proceedeth out of the mouth of the Lord doth man live" (Deut. 8:3) as referring both to Halakot *and* Haggadot.[12] Younger scholars were stimulated toward becoming skillful in *Haggadah* as well as in *Halakah*.[13] True, as Lieberman points out, the Rabbis were mindful of their audience, suiting the style and content of their message in accordance with the background of their hearers.[14] In contrast, for example, to one interpretation of Koh. 12:2 R. Levi had given the scholars, he gave another for the masses which was more "earthy."[15] But such differences in approach do not vitiate the factors which all types of *Haggadah* have in common. Whether any particular midrashic statement was intended for the scholars or for the masses, it contained value-concepts that were common to all, scholars and masses alike.

Seldom do we find the gap between the scholars and the folk, as here, all but closed, and still more seldom over so extended a period. In fact, the tendency in the western world has been the other way. The medieval scholars and thinkers spun out abstract doctrines, far beyond the ken of the common folk, and insisted that these are the truths of religion and morality. Nor are we closing the gap today. A philosopher like Bergson, much in vogue among the intellectuals, divides the world into "society," on the one hand, and mystics and saints, on the other. Society only develops obligations, and it exacts obedience to these obligations through pressure; new moral and religious ideas, which are also warm, all-pervasive emotions, are achieved by the mystics through intuition; these new ideas do not compel, but attract and inspire.[16] Bergson merely substitutes in persuasive and glowing terms his mystic for the medievalist's philosopher, but society is stigmatized in either case. Now if Bergson does not realize that the all-pervasive, warm emotions are, in truth, social value-concepts, it is perhaps not his fault. The literary works of western civilization are not, on the whole, produced under the conditions or by the type of men that produced the *Haggadah*. The *Haggadah* is a unique literature. Containing the value-concepts of the people as a whole, including the scholars and thinkers, it is a reflection of how these concepts functioned in daily life.[17]

Halakah and its Nexus

Haggadah made the value-concepts vivid, and by means of sermons nurtured and cultivated them. The other product of the Rabbis, *Halakah,* had an altogether different function. It prescribed ways for the concretization of the concepts in day-by-day living. Does *Halakah* also reflect the qualities of the value-concepts, and if so, how?

In contrast to *Haggadah, Halakah* does not consist of independent units or entities. Definite forms of haggadic composition—literary, aesthetic forms—enabled the Rabbis, as we saw, to build up larger structures out of the independent haggadic statements. The literary forms overcome the barrier which the independence of the haggadic statements places in the way of any organization of haggadic material. But the halakic material—the laws—presents no such barrier. There is an internal nexus between the laws themselves which, in the first instance, allows them to be classified and organized in accordance with their content. In other words, the various subjects with which the laws deal—tithes, the Sabbath, divorce, damages, and so on—constitute natural classifications and can be used for that purpose and for the more detailed organization of the laws. By and large, this is the principle of classification and organization employed by the Mishnah as we have it, with its six major divisions and sixty-three tractates.[18] It was on the basis of this principle that the Rabbis of the Talmud, the *Amoraim,* would account for the presence of an identical law in two different tractates of the Mishnah. That particular law primarily belongs in the one tractate, they would say, because of its subject matter, and is repeated elsewhere only incidentally.[19]

The nexus between the laws, unless brought to light, is always merely implicit. It becomes increasingly explicit only as the result of the work of individual Rabbis and, especially in the Talmud, of discussions among the Rabbis. Thus, though the organization of the laws was implicit in the natural classifications of the subject matter, it remained for a great mind to bring these classifications to light. This, it appears, was achieved by R. Akiba, whose work was continued by his pupil, R. Me'ir, and was utilized by Rabbi Judah the Prince in his authoritative edition of our Mishnah made at about the end of the second century.[20]

Apart from the classification of the laws according to subject matter, the task of establishing the nexus between the laws was not undertaken by the Rabbis for its own sake. It was a concomitant of their efforts to formulate and elucidate the laws, although not a necessary concomitant. In the mishnaic period, the laws were often formulated with the aid of hermeneutic rules, methods for deriving laws from the Bible[21], and it is in the course of the application of these rules that the nexus between specific laws may be brought to light. The application of a certain hermeneutic rule, for example, results in the formulation of a general law based on four distinct classes of damages.[22] But that general law also reveals the nexus between these four classes: it describes the characteristics common to them all. The famous rabbinic interpretation of *lex talionis*—"an eye for an eye" (Exod. 21:24)—offers an instance of another type. Here the use of hermeneutic rules by R. Ishmael and by R. Isaac apparently but confirms what was already accepted as law—namely, not *lex talionis* but monetary compensation. The use of hermeneutic rules elicits in this instance too, however, a relation between this law and other laws.[23]

Nevertheless, the nexus between the laws is not made fully explicit in the mishnaic period. It was not always brought to light when the hermeneutic rules were employed. The very passage just cited contains a third interpretation of "an eye for an eye" which also applies a hermeneutic rule, but one that does not involve relations between laws.[24] Moreover there were laws, representing an older tradition, unsupported by any hermeneutic rule at all.[25] The classification of the laws, it is true, marks an advance in the direction of establishing the nexus between the laws. But it is an advance limited by its own objective. It relates the laws within any classification but not across classifications. We may say, therefore, that though the nexus between the laws becomes evident in the mishnaic period, it is still somewhat implicit.

It becomes more and more explicit in the talmudic period. As Krochmal has pointed out, there is a distinction, so far as the Babylonian Talmud is concerned, between the kind of discussion engaged in by the earlier generations of *Amoraim* and that engaged in by the later. The earlier discussions, initiated by Rab and Samuel and hence associated with their names,[26] were directed toward the clarification of the Mishnah, and this involved comparing the manner in which a law is stated in our Mishnah with the manner in which it is stated in extra-mishnaic collections, tracing a dispute back to its earliest protagonists, and similar matters.[27] The later discussions, initiated by 'Abaye and Raba and hence associated with their names,[28] were often based on the earlier discussions but exceeded them in the minute analysis of the law. They deal with the discrepancies between the mishnaic and the extra-mishnaic statements of the laws, with the reasons that may be attributed to a law, with the assumptions or principles apparently underlying conflicting views or disputes among the older authorities.[29] It is in the course of these discussions that a nexus may be established between laws in different classifications. Thus, it is elicited in a discussion that an identical principle underlies both a law concerning the building of the booth for the Festival of Tabernacles and a law in a totally different classification, that of tithes.[30] When relations are established among laws in different classifications, the nexus between the laws is being made fully explicit.

We have depicted *Halakah* as the most important product of the value-concepts' drive toward concretization.[31] And now we shall see that, like *Haggadah*, *Halakah* also reflects the qualities of the value-concepts, although in its own way. *Haggadah* is characterized by diversity of opinion. But *Halakah* differs from *Haggadah* in not being composed of discrete, independent entities which encourage diversity of opinion. There is a nexus between the laws, an implicit nexus that becomes more and more explicit. Does *Halakah*, nexus and all, nevertheless have room at any time for wide divergence in law? It does, and so reflects in its own way the organismic, nonrigid nature of the value-complex.

During the mishnaic period, there was achieved the classification of the laws. To this degree only had the nexus been made explicit for the laws in general. Classification according to subject matter, however, is one thing and the elimination of controversial opinion quite another. The "code" may simply be a collection of divergent opinions organized according to subject matter, and this is indeed what the Mishnah, until its final redaction, tended to be. There are only six complete chapters in the Mishnah which are "anonymous," that is, chapters in which no controversies are recorded.[32]

But divergence in law is not only a matter of diversity of opinion; it means that and much more. The differences of opinion which the Mishnah exhibits pertain not to theoretical questions alone. They often represent actual divergence in practice, Ginzberg has shown, even when it is the view of one authority as against that of the majority of his colleagues. Providing the law was not fixed, the individual authority had the right—the duty—to render a decision in accordance with his

own view, although knowing that the majority disagreed with him.[33]
Thus, for a long time the School of Shammai differed from the School
of Hillel in respect to hundreds of *halakot,* and both decided cases in
accordance with their own views, though the School of Shammai recognized that it was in the minority.[34] That this was true of individual
opinions also we can see from the instances of R. Eliezer and R. Jose.[35]
Naturally, there were certain limitations on divergence in practice.
When a case came before a group of Rabbis, the decision was by a majority vote, and dissenting opinions in that case had no validity.[36] A
further limitation consisted of the ordinances and verdicts of The
Great Court. An ordinary court was obliged to decide a case as it saw
the law, notwithstanding the fact that another court may have decided
a similar case differently;[37] but the ordinances and verdicts of The
Great Court were binding on all other courts and on all individuals.[38]
Since, however, the decisions of The Great Court were comparatively
few, and usually made only in times of extreme national danger, ample
room was left for decisions by the individual authority in accordance
with his own views.[39] As Ginzberg sums it up: "Hence we need not
wonder at the many conflicts of opinion among the Rabbis from the
days of Shammai and Hillel to the close of the Mishnah. Not only
could each of the Rabbis differ from the majority when dealing with
theoretical questions, but the individual authority could decide according to his own opinion without regard to the opinion of the majority in any specific case that came before him, outside of those matters
already decided by The Great Court."[40] In the course of time conflicts
of opinion among the Rabbis became so numerous that there was hardly a law which was not indefinite. The rule was then made that, if an
individual authority could not decide a specific case either on the basis
of a tradition he had received or on that of legal reasoning, he must decide the case in accordance with the view of the majority of the Rabbis.[41]

Halakah reflects the organismic character of the value-concepts in
other ways as well. But we shall not pursue them here. Some of them
will become apparent in subsequent discussions.

The value-concepts are concretized in *Haggadah* and *Halakah.* Because of the intimate relation of the Rabbis to the folk, rare among crea-
tors of written literature, the sermons of the Rabbis as preserved in the
Haggadah constitute a unique literature. Informed by the value-concepts common to the whole people, these sermons reflect the manner in

which the value-concepts functioned in everyday speech and action. In speech, the value-concepts are inseparable from the data which they interpret, and render every valuational statement a fused, independent entity. Only by means of literary forms were the Rabbis able to overcome the atomistic nature of the haggadic statements and to organize these statements into sermons. The value-concepts affect not speech alone, however, but the whole personality. If the independence of the valuational statement encourages diversity of opinion, reflects the *differentia* of individual minds, it is because the entire value-complex encourages and makes possible the development of distinctive personalities. The common character of the group and the differentiated personality of every individual member of it go hand in hand, and both derive from the value-concepts.

The value-concepts have a drive toward concretization, and *Halakah* is the most important product of that drive. It ensures the steady concretization of the concepts. In contrast to *Haggadah, Halakah* does not consist of independent entities. There is an implicit nexus between the laws, a nexus that becomes fully explicit only in the talmudic period. Yet so long as the nexus remains more or less implicit, there is room for wide divergence in law, and this is actually the case in the mishnaic period. *Halakah,* too, thus reflects in a measure the nature of the value-concepts. It is because *Halakah* is a manifestation of the value-concepts that the practice of the laws can be so whole-souled an expression of the self.

The Category of Significance

Value-concepts made for the distinctiveness and uniqueness of the self. They supply the means of expression to each individual personality. This is to say that every action or situation fraught with value-concepts is unique and original, holding however briefly the distinctive essence, as it were, of a personality. A true work of art is likewise unique and original—in fact, valuational expression and artistic expression are but different modes of one great category. In the present chapter we are attempting a description of that category, largely in connection with valuational expression but touching also on aesthetic expression.

Concepts supplying the means of expression to each individual personality are bound to be, in some degree, subjective. How could they be otherwise and still respond to the unique quality of each individual personality? But these value-concepts express personality only when they are embodied in a concrete situation or action. The subjective value-concepts act not by themselves but always in concert with objective, concrete, cognitive concepts, and even with defined concepts. As we noticed above, value-concepts are fused with cognitive concepts in any concrete situation. Does this "acting in concert" make for a kind of coalescence of conceptual types, blur the demarcations between them? We expect to show that the contrary is true. A value-concept functions easily only when it is free from admixture with a concept of a different type. Subjective valuational experience goes together with a firm grasp of the impersonal, objective nature of things that contribute to that experience. When concepts of various types can act steadily in concert, it is because they do so as a category of thought, speech and action in which each conceptual type remains pure. This category, which we call "the category of significance," is a hallmark of civilized societies; valuational expression in primitive societies, we shall see, manages without it.

Situations fraught with value-concepts have their literary parallel in the discrete haggadic statements. This means that the problems raised by the consideration of these discrete statements are not primarily literary but valuational. For example, is not belief involved in the acceptance of haggadic statements? What kind of belief was it that could also be inspired by legend? This is a problem in religious psychology, and its solution will throw light on the nature of the category to which the rabbinic statements and legends belong. Even what is a genuine literary device—the peculiar manner in which haggadic statements are attached to the Bible—is also much more than that. To account for it we shall have to describe a major aspect of "the category of significance," a description comprehensive enough to include the reasons for that name. With this "literary" problem we shall therefore begin.

Category of Significance—Halakah

Does *Halakah*, too, belong to the category of significance? It would be easier to answer this question had a complete and thorough study been made of the relation of the Halakic *Midrashim* to the *Mishnah* and *Tosefta*. The Halakic literature of the mishnaic period has come down to us in two forms. There is the midrash form, wherein the *halakot*, laws, are given as interpretations of biblical texts, and there is the

Mishnah form, wherein the *halakot* stand by themselves and are not interpretations of biblical texts. *Halakot* in the Midrash form are contained in the Halakic *Midrashim*—the *Mekilta, Sifra* and *Sifre; Halakot* in the Mishnah form are the rule in the *Mishnah,* although the latter contains also some *halakot* in Midrash form.[42] Now a great many *halakot* of the Mishnah have parallels in the Halakic *Midrashim,* and these parallels are thus in Midrash form.[43] The question is: which form is the earlier—Mishnah or Midrash? If the Midrash form is the earlier, then the biblical texts were in some sense the points of departure for the *halakot.* Opinion among modern scholars is divided, some holding the Midrash form and others the Mishnah form to be the earlier.[44] There can be no solution to this complicated problem, as Ginzberg has said, until a detailed comparison has been made of the Mishnah and the Halakic *Midrashim.*[45]

A comparison of the haggadic with the halakic approach to the biblical texts need not wait on this study, however. It can be seen that the methods of halakic interpretation of texts differ widely from those employed in haggadic interpretation. Not only do the methods of interpretation differ, but the basic approach to the texts differs as well.

In *Haggadah,* it is sufficient if a sequence is established between the biblical text and a haggadic idea, any kind of sequence. We must be made aware of how the text suggests the haggadic idea, and that is all that is required. If rules of interpretation were in any wise employed, it was only as helpful guides. But in *Halakah,* the rules of interpretation were much more than that, and were introduced at a very early period. A large number of *halakot* were derived from the Bible by the application of the Thirteen *Middot* of R. Ishmael, rules of interpretation based on those formulated by Hillel, but probably going back beyond him. From very early times, therefore, inference, analogy and literary considerations were factors in the derivation of *halakot.* Even the methods of R. Akiba, with far less emphasis on logical procedure than those of R. Ishmael, require more than mere sequence.[46]

The entire approach to the biblical text is different in *Halakah* from what it is in *Haggadah.* In *Haggadah, derash* is set off against *peshat,* and this demarcation is kept to, by and large. Such a demarcation is not possible in *Halakah.* Biblical texts may contain implications that have to do not only with the law in question but that are in the nature of general principles. Yet these principles can only be drawn forth by means of inference or analogy; they are not explicitly given in the biblical text itself. The biblical law regarding the paschal lamb, for example, states that "they shall take to themselves every man a lamb, according to their fathers' houses, a lamb for a household" (Exod. 12:3). This law, enjoining that "every man" take a lamb, is modified in the same verse by "according to their fathers' houses, a lamb for a household," since a household contains a number of other persons besides the one who does the taking or the buying. The injunction is upon "every man," yet it is not necessary for each to take or buy a lamb for himself; hence the Rabbis deduce the principle that a man's agent is like a man himself.[47] This far-reaching principle of agency, of prime importance to the urban, commercial centers of rabbinic times, is certainly not explicitly given in literal terms in the biblical law. Yet can we say that it is altogether *derash*?

We have no parallel in *Halakah* to the dichotomy of *peshat* and *derash*. It is true that the Rabbis differentiate among halakic interpretations. Some *halakot* they describe as ordained by the Rabbis, and they designate a verse used in "deriving" such a non-biblical law as *'asmakta*, "support."[48] (This is the term employed in the Babylonian Talmud; the same idea is conveyed in tannaitic literature by a Hebraic term— *Zacher l'davar*.[49]) So far as the sheer approach to the biblical texts is concerned, however, there is no marked difference between those halakic interpretations designated *'asmakta* and those not so designated. This becomes evident as soon as we attempt to classify halakic interpretations on the basis of their approach to biblical texts. A study of this kind has been made by Michael Guttmann, and his three major classifications—*derashot* explanatory of the text, *derashot* eliciting halakic principles, and "symbolic" *derashot*—hold, in his analysis, for the one group as for the other.[50] No doubt other ways of classification are also possible, and here and there objection may be raised in regard to details;[51] nevertheless, his study as a whole, broad in scope and bold in method, is highly indicative. There is no basic difference in method between interpretations labeled *'asmakta* and other halakic interpretations.

We reach a similar conclusion when we consider halakic interpretations designated as implications "from the Torah." In several such instances, there are Rabbis to whom the particular interpretations are not acceptable, and who regard them as invalid. These interpretations are, therefore, no different in kind from other disputed halakic interpretations. For example, a biblical law prohibits the use of the new products of the field before the Omer-offering, and the law concludes with the statement: "It is a statute for ever throughout your generations in all your dwelling-places" (Lev. 23:14). The Mishnah takes this law to apply "everywhere," that is, not only to the land of Israel, and designates the wide application of the law as being "from the Torah."[52] The Mishnah here sides with R. Eliezer,[53] who alone gives this wide interpretation to the phrase "in all your dwelling-places."[54] His colleagues disagree with him[55]; for them, his interpretation does not represent an implication of the Torah. Another example is the interpretation of Deut. 6:7—"And thou shalt talk of them . . . when thou liest down and when thou risest up." From the Mishnah onward, that verse was taken as the warrant for the recital of the *Shema*,[56] and the recital to be thus enjoined by the Bible.[57] A view in the Talmud, however, has it that the recital was ordained by the Rabbis, and that "And thou shalt talk of them . . ." refers to "words of the Torah," that is, to general Study of Torah.[58]

It would seem, therefore, that the textual methods and approach are quite the same, whether the halakic interpretation be designated *'asmakta* or as an implication "from the Torah". This is again reflected in the discussions pertaining to this matter in the Middle Ages. Maimonides states that laws not found in the Bible but derived by the Rabbis by means of any of the Thirteen *Middot* are to be regarded as biblical only if the Rabbis themselves explicitly declare or explain them to be so.[59] Nahmanides takes issue with this view of Maimonides. He brings proof to the contrary, namely, that all matters derived by means of the Thirteen *Middot* are to be regarded as biblical unless the Rabbis explicitly declare a "derivation" to be an *'asmakta*.[60] These great authorities could differ so radically only because there is no way to distinguish, so far as interpretation of text goes, between an implication "from the Torah" and an *'asmakta*.

Halakic interpretation is, then, altogether different from haggadic interpretation. In haggadic interpretation the biblical texts serve as a spring-board merely as a stimulus, whereas halakic interpretation of Scripture employs logical procedures expressed in hermeneutic rules. The very dichotomy of *peshat* and *derash*, so basic in *Haggadah*, does not hold for *Halakah*. A general principle may be inherent in a specific biblical law, even if it is not explicitly stated there but only drawn forth by inference or analogy. Nor is there a halakic parallel to *peshat* and *derash* in the fact that some laws are designated as "from the Torah" and others as *'asmakta*. The same methods of textual interpretation are employed in order to "support" laws labeled *'asmakta* as to "derive" laws described as "from the Torah."

Yet there are halakic interpretations that do exhibit the characteristics of haggadic interpretation. Thus there are some halakic interpretations that are related to biblical texts by nothing more than bare sequence, and hence that are quite analogous to haggadic *derash*. It is on that very ground, in fact, that objection to such interpretations is voiced at times. At R. Eliezer's interpretation of Lev. 13:47, his colleague R. Ishmael exclaimed: "Thou sayest to the verse, 'Keep silent until I shall interpret (thee)!'" And the root of the verb "I shall interpret," be it noted, is *derash*.[61] When, in a passage cited above, R. Akiba's rendering of Deut. 20:8 is designated *kemashmao* (its literal meaning), we must infer that R. Jose's interpretation of that verse is regarded as not *kimashmao*.[62]

But ordinarily halakic interpretations that exhibit the characteristics of haggadic interpretation do so in a form greatly modified. Sometimes a law in its general aspect, as Guttmann points out, is implied in a text of the Bible, but not the details of that law. These details, such as the number and order of *teru'ot and teki'ot* on Rosh Ha-Shanah, of the four benedictions in the grace after meals, are connected with the texts by no more than the barest sequence.[63] Many derivations of this type are, however, only midrashic support for laws previously established. When the Rabbis ask as to why there should be exactly eighteen benedictions in the daily *'Amidah*, different reasons are given, all of them warrants from Scripture and all of them characterized by mere sequence.[64] Obviously, the eighteen benedictions had long ago been established; the Rabbis are here but seeking biblical support for that number.[65]

We meet also with halakot that are influenced by *Haggadot*. For example, a certain rite prescribed for fast-days during a drought is regarded by the Rabbis as a symbol. Two authorities disagree as to the specific meaning of the symbol; and the difference in these haggadic ideas spells also a difference in the halakah concerning the rite.[66] The haggadic ideas, we may add, are connected with a biblical text by mere sequence. But, again, very often *Halakot* that are associated with *Haggadot* have not actually been influenced by the latter. The *Haggadot* may be only either interpretations of, or else support for, the *Halakot*. Why is a *shofar* made of a cow's horn not a proper *shofar*? A sound halakic reason is given in the Mishnah.[67] But the Midrash supplies another reason, a haggadic interpretation of the law as manifestly already known and practiced.[68] R. Joshua b. Levi's statement which associates the patriarchs with the morning, afternoon and evening prayers[69] is an instance of a haggadic support for a *Halakah*. The wording of this statement in the original source, to which Ginzberg has called attention, indicates that R. Joshua b. Levi himself regarded the *Haggadah* here as only a support for the *Halakah*. In the original source—the *Yerushalmi*—the words *me-avot lamdum* (they learned from the fathers) imply that those who ordained the prayers "learned" to do so from the examples provided by the patriarchs, and not that the patriarchs themselves ordained the prayers.[70] The examples provided by the patriarchs are adduced, as in *Haggadah* generally, by mere sequence.

It is thus in a modified form that *Halakah* employs the type of interpretation characteristic of *Haggadah*. However tenuous the sequence between a biblical text and a haggadic idea, the text actually serves as a stimulus to the idea. This is rather seldom true when *Halakah* employs that method of interpretation, whether directly or through the medium of a *haggadah*. In most cases, a tenuous connection between a biblical text and a *halakah* is a fairly good indication that the *halakah* in question existed before it was connected with the biblical text in that fashion.[71] *Halakah* occasionally employs the method of haggadic interpretation, but in a manner greatly modified.

Halakah also employs the principle of multiple interpretation; in fact, the principle itself is stated in a halakic context.[72] *Halakah* presents multiple interpretation of texts when the Rabbis differ on the halakic interpretation of a verse, as they often do. We noticed, for example, that different authorities give different halakic interpretations to Lev. 23:14 and to Deut. 6:7.[73] But this principle, too, is employed by *Halakah* in a modified manner as compared with its use in *Haggadah*. In *Halakah*, a text cannot bear more than one halakic interpretation for the same authority,[74] whereas there is no such limit to haggadic interpretation.

The characteristics of haggadic interpretation, we must remember, are not just peculiarities of style. They are conditioned by the category of significance. Greatly modified, these characteristics are found, frequently enough, in halakic interpretation. If these characteristics are to an extent also found in halakic interpretation, *Halakah* is certainly at least affected by the category of significance.

This is indeed what we might have expected. *Halakot*, like *haggadot*, are concretizations of the value-concepts, and must therefore in one way or another reflect the organismic character of the value-concepts. *Halakah* reflects that character despite the fact that there is an implicit nexus between the laws, a nexus that becomes more and more explicit. We saw above how *Halakah* leaves room not only for diversity of opinion, a prime quality of the organismic complex, but for divergence in practice.[75] The characteristics of haggadic interpretation likewise derive from the organismic nature of the value-concepts. By virtue of the manner in which the value-concepts function, each haggadic idea is an independent entity; each haggadic idea therefore has need of a stimulus, and it is thus that the characteristics of haggadic interpretation are called into play. We cannot, of course, expect that *Halakah*, with its laws connected by an inherent nexus, should exhibit to the full the characteristics of haggadic interpretation; it reflects the organismic nature of the value-concepts if it exhibits some of the characteristics even in modified form. Examples wherein *Halakah* reflects most clearly the nature of the value-concepts have to do not with halakic discussion or interpretation but with actual practice, and especially with the liturgy. In the latter we often have that interweaving of concepts which is the chief characteristic of the organic complex. The recital, for instance, of the first verse of the *Shema'*, Deut. 6:4, involves at one and the same time the concepts of *Malkut Shamayim*, Torah and *Mizwot*.[76]

Notes

1. L. Ginzberg, *Students, Scholars and Saints* (Philadelphia: Jewish Publication Society of America, 1928) pp. 48–50. The Rabbis recognized and emphasized the creative function of the *bet ha-midrash*—see OT, p. 38, bottom, and the references there.

2. L. Ginzberg, *Students*, etc., p. 51.

3. See OT, p. 283, note 291 and references; and Ginzberg, *Students* etc., p. 55.

4. L. Ginzberg, *Students* etc., p. 40.

5. Solomon Goldman, *The Jew and the Universe* (New York: Harper and Bros., 1936), p. 191, note 50 and the references there.

6. L. Ginzberg, *Students* etc., pp. 40–41. See also his fine characterization, illustrated by incidents, ibid., pp. 52–57.

7. On the relation between the two concepts see *The Rabbinic Mind*, p. 43.

8. See *The Rabbinic Mind*, p. 29.

9. See L. Zunz, *Die gottesdienstlichen Vorträge der Juden* (Berlin, 1832), pp. 334–336.

10. Ibid., pp. 336–340. These homilies sometimes included instruction in law—the Yelammedenu and She'eltot types, (ibid., p. 354 f.); cf. above, p. 64.

11. N. Krochmal, op. cit., pp. 242–245.

12. Sifre on Deut. 11:22. See also end of that paragraph—By studying Haggadah you know the Holy One blessed be He and cleave to His ways.

When the Rabbis object to *Haggadah*, they have in mind, as Krochmal has shown, not genuine but spurious *haggadot*. See his treatment of the subject, op. cit., pp. 246–248, 250–255. See also OT, pp. 217–18, where the point is made that these spurious *haggadot* do not embody value-concepts.

13. Bacher, *Aggadot ha-tanaim* (Jerusalem: Dvir, 1932), trans. Rabinowitz, p. 26 (R. Johanan b. Zakkai), p. 68, (R. Gamaliel of Yabne).

14. S. Lieberman, *Greek in Jewish Palestine*, pp. 161–2.

15. Ibid.

16. H. Bergson, *The Two Sources of Morality and Religion* (Eng. trans.) (New York: Henry Holt and Co., 1935), Chap. I.

One of the "new" religious emotions, according to Bergson, is "the emotion introduced by Christianity under the name of charity" (ibid., p. 40). But the term is already found in the Book of Ben Sira and in the Book of Tobit—see OT, p. 303, note 194.

17. Modern democratic values would be far more vivid were there a genuine interaction between the intellectuals and the people at large. We have not yet produced a supplement to the speech of ordinary social interaction embodying democratic value-concepts. Educators attempt to offset this lack by encouraging democratic procedures and conditions in schools and clubs. These worthwhile enterprises must remain, however, quite limited in scope; it is hardly possible to duplicate on this small scale the varied opportunities for the expression of democratic values in everyday life. More promising is the attempt to develop neighborhood organizations in which the adults of the community will find a much wider scope for democratic action. Such a movement, if it gathers momentum, may in time call forth a supplementary form of communication that will evoke the democratic concepts and make them more vivid.

A development of this kind will be arrested if its proponents are influenced either by the definition seekers (see above, p. 83, note 10) or by the educators who abhor "indoctrination." The latter have gone to the opposite extreme of the definition seekers. There is a denial here of all that we have found to be true of the value-concepts, of their role in the popular vocabulary, and of the need for their deliberate maintenance.

18. Strack, op. cit., pp. 26–64, gives a summary of each tractate.

By and large, the principle of classification and organization we have described holds for the Mishnah. But there are occasionally departures from it. On departures in the sequence of the tractates, see ibid., pp. 27–28 and the references; on departures within a tractate, see ibid., 24–5 and the references. Add to the references on the order in the Mishnah, L. Ginzberg, "Tamid the Oldest Treatise of the Mishna," *Journal of Jewish Lore and Philosophy*, I, pp. 33–44, 197–209, 265–295.

19. *Shebu'ot* 40b—see also Rashi, a. l. Cf. *Baba Mezi'a* 4b. So also in regard to a law apparently given in two different chapters of the same tractate— *Zebaḥim* 11b. For another type of repetition, see *Ketubbot* 72a.

20. See Z. Frankel, *Darchey Hamishnah*, second ed., (Warsaw, 1923), pp. 220–228.

21. For a description of the hermeneutic rules, see M. Mielziner, *Introduction to the Talmud*, third ed., (New York: Bloch, 1925), pp. 130–176; Strack op. cit., pp. 93–95.

22. *Baba Kamma* I.I. This is an application of *binyan 'ab*; cf. Mielziner, op. cit., pp. 161–162.

23. *Mekilta*, III, 67–68.

24. Ibid., pp. 68–9. This interpretation by R. Eliezer, as many have said, does not mean that he does not accept the rabbinic law, but only that he insists that the biblical meaning was otherwise.

25. Such laws were designated *halaka l'moshe miSinai* or else were introduced by *B'emet omru* or by *omru*—see Frankel, op. cit., pp. 20, 304–305, and Krochmal, op. cit., pp. 213–214.

26. *Havayot d'rav v'shmuel.*

27. Krochmal, op. cit., p. 234.

28. *Havayot d'abaye v'rava.*

29. Krochmal describes these later discussions as characterized by: *Hakushia vhateyrutz hatashuva vhapiruk bichlal, hapilpul veyun hasvara b'chal hanimtsa mikvar*—op. cit., p. 234.

30. *Sukkah* 23a–24b; see a. l. the commentary of R. Hananel, beg.: *v'shaninun.* See note, *The Rabbinic Mind*, p. 369.

31. See *The Rabbinic Mind*, p. 80.

32. See L. Ginzberg, *A Commentary on the Palestinian Talmud*, I, p. 83, where these chapters are listed. See *The Rabbinic Mind*, notes, p. 369.

33. Ibid., I, pp. 81–2, 90.

34. Ibid., p. 82.

35. Ibid., pp. 81–2.

36. Ibid., p. 81 and p. 91, note.

37. Ibid., p. 82.

38. Ibid.

39. Ibid., pp. 82–3.

40. Ibid., p. 83.

41. Ibid.—a later and enlarged application of *Yachid v'rabim halacha kerabim.* See *Rabbinic Mind*, p. 369.

42. On the Mishnah and Tosefta, see Strack, op. cit., Chaps. III, IV, and VII; on the Halakic *Midrashim*, ibid., Chap. XVI.

43. See the parallels from the first five chapters of the *Mekilta*—L. Ginzberg, "On the relationship between the Mishna and the *Mekilta*" (Hebrew) in *Memorial Volume For Moshe Schorr* (Hebrew) (New York, 1945), pp. 57–95; also the parallels in C. Tchernowitz, *Toldot Hahalakah*, I (New York, 1934), pp. 51–53, 56–58.

44. See the summary of these opinions in Tchernowitz, op. cit., pp. 37–49.

45. Ginzberg, op. cit., p. 57. In this article, he begins the publication of such a detailed comparison.

46. On the references to the hermeneutic rules, see above, p. 91, note 4. On the norms of interpretation associated with Hillel and with R. Ishmael, see now S. Lieberman, op. cit., pp. 53 ff. Lieberman here shows that there is a decided kinship between these norms and the methods of the rhetors in Alexandria, and even in the terminology.

47. *Mekilta*, I, p. 25; comp. ibid., p. 40. See notes, p. 370.

48. Yoma 74a; Hagigah 4a; and elsewhere. Verses supporting *Halakah L'Moshe Mi-Sinai* are also designated as *'asmakta*—see *Sukkah 6a. (The parallel in Berakot 41b has an incorrect reading*—see Rabbinovicz, *Dikduke Soferim a. 1.)*

49. See Bacher, *Terminologie*, Hebr. trans. *arche midrash, p. 152, s. v. 'asmakta* and p. 38, note 11, end.

50. Michael Guttmann, *Mafteah Ha-Talmud*, Vol. III, Part I (Breslau, 1924), supplement, *'asmakta*, pp. 1–48.

51. See, for example, Tchernowitz's objection (op. cit., p. 66, note) to Guttmann's taking *somchu* to refer to an *'asmakta*. We have here, by the way, another instance in rabbinic terminology of how careful we must be before assuming that verb-forms of a root have the same sense as the nominative.

52. *Orlah* III.9.

43. *Kiddushin* I.9. See Bertinoro a.1.

54. *Yer. 'Orlah* III.8 (9), 63b.

55. Ibid.; cf. *Kiddushin* 37a.

56. The *Shema'* consists of Deut. 6:4–9; ibid., 11:13–21; and Num. 15:37–41—see *Berakot* II.2.

57. See the discussion in *Tosafot to Sotah* 32b, s. v. *v'rab*.

58. *Berakot* 21a.

59. Maimonides, *Sefor Hamitzvot, shoresh sheni*.

60. Nahmanides' comments, ibid.

61. *Sifra* to Lev. 13:47—*ad she'edrosh*. Malbim's explanatory comment a. l. is: "Thou sayest to the verse that it keep silent until thou shalt interpret according as thy wish."

62. See above, p. 100.

63. See Guttmann, op. cit., supplement, pp. 25–6, and the references there. Several such derivations are to be found in Sanhedrin 3b–4b.

64. Yer. Berakot IV.3, 7d. The same query is raised in regard to the number of benedictions on other occasions, and the same type of answer is given—ibid.

65. Ginzberg remarks that the Rabbis deliberately searched in Scripture until they found support of one kind or another for the number and order of the benedictions—Commentary, III, p. 248.

66. *Yer. Ta'anit* II.1, 65a, cited by Guttmann, op. cit., p. 28.

67. *Rosh Ha-Shanah* III.2.

68. *Leviticus R.* XXVII.3.

69. *Yer. Berakot* IV.1, 7a. The parallels are given by Theodor, op. cit., p. 778.

70. Ginzberg, op. cit., III, pp. 24–7. R. Joshua b. Levi's statement is, moreover, later than the one which attributes the prayers to Daniel and also found in *Yer. Berakot* IV.1, 7a—Ginzberg, op. cit., III, p. 25.

71. Scholars sometimes assume that a *Halakah* is based on a *Haggadah* because they have not read the passage correctly. Guttmann so understands a passage in *Shabbat* 119b which has to do with the interpretation of Gen. 2:1 (op. cit., p. 27). Guttmann's text was faulty. As can be seen from the *mesoret hashas* a. l., the authorities for this particular *Halakah* preceded by several generations the authority for the *Haggadah*, and the *Halakah* is, therefore, older than the *Haggadah* in this instance. Similarly, some medieval scholars have assumed that Ps. 103:3, as interpreted in *Yer. Berakot* II.3, 4c, conveys the idea that illness purifies the body of sin, and that a certain procedure of R. Yanai's recorded there is based on this haggadic idea—see Ginzberg, *Commentary*, I, p. 259. But Ginzberg has demonstrated that this entire assumption is erroneous—ibid., p. 265 f. In the light of his explanation, there is no haggadic element in the passage.

72. *Sanhedrin* 34a.
73. Above, p. 125.
74. See, for example, *Sukkah* 9a. See notes, p. 370.
75. Above, pp. 93–95.
76. The recital of "Hear, O Israel, the Lord is our God, the Lord is One" (Deut. 6:4) is the affirmation of *Malkut Shamayim*— TE (above, p. 15, n. 2), p. 60. This is emphasized by an insertion the Rabbis made between Deut. 6:4 and ibid.

To ERNST SIMON, halachah advocates, above all, "sober drunkenness" (Philo) or "normal mysticism" (Max Kadushin). It does not
demand self-negation, but "tempers self-surrender with self-control." Halachah is also "non-totalitarian totality," in that it
"leaves room for doubt, discussion, and disagreement." Its principles and conclusions are not fixed or frozen. There is no central
authority to enforce observance. The sanctity of one's deeds is
stressed, not the conformity of one's beliefs.

Rabbinic Judaism emphasizes the middle way between Greek
non-asceticism and Christian asceticism. One must "enjoy the
fulfillment of life" without falling prey to instant roads to utopia.
To live as a Jew demands "critical identification" with the Jewish
people and their land. In the tension between tradition and life,
halachah is in danger of "petrification," "esthetic deficit," "emotional deficit" (excessive legalism) and "chauvinism." But halachah has demonstrated time-worn effectiveness in preserving Jewish religious society, in inculcating a sense of religious obligation,
and in cultivating chastity of the soul. It can yet cultivate one's intellect, discipline, and sense of direction with its constant sanctity.

237

The Halachic Dimension: Law and Observance in Jewish Experience

ERNST SIMON

Shlomo Alkabetz opens his famous Sabbath hymn, *l'cha dodi,* with the words, *shamor v'zachor b'dibur echad,* "observe and remember the Sabbath day—these commandments God caused us to hear in a single utterance." Alkabetz's phrase recapitulates a formulation of the Talmud[1] where the rabbis seek to explain the discrepancy between the two versions of the fourth commandment in the Torah—the one in Exodus 20:8 which says, *zachor et yom ha'shabbat,* "*remember* the Sabbath day," the other in Deuteronomy 5:12 which reads, *shamor et yom ha'shabbat,* "*observe* the Sabbath day." The rabbis of the Talmud felt that both terms belong together. They are "a single utterance" and represent a unity which in turn reflects God's unity and indivisibility in space and time.

I believe these terms can also serve as a meaningful description of my task. In the act of *zachor*—by evoking the past and recapitulating it—we can discover the rationale for *shamor,* our observance of halachah.

Sobriety and "God-intoxication"

Halachah has several characteristic features which reflect Judaism's distinctive attitude towards life and the world. One of these characteristic features is that halachah makes a plea for sobriety in religion. Philo, the first Jewish philosopher (about 25 B.C.E. to 50 C.E.), who wrote in Greek but is usually quoted in Latin, once spoke of *sobria ebrietas,* sober drunkenness. A contemporary scholar, Dr. Max Kadushin, de-

238

scribes the same phenomenon by using the term, "normal mysticism."

Both terms describe the spiritual and intellectual climate which ha-lachah seeks to create—sober drunkenness. We cannot help but be drunk when we come near to God. Yet classical Judaism has always in-sisted that this intoxication be kept within the limits of sobriety.

But how can drunkenness be sober? To use Dr. Kadushin's phrase, how can mysticism be normal? Is drunkenness not a state in which you seek to gain yourself by losing yourself? Is mysticism not a posture in which man seeks what the philosophers have called a *unio mystica,* a union with God which can be achieved only by means of ecstatic con-templation and the complete abandonment of the self? In the ecstasy of the mystic experience, the distinction between God and man disap-pears and the danger arises that in this experience God will lose His di-vinity and man, his humanity.

Precisely because the danger of a complete abandonment of self is always present when man seeks to approach God in prayer, Judaism has attempted to "normalize" mysticism. Halachah is our means to maintain the delicate balance between sobriety and God-intoxication. It tempers self-surrender with self-control and preserves the distinc-tion between God and man: man's relationship to God is achieved not in a mystical union but in the fulfillment of God's commandments in the here and now. And unlike mysticism, which restricts the mysteri-ous experience of a union with God to a select few, halachah obliter-ates the distinction between the few select who can experience God, and the masses who cannot. Law and observance are a way to God which is open to all without distinction.

Non-Totalitarian Totality

A second characteristic of halachah is what I would like to call its non-totalitarian totality. Jewish law is all-embracing. It is total: it governs all aspects of man's life. No province in the kingdom of man and his life is beyond the reach and discipline of Jewish law. In this respect, Judaism differs from the philosophy of the Stoics who maintained that there is an *adiaphoron*—things which are neither good nor bad, neither commanded nor forbidden. The *adiaphoron* represents an area of neu-trality and hence of freedom in the moral realm. Classical Judaism does not know such a neutral sphere. No things or actions can ever be morally neutral. Halachah regulates every area of life—eating, drinking, prayer, work, our relationship to family and fellow man, even our love life, the most intimate sphere of human experience. It is a total system. It aims at the sanctification of every action and moment of man's life. I find this aspect of halachah expressed with particular poignancy in the order of worship which requires that the daily evening prayer be said immediately upon the conclusion of the Ne'ilah service on Yom Kippur. We have prayed and fasted throughout the entire day. Now the day is ended. Everyone is eager to go home and break the fast. People are rushing out. Yet there is always at least a small group of persons who remain behind to recite the regular daily evening prayer. Having just cleansed and purified ourselves, we again pronounce the daily bid for forgiveness. The Jewish year, time, has no pauses. Halachah governs the totality of man's life and time.

Nevertheless, this totality is non-totalitarian. Halachah is demanding and commanding but not despotic. It could not become totalitarian because it leaves room for doubt, discussion, disagreement. Its principles and conclusions are not fixed or frozen into immutable finality. The Talmud is not a book but a record, in twenty volumes, of discussions which were going on in Babylonia and Palestine for a period of at least 600 or 700 years. It does not mention the year or period when certain discussions took place. All the generations talked with each other. Every question may become an answer, and many answers turn out to pose new questions.

Yet the Talmud is not only a record of discussions. It actually can be studied only through discussion. A man can read or study every book in world literature by himself except the Talmud. The Talmud can be studied only by the same oral method—the method of discussion—in which it was developed. Questions and answers are not indicated by punctuation marks. There are no commas, no question marks, and only rarely periods. Questions and answers or the end of sentences must be indicated by the rise or fall of the speaker's voice. Rashi, the most famous of all Talmud commentators, gives us a clue to this almost hidden treasure. Whenever a sentence or phrase in the text should be read not as a question but as if there were a period, he says, *binichuta*, an aramaic term which means: "Say it in a lowered voice." Rashi uses an acoustic notation to describe a non-existing but needed graphic or visual symbol. The melody of speech has become the melody of learning. Hence the Talmud is not a dry book. It has music. And it could never become totalitarian because it contains the music of discussion, the staccato arguments of debate, the counterpoint of disagreement, the final harmonization of differing views.

There is a second reason for which this total system is not totalitarian. Since Talmudic times, Judaism has had no central religious authorities, no ecclesiastic hierarchy. When I began my career as a high-school teacher in Germany before my *aliyah* to Israel, I asked my principal on the first day of school to permit me to take Shabbat off altogether or at least those morning hours which I needed to attend synagogue services. He denied my request. The regulations left him no choice. When I told him that I would neither write nor carry my books on Shabbat, he suggested that I consult my rabbi and ask him to give me permission to do both. There was only one answer I could give him. A rabbi who would give me permission to violate the Sabbath could not be a rabbi for me. Unlike the Roman church, Judaism makes no distinction between priesthood and laity. There is no special group of persons who are entitled to perform particular priestly or sacerdotal functions for others. The entire people is to become a "kingdom of priests"—every Jew, be he the Chief Rabbi of Israel or a simple unlearned Jew in the streets of New York City, is required to fulfill all *mitzvot.* Jews may—and do—differ in the degree of conscientiousness with which they fulfill the religious commandments. Traditional and liberal Jews and their various sub-groupings differ in the way they define the nature and implications of *mitzvah* and law in Judaism. These are legitimate differences of conviction. But to establish a difference in the standards of observance between rabbi and "layman" would be illegitimate. We have no ecclesiastical hierarchy or caste of priests ordained to do the job for us. One cannot be a Jew by proxy. Every single Jew bears full responsibility for the observance of the law.

In Talmudic times, the Jewish community had a central authority, the *Beit Din Ha'gadol.* It served as the Supreme Court of the Jewish community, and its decisions, proclaimed in a certain place in the sanctuary, were law. Nevertheless, a scholar who disagreed with the pronouncements of the court was still permitted to question the law and to express his disagreement with it when he taught his students in the academy. He was not permitted to advocate that the law be violated, but he retained the freedom of intellectual dissent. Jewish law is not totalitarian.

There is still another factor which assures the non-totalitarian character of halachah. There is a relative freedom of teaching and opinion in Rabbinic Judaism. Near the beginning of his famous codification of the law, the *Mishneh Torah*, Maimonides makes the statement that anyone who believes that God has a body like a human being is a sectarian. He is not a good Jew. Maimonides was a rationalist, the leader of the enlightenment of his day. His philosophic training had convinced him that the anthropomorphisms of the Bible could not be taken literally. However, his views did not remain unchallenged. One of his contemporaries, Rabbi Avraham Ben David (the RaViD), dissented sharply: better and wiser men than this author believe that God has a body, yet they do not call the people sectarians. The people are entitled to their beliefs, even though they may be erroneous. They have derived their beliefs from the *Aggadah* and the *Midrashim,* our traditional sources. Maimonides' antagonist fought for the freedom of belief of people whose beliefs he himself did not share. Like Maimonides, Avraham Ben David was anti-anthropomorphic and could not accept the belief that God has a body. Yet he insisted that one can be a good Jew and affirm this belief. Judaism regulates man's acts but not his thoughts. No one has the right to read someone else out of Judaism or to consider him a less adequate Jew because their views of God's nature may differ. Judaism must be able to accommodate both views. Both are authentic expressions of Jewish tradition and Jewish faith even though they may contradict each other. The unity of the Jewish people is based not on everyone's acceptance of the same dubious results of philosophical speculation but on every single Jew's faithful performance of the mitzvot. God's commandments are addressed to man's will, not to his mind. Man's notions or thoughts may well be mistaken or erroneous. God's nature is beyond our grasp. But His commandments are neither hidden nor far off.[2]

This relative freedom of thought and teaching is one of the characteristic features of Rabbinic Judaism. Luther and Zwingli, two of the giants of the Protestant Reformation, were troubled by a problem which was similar to that which had troubled Maimonides and Avraham Ben David, when they discussed the question whether the host, the consecrated wafer, merely *symbolizes* God's body or actually *is* God's body. If God has a body, why could He not be in this holy bread? When Zwingli insisted that the bread was more than a symbol and that it actually was God's body, Luther broke off the discussion and said to his colleague, *Wir haben nicht denselben Geist*—"ours is not the same spirit." As a result of this disagreement, the Reformation movement was split into two parts—divided by a question which had been settled by Maimonides and the RaViD through a single side-remark stating their disagreement but accepting both views as authentic. The controversy did not destroy the unity of Judaism, and every reader of the *Mishneh Torah* today can study both views and reach his own conclusions. Halachah does not impose specific views upon you. It is not a totalitarian system.

The Middle Way

A third characteristic of Rabbinic Judaism is its partial asceticism. In this respect it differs from the Greek world which, with some noteworthy exceptions, was non-ascetic. According to the Greek view, man realizes his humanity by living out his life to the fullest, physically and intellectually, even though this course of action might involve indulgence and physical excess. This concept became a dominant ideal once again in the Renaissance which spoke of *uomo universale,* universal man. The universal man is the person who actualizes his potential of body and mind to the fullest. Renaissance man thus obliterates the distinction between virtues and vices; he is less interested in whether an act is good or bad than whether it is authentic or inauthentic. The same criterion is usually applied in the realm of esthetics. Its highest value is authenticity of expression. Shakespeare's *Richard the Third* is an authentic person; Shakespeare would never have been able to create him without a deep empathy for authentic evil. What matters is not whether a man's conduct and life are morally good or bad but whether they are an authentic expression of his personality. This is one approach to life. Its most recent form is existentialism.

Christianity advocates the opposite way of life: complete asceticism. Echoing a statement of ancient Greek mysticism that "the body is a tomb," Christianity, again with important exceptions, considered the experiences of the senses sinful and insisted that the desires of the body corrupted and destroyed the soul. The ideal Christian personality type was not universal man but the monk and the nun, the person who withdraws from family and the world to avoid temptation and to achieve purity from the desires of the body.

Judaism represents a middle way. It posits partial asceticism. It rejects uncontrolled indulgence of desire just as vigorously as it objects to complete asceticism. The body is no less the work of God than is the soul, and it can therefore not be inherently evil. Self-negation is not necessarily a virtue. On the contrary, it may turn out to be an evil by destroying man's ability to enjoy the fulfillment of life. According to a rabbinic interpretation, the biblical verse, "Thou shalt rejoice before the Lord thy God," refers not only to the joys of the spirit—study, worship and good deeds—but also to the joys of the body, "food and drink, raiment and fellowship."[3]

According to the Talmud, we are not forbidden but actually bidden to enjoy food, drink, love. They are God's gifts. In the last analysis, the complete ascetic who rejects these gifts rejects God.

Jewish tradition posits partial asceticism—a way of life which is neither surrender to unbridled hedonism nor an ascetic withdrawal from the world. It is a way of life that enables us to live in this world, to enjoy it fully and with all our senses. At the same time, it demands that we always remain in control of ourselves and invest everything we do with k'dushah, with holiness, with intimations of the divine.

Non-utopian Messianism

A fourth element which characterizes Rabbinic Judaism and is embodied in Jewish law is its non-utopian messianism. Messianism is a pointing to the future. Why then do I call Jewish messianism, the Jewish drive for the millenium and its hope for a better future for Israel and mankind, non-utopian? Utopia, a Greek term, was coined by Thomas More in 1516 when he wrote his *Utopia* as an answer to Machiavelli's *Principe*. Utopia, literally, means "no-place," and More's book describes the ideal society which is on no-place but which is to serve as a model for the earthly place and society of the man who envisions it. The author speaks of something that is far away (and perhaps unattainable) in order to influence the society which is near, and to introduce changes in accordance with the image of the ideal. The ideal society does not exist. Hence all utopian thinking is pseudo-messianic: the redeemer has not yet come. Utopia always remains something that still has to be achieved.

Judaism represents a non-utopian messianism. Jews exist today, and we are able to define ourselves as Jews, because our forefathers, in a decisive moment of our history, said "no" to various utopias, whether it was the utopia of Christianity or that of Communism.

Someone once said that through the *nays* you can hear the *yeas* of the Jewish people. That which is rejected by Judaism often gives us a clue to what Judaism affirms. Judaism rejected Christianity. Among the people who rejected Jesus and refused to accept Christianity were some of the best as well as some of the worst Jews. The worst were the cynics who rejected the new faith because they could not believe in the possibility of a better future. The best were the believing realists who rejected the promise of utopia precisely because they saw the world as it was—still unchanged, still incomplete, still in need of fulfillment and redemption.

The Jewish attitude is compellingly illustrated by a story of a Chassidic rabbi who had gone to *Eretz Yisrael* and had made his home near the Mount of Olives. One morning, he heard the sound of the *shofar,* on a day on which the sounding of the *shofar* is not prescribed by Jewish law. He left his little hut wondering whether the Messiah had come, for, according to an ancient tradition, the arrival of the Messiah is heralded by the sounding of the *shofar.* But as he looked around, he responded to what he saw in the streets in just a single sentence, "The world has not changed." The Messiah could not have arrived. And he returned home to pursue his life of study and piety.

The power to resist pseudo-messianic movements and promises has made us the people that carries with it the message of *ge'ulah,* of final redemption. Had we fallen victim to one or the other type of utopian messianism we would today be disappointed Christians or disappointed Communists. Our non-utopian messianism has enabled us to remain hopeful, actively hopeful Jews.

People and Nation

A fifth and last characteristic of the Jewish posture is a critical identification with a religiously defined nation or people. Associated with this identification is what I consider to be this generation's main task, the building of *Eretz Yisrael.*

"Critical identification" is a dialectical combination of terms. How can identification be critical? And how can a critic be identified with the cause he criticizes? To paraphrase Pascal's distinction, criticism is a function of the mind, identification is an involvement of the heart. How can the heart become critical and the mind, identified?

The answer can be found in another, more familiar phrase. We sometimes speak of "critical love" in order to characterize a relationship in which love and criticism, attachment and detachment are fused together indissolubly. Love is not so blind as to silence criticism, criticism not so detached as to destroy love.

This is what I mean when I speak of critical identification with the
Jewish people. It is possible to remain critical from without—without
love, without identification with our people and the country which
once again has become our homeland. In this case, our criticism will
remain external and ineffectual. Obversely, we can permit our glowing
hearts to become identified with our people's life and work in Eretz
Yisrael to such an extent and with such intensity that our love will silence even justified criticism of ourselves and our work. In this case we
tend to become chauvinists, and all we do today may ultimately lose its
meaning because the Jewish people and the Jewish state will no longer
be and represent what we hoped and worked for in order to stem the
danger of collective assimilation in Israel and to make this land the setting for the fulfillment of an age-old dream.

Critical identification is characteristic not only of the attitude of Rabbinic Judaism but expecially of the prophets. No prophet ever dreamt
of leaving his people. No prophet ever claimed that everything Jews
did or do is good because it is being done by Jews. They criticized their
people precisely because they loved them; and they suffered deeply because their concern for their people's welfare and destiny compelled
them to silence their love and compassion and to criticize. The prophet
Jeremiah personified this attitude.[4] Hananiah, who turned out to be a
false prophet, came to besieged Jerusalem whose capture and destruction by the Babylonians had been predicted by Jeremiah. Hananiah
proclaimed that the yoke and stranglehold of Nebuchadnezzar on Jerusalem would be broken, that the city would be freed and that the cap-
tives would return. Jeremiah was present when Hananiah spoke. He
listened carefully. He wished from the bottom of his heart that Hananiah were right and that his own prophecies of doom were wrong. He
loved his people. He did not want them to suffer. Yet he also knew that
Nebuchadnezzar's yoke would not be broken and that the suffering
that lay ahead was God's punishment for the moral corruption and decay of the people and its disobedience to God. He loved his people yet
he had to criticize them. He wanted to comfort them, yet he had to admonish them for the sake of their welfare and their responsibilities under their covenant with God. But he never lost his feeling of identification with his people even though he had to chastise them. He remained
one of them and was among the pitiful remnants of the people that
were led into exile in Egypt.

This is critical identification. One can be the sharpest critic of one's
people yet remain fully identified with it and wish to share its life and

tasks. At the end of the volume which deals with the destruction of the Second Temple by the Romans in the year 70, Heinrich Graetz (1817-1891), probably our greatest Jewish historian, asked why Jeremiah, who had predicted the destruction of the First Temple, had been accepted by the Jewish people as a true prophet, while Flavius Josephus, who quoted one of Jeremiah's speeches when he was standing among the Roman legions before the walls of Jerusalem that were besieged by Titus and Vespasian, was considered a traitor. Graetz's answer makes the point that "Jeremiah spoke from within; Josephus spoke from the tent of the Roman general." Where you stand when you speak—that makes all the difference. It makes either for identification or lack of it.

Dangers and Balance

Law and observance provide the climate of Jewish life that safeguards and sustains its distinctive features: its emphasis on sobriety in religion, its non-totalitarian character, its partial asceticism, its non-utopian messianism, its demand for critical identification with the Jewish people. Nevertheless, law and observance may also involve certain dangers to the health of Jewish life.

One possible danger is petrification, arrested development. The term halachah is derived from the verb, *haloch*, to walk. Halachah is a way of life, not a standpoint of life. It involves movement, change, progression, not immobility and standing still. Yet many of us use the Talmud or the *Shulchan Aruch* and our other codes in the same way in which the Sadducees and the Karaites used the Bible. The Karaites rejected the Rabbinic tradition and claimed to base their teachings solely on the text of the Bible, disregarding the outer and inner developments that had taken place between the time of the Bible and their own time. Many of us have become Karaites of the most recent codifications of the oral law. We act as if nothing had taken place since they were published. Thus we have what I like to call an *evolutionary deficit* in halachah. Orthodoxy does not reject the principle of change as such. But its method of change has become so ineffective and slow that the danger of petrification is very real.

A second danger lies in the *esthetic deficit* that can be found in Jewish tradition. Martin Buber once said that the Jews were not a people of the "eye and imitation" but of the "ear and obedience."[5] According to

Jewish tradition, God can only be heard, not seen. Visual art was largely neglected. One of the reasons might have been that the Jew met visual art only in the context of pagan worship and idolatrous practices which were often hideously immoral. The esthetic realm had no autonomous existence in ancient times. Even in Greek civilization, art was intimately related to religious practice, worship and cult. The Jew rejected visual art because he rejected the religious and moral aberrations of the idolatrous practices for which the artist's handiwork was used.

Whatever the reasons for the absence of a concern with visual art in Jewish life may be—the point is that there is an esthetic deficit in Jewish tradition. We must try to reduce it. I do not propose that we place esthetic values at the top of the pyramid of Jewish values. But we must place them higher than we have done in the past.

A third danger which threatens meaningful observance is excessive legalism, an *emotional deficit* that can occasionally be found among strictly observant Jews. Some years ago I wrote an article for a Hebrew journal in which I attempted to show that a religious experience encompasses peaks as well as valleys of intensity. We oscillate between moments of greater and lesser spirituality and emotion in prayer and observance. In the same way, we respond with varying degrees of intensity to different parts of the Torah. There are some ideas and *mitzvot* which we stress more, which we can "feel" more deeply and with which we can identify ourselves more adequately than with others. A very observant rabbi, in answer to my article, wrote that I was wrong: All parts of the Torah are of equal value and religious importance. We have no right to make a distinction between the Sh'ma Yisrael, for instance, and a biblical sentence dealing with the status of a woman who was a concubine. In my answer, I pointed out that I had never heard or read that our martyrs, in the Spanish period or our own time, went to their death proclaiming their faith in a sentence such as *vetimnah hayta pilegesh*—"and Timnah was a concubine." The cry that rose from their lips at the moment of agony was the *Sh'ma Yisrael*. Emotionally and existentially, there is a vast difference between these notions. Yet it is not easy to accept the validity of such a distinction from a purely legalistic, halachic point of view.

There is a last danger. It is the danger of chauvinism.° Numerous people claim, for instance, that a true Jew must be a pacifist—Judaism

°See the author's recent article "The Neighbour Whom We Shall Love" in *Modern Jewish Ethics* edited by Marvin Fox, Ohio State University Press, 1975, pp. 29–56.

has always identified itself with the unconditional quest for peace. This claim is, however, not supported by the facts. According to its classical sources, Judaism is neither for peace nor for war. Our tradition—the Bible, Rabbinic Judaism, even the Rambam and our prayers—contain notions and events which support both positions. The opening prayer of the *S'lichot* service contains a phrase in which we forgive our enemies and adversaries and ask that no man should suffer or be punished for our sins and the sins committed against us. Yet a few moments later, the entire congregation join in a recitation of the *ashrey* in which we say, *v'et har'shaim yash'mid*—"and the wicked people God will destroy." Our sources are inconsistent. We must have the courage to face the fact that our definition of the ideas and commitments of Judaism depends on the sources which we use. Judaism contains contradictory notions, and the decision which element of the Jewish heritage to choose or stress depends on our interests and concerns. Only a chauvinist can claim that everything which is recorded in our tradition is good or that nothing Jews ever said or did is wrong. Sometimes, when certain parts of the Torah are read in the Sabbath service, I have the fervent wish not to be called upon to recite the blessing over the Torah. I do recite the *b'rakhah* when I am called to the Torah because I am a good soldier and perhaps do not have enough courage. But I do not always find it easy to reconcile the benediction with the content of the passages which are being read.

Halachic observance poses certain dangers; but these dangers are out-balanced by the capacity of halachah to create and strengthen the distinctive quality of Jewish life.

Only halachah gives us the possibility to become a religious society and not merely to remain unrelated religious individuals. It is difficult to be a religious Jew as an isolated individual, divorced from the community. This is one of the significant differences between Judaism and Christianity. Both religions bear the mark of their native hours. Judaism was born in a collective experience, the experience of an entire people at Mount Sinai. Christianity was born in an individual experience, the experience of one person believed by his believers to be the son of God. Therefore the believing individual is central to Christianity while Judaism, be it traditional or Reform Judaism, has always stressed the community. Judaism and Christianity represent two different approaches to the life of faith, and we may conceivably have something to learn from one another. We can learn from the Christians how to become a believing individual. They can try to learn from us how to

become a religious society. One could write a history of Christianity as
a sequence of experiments to achieve a religious society. When Christians tried to establish such a society, as Cromwell and other Puritans
sought to do, they took their guiding principles from the Hebrew Bible. The New Testament does not contain those principles of communal life and organization which could serve as a foundation for the establishment of a Christian society. The Hebrew Bible and our halachah contain these features. The achievement of a genuinely religious
society remains an unfulfilled need.

A second aspect of halachah which contributes to its efficacy, is a
phenomenon which I want to call "obligating prose." I mentioned earlier that Jewish tradition is characterized by an esthetic deficit. Nevertheless, modern Judaism still possesses too much poetry and not
enough obligating prose. In religious life prose is more important than
poetry. Poetry addresses itself to the imagination. Prose addresses itself to the will. Poetry can get away with the beauty of expression.
Prose obligates you. It makes a claim upon you. It demands action and
sustained effort. Chaim Nachman Bialik, who succeeded in capturing
the poetry of the *Aggadah* and made it accessible to a wide public in
his *Sefer Ha'aggadah,* had the courage to say in his wonderful essay on
"Halachah V'aggadah," "We have too much *chibah,* too much lovingkindness, and not enough *chovah,* not enough obligation." If I were
able to compose prayers, I would perhaps pray, "Give us *mitzvot;* give
us obligations."

What I mean when I speak of "obligating prose" can be illustrated
by two examples from the Responsa literature of the time of the recent
European holocaust. Our Responsa literature contains the answers to
halachic questions which rabbis are asked. Among the volumes record-
ing the questions and answers of our people during the holocaust, is a
Hebrew volume by Rabbi Oshri, formerly of Kovno, entitled *Min Ha-
ma'amakim,* "Out of the Depths." The book contains the answers
which Rabbi Oshry and some of his colleagues gave to the questions
the Jews of Kovno asked of them during the time of the Nazi occupa-
tion and at the height of persecution—for instance, whether it was permissible to eat non-kosher food in order to maintain one's strength, or
to break the Shabbat in order to escape death. The questioners were
prepared to accept whatever answer the rabbis would give them. They
sought guidance. Therefore the answers were obligating prose, guidelines for conduct in the face of danger and the threat of imminent
death. As far as I can remember, there were only two cases in which the

court did not grant permission to do what people had asked for. In response to the question whether a young man was permitted to kill himself in order to escape torture and death at the hands of the Nazis, the rabbis answered, "No, my son. We should never do their evil work for them. We have to live to our last moment." Suicide is the ultimate abdication of faith. It means final despair, the conviction that God can no longer help.

In the second case they said "no" to a young girl's question whether she was permitted to register, dress and act as a gentile in order to save her life. Again the answer was in the negative, despite the fact that Maimonides, in his *"Iggeret Hash'mad,"* had made a different ruling. Rabbi Oshry's rationale and motivation—as difficult as their acceptance may be for us—were based on his unshakable conviction that no person should desert the Jewish people even under extreme stress. Halachah is obligating prose. It deals with man's ethical and religious obligation, not with esthetic values which do not ask for a commitment.

A third characteristic of halachah is its tenor of religious chastity. I do not mean the chastity of the body, an important concept in Rabbinic thought. I mean the chastity of the soul. When you study the Talmud, you discover that it says little about God. He is rarely mentioned in the really indispensable passages of the Talmud which are studied customarily and with regularity. Unlike the Billy Grahams of today, the Rabbis rarely spoke of God, not because they lacked faith but because their faith was so profound and secure that it did not require verbalization. God's presence was felt in all they thought and did. A man of tact and sensitivity does not discuss his love for his wife with others. In the same way, the Rabbis of the Talmud rarely spoke of their deepest love, their love of God. The atmosphere of the legal parts of halachic discussion is one of religious chastity.

Jews and Jewish Law

Can a modern Jew still find a rationale for the observance of halakhah? Specifically, can a non-Orthodox Jew take a positive stand with regard to halakhah, and on what grounds can he affirm its validity and accept its claims for himself and his community?

I believe such a rationale can be formulated. Halakhah safeguards the identity of the Jewish faith and the Jewish people. Judaism is a religion that is practiced by Jews. Judaism accepts proselytes but does not seek them. Persons who profess a Christian faith cannot be Jews. A Jew who embraces another faith leaves the Jewish people. He may be a deeply moral person, yet his conversion terminates his membership in the Jewish people. There is a relative identity between the faith and the people, and this relative identity can be established and maintained only by a sanctified way of life. Halakhah is our only means to establish and maintain this sanctified way of life.

Above all, however, halakhah can have profound relevance for the modern Jew because it embodies and represents an attitude toward life which emphasizes the need for a restitution of the intellect in a partly anti-intellectual society, for discipline in a partly libertarian world, for orientation and a sense of direction in a chaos of over-information, and for a rational religion in the face of the inroads of mysticism and obscurantism.

Halakhah stresses the use of the intellect and its restitution in a partly anti-intellectual society by virtue of its uncompromising emphasis on study and the life of the intellect as a mode of worship and religious expression. Dr. Robert Hutchins, the former chancellor of the University of Chicago, concluded the fifth of a series of lectures which he delivered in Jerusalem by saying that the Jewish people had always had his unconditional support and admiration because it was the only people he knew which had made learning a religious duty. Hutchins was not wholly correct; the Chinese had a similar emphasis. Nevertheless, he was right in pointing out that halakhah has always and vigorously insisted on the primacy of intellectual activity and concerns over against emotionalism—an emphasis which can serve as a vitally needed antidote to the anti-intellectual trends in contemporary society.

Halakhah calls for the restoration of discipline in a partly libertarian world and for the recovery of a perspective and a sense of direction in the chaos of over-information. To use the title of a well-known book by Professor Wolfgang Koehler, it calls for a "place of values in the world of facts." Halakhah teaches the place of values in a world of facts. We live in a world that lacks equilibrium between too much and not enough information. We know too much, yet, at the same time, too little. We know too many details but do not have sufficient principles to organize them meaningfully. One function of revelation is to provide orientation and direction. When Jews pray, they turn East in order to face Jerusalem. They have a point of reference by which they orient themselves. It gives them direction and helps organize the data of their experiences. Halakhah provides such orientation, occasionally too much so. But it is easier to reduce a surplus than to fill a vacuum.

Lastly, halakhah represents the unceasing demand for relative rationality in religion, for a rational religious way of life in a world challenged, on the one side, by shallow secularism and, on the other side, by religious obscurantism. The concluding verse in the twenty-ninth chapter of Deuteronomy says, "The hidden things belong unto the Lord our God, but the revealed things belong to us and our children for all eternity, that we may fulfill all the words of His Torah."[6] When I spoke at an academic convocation honoring Professor Gershom Scholem, the foremost authority in the field of Jewish mysticism, on the occasion of his sixtieth birthday, I concluded my address with the words, "At a time when the hidden things are being revealed, the revealed things are being hidden."

Halakhah stands not for what is hidden but for what man can know and do. My plea is for the revealed things—to study them and to fulfill them.

Notes

1. *Rosh Hashana* 27a; cf. *Y. Nedarim* III, 5:37d.
2. *Mishneh Torah, Hilkhot Teshuvah* 3:7, and RaBAD there.
3. Deut. 30:11.
4. Deut. 12:18; 16:11, cf. Lev. 23:40.
5. Milton Steinberg, *Basic Judaism* (New York, 1947) p. 72.
6. Deut. 29:28.

Part II

LAW AS GUIDANCE

In this section we present some of the *teshuvot* (responsa) that have been prepared by members of the Committee on Jewish Law of the Rabbinical Assembly. They deal with issues of *kashrut*, bioethics, and the role of women in the synagogue. These *teshuvot* illustrate the approach of Conservative Judaism to practical issues of halachah.

This process involves: 1) searching out precedents in the traditional literature which apply to the current problem, 2) analyzing these precedents as to their basis and assumptions, 3) deciding whether under the present conditions these assumptions can be accepted. The conclusions drawn are sometimes different than those of the traditional authorities. This is because the scientific or sociological assumptions of the past cannot, with good conscience, be accepted in the present. Though the results may differ from those who hold more traditional views, the process is the same one that has characterized Jewish law-interpretation from time immemorial.

It will also be noted that different opinions may be reached by various writers of the *teshuvot* (as, for example, the role of women in the synagogue ritual). In the view of Conservative Judaism, when two authorities have differing views, the individual, local rabbi (the *mara d'a-tra*) makes the decision for his congregation. The Conservative movement attempts to achieve an over-arching unity which can include diverse views and interpretations of individual matters of Jewish law.

The function of a *teshuvah* is to clarify an issue of Jewish law. The material found in this section represents only an extremely small proportion of the answers to questions asked of the members of the Committee on Jewish Law. Although the responsa we selected deal with is-

255

sues that are among the most lively and controversial, the archives of
the Committee on Jewish Law reflects decisions covering almost every
facet of Jewish life. Many of the *teshuvot* have appeared in *Conservative Judaism* and in the *Proceedings of the Rabbinical Assembly.* An
earlier collection of *teshuvot* appears in *Tradition and Change,* and
many of Rabbi Isaac Klein's responsa can be found in his *Responsa
and Halakhic Studies.*

RABBI ISAAC KLEIN, one of the leading poskim, decisors, of Conservative Judaism presents the Jewish view on abortion in this responsum. His conclusion is that abortion be permitted only for therapeutic reasons.

Though this teshuvah was written some time ago, and much new material has accumulated since its publication, it is a succinct expression of the view on abortion by one of the leading authorities in the Conservative movement.

Teshuvah on Abortion

ISAAC KLEIN

Is abortion permitted according to Jewish law?

We first have to define the word "abortion." Medically, abortion is the term indicating the spontaneous or artificial termination of a pregnancy before the twenty-eighth week, when the infant, theoretically, first becomes able to carry on an independent existence.[1] In our case the question applies only to the artificial (not spontaneous or natural) termination of the pregnancy at any time before the complete birth of the child and involving the death of the embryo or the foetus.

The main talmudic source for this question is found in the Mishnah which states: "A woman that is having difficulty in giving birth, it is permitted to cut up the child inside her womb and take it out limb by limb because her life takes precedence. If the greater part of the child has come out it must not be touched because one life must not be taken to save another."[2]

This is repeated in the *Tosefta* with slight variations: "A woman that is having difficulty in giving birth, it is permitted to cut up the child in her womb even on the Sabbath, and take it out limb by limb because her life takes precedence. If its head came out it may not be touched even the second day because one life may not be taken to save another."[3]

On the above Mishnah we have the following comment of the Talmud: "Once his head has come forth he may not be harmed because one life may not be taken to save another. But why so? Is he not a pursuer? There it is different, for she is pursued by heaven."[4]

What is the reason that we permit taking the life of the unborn child when it endangers the life of the mother? Rashi in his comment on the above passage gives the following reason: "For as long as it did not come out into the world it is not called a living thing and it is permissible to take its life in order to save its mother. Once the head has come

258

forth it may not be harmed because it is considered born, and one life may not be taken to save another."[5]

Thus according to Rashi the reason for the permission to take the life of the unborn child is that the embryo is not considered a living thing, and hence, taking its life cannot be called murder.

This view is supported by the biblical law concerning harm done to a pregnant woman in which case the Bible prescribes: "If men strive, and hurt a woman with child, so that her fruit depart from her, and yet no mischief follow: he shall surely be punished, according as the woman's husband will lay upon him; and he shall pay as the judge determines. And if any mischief follow, then thou shalt give life for life."[6]

The mischief in the verse refers of course to the death of the woman. It is only if death to the mother results from the hurt that capital punishment follows. The death of the unborn child is punishable by fine only.

From Maimonides it would appear that the reason the life of the unborn child may be taken when it endangers the life of the mother is based on the law of the "pursuer". In his code Maimonides says: "This is, moreover, a negative commandment, that we have no pity on the life of a pursuer. Consequently, the Sages have ruled that if a woman with child is having difficulty in giving birth, the child inside her may be taken out, either by drugs or by surgery, because it is regarded as one pursuing her and trying to kill her. But once its head has appeared, it must not be touched, for we may not set aside one human life to save another human life, and what is happening is the course of nature."[7]

This opinion of Maimonides is followed by Joseph Karo in the *Choshen Mishpat*.[8]

There is, then, a clear distinction between the reasoning of Rashi and that of Maimonides. According to Rashi the embryo is not considered a living being and therefore the life of the mother takes precedence. According to Maimonides the life of the mother takes precedence because the embryo is in the position of a "pursuer."

From this difference in interpretation may result also differences in legal decisions. According to Maimonides we would permit abortion only where there is clear danger to the life of the mother.

The interpretation of Maimonides offers many difficulties. There is no indication in the Mishnah that in the case of an embryo the law of the pursuer applies. On the contrary, the Mishnah clearly states that the life of the mother takes precedence as long as the child is unborn. The Talmud suggests the reason of the "pursuer" only where the child is already born. The answer that the Talmud gives for not applying the reason of the "pursuer" in the case of a child already born applies just as much to the unborn child. Many of the commentators try to give answers but they seem forced.[9] Hence we prefer to follow the reasoning of Rashi that the whole problem revolves around the question whether the foetus is considered a living being.

The ancients spoke of this in their idiom, e. g., the following conversation between the compiler of the Mishnah and the Roman Emperor: "Antoninus said to Rabbi: When is the soul given unto man, at the time that the embryo is formed, or at the time of conception? He replied, at the time the embryo is already formed. The emperor objected: Is it possible for a piece of meat to stay for three days without salt and not putrify? It must therefore be at conception. Said Rabbi: This thing Antoninus taught me and Scripture supports him, as it is said; And thy visitation has preserved my spirit, i. e., my soul (Job 10.12)."[10]

According to Aristotle the rational soul is infused the fortieth day after conception in the case of a male and the eightieth day in the case of a female. The Platonic tradition was that the soul entered at conception. The Stoics believed that the soul entered at birth. Roman jurists followed the Stoics and held therefore that abortion was not murder. According to Common Law too, taking a life is punishable only after there has been complete extrusion of the child from the body of the mother.

The Catholic Church evidently followed the Platonic tradition because it forbade all abortions. Even in the case of ectopic pregancies the official ruling of the church issued by the Congregation of the Holy Office, March 5th, 1902 is: No, it (abortion) is not lawful. Such a removal of the foetus is a direct killing of the foetus and is forbidden.

A *fatwa* of the Grand Mufti of January 25th, 1937, states that therapeutic abortions are absolutely forbidden after the embryo has "quickened."

Medical science considers the foetus a living thing from the moment the ovum is fertilized.[11]

Actually being a living thing and being a separate entity are two separate matters. Even if it is a living thing we can say that the foetus is *pars viscera matrum,* or to use the talmudic expression, "the foetus is accounted as the loin of its mother." When abortion is therapeutic there can be no objection to it because like in any surgery, we sacrifice the part for the whole.

This is the attitude the Rabbis have taken. Abortion is forbidden.

Though it is not considered murder, it does mean the destruction of potential life.[12] If, however, the purpose is therapeutic this objection is removed. I have chosen a number of Responsa dealing with the question.

Rabbi Yair Hayyim Bachrach (1639–1702) has this strange case. A married woman committed adultery and became pregnant. She had pangs of remorse and wanted to do penance. She asked whether she could swallow a drug in order to get rid of the "evil fruit" in her womb. In answer Rabbi Bachrach makes it clear immediately that the question of the permissibility of abortion has nothing to do with the legitimacy of the child to be born. The only question involved is whether abortion is accounted as taking a life or not. Rabbi Bachrach draws distinctions between the various stages of the development of the foetus, i.e., forty days after conception, three months after conception. Then he concludes that theoretically it might be permitted at the early stages of the pregnancy but we do not do so because of the custom adopted both by the Jewish and the general community against immorality.

Rabbi Meir Eisenstadt (1670–1744) in Panim M'eirot has the following question: A woman that had difficulty in giving birth, and the child came out feet first, is it permitted to cut up the child limb by limb in order to save the mother. This seems to be the very question explicitly answered in the Mishnah. The only problem that is introduced is a discrepancy between the Mishnah and Maimonides. Whereas the Mishnah mentions that if the greater part of the child has come out we do not take the life of the child in order to save the mother, Maimonides says that if the head of the child or the majority thereof came out first it is considered as born and we do not take its life in order to save the mother.

The commentators tried to resolve this contradiction by saying that the extrusion of the head or the majority thereof, or in the case where the head came last, the extrusion of the majority of the body, constitutes birth. The author then poses the question, supposing if at this stage death could result to both if we should let nature take its course, is it still forbidden to take the life of the child in order to save the mother. He leaves the question unanswered.[13]

Rabbi Eliezer Deutsch (1850–1916) treats the following problem. A woman who has been pregnant a few weeks began to spit blood. Expert physicians said that she must drink a drug in order to bring about a miscarriage. Should she wait, it will become necessary to bring out the child by cutting it up and also endanger the life of the mother, whereas now it is possible to bring forth the child with a drug. Is it permissible to do so?

Rabbi Deutsch answers that in this case it is certainly permitted. He also makes a distinction between the various stages in the development of the foetus, between the use of drugs and the use of surgery, and between another person doing it or the woman herself. The conclusion is that it is permitted in this case for three reasons: a) Before three months after the conception there is not even a foetus, b) There is no overt act involved in this case, (i.e., surgery) c) The woman herself is doing it and it is thus an act of self-preservation.

In current literature I found a Responsum by Rabbi Yitzhak Oelbaum of Czechoslovakia, now of Canada. The question is as follows: A woman has a weak child. According to the doctors it will not live unless it is breasted by the mother. The mother has now been pregnant four weeks and has felt that there was a change in her milk. Could she destroy the child, she asked, by means of an injection in order to save the child that she nurses.

The author discusses first of all the reliability of doctors in these things (they sometimes exaggerate) and whether the fact that a proper formula for bottle feeding could be substituted. He concludes that if there is expert evidence that danger might result if there be no abortion, then it is permitted.

In this Responsum a new issue is introduced. Until now we have spoken of danger to the mother. Here there is no danger to the mother but to another child. This opens new possibilities which we shall not pursue here.

An even more recent Responsum on the subject is by Rabbi Gedaliah Felder of Toronto published in the current issue of a rabbinic periodical published in Jerusalem. Here the question is as follows: A pregnant woman is afflicted with cancer of the lungs. The doctors say that if a premature birth will not be effected the cancer will spread faster and hasten her death. Is it permissible to have an abortion where the mother is saved only temporarily?[14]

Before we sum up, it would not be out of place to bring in a comment from the medical profession. This was called to my attention by Dr. Hiram Yellen, a most prominent obstetrician of the City of Buffalo.

There is abundant evidence that the frequency of criminal induction of abortion is increasing at an alarming rate, although accurate statistics cannot be obtained. Numerous reasons may be advanced for this deplorable situation, the most probable being: 1) Twentieth century standards of living have made children an economic liability for a large percentage of the population. This may be contrasted with more primitive rural conditions where a large family was considered an economic asset. 2) As a by-product of the woman's freedom-movement, a very large number of women have come to believe that pregnancy should be regulated by their personal desires. 3) The present day lack of religious feeling and the wide teaching that pregnancy may be controlled have contributed to a lowering of moral standards among women, with a resulting increase in the number of undesired pregnancies. . . .[15]

Our conclusion, therefore, must be that abortion is morally wrong. It should be permitted only for therapeutic reasons.

Notes

1. *The Management of Obstetric Difficulties*, by Titus and Wilson, New York, 1955, p. 210.

2. *Ohalot 7:6.*

3. *Tosefta Yevamot 9:9.*

4. *Sanhedrin 72:b.*

5. Rashi, *Sanhedrin* 72b, s.v. *yatzah rasho.*

6. Ex. 21.22-23.

7. Rambam: The Laws of the Murderer (*rotseach*) 1:9.

8. *Chosen Mishpat, 424:12.*

9. See the *Tosefot Rabbi Akiva Eger* on the *Mishna* in *Ohalot* and the *Chidushei Reb Hayyim Halevi, ad loc.*

10. *Sanhedrin 91b.*

11. See Joseph B. De Lee, *Obstetrics*, 4th edition, p. 274.

12. See the *Tosefot Chullin, 33a s.v. Echa Akum.*

13. See, however, *Melamed Lehoil*, Part II, Responsa 69.

14. See *Kol Torah, Cheshvan, 5, 719.*

15. Carl Henry Davis, *Gynecology and Obstetrics*, 1937, Chap. X, p. 1.

RABBI AARON BLUMENTHAL *argues that women be permitted to be called to the Torah. He points out that there is talmudic precedent for this in the statement,* Anyone may ascend (for an aliyah) *for the seven honors, even a minor, even a woman. Rabbi Blumenthal exhaustively analyzes the second part of the talmudic statement* "but the sages have said that a woman shall not read in public because of K'vod hatzibbur (the dignity of the congregation)." *He believes that in today's congregations there is no breach of K'vod hatzibbur in calling women to the Torah.*

265

An Aliyah for Women

AARON H. BLUMENTHAL

The practice of reading the Torah regularly at synagogue services is so old that its origin is attributed to Moses and Ezra. *"Moses instituted the reading of the Torah on Sabbaths and holidays, and Ezra instituted it on Mondays, Thursdays, and at Minhah services on Saturdays."*[1] By the time of the Mishnah many of the regulations governing the reading of the Torah had become fixed, especially the principal regulations dealing with *aliyot*. The Mishnah seems to imply that only males may be accorded the privilege of an *aliyah*. It says specifically *"A minor may read the Torah or serve as translator,"* but there is no reference in the Mishnah proper to a woman's right to an *aliyah*.

The classic reference is found in a *B'raita* quoted in *Meg.* 23a. *"Anyone may ascend* [for an aliyah] for the seven honors, even a minor, even a woman, but the sages have said that a woman shall not read in public because of K'vod hatzibbur [the dignity of the congregation]."* This law is repeated almost verbatim in the *Alfas*, the *Tur*, and the *Shulchan Aruch*. Its very phraseology has become hallowed and any discussion concerning a woman's right to an *aliyah* must begin with it.

Please observe that our text is a composite sentence with two parts, one of which is subordinate to the other. The first part is a simple declarative statement *"Anyone may ascend...even a minor, even a woman."* Were the sentence to end here, there would be no room for misunderstanding. However the *B'raita* adds a subordinate clause *"But the sages have said that a woman shall not read in public..."*

We shall try in a moment to discuss what this text might have meant to the *Tannaim in their day, and to bring to it the comments of later au-*

---

*The platform where the reading was conducted was elevated.

thorities. For the present, let us note that the permission is granted, and only K'vod Hatzibbur (the dignity of the congregation) interposes to prevent the exercise of the permission.

What is the meaning of *K'vod Hatzibbur?* The phrase occurs only five other times in the talmudic literature.

1. *"A naked person may not read from the Torah because of K'vod Hatzibbur."*[2]

2. *"One who is clad in rags may not read from the Torah because of K'vod Hatzibbur."*[3]

3. *"One may not roll up the Torah scroll in public because of K'vod Hatzibbur.*[4]

4. *"The cantor may not disassemble the ark in public because of K'vod Hatzibbur.*[5]

5. *"One may not read from a printed Pentateuch in the synagogue because of K'vod Hatzibbur.*[6]

The first two are obvious. It is offensive to the dignity of the congregation for one who is improperly clothed to officiate in the synagogue. (The word *"arum"* does not always mean stark naked. Cf. *Targum* to Is.20:2). The third case involves the High Priest on Yom Kippur. The Mishnah requires that he read a portion of the Torah from Leviticus, roll up the scroll, and then recite the *maftir* by heart. Among other questions, the Talmud asks, "Why does he not roll the same scroll to Numbers and read from the text instead of reciting by heart?" The reply, according to all the commentators is, that this would require keeping the worshippers waiting and that is an offense to *K'vod Hatzibbur*.

The fourth case is another instance of keeping the congregation waiting. It was customary to bring the scrolls from the outside into the house of worship. The ark was decorated with drapery before placing the Torah in it. At the end of the service, the Torah was removed to its place outside the synagogue. Was it permitted to dismantle the drapery before the Torah was removed? The Talmud says that one may not keep the congregation waiting for this purpose because of *K'vod Hatzibbur*. This should be done later after the worshippers have departed. The fifth instance implies that the dignity of the congregation requires that every synagogue possess a Torah scroll that is kosher in every respect and that it is improper to read from any other kind.[7] The same words which Rashi and the Raav use in the case of the "person clad in rags" are used by the Mordecai to explain the objection to reading from a printed Pentateuch. The words are, "It is a disgrace to the congregation."

All five cases have this element in common—they involve an offense to the dignity of the congregation. It is improper for one inadequately dressed to officiate in public. It is improper to delay the congregation unnecessarily, and it is improper or undignified for the Torah reading to be conducted from anything less than a complete and valid scroll.

This definition of *K'vod Hatzibbur,* which is valid for these five cases, must apply to the only other case in the Talmud, that of a woman reading from the Torah—it is offensive to the congregation. What makes it offensive? The implication that there is no man present who can read from the Torah. For all practical purposes, however, the important thing is that the privilege is denied the Jewish woman only because it was considered to be offensive or improper.

Perhaps the most direct approach to our problem is to compare the talmudic concept of propriety regarding women with our own. The Talmud abounds in lofty and reverent sentiments about women, but halachically she suffered from a number of disabilities. She was not permitted to testify in court[8], to inherit from her father equally with her brother[9], or to serve as a judge[10]. She did not have equality under the law in marriage or divorce. Almost a thousand years were to elapse before her husband was denied his polygamous rights, and that, only in Western countries.

None of these sentiments or disabilities can stand the test of scrutiny today. To continue to act as if they were still valid is the height of folly. We could solve our problem very expeditiously by saying that many of the things which offended *K'vod Hatzibbur* in talmudic times no longer offend us. The Jewish woman who works side by side with her husband for the welfare of the synagogue and the Jewish community, who is active in the UJA, in Zionist effort, in both Jewish and secular education, whose sense of social responsibility usually is keener than that of her husband, deserves this equality of status in the synagogue. This would be an obvious act bespeaking both gratitude and recognition to the Jewish woman for the indispensable role which she plays in the modern synagogue.

To adopt such a course of action would be consistent with the procedures espoused by the classic halachic tradition. We are faced here not with a law of the Torah, only with the rabbinic concept of *K'vod Hatzibbur.* Jewish law, faced with a valid and pressing need, has re-interpreted the law, even where it contravenes a Biblical commandment. When the economic development of society rendered the Biblical law of *Sh'mittah* impractical, Hillel's *Prozbul* received the approval of his contemporaries. When the Biblical law of ordeal for the *Sotah* became obsolete, Johanan ben Zakkai abolished it, though one wishes that the Talmud had more to tell us about the circumstances of its abolition. The Rabbis whittled away the law of "the rebellious son" limiting its application and hedging it about with so many impossible circumstances that despite the eye-witness testimony of Rabbi Jonathan *"I saw one and sat on his grave"* the *B'raita* insisted *"There never was and there never will be a rebellious son."*[11] Again despite the testimony of Rabbi Jonathan *"I saw one and sat on its mound"* the *B'raita* proclaims *"There never was and there never will be an apostate city"*[12]! Despite the Biblical injunction of levirate marriage, the rabbis made *chalitzah* mandatory instead of optional. Despite the Biblical permission of polygamy, Rabbenu Gershom, sensing the need of his times, abrogated it.

If the Halachah could modify laws enunciated in the Torah, it certainly can re-define the rabbinic concept of *K'vod Hatzibbur*. This is the most direct and most obvious approach to our problem.

It would be profitable, however, to trace the historical developments of the law, to inquire whether *K'vod Hatzibbur* is the only consideration, and whether the prohibition is as old or as fixed as it seems to be.

History

There is an earlier version of our text which is found in the *Tosefta*, whose wording is significantly different from the *B'raita* in the Babylonian Talmud. It consists of two simple sentences: (1) *"Anyone may ascend for the seven honors, even a minor, even a woman."* (2) *"One may not bring a woman to read in public."*[13] Notice that there is nothing here about *K'vod Hatzibbur*.

There are several difficulties about our two texts.

(a) Had the *B'raita* or the *Tosefta* meant to say that a woman may not receive an aliyah, it would have been so much simpler to follow the example of the Mishnah by saying *"A minor may read from the Torah,"* and remaining completely silent about a woman's rights. Or, it might have said, *"Anyone may ascend for the seven honors even a minor, but not a woman."* Why this round-about and back-handed way of saying

something that is very simple? Maimonides, whose genius lay not only
in his logical arrangement of the law, but also in his ability to select the
appropriate words to convey very fine shadings of meaning, senses this
difficulty. He refuses to say, as do the Alfas, the Tur and the *Shulchan
Aruch: "Anyone may ascend . . . even a minor even a woman, but the
sages said a woman may not . . ."*14 He rephrases the law in simple
terms, *"A woman may not read in public because of K'vod Hatzibbur.
A minor who can read and knows to Whom prayer is addressed may ascend.*

(b) We have been so bedazzled by the *negative,* the denial of permission, that we have failed to see that the *positive,* the granting of the permission, must have had some relevance. Rabbi Jacob Emden who died
less than 180 years ago, in his notes on the Talmud, has this to say
about the last sentence of the B'raita. *"It seems to me that a woman
may not read in public whenever this is possible. But the first sentence
(granting her permission) would apply when there are not seven men,
among the ten who constitute a minyan, who can read and there is a
woman who can read, that they cannot do without her."*15

(c) What is the meaning of the phrase, "bring to read in public" in
the *Tosefta?* Why the phrase *"read in public"* in both the *B'raita* and
the *Tosefta* Maimonides uses the simple word *"reads".*

I have not been able to find a parallel to the phrase *"bring to read in
public"* but the phrase *"read in public"* occurs in the *Tosefta.* With reference to the reading of the *Megillah* of Esther the *Tosefta* says,
*"Women, slaves, and minors are exempt from reading the megillah and
cannot discharge that responsibility for the congregation (who are obligated to hear it.)"* Then the *Tosefta* continues *"Rabbi Judah said,
'When I was a minor, I read it before Rabbi Tarfon at Lud and he
praised me.' Rabbi said, "When I was a minor I read it before Rabbi Judah at Usha, and some Elders were present and not one of them objected.' They said to him, 'Proof from a permissive teacher is not acceptable.' Thereafter they instituted the practice that a minor may read it in
public."* Neither the *Tosefta* nor the Mishnah uses the phrase *"reading
in public"* with reference to the reading of the *Megillah.* Both are content to use the word *"reads"* alone. However, because the decision to
permit a minor to read is a departure from the earlier law, it requires
emphasis, and therefore, the phrase *"reading in public"* is used. So, I
think, does the phrase *"reading in public"* have a special emphasis
when applied to the reading of the Torah. An ordinary *aliyah* usually is

referred to with one word *"reads,"* e.g., *"He who reads from the Torah shall not read less than three sentences,"* but *"reading in public"* must mean something else.

After theorizing for some time about the meaning of both the *Tosefta* and the *B'raita* I consulted one of the professors at the Jewish Theological Seminary, and he was kind enough to discuss it with me at some length. It seems obvious to me now that the *Tosefta* means that whereas a woman is permitted to be called to the Torah when she is present in the synagogue, it is considered improper to invite a woman from the outside to read the scroll. It reflects on *K'vod Hatzibbur* that they have no man who can read the Torah, and that they have to resort to inviting a woman for this purpose. This was the practice in Palestine. The *B'raita* reflects the Babylonian practice. In their time and place it was already customary to have a special reader for the Torah. They permitted an *aliyah* to be given to a woman, but they did not permit a woman to be the official reader for the entire congregation.

The *Tosefta* and the *B'raita* therefore, reflecting the practice in both Palestine and Babylonia, indicate that a woman was called to the reading of the Torah in talmudic times. *K'vod Hatzibbur* drew some distinctions between the privileges of a man and those of a woman, but not enough to deny her an *aliyah*. There is no other explanation for what otherwise becomes an inexplicable and circuitous phrasing of the law.

Later Development

The Alfas (1013–1103), the Tur (died before 1340) and the *Shulchan Aruch* (written by Joseph Karo, 1488–1575) all quote the *B'raita* almost verbatim. Only Maimonides changes the language as indicated above.

However, the *Ran,* (who flourished in Toledo from 1340 to 1380) writes as follows (commenting upon the Alfas, *Meg.* 13a).

> *"All May Ascend . . . For The Seven Honors; This means to complete the number of seven but not that all may be minors or women. For, since they are obligated they cannot be exclusive. Essentially, since the law requires only the first and the last readers to recite the benedictions, a woman and a minor may not read first or last, because the other readers are not fulfilling their obligations to have the benedictions recited through their (minors or*

women) recital of them. However, nowadays, that the Rabbis have or-
dained that all the readers should recite the benedictions, a woman and a
minor may read even first and last. And since they may read, they certainly
may recite the benedictions."

The Ran is among the first to use the phrase *"ascend to complete"* and
most of the later commentators follow this example, to indicate that
while a woman *may* be called, it is forbidden to discriminate against
men by calling only women! The Rama (Rabbi Moses Isserles
1530–1572), basing his opinion on the *Ran* and the *Rivash* says, *"They*
may be counted among the number of seven, but all of them may not be
women or minors." [16]

The Gaon of Vilna (1729–1797) more than two centuries after the
Rama says, *"The version of the authorities is 'to complete' . . ."*

How Many Women?

The question of how many women may be called to the Torah is an interesting one.[17] On the phrase *"All may ascend for the number of sev-*
en", the *B'er Hetev* (Rabbi Judah b. Simon Ashkenazi, Tiktin, first half
18th century) writes, *"But not for the number of three."* Rabbi Akiba
Eger (Posen 1761–1837) comments as follows:

> *"This means that whenever less than seven ascend, as on the festivals or on*
> *Yom Kippur, they (women) may not ascend. Only for the number of seven*
> *may they ascend. Accordingly it seems obvious that on the Sabbath only*
> *one woman may ascend but not two women since (without the second wom-*
> *an) there would not be six males. For the Sabbath is not to be treated more*
> *lightly than Yom Kippur [which requires six males. The principle is that a*
> *woman may not be counted among the three [or four, five or six]."*

The Gaon of Vilna expressed this opinion even earlier. He writes,
"In discussing those who ascend, it says, even a minor, even a woman.
It does not say women and minors."

The Rama, as we have seen, places no limit upon the number of
women who may be called to the Torah except *"all of them may not be*
women." Rabbi Akiba Eger notes that his own restriction of the privilege to one woman contradicts the Rama and refers to a discussion in
Panim M'irot. As is to be expected, this latter *T'shuvah* agrees that only
one woman may be called to the Torah at the Saturday morning ser-

vices. On the other hand Maharam Rothunberg quotes *Rav Simchah* [*Simchah ben Samuel of Speyer, 13th century*] as follows: "*All may complete the number of seven even a male slave, a female slave and a minor. Rav Simchah of blessed memory explained that this applied not only to the number of seven but even to three. For it is taught in the third chapter of Megillah simply that a minor may read* [*without limitations*]."[18]

Other Halachic Considerations

The Ran seems to raise four other halachic considerations: (a) "*They are not obligated*". The obligation is that of "*the study of Torah*". Participation in the reading of the Torah in the synagogue is considered to be a fulfillment of the mitzvah to study the Torah. Since women are not obligated to study they are not obligated to ascend. (b) This raises the corollary question whether those who are exempt from the performance of a mitzvah, are permitted to observe it voluntarily. The principle of "*Ye may not add to it*" is involved here. (c) If they are permitted to observe it, may they recite a *b'rachah* or would it be an unnecessary *b'rachah* and (d) If the woman may receive an *aliyah,* and her *b'rachah* is not an unnecessary *b'rachah,* there still is the principle that, "*Whoever is not personally obligated to perform a mitzvah cannot fulfill the requirement for others.*"[19] The congregation is under obligation to *hear* the *b'rachot.* How can the woman who is not obligated to study the Torah recite the *b'rachah* for the congregation and have them fulfill their obligation thereby?

The Ran himself disposes of this last difficulty and uses this principle to permit an *aliyah* for a woman. Since the worshippers fulfill their obligation by the *b'rachah* recited by some of the men, says the Ran, there is no harm in having the woman called to the Torah.

To consider the other three difficulties we must turn to the opinions of the Ashkenazic school of *Rashi* and the *Tosaphists.*

The following *T'shuvah,* dated approximately 1064–1070 is reported in the name of *Rabbi Isaac Halevi,* one of the teachers of Rashi (1040–1105). It is published in *T'shuvot Rashi* by Elfenbein.

Rabbi Isaac Halevi taught that one does not prohibit women to recite a b'rachah over the Succah and the Lulav. For when we say that women are exempt from all positive mitzvot which are contingent (for their perfor-

*mance) upon a specific time this means only that they are not obligated. But
if they wish to place themselves under the yoke of the mitzvot that is their
privilege and no one may interfere with them. They are no different than anyone who is not obligated but still performs a mitzvah. Furthermore, since
they wish to observe the mitzvah it cannot be done without a b'rachah. Therefore when we say that all may ascend for an aliyah to the number of seven
even a woman, though she is exempt from the mitzvah of Talmud Torah, she
may ascend, she may recite the b'rachot and there is no suggestion of* b'ra-
chach l'vatala *(an unnecessary b'rachah).*[20]

Two of the problems disappear immediately: (1) *"If they wish to
place themselves under the 'yoke of the mitzvot' that is their privilege
and no one may interfere with them." (2) "There is no* b'rachah l'vatalah.*"*

That Rashi's pupils and their school approved of this *t'shuvah* is evidenced by the fact that both the *Mahzor Vitry*[21], and *the Siddur Rashi* [22], the standard codes which emanated from Rashi's school of
thought, incorporated it with only minor variations in language.

Rabbenu Tam (Jacob ben Meir 1100–1171) is quoted twice in the
Tosefot on this issue.[23] The question under discussion is whether a
woman who performs a *"positive commandment, whose performance
is contingent upon a specific time,"* is permitted to recite a *b'rachah.*
The following is from the citation in Erub: 96a and b. *"Rabbenu Tam
says that one cannot find support from the fact that a woman ascends
for an aliyah and recited the benedictions though she is excused from
the mitzvah of Talmud Torah. For the* b'rachot *at the Torah reading are
not in observance of the mitzvah to study Torah."* Almost the same language is used in quoting Rabbenu Tam in R.H. 33a. The interesting
thing here is not only that Rabbenu Tam quotes *"a woman may ascend . . . and she recites the* b'rachot" but his insistence that *"the* b'rachot *for the reading of the Torah are not in observance of the mitzvah of
Talmud Torah."* The purpose of the *b'rachah* at the reading of the Torah is *"To honor the Torah".* This same thought finds expression in the
Abudarham—*"R. Judah of Barcelona said in the name of Rav Saadya
Gaon that the b'rachah before the reading of the Torah in public was
designed to honor the Torah. And it is not* a b'rachah l'vatalah."[24]

Since we are not concerned here with the mitzvah of *talmud torah*
but rather with a *b'rachah* for the honor of the Torah, there is no problem at all about not being obligated.

This is as good a place as any to remind ourselves that originally
each portion was reach by the person called to the particular *aliyah.* To-

day all that any one who ascends to the Torah does, is recite the *b'rachot*. At no place does the law indicate that a woman is forbidden to recite the *b'rachot*. Quite the contrary . . . in enumerating those portions of the morning service which a woman is required to recite the *Shulchan Aruch* states very clearly *"Women are required to recite the b'rachot to the Torah* (which are part of every morning's prayers)."[25]

In Practice

It should be obvious by now that there is no halachic objection to granting modern woman the privilege of an *aliyah*. But, was it ever practiced? Though the argument from silence is by no means conclusive, it should be noted that there is no recorded instance of a woman called to the Torah either in the Talmud or in the Gaonic literature. However, there is a medieval decision which seems to be practical *halachah*. It deals with the problem of *"A city whose men are all Cohanim."*

This problem is not as far-fetched as one might think. Rabbi L. Rabinowitz, in his essay "France in the 13th Century" in a volume edited by H. Loewe, entitled *Judaism and Christianity*, writes as follows:

> *"The Jews of Northern France, from the eleventh to the fourteenth centuries, formed a widely and sparsely distributed community throughout the length and breadth of France. There was hardly a village without its Jews, many had but a single Jewish resident in them, and the number of communities which numbered more than a hundred Jews was negligible. It is doubtful whether, apart from Paris, there was any. The same state of affairs prevailed in England during this period."*

Under such circumstances, it probably was not unusual for a father and his sons, all Cohanim, to be the only Jewish family in a community. They might have had a *minyan* for religious worship but was it permissible for them to read the Torah? Rabbi Meir of Rothenburg (1220–1293) writes as follows in one of his T'shuvot: *"In a city whose men are all Cohanim and there is not even one Israelite among them, it seems to me that one Cohen takes the first two aliyot and then women are to be called, for, 'All may ascend . . .'"*[26]

Maharam's pupils, the authors of *Hagaot Maimuniyot* quote this decision, and carry the discussion one step further. *"In a city where all are Cohanim which has no women or slaves or minors, the Torah may not be read at all.''*[27]

It should be added that the segregation of the sexes in Jewish worship is a late manifestation. Israel Abrahams in his *Jewish Life in the Middle Ages* writes as follows:

> *"In the separation of the sexes, the synagogue only reflected their isolation in the social life outside. The sexes were separated at Jewish banquets and home feasts no less than in synagogues. If they did not pray together, neither did they play together. The rigid separation of the sexes in prayer seems not to have been earlier, however than the 13th century. The women had their own "court" in the Temple, yet it is not impossible that they prayed together with the men in Talmudic times.* (Abrahams cites as his authority for this statement Low, Monatsschrift, 1884, pp. 314, 463). *Possibly the rigid separation grew out of the medieval custom—which induced men and women to spend the eve of the Great Fast in the synagogue.''*[28]

Perhaps we ought to turn about and ask ourselves when and where there are evidences of the *denial* of the privilege. Rabbi Abraham Gumbiner of Poland (1635–1683), in his *Magen Avraham,* discusses the law, quoting the Rivosh and the Tosefot, among others, and concludes as follows: *"And here it is customary for the women to leave the synagogue."* Even more interesting is the statement of Rabbi Joshua Falk (died 1614, Lublin) author of both the *P'risha* and the *D'risha* to the Tur. In accordance with his usual procedure he reviews the earlier arguments, for according a woman an *aliyah,* and he concludes as follows: *"I have elaborated here in order to explain our* minhag *of not calling a woman or a minor . . .".*

Conclusions

What are our conclusions then? (1) That in Tannaitic times a woman was accorded the privilege of an *aliyah,* but that we do not know how late the practice was observed. At the very latest, if Abrahams is correct, the practice was abolished in the 13th century. One must remember that there was no uniformity of practice among the various countries in which Jews lived. Local customs in the treatment of women among the non-Jewish community might have exercised an influence. (2) There is ample testimony to indicate that the practice was abolished and has not been revived for several hundred years. That which the early authorities permitted, the later ones withdrew.

For Today

What shall we do in this matter? Stated in its strongest terms, the refusal of our ancestors to implement the halachah over a period of centuries has acquired the sanctity of a strong *minhag* and *"the minhag of our fathers is Torah."* However there is another matter which is of commanding concern to modern Jewish life—the emancipation of the Jewish women under Jewish law.

Somehow, one does not know quite how, there were grafted onto Jewish law many offensive characterizations of woman. The contrast with the classic period of Jewish law is illuminating. The Rabbis of the Talmud so restricted the Biblical rights of the father to sell his daughter into slavery or to marry her off against her will, until they virtually disappear. The marriage law is changed frequently through the institutions of the *ketubah,* the restrictions upon the husband's rights to divorce at will, the requirement of women's consent to divorce, and eventually the elimination of polygamy, all designed to protect and elevate the woman in the marital relationship. This is dynamic and creative halachah at its loftiest and we can be proud of it. But what about the later halachah?

One of the first problems, in connection with women at the Torah is that of her menstrual impurity. The Talmud says specifically, *"R. Judah ben B'teyrah says Torah scrolls cannot receive impurity'"*[29] That the opinion of R. Judah ben B'teyrah became the accepted one is evident from the following quotation. *"Nowadays everyone accepts the practice of following three old sages . . . and R. Judah ben B'teyrah about Torah scrolls . . . who says that Torah scrolls do not receive impurity."* This law is expanded by Maimonides as follows: *"All the impure ones even menstruants and heathens may take hold of* a Sefer Torah *and read from it, for Torah scrolls cannot receive impurity."*

Rashi is of the same opinion.[30] The *Tosefot* agree. On the statement in the Talmud that before a *"man who has had an emission"* may study Torah he has to undergo *T'villah,* the *Tosefot* say, *"We follow the opinion of R. Judah b. B'teyrah who says that Torah scrolls cannot acquire impurity."*[31] Joseph Karo in the *Shulchan Aruch* follows this tendency:

"All the impure ones may read from the Torah and recite the Shema *and pray . . ."*

The law is clear, isn't it! But listen to the Rama: *There are some who have written that a menstruating woman may not enter a synagogue, or pray or mention the name of God or touch a* Sefer,*(Hagaot Maimunyiot). Others say that she is permitted all of these, and this is the law. (Rashi, Hilchot Niddah). However the Minhag in these lands follows the first opinion.*[32]

It has been indicated that in matters of *"prohibitions"* the Ashkenazic practice of the Rama is much more severe than the classic and Sephardic practice. This may account for the unfortunate deterioration in this area of Jewish law, but what is worse is that this later formulation, the decisions of the Polish Ashkenazic authorities, constitute Jewish law today and not the Talmud, Rashi, Tosefot, and Maimonides.

Is a woman permitted to recite the *kaddish* for her father? Listen to *"T'shuvat Chavat Yair" (Yore Deah,* 276): *"If, in his will, a man requested his daughter to recite the Kaddish for him, according to the law she may do so . . . however there is reason to fear that this may lead to a weakening of Jewish practice . . . therefore she should be prevented from doing so."* Such reasoning is outrageous. May a woman serve as a *mohel?* The Bible informs us that Zipporah, the wife of Moses, *". . . took a flint and cut off the foreskin of her son"* (Ex. 4:25). The Talmud adds *"This teaches us that a woman may serve as a* Mohel" (A.Z. 27a). That ought to settle the matter, but it doesn't. The *Torah T'mimah* comments *"It is agreed that a woman may serve as a* Mohel, *but that is not our practice."*

May a woman serve as a *shochet?* The first Mishnah in *Hullin* is very clear. *"All may slaughter, and what they slaughter is kosher, except a deaf-mute, an imbecile and a minor."* The Mishnah in *Zebahim* (3:1) is even more explicit *". . . slaughtering is valid if it is done by those that are not priests, by women or by bondservants . . ."* This is good enough for Maimonides (*Hil. Schechita* 4:4); the Tosafot (*Hullin* 2a; *Zeb.* 31b; *Kidd.* 36a, etc.); Rabbi Meir of Rothenburg (*Responsa Maharam ed.* Prague p. 286); the Rosh (Comm. to *Hullin* 2a); and the *Shulchan Aruch* (Y.D.1:1); among others. But not for the Rama, the Ashkenazic commentator to the *Shulchan Aruch* who says *"Some are of the opinion that women may not slaughter and it already has become a rule that they do not . . ."* It does not matter that there is clear evidence that in Italy women served as *shochtim.* Their certificates as *shochtim* were discovered by the late Prof. Alexander Marx who made them available to Dr. C. Duschinsky, who published them in the Dr. Moses Gaster 80th Anniversary Volume. We are stuck with the Ashkenazic decision which forbids it.

The statements in the Talmud, *"The sound of a woman's voice provokes lust: the sight of a woman's hair provokes lust"* are nothing more than inconsequential individual opinions, which, in the vast sea of the Talmud are submerged deep below the surface, where they are available only to the student-diver. To drag them up from the deep, to magnify them beyond all reasonable proportions, and to make of them treacherous reefs and rocks to wreck piety and saintliness requires an earthquake of staggering proportions. And that is exactly what has happened to our *halachah.*

The time has come for someone to reverse the direction in which the *halachah* has been moving for centuries. In referring to the law which requires one to recline at the *Seder* table, the question arose whether a woman too, should recline. The answer was that only "an important woman" was permitted to do so. The Maharil protests with a statement which we might set as the foundation stone of the activity of the Law Committee: *"Today all of our women are important."*

In view of all these considerations, the precedent in Tannaitic times, the classic halachic permissibility, and the contemporary need to extend equality of status to the Jewish woman under Jewish law, we declare that it is proper to grant the privilege of an *aliyah* to a Jewish woman during the reading of the Torah in the synagogue.

"If they wish to place themselves under the yoke of the law, that is their privilege, and no one may interfere."

Notes

1. *Jer. Meg.* 4:5
2. *Meg.* 24b
3. *Meg.* 24b
4. *Yoma* 90a
5. *Sotah* 39b
6. *Gittin* 60a
7. *Mordecai,* ad loc; *Yer. Meg.* 74a
8. *Shabuot* 31a
9. *B.B.* 80a & b; 109a
10. *Jer. Yoma* 6:11
11. *San.* 71a
12. Ibid.
13. *Meg.* 3

14. *Laws of Prayer* 12:16
15. *Meg.* ad loc.
16. *Orach Chayim* 282:3
17. All references here are to *Orach Chayim* 282:3
18. Responsum, *Orach Chayim* 108
19. *R.H.* 3:8
20. Pp. 80–81 section 68
21. Pp. 413–414 section 358
22. Pp. 127–128 section 267
23. *R.H.* 33a; *Erub.* 96a & b
24. *Laws of Week-day Morning Services*
25. *Orach Chayim* 47:14
26. Responsum. *Orach Chayim* 108
27. *Laws of Prayer* 12:19
28. Page 25
29. *B'rachot* 22a
30. Elfenbein, *T'shuvot Rashi,* p.81 section 69
31. B.K. 82b
32. ad loc.

RABBI PHILIP SIGAL argues in this teshuvah *for the inclusion of women in the* minyan, *the prayer quorum. He bases his views on the vital importance in Judaism of public worship; the feeling that women should be equal in this obligation; and on halakhic precedents.*

281

Women in a Prayer Quorum

PHILLIP SIGAL

A New Question

In his book, *Jewish Worship*, Abraham Millgram relates the story of Dubrovnik, Yugoslavia. Only seventeen Jews, seven men and ten women, have survived the Nazi "final solution." They continue to hold Sabbath and Festival worship and a spokesman of that remnant told Millgram that they continued those services "even though we do not have a *minyan*." Their hope is that one day more Jews will settle there and, so, they feel a deep obligation to preserve a viable synagogue which dates back to Roman times. Millgram then asks: "Should such communities be granted official permission to revert to the ancient Palestinian practice?" One view, expressed in a medieval compilation, *Soferim*, maintained that, in Palestine, seven, and even six, were sufficient for a public quorum.[1] Millgram asks further, "Or should they act independently as do the Jews of Dubrovnik?" By this is meant, should such communities which do not possess the traditional quorum, the *minyan* of ten males, pray without a *minyan as if* there were a minyan?[2] What does not seem to occur to Millgram is to ask a third question: Should such communities (if not all) count the women?

We live in a radically changing world, and foremost among the transformations taking place is that of the status of women. The equalization of women with men has been progressing at an accelerating pace in recent years in various phases of the socio-economic context of society, as well as in new attitudes toward women in the sexual-moral sphere. Over the years, the Reform and Conservative Movements in Judaism have introduced a variety of ritual and liturgical revisions that have made the position of women more rational and more closely approximating that of men. The Reform Movement has seen the ordination of its first female Rabbi. In the Conservative Movement, on the other hand, although the rights of a woman to sing in a choir, to lead services, to be called to the Torah, or to receive an annulment of her marriage if her recalcitrant civilly-divorced husband refuses to offer her a Jewish divorce, have been normalized, the question of her being counted as part of the prayer quorum is not yet definitive. The Rabbinical Assembly Committee on Jewish Law and Standards decided on May 13, 1970 that to include women in the *minyan* is not a violation of the Preamble to the Constitution of the United Synagogue, which requires congregations to remain loyal to "tradition"—an undefined term. But in this negative posture, it did not arrive at the conclusion that asseverates that women *should* be included *as of right.* *

Furthermore, it is imperative that we see this in a comprehensive halakhic context. This should not imply that only one view has validity. In the halakhah, a permissive conclusion does not invalidate the right to be *maḥmir*, to accept a greater stringency upon oneself, to fulfill *lifnim meshurat ha'din*, to accept an observance that goes beyond the requirement of the precise limits of the halakhah.[3] But it is one thing to refuse personally to participate where women are included in a prayer quorum out of one's personal conviction, or because one is *maḥmir*. It is quite another thing to insist that everyone else conform to that standard, to argue that women must not be included as part of the ten who make up a public prayer quorum.

This essay will, therefore, show that, in Judaism public worship is a mandatory requirement of high priority, for women as well as men, and that for valid public worship to take place there is a specific requirement of a "community" of worshippers numbering no less than ten, and that, on the basis of the attitude of the halakhah toward women in liturgical and other ritual matters, there is adequate precedent for modifying the existing *minhag* of not counting women as part of the prayer quorum.

Importance of Public Worship

Public worship is mandatory in Judaism despite all modern speculation to the contrary. This unquestionable requirement is quite specifi-

---

*The author's responsum on this question was instrumental in a vote being taken by the Rabbinical Assembly Law Committee on August 29, 1973 (after preparation of this article) to approve formally the inclusion of women in a minyan.

cally stated, not merely in a large variety of philosophical or aggadic passages which might occasionally be contradicted or not taken at face value, but, more to the point, in the halakhic passages of the Talmud. Furthermore, the mandatory nature of public worship was accepted in subsequent halakhic compilations with uninterrupted unanimity.

The requirement of public worship is stated lucidly in the Babylonian Talmud where we read "a person's *tefilah* (prayer) is listened to (by God) only in the Synagogue." R. Akiva Eger, the 18th century scholar of Posen, noted, in a marginal gloss, the variant reading "that a person's prayer is listened to *only* in a *Tzibbur*," Prayer is listened to when it is recited in a public quorum, in a congregation. This view is fortified several pages later where we read that the favorable moment of prayer is "when the community (*Tzibbur*) worship." A parallel emphasis was placed upon praying at the *same hour* as a quorum if one cannot be present at the synagogue.[4]

The talmudic view was cogently reformulated by Moses Maimonides in his *Mishneh Torah*. Furthermore, he stated that public worship consists of one praying aloud with the congregation listening, this "congregation" being constituted of no less than ten free persons who have reached the age of religious majority. The basic explanation for the significance of public worship over private devotions was summarized by Maimonides when he wrote "for even if there were sinners among them, God would not despise the prayer of the group." In other words, collective virtue will outweigh individual inadequacy.[5] As a matter of fact, the halakhic tradition branded one who does not join in public worship as an "evil neighbor" who is to be shunned by a pious Jew.[6] It is clear that public worship is not a mere option in the halakhah but a mandatory requirement.[7]

The Minyan

The cursory review of the question establishes the premise that public worship is regarded as a *sine qua non* of the Jewish religion. R. Joel Sirkes (1561-1640), author of *Bayit Ḥadash*, a commentary on R. Jacob b. Asher's *Turim*, ruled that Jews can be compelled to attend Synagogue worship on pain of fines, in order to assure the prayer quorum, which was also the ruling of Moses Isserles.[8] The task is to define precisely of what a quorum was understood to consist. From that point we can proceed to examine the status of women.

In the Babylonian Talmud we read that all passages of *kedushah* in prayer, all passages that fit under the rubric of "holiness-passages" may be said only if a quorum of *ten* is present. As delineated, this meant the *shema* segment of the liturgy, the Torah reading, the *haftorah*, the *kaddish*, *kedushah* and the public recitation of the *amidah*, among other things. The need to say the mourners' kaddish in public quorum arose only in later centuries when it became one of the regular "holiness-passages."[9]

Why was the number "ten" seized upon? We read in the Babylonian Talmud that the number "ten" is derived from a *gezerah shavah*, a term which means a decision based upon the likeness of two parts or, more tersely stated, "an analogy of expression."[10] The analogy is taken through several separate stages and is dealt with somewhat differently and not always lucidly.[11]

Logic also supports the analogy to determine the public prayer quorum at ten. There were ten spies who brought calamity upon the *edah*, the community; consequently, ten praying people, exercising their fund of collective virtue, were regarded as competent to bring salvation to an *edah*. As a matter of fact, we read in Midrashic literature that ten persons have the power to prevent adversity.[12] There the reference is related to the story of Abraham pleading for the salvation of Sodom and Gomorah where God was willing to spare the towns if a minimum of ten worthy people were to be found.

Despite the ups and downs of the nature of support rendered, it is clear that the halakhic tradition, from the outset, defined "public worship" as being constituted of ten persons. Tannaitic literature delineated the liturgical series which required such a quorum. Maimonides asserted that this means nine persons plus the leader. That these ten people had to be males was not explicitly stated. It may have been an assumption, at first, in the light of women's exemption from certain *mitzvot*. But this cannot be stated unequivocally. Only in the *Shulḥan Arukh* was the term "males" specified when the *halakhah* of ten was noted.[13]

The Obligation to Pray

We have now reviewed key sources which indicate that public worship, or worship-in-community is mandatory, and that a "community" of a prayer quorum is ten persons.

We must now raise the general consideration of the role of women in the liturgy. First, we must establish that women are obligated to pray. For if they are not obligated to pray, we could neither urge their attendance nor expect them to participate. Furthermore, if they are not bona fide worshippers, there would be no grounds to count them in a quorum to legitimize worship for others, since if one is not obligated he cannot serve as the instrument that enables others to fulfill their obligation. We will find, however, that the *halakhah* clearly established the obligation of women to participate in public worship.[14]

There are differences of opinion among medieval scholars whether the obligation for a woman to pray is Torahitic or Rabbinic, but there is unanimity on the idea that it *is* an obligation and that women are not excused on the basis of prayer being a *mitzvat aseh she'ha'zman gramah*, a *mitzvah* determined by a time factor, which must be conducted at a specific time. Certainly Maimonides considered the woman's obligation as a Torahitic one.[15]

It has to be assumed that this obligation, stated by the Mishnah and reiterated in the Talmud and in halakhic writings, was understood to apply to public worship or their exemption would have been noted. Furthermore, it is evident that the *halakhah* took it for granted that the women were in the place of worship and, therefore, could consider whether or not to use them when needed. When the Talmud informs us that women can be one of the seven that ascend to the Torah or that they can sound the *shofar*, it is evident that they were in the place of public worship. And they were there because they were obligated equally with men. In his inimical conservative style, Maimonides omitted the right of women to ascend to the Torah and merely cited the end of the Rabbinic statement, that women do not read the Torah in public because the honor of the community is at stake.[16]

R. Isaac Alfasi (11th century) cited the *beraita* that women may be included in the seven called to the Torah and R. Nissim conceded that "now" (the 14th century), when each person called to the Torah says his own blessing, women can say the blessing when called to the Torah, although, originally they were never called first or last when the opening and closing blessings had to be said. Whether the limitation of the ratio of women would today be any more justified than the limitation which denied them first or last place previously, and was later changed, is open to question.[17] Despite this participation of women in the Torah service, however, Karo prohibited them from being included in the prayer quorum.[18]

Furthermore, on the question of whether a woman may be included in the mandatory quorum for the public reading of the Scroll of Esther on Purim, Moses Isserles (16th century) cautiously raised that possibility in the light of differences expressed in previous centuries. Referring back to opinions cited in Jacob ben Asher's *Tur*, Isserles speculates that when a woman participated in the quorum for the reading of the Megillah it was a correct quorum for the town.[19] But even more explicit was the 13th century Mordecai who cited an earlier scholar, R. Simḥah (probably the compiler of *Maḥzor Vitry*), that a woman may be included in the *minyan* for prayer and when ten are required for grace after meals for purposes of including the name of God in the formula.[20]

The status of *mamzer*, the product of an adulterous or incestuous sexual relationship, of the Karaite and of the slave, might be of some interest in relationship to that of women. It would appear that a woman was either beneath them or no better than these classes of disqualified Jews. Certainly contemporary halakhah should avoid such an anomaly.[21] As a matter of fact, not to recognize a woman's right to constitute part of the worship quorum is to place her in the same category as a Karaite who was barred by Maimonides from being included in the quorum.[22] It might be of interest to extend the view of Asher (in his compendium on Babylonian *Berakhot*), regarding a slave, to a woman. There, R. Asher suggested that anyone who is under the obligation of mitzvot, including a circumcised slave, can be included in a minyan, for any such person is subsumed under the verse in Leviticus 22:32 which ways that God will be "sanctified in the midst of Israel." In accord with the view expressed on the text by R. Yom Tov Lipman Heller, that a woman is equated with a slave in ritual matters, this would imply that a woman, like a slave, obligated to *mitzvot,* may be included among those in whose midst God is sanctified. Above all, in respect to the specific question of public worship, a woman is obligated, and, hence, is entitled to be part of the quorum.[23] R. Asher supported this idea when he argued that although a person who is not obligated to a certain *mitzvah* cannot be a *motzi,* cannot enable others to fulfill that *mitzvah,* nevertheless, a woman may be called to he Torah as one of the congregation's mandated seven, thus enabling the public to fulfill its obligation, although she is not obligated to study it, because the blessing she recites is not for its study, but for the Election of Israel and the Revelation. How much more so, if she is obligated to public worship, she can count in the quorum to enable a congregation to fulfill its obligation of public worship.[24]

Women were permitted to perform ritual slaughter and they were permitted to read the *Megillah of Esther* on Purim for the public. These rights follow naturally the reasoning of R. Asher, cited previously, that, since they were obligated to observe the *mitzvah* of *kashrut* or of hearing the *Megillah* they could enable the public to fulfill its obligation. Maimonides, after first stating that a woman is obligated, has asserted that as long as one hears the *Megillah* read by one who is obligated, he fulfills the *mitzvah*. The same reasoning would logically imply that since a woman is obligated to public worship, one can fulfill his public worship obligation in a quorum which is constituted of both men and women. Lest anyone doubt that a woman's right to read the *Megillah* follows from the fact of her obligation, this is explicitly stated by Joseph Karo in his commentary on Maimonides.[25]

A Necessary Change

From the foregoing, it is clear that public worship in a community of ten persons is a mandatory *mitzvah* of high priority in Judaism. It is evident in the *halakhah* that women are obligated to it equally with men. Various segments of the halakhah give women the right equally with men to participate publicly in a wide variety of rituals and, therefore, to enable the public to fulfill its obligation. Furthermore, a number of categories of persons who suffer from certain halakhic restrictions or disabilities, such as a *mamzer*, may be counted in a *minyan*. Persons excluded from qualifying for a quorum are minors or Karaites and there is even a degree of controversy over minors. To disqualify women from sharing in the right to constitute an assembly or a worship community is to offend them without reason. Even if we categorize the disqualification of women to constitute a quorum as *minhag*, it is a *minhag* which has lost its reason and its appeal. It is a *minhag* which often runs counter to the best interests of Jewish communities, especially the small ones, not only on Friday nights but on Saturday mornings, at daily services and in houses of *shivah*. When a *minhag* is no longer of spiritual benefit it may be modified or abolished. Although Moses Isserles was firm about preserving a *minhag*, he held that when "circumstances change" the *minhag* may be modified to suit current standards. In the sources referred to we find that the commentators hold that the strength of *minhag* obtains where there is some support for it in the Torah. But where there is no support for it in the Torah, to preserve an obsolete *minhag* is merely "to err in logic," or, in their words, to be *toeh b'shikul ha'da'at*.[26]

In the light of all of these considerations:—that a woman is obligated to public worship; that when one is obligated, one can contribute to the public's fulfilling its obligation; in order to remove the stigma of a woman not even enjoying the ritual status of a *mamzer* who may be counted in a minyan; and not to classify her with a Karite who may not be counted—it would appear that the time has come to declare that women may help constitute a community of worshippers in order to fulfill the great mitzvah of public worship.

Notes

1. Tractate *Soferim* 10:8.

2. Abraham Millgram, *Jewish Worship* (Philadelphia: Jewish Pub. Soc., 1971), p. 343f.

3. Cf. *Mekhilta, Ex.* 18:20. That it is meritorious to observe more than the minimum standard. On the other hand, no individual should seek to impose his personal standard of piety upon the community. See *Tosephta Makhsihirin* 3:3-4.

4. Ps. 69:14. Babylonian *Berakhot* 6a, 8a. See *Gilyon ha'Shas* on the text. Cf. B. *Avodah Zarah* 4 b. *Tosafot*, passage beginning *Keevan*. See R. Asher b. Jacob, the *Rosh*, on *Berakhot*. Chapter one, Section 7, p. 3a and *Divrei Hamudot* (by Tom Tov Lipman Heller) on the *Rosh*, note 26.

Elijah of Vilna drew to our attention that both Alfasi and R. Asher ben Jacob included the proposition that "a person's tefilah is not listened to except in the Synagogue" because of the verse "the favorable moment is when the community worships." The 16th-17th century R. Yom Tov Lipman Heller, commenting on the words of R. Asher, noted that his son, R. Jacob, author of *Tur*, interpreted the term "synagogue" to mean "congregation," accenting the presence of a quorum rather than a location. Nevertheless, as he added, in the view of Gaonim, the importance of the quorum-concept is so great that even if a quorum is not physically present, a person should pray in a Synagogue since that is the usual locale of a quorum.

5. Moses Maimonides, *Mishneh Torah, Hilkhot Tefilah* 8:1, 4. Cf. Mishnah *Megillah* 4:3, and the Babylonian Talmud 23 b. See also R. Joseph Karo, Shulḥan Arukh Orah Ḥayyim 55:1.

6. B. *Berakhot 8* a, Maimonides, *loc. cit.; Avot* 1:7.

7. Actually, this idea was taken so seriously that it was used as a basis for negating the general principle that *mitzvah ha'ba'ah b'averah* a *mitzvah* which results from a transgression is not a *mitzvah*: Thus, R. Eliezer freed his gentile slave, contrary to the Torah *halakhah,* so that he might serve as the tenth member of a *minyan*. Normally, this would not be considered a *mitzvah* because it

ran counter to the Torah (Lev. 25-46), but, in this case, it was deemed meritorious because the Talmud held *mitzvah d'rabam shani,* "a public *mitzvah* is different." In other words, the requirement of public worship is so vital, that to help the public fulfill this significant requirement one may even violate the Torah to be able to conduct it. R. Asher commented that *d'alim aseh d'rabim,* a public *mitzvah* is even stronger than the individual's obligation to a verse in the Torah. For this reason alone, even if we found no independent reason to count women, it would be advisable for *all* congregations to do so at least when that is the only way to constitute a quorum.

See B. *Berakhot* 47 b; R. Asher on *Berakhot,* Chapter 7, Section 20. The importance of public worship was one of the factors that influenced the Rabbinical Assembly to permit travel to the Synagogue on the Sabbath, as can be seen in the Sabbath Responsum of 1950.

8 *Bayit Ḥadash* on *Oraḥ Ḥayyim* 150. Cf. Moses Isserles on *Shulḥan Arukh, Oraḥ Ḥayyim* 15:22.

9. B. *Berakhot* 21b, *Megillah* 23b. The Talmud makes no mention of the ten to consist of males specifically. But Joseph Karo, in his *Shulḥan Arukh Oraḥ Ḥayyim* 55:1, where he also introduced the need for a quorum for *kaddish,* added the requirement that the ten be males. Naturally, he did not originate the idea. It came down in the discussions of the scholars from the early Middle Ages on, as will be indicated later in this essay. But Maimonides did not specify "males." See Maimonides, *Mishneh Torah Hilkhot Tefilah* 8:4, 5, 6, Cf. Mordecai on *Berakhot* 21b, note 69.

10. For an exposition of *gezerah shavah* see Moses Mielziner, *Introduction To The Talmud,* p. 142 ff.

11. The Scriptural sources involved in this are Leviticus 22:32, and Numbers 16:21, 14:27. The *gezerah shavah* is expounded in B. *Berakhot* 21b and *Megillah* 23b. This *gezerah shavah* as expounded in the Babylonian Talmud is somewhat less than adequate.

It is pointed out that Leviticus 22:32 uses the term *tokh* in stating that God will be sanctified *b'tokh,* in the midst of Israel, and Numbers 16:21 uses the same term, *tokh,* when referring to Korah and his fellow mutineers, when God tells Moses and Aaron to separate themselves *m'tokh,* from the midst of that *edah,* the assemblage, in order that He may destroy it. The term *tokh,* becomes the subject of analogy. The second step is then propounded. The term *edah,* "assembly," is taken to signify ten, but this is where the *gezerah shavah* falters. The assessment of *edah* in Numbers 16:21 to be ten is erroneous, and this error on the part of the Talmud is naturally puzzling, for Numbers 16:21 refers to Korah and his associates, who numbered over 250.

The *gezerah shavah* is then taken into its second stage, where we are told that the minimum number of *edah* is ten because in Numbers 14:27, where God deplored "the wicked *edah*" he was referring to the ten spies whom Moses had sent to Canaan and who returned to discourage Israel from proceeding with the conquest and thereby set in motion a disastrous mutiny. In reality, however, that verse refers to *all* Israel! In the light of this analysis, the *gezerah shavah* designed to establish *ten* as a public worship quorum might be regarded as inadequate. (On the other hand, Rabbi Robert Gordis, in a communication to the author, sees *mallinim* in Numbers 14:27 as possibly causative, and, therefore, might refer to the ten spies.) If the Babylonian Amoraim did not adequately explain the Tannaitic innovation, the *gezerah shavah* is redeemed in the Palestinian Talmud. (*Megillah* 75b, *Berakhot* 11c.) There we are first given the erroneous one based on the term *edah*, "assembly," used in Numbers 14:27 and 16:21, neither one of which refers to "ten," the former referring to the 250 of Korah and the latter to all Israel. But, then, an analogy is offered between Leviticus 22:32 and Genesis 42:5. In the latter passage, we have reference to Jacob's *ten* sons coming *b'tokh*, among all the other purchasers of grain in Egypt, and in the former that God is to be sanctified *b'tokh*, in the midst of Israel. There in Genesis 42:5, the Israelites are "ten" and, so, the minimum for "Israel" in Leviticus 22:32 is defined as ten.

12. Midrash *Tanhumah va'yera* 8. Cf. Genesis 18:32. In *Tanhumah*, we read that ten can save from *pooraniyut*, from "adversity." That is the correct meaning of the term, as it is seen in the context of the standard *tefilah la'derekh*, the prayer one recites before taking a journey, and how it should be understood in *Avot* 1:7 rather than as "retribution."

13. Mishnah *Megillah* 4:3; Maimonides, *Hilkhot Tefilah* 8:4, *Shulhan Arukh Orah Hayyim* 55:1.

14. Mishnah *Rosh ha'Shanah* 3:8; Babylonian R.H. 29 a; Mishnah *Berakhot* 3:3; B. *Berakhot* 20 b; Maimonides *Mishneh Torah Hilkhot Tefilah* 1:2, 6:10; *Shulhan Arukh Orah Hayyim* 106:2.

15. See Maimonides *Op. cit.* 1:1. *Tosafot Berakhot* 20 b, passage beginning *b'te-lah*. Cf. Psalm 55:18. B. *Kiddushin* 29 a. B. *Sukkah* 38 a. The Talmud declares that prayer is not in this category of *mitzvah* from which women are exempt, despite the Psalmist's reference to prayer at night, morning and noon. Rashi further elucidates that prayer is Rabbinic *mitzvah* and the Rabbis instituted it equally for women, although Hallel, which is recited only at specified occasions, is so considered and women are, therefore, exempt from reciting Hallel.

Actually, the whole quesion of a *mitzvat aseh she'ha'zman gramah*, a mitzvah determined by a specific time, is under an ambiguity which defies absolute definition. Even Maimonides was not sufficiently lucid in his various attempts to define it, and classical halakhic literature offers examples rather than a definition. But there is unanimity in all the sources for the obligation of women to engage in daily prayer.

Maimonides, *Perush haMishnayot* on the first chapter of Mishnah *Kiddushin*. The passages from 20a through 35a. Cf. also his *Hilkhot Avodat haKokhavim* 12:3.

16. *Tosefta Megillah* 3:5, B. *Megillah* 23a, B. *Rosh ha'Shanah* 33a. Maimonides, *Hilkhot Tefilah* 12:7. Cf. *Shulhan Arukh Orah Hayyim* 282:3. In 12:3 Maimonides specifies that we require ten *males* as a quorum for Torah Reading. The fact that he regards women as *obligated* to pray but *not privileged* to be part of the quorum is the natural result of Maimonides' Islamic approach to rights of women.

17. R. Isaac of Fez (Alfasi) on *Megillah* 23a and R. Nissim on the text, passage beginning *ha'kol olin*.

18. R. Joseph Karo, *Shulhan Arukh Orah Hayyim* 55:4. See *Biyur ha'Gra* (the notes of Gaon R. Elijah) on the text, beginning *V'eesha*. The 18th-century

Elijah of Vilna comments on Karo's text saying, "A woman's status is always like that of a slave." We might argue that since a manumitted slave can be used in a minyan, a woman who is always free can be considered as a manumitted slave.

19. Karo, *Shulḥan Arukh Orah Hayyim* 690:18, and Isserles' note thereon. See also, R. Abraham Gumbiner (17th century) *Magen Avraham,* note 24 and *Maḥatzit ha'shekel* thereon.

20. Mordecai on *Berakhot,* note 173. This citation has stimulated much public discussion. It has virtually been denied that the reference is accurate. However, the words are explicit in R. Mordecai Ashkenazi's word: "I have found in the name of R. Simḥa, 'a slave and woman may be added (to a group) both for *tephila* (prayer) and *barukh elohainoo . . .'"* It is true that many scholars differed with this view. But Rabbi Abraham b. David of Posquieres, (12th century) long ago wrote: ". . . . There are matters concerning which the *gaonim* disagree . . . why should I rely upon his (Maimonides') choice when it is not acceptable to me . . ." (*Hasagot* on Introduction to *Mishneh Torah*). We, too, should feel as free and as self-confident as *Ravad* to set aside the choices of other halakhists and follow those precedents that apply most significantly to our time and circumstance.

21. Moses Isserles on *Orah Ḥayyim* 282:3, and Elijah of Vilna's comment, passage beginning *u'mamzer.* Cf. Babylonian *Horayot* 13a and *Sefer haḤinukh, Mitzvah* 560.

In connection with the ritual of Sabbath Torah reading, Moses Isserles indicated that a *mamzer* may be called to the Torah. On that text, Elijah of Vilna explaind that a mamzer is regarded as a full Jew for all purposes (except marriage to a non-*mamzer* fellow-Jew). This would, incidentally, also mean that a *mamzer* is eligible to be counted as part of a *minyan.* Certainly, if, as is stated in the Talmud, a *mamzer* who is a scholar takes precedence over a high priest who is not, it becomes quite clear that his rights are assured. And, as a matter of fact, the tradition explicitly asserted that the only disability the *mamzer* suffered was in the matter of marriage.

22. A responsum cited by R. Gedaliah Felder, *Yesodei Yeshurum* Vol. I, p. 56.

23. R. Asher on *Berakhot* 48a, Section 20, and R. Yom Tov Lipman Heller in *Divrei Ḥamudot,* note 53. Heller, however, arrives at a reverse conclusion from that which logic would dictate. R. Tam said that the *halakhah* is according to R. Joshua b. Levi that a slave counts, and Heller says that, nevertheless, R. Tam did not practice it. The same could be true of woman: she should count, but it was not practiced.

24. B. *Rosh ha'Shanah* 29a, R. Asher, *loc. cit.*

25. *Mishnah Ḥulin* 1:1. See *Tosafot* there, first passage on B. *Ḥulin* 2a. Mishnah *Megillah* 2:2, Maimonides, *Hilkhot Megillah* 1:2, 1:1, and the *Kesef Mishnah* on 1:2. Cf. also *Hagahot Maimuniyot,* note 1.

26. Cf. *Magen Avraham,* note 22, and *B'er Hetev,* note 15, on Karo's *Orah Ḥayyim,* 690:17, and their citation of a responsum by Moses Isserles on the matter.

RABBI DAVID M. FELDMAN argues in this teshuvah that women should not be included in the minyan, the prayer quorum. He bases this view on the fact that since women are not obligated to pray in regular minyanim, it would not be proper, according to the law's own categories to include them in the prayer quorum. This is because the minyan includes only those who are obligated to pray. This does not, in Rabbi Feldman's view, involve any notion of inequality, rather it recognizes the differing roles of men and women in the religious life of Judaism. He believes that the retention of these differences is sound from the halachic point of view and also is sound from a psychological and sociological viewpoint.

293

Woman's Role and Jewish Law

DAVID M. FELDMAN

Under the felicitous name of *Ezrat Nashim,* a delegation of young women appeared at the 1972 Rabbinical Assembly convention. They presented a manifesto declaring, among other things: "Although the woman was extolled in Judaism for her domestic achievements and respected as the foundation of the Jewish family, she was never permitted an active role in the Synagogue, court, or house of study. These limitations on the life patterns open to women, appropriate or even progressive for the Rabbinic and medieval periods, are entirely unacceptable to us today . . . It is time that women be granted membership in synagogues, that women be counted in the *minyan,* that women be allowed full participation in religious services, including *aliyot* (called to the Torah), serving as Torah readers and Cantors, among other responsibilities."

At the *minyan* the next morning, which happened to be *Rosh Hodesh,* I addressed myself, in a *D'var Torah,* to their plea by referring to the circumstance that four persons were to be called to the Torah that morning. When the Torah is read each week on Monday or Thursday, only three are called; on a Sabbath or *Yom Tov,* there are five, six or seven *aliyot.* But four are called on *Rosh Hodesh* because, say Rashi and *Tosafot,* of the women. For women have inherited the custom of treating the day more like a *Yom Tov.* This custom, we are told, is their reward for the superior piety and wisdom they showed in refusing, unlike the men, to hand over their gold to Aaron for the fashioning of the Golden Calf.[1]

An added *aliyah* in honor of women, but a woman herself would not be given the *aliyah!* Yet the irony here does say something on both sides of the question of Judaism's attitude to women. It shows, at least, that "equality" is too facile a concept, perhaps even an irrelevant one, in this context. A deeper look into the halakhic structure and criteria seems called for in the light of modern ideas of equality, to assess what can be done within that structure to make for fuller participation of women.

Aliyot and K'vod Ha-Tzibbur

The subject of *aliyot* to the Torah is a helpful starting point. In the Talmud we read, "All are included in the seven called to the Torah, even a woman, even a minor. But," the passage continues, "the Sages said: A woman should not read the Torah (for the public; originally the one called to the Torah did the reading of his portion himself), because of *k'vod ha-tzibbur*, the honor of the congregation."[2]

How are we to interpret *k'vod ha-tzibbur?* Neither the Talmud nor the Codes, nor their Commentaries, defines the term in our specific case.[3] The same term is used in connection with other practices such as: not calling an improperly dressed person to the Torah (a *poheah*)[4] or sparing the congregation the delay when just one Torah Scroll is used, then rolled for reading widely separated sections.[5] The meaning of *k'vod ha-tzibbur* in connection with *aliyot* for women must be deduced from its use elsewhere, and we are left to conjecture just what the considerations were—sexual distraction, sexist male chauvinism, or something else—that occasioned the qualifying clause.

Whatever *k'vod ha-tzibbur* does mean, we can be certain of one thing. Despite prevalent misconceptions to the contrary, it does not mean that a woman is to be kept from reading the Torah because of her periodic "uncleanness." For, "the Torah is immune to being rendered unclean by contact," says Rabbi Judah ben Bteira, whose view in the Talmud is accepted as standard and operative.[6] Any suggested relationship in the Codes between Torah reading and uncleanness must be understood to apply, if at all, equally to men who may be in a state of uncleanness; it is simply not involved in any halakhic distinction between men and women with respect to public or private Torah reading.

This is evident as well from a major post-talmudic ruling, which seems to implement the original provision for including women among the seven *aliyot*. It comes from Rabbi Meir of Rotenburg (d. 1293), who addressed himself to the question of a community made up entirely of *kohanim*.[7] Unlikely as it may seem, the existence of such communities was not unknown in Jewish history, although we have no evidence that Rabbi Meir's responsum was anything more than academic. He ruled that in such a community, a *kohen* should read the portion for both *kohen* and *levi*. However, since calling a *kohen* for the subsequent *aliyot* would be casting aspersion on him as a *kohen*, the remaining *aliyot* should be given to women. In such cases, he says, the concern for *k'vod ha-tzibbur* should be "set aside." Though this recommendation did not occur to the Spanish codifiers dealing with the same question,[8] Rabbi Meir's ruling is cited in a goodly number of Codes and Commentaries, in both *Ashkenaz* and *Sefarad*.[9] It demonstrates, among other things, that any consideration of "uncleanness" is not an issue in regard to *aliyot* for women.

Aliyot and Obligation

An examination of the halakhic sources indicates that, social or historic factors aside, the difference between men and women with respect to *aliyot* is predicated on their respective obligations to study and to participate in the public reading of the Torah. Indeed, our talmudic *baraita* has a parallel passage in the *Tosefta*, where the second clause reads differently: "All are included in the number seven, even a woman and a minor . . . but a woman is not brought in to read for the public." According to Professor Saul Lieberman, this means that while a woman may be included in the seven, she is not to be "brought in" for this purpose in the absence of a qualified adult male, for only males have the statutory obligation to read, and can thus discharge it for others.[10] This would lend a legally specific, as opposed to a sociologically variable, meaning to *"k'vod ha-tzibbur."*[11] Along similar lines, Rabbenu Tam (d. 1171) suggests that women were called to read the Torah only in that historical period when the first and last honoree alone recited the *b'rakhah* (benediction); hence a woman could be honored with any of the intermediate *aliyot*. Now that the custom is for all seven to pronounce the *b'rakhah* (which has the function of discharging the reader and the other congregants of their formal obligation), perhaps this is what excludes the women.[12] This reasoning is cogent enough for Rabbi Menahem HaMe'iri of Provence (d. 1306), who asks: "How can she say the *b'rakhah* when she herself has no obligation (to study Torah)?"[13] Rabbenu Tam's contention is cited by Rabbi Joshua Falk (d. 1614), a Polish authority, who then adds: "I have relayed this point in order to explain our present custom, whereby a woman is not called to the Torah . . ."[14]

Which obligation, now, are we talking about? The study of Torah? Rabbi Eliezer's exclamation in the Mishnah against "teaching one's daughter Torah" cannot be taken as eliminating the necessity of her knowing the Written Torah and that part of the Oral Torah which relates pragmatically to her areas of observance.[15] Accordingly, Rabbi Jacob Landau (d. 1487) rules that women as well as men must say the *Bir'khot HaTorah* in the daily morning service (before reading the passages of Torah in that service and in anticipation of fulfilling the ongoing mitzvah of Torah study). From Rabbi Landau's Code, this ruling entered our *Shulhan Arukh*.[16]

The balance of Rabbenu Tam's statement, on the other hand, implies that the *b'rakhot* now recited by those called to the Torah are not for the purpose of discharging one's obligation of Torah *study*, but that of Torah *reading* in public. (Hence a *kohen* who is called twice recites the same *b'rakhot* twice.) If the obligation, then, is that of public reading, Ha-Me'iri himself had suggested that the "Mosaic" requirement of public Torah reading is fulfilled by even a token amount, that the multiple *aliyot* were required only by an Enactment of Ezra. Hence, women are included in the number seven, even if only one male is called, in line with what was said above regarding the *Tosefta*.

Is *hearing* the public reading, then, the *hiyyuv*, the obligation involved? Rabbi Abraham Gumbiner (d. 1683), in his Commentary to the *Shulhan Arukh* writes: "This (that women may be included among the seven *aliyot*) implies that women are obligated to hear the public Torah reading. Even though it was instituted to help us fulfill the duty of (theoretical) Torah study, from which women are exempt, they are nonetheless obligated to hear the public reading, as in *Hak-hel* ("gather the people—the men, women, and children"—Deuteronomy 31:12)." Rabbi Gumbiner, alone among later authorities, then cites an early passage of almost talmudic provenance, and contrasts the contemporary practice: "In *Massekhet Soferim* it is written: Women are obligated to hear the reading of the Scroll just as men are, and it is a duty to translate for them so that they may understand. But here the women are accustomed to going outside."[17] We come full circle, now, with the observation by the eminent Hayyim Y. D. Azulai (d. 1806). The extra *aliyah* on *Rosh Hodesh*, he reasons, does indicate that women "belong" at the Reading of the Torah.[18]

On Assuming Obligation

Assuming formal obligation to be the important halakhic, as opposed to social or historic[19] factor, our question is: Can the ultimate demand of *Ezrat Nashim* be met, that "women be considered as bound to fulfill all *mitzvot* equally with men"?

There are, halakhically speaking, at least three levels to that question. First, can one voluntarily assume obligations not imposed upon him or her by the Torah and recite the accompanying benedictions? Since women are "exempt from the performance of affirmative *mitzvot* that must be fulfilled only at a specific time," may they choose to perform them anyway—and with a *b'rakhah?* As if both to beg the question before us and to answer it, early authorities point to the example of *aliyot* to prove that women may recite the *b'rakhah.* The eleventh-century Rabbi Isaac Halevy is quoted by his illustrious pupil, Rashi (d. 1105), as follows: "If women wish to bring themselves within the yoke of the commandments, that is their privilege; and no one ought to protest. Once they do this, the *b'rakhah* is required. The proof is that they are included in the seven *aliyot,* which entails a *b'rakhah,* even though they are exempt from *Talmud Torah.*"[20] The same point is made in *Tosafot* and in the compilation called *Mahzor Vitri*[21] of the School of Rashi (although Rashi himself seems not to have accepted it).[22] In language redolent of the modern *Ezrat Nashim,* Rabbi Shimeon ben Tzadok, of the disciples of Rabbi Meir of Rothenburg points out: "women can obligate *themselves (y'kholot l'hayyev atzman)."*[23]

Though Rabbenu Tam, Rashi's grandson, dismisses the evidence of *aliyot,* he arrives at the same conclusion on other grounds. He notes that the talmudic sage Rabbi Joseph rejoiced in performing *mitzvot* from which he, as a blind man, was legally excused;[24] Rabbenu Tam thus deduces that where women similarly elect to perform *mitzvot* from which they are exempt they can say the accompanying *b'rakhot* as well.[25] He argues that Rabbi Joseph would not have rejoiced if he had been denied the reciting of these *b'rakhot* on the grounds of "taking God's name in vain." The opposing point of view is associated with Maimonides, who rules that while a woman may choose to don a *tallit* or *tzitzit,* or perform other acts from which she is exempt, she may not recite the accompanying *b'rakhot.*[26] The question thereafter has a long history, with authorities aligning themselves on the side of either Rabbenu Tam or Maimonides.[27] Some commentaries on Maimonide's Code echo the objection: "How can she say 'Blessed art Thou . . . Who hath sanctified us with His commandments and commanded us . . .' when she was not commanded in either the written or oral Torah?"[28] Such arguments had, however, been forestalled by Rabbi Nissim of Gerona, known as *RaN* (d. 1380), who reasoned that women are

included, as it were, in the nation that was sanctified by these commandments (for even males say "commanded us" rather than "me").[29]
The *Shulḥan Arukh* in these matters follows Maimonides, while Rabbi
Moses Isserles, whose authority determines our practice, follows Rabbenu Tam.

Proceeding now to a second level of our question, one can even say
that a woman performs the voluntarily assumed *mitzvah* as a *mitzvah*,
not as a privilege. To illustrate, sounding the *shofar* on Rosh Hashanah
for purposes other than fulfilling the commandment violates the rabbinic ordinance *(sh'vut)* against handling the *shofar* on a holy day.
Does a woman's use of the *shofar* to fulfill a voluntarily assumed *mitzvah* qualify to set aside the ordinance? It does, according to Rabbenu
Tam's school of thought.[30] Again, according to Rabbinic interpretation, the prohibition of *sha'atnez*, mixing wool and linen in garments,
is to be suspended when the mitzvah of *tzitzit* is involved. If a woman
chooses to don a *tallit*, does she do so as mere privilege or as a real
mitzvah, which can set aside the injunction of *sha'atnez?* According to
a halakhic commentary by Rabbi Abraham ben David (d. 1198) the injunction is here, too, set aside.[31]

Within the halakhic structure, then, can women assume the obligation, specifically, of *aliyot* and say the benedictions? Yes, says Rabbi
Nissim, who shares Rabbenu Tam's earlier theoretical argument, but
takes it to an affirmative conclusion: When only the first and last called
to the Torah said the *b'rakhah*, women would have to be called for the
middle *aliyot*. Now that each person called recites the *b'rakhah*, says
Rabbi Nissim, women should be permitted to be called first, last, and
in-between. She may certainly say the *b'rakhah* on her own behalf, if
not for others.[32]

The third level of our question gives us pause. The *Mishnah* states:
"One who is not formally obligated (in a specific matter) cannot discharge (for them) the obligation of those who are."[33] This remains a
problem where obligation is voluntarily assumed—as does the following factor: What is the difference, asks *Tosafot*, between one who
fulfills the commandment out of obligation, and one who fulfills it voluntarily? The answer is that the former is "anxious" about it, makes
sure not to neglect it; while the latter can "take it or leave it."[34]

"Be fruitful and multiply," for example, is interpreted as a *mitzvah*
devolving upon the male to fulfill.[35] It is he who must "worry' about
it; yet, says Rabbi Nissim, the woman who voluntarily shares in the act

"shares in it as *mitzvah*."[36] Rabbi Meir Simḥah of Dvinsk (d. 1927), moreover, gives the following as the reason for the discrimination here: the man can be "commanded" to propagate, but not the woman— for whom pregnancy and childbirth are often dangerous or painful. *She* cannot be commanded by the Torah, whose "ways are ways of pleasantness," to enter into such a state; for her it must be a matter of privilege and choice.[37] Thus is the principle of obligation, and of discharging it for others, so very much part of the halakhic structure. If it does not loom large as a problem with respect to *aliyot* to the Torah, it may do so in other areas.

Obligation and the Minyan

It also helps illuminate those areas. The *minyan* is made up of ten people who share the same degree of obligation. Not only a woman, but an adult male, to whom the obligation of statutory prayers does not apply, cannot be counted in the *minyan*. For example, during the time between the death and burial of a close relative, a man *(onen)* is exempt from *t'fillin* and from public prayer, and by that token is *not eligible* to be counted in the *minyan*.[38] Equality of men and women is not at stake here but equality of obligation. This accounts for the paradox, noted by Rabbi Jacob Emden (d. 1776), that a woman may be part of the seven aliyot but not part of the ten who make up the *minyan*.[39]

The ordinary *minyan* for daily prayers is made up of ten people who share the obligation of public prayer, of *t'fillin,* and of reciting the *Sh'ma.* Women are exept from all three since these are time-based affirmative commandments. *T'fillin,* by the way, is in a category by itself. Although the Talmud tells us that Michal, King Saul's daughter, "put on *t'fillin* and the Sages did not protest,"[40] and although Rabbenu Tam used this as additional evidence that women can "obligate themselves" and say the *b'rakhot,*[41] the law today as codified by Isserles is that "we do protest."[42]

But if there is a *minyan* for purposes other than public prayer, it can be argued that women are to be equally included. One view in the Talmud, for example, requires a *minyan* for reading the Purim *Megillah.* And, says Rabbi Joshua ben Levi, "Women are obliged to read the *Megillah* because they, too, were included in the miracle of deliverance."[43] On this basis, Rashi and Rabbi Nissim reason that women, by their reading the *Megillah,* discharge the obligation of the men present.[44] More important for our purposes, Rabbi Nissim, emerging as a fourteenth-century hero of women's liberation, argues: "How can it be that women may help fulfill the men's obligation and not be counted as part of them in the *minyan* for this purpose? Rather, they are definitely to be counted."[45]

The requirement of ten for a *minyan* is connected with the Biblical verse (Leviticus 22:32): "And I will be sanctified among the people of Israel." *B'nai yisrael* here is then associated with its first occurrence in the Bible, where it meant the ten sons of Jacob (Gen. 42:3,5).[46] Also, the "twelve men" sent by Moses as spies or scouts to Canaan were, minus Joshua and Caleb, known as "this congregation."[47] (The medieval preacher, Chief Rabbi of Prague Ephraim Luntshitz (d. 1619), advances the idea that had Moses sent women instead of men in that "congregation," the result would have been far more favorable.)[48] But the requirement of ten men for a minyan is not based on arbitrary textual or historical precedent, but on the degree of obligation. This is indicated by another instance of a *minyan* for purposes other than daily prayer. The verse, ' And I will be sanctified among the people of Israel" is also interpreted to mean that martyrdom, *kiddush ha-shem*, takes place in the presence of a *minyan*.[49] Since the obligation of martyrdom rests upon women as well, it follows, according to Rabbi Joseph Engel of Cracow (d. 1920), that they should be counted in this *minyan* as well.[50]

Conclusions

Patterns of Jewish religious observance may indeed have taken shape against the background of a strongly patriarchal society, with the resultant delineation of male and female roles in Torah study, ritual observance, and community life. But on the level of halakhic analysis, for new directions in the future as well as an understanding of past and present, an appreciation of obligation differences is essential. Even if, for example, a way is sought to include women in the *minyan,* this principle would be the starting point.

The most forbidable problem, from a strict halakhic point of view, is that of sex segregation and the attitudes and practices associated with it. This is illustrated by the incongruous suggestion of Professor Meir Friedmann, written as a Responsum to the President of the Jewish Community of Vienna in 1893. If you want to institute, or re-institute, *aliyot* for women, he wrote, "it goes without saying" that a special, covered stairway should be set up, leading the women, unseen, from and to the women's gallery![51] The problem reflected here—"mixed-pew" usage notwithstanding—is not at all simple of resolution. Sex equality is one thing, the halakhic concern with sexual distraction quite another.

This latter point is well demonstrated by consideration of just one more area of ritual observance, that of joining together (m'zumman) for Grace after Meals. Women, the Talmud concludes, are also under obligation to recite Birkat HaMazon; hence they, too, should form "the three" who "join" for this purpose.[52] Yet, the Talmud decrees that women make their own, separate m'zumman, that the sexes should not mix even for this occasion. The reason for separation is alternately given as the possibility of sexual laxity[53] or that the text varies for women. The second paragraph of the Birkat HaMazon relates thanksgiving for food to that for the gift of the Land, the Torah, and the Covenant of Circumcision. Whereas a woman nevertheless recites the text as is—because here, too, she is part of the nation to whom it more literally applies[54]—her ḥiyyuv is thus of a different order.[55] Be this as it may, important for our purposes is the reason stated for the equality of numbers: When one leads two others in reciting Grace ("Magnify ye [two] the Lord with me [one]," Psalms 34:4), not three people with an obligation are required, but simply three people with da'at," with mature awareness. "And women," says the Talmud, "have da'at." Two men would not suffice; either three men or three women, Rashi explains. (Similarly, the aforementioned Rabbi Joseph Engel again severs the customary legal link between the woman and a minor. For kiddush ha-shem, where the obligation is equal, women, unlike minors "who lack da'at," should be counted in that minyan.)[56]

If the women's movement is seen as another struggle for civil rights, and the goals of one movement confused with those of the other, then a situation of "separate but equal" is obviously unacceptable. But this is not the case where sex-role differences and sexual distraction are intrinsic factors. The demands of Ezrat Nashim should be viewed in the perspective of past—and future—categories of sex segregation and role functions. When we distinguish these legitimate values from oppressive sex discrimination, we can begin to respond.

Notes

1. Rashi, Tosafot to Megillah 22b; based on Pirkei D'Rabbi Eliezer, Ch. 45.
2. Megillah 23a.

3. Nor the Responsa: One by R. Isaac ben Sheshet of Spain (d. 1408) offers only the following: Since not everyone in the *minyan* may be capable of reading the Torah publicly, the Rabbis allowed a minor to help fill the quota. "Otherwise, a full seven who are capable may not be found. Similarly, he goes on to say, "they permitted a woman to do so, were it not for *k'vod ha-tzibbur.*" *Responsa Rivash,* No. 326.

4. *Megillah* 24b.

5. *Yoma* 90a.

6. *B'rakhot* 22a.

7. *Responsa Maharam Rotenburg,* Prague ed. No. 108; ed. Cahana, pp. 66, 100. Cf. *Yerushalmi Gittin,* Ch. V.

8. *Ravyah,* in *Mordecai* to *Gittin* (V) No. 405; *Responsa Rashba,* No. 13; *Ritva* to *K'tubot* 25b.

9. *Sefer HaParnas,* No. 206; *Mordecai* to *Gittin,* Ibid., No. 404; *Hagahot Maimuni* to *Tefillah,* Ch. 12 (No. 200); *Avudraham,* ed. Kemper, p. 71; *Adam V'Havvah,* I, 3; *Beit Yosef* to *Tur,* O.H. 282.

10. *Tosefta Kif'shutah, Moed,* pp. 1176–77. See also Note 45, below.

11. In the words of *Tos'fot RiD* to *Megillah* 23a: "This *Tosefta* is explained by the *baraita.*" An alternate version or interpretation is *ha-kol mashlimim* instead of *ha-kol olin,* which means that women may be "included," but not exhaust the seven. This version is cited by *RaN* and others, including *Beit Yosef* to *Orah Hayyim* 282, but the *Shulhan Arukh* disregards it. Isserles restores it: women make up the seven but not all the seven. Which implies, says *Magen Avraham, ad loc.,* that women cannot be part of the basic three, e.g., when only three are called. The *Gaon* of Vilna, *ad loc.,* concludes, moreover, that just one such may be called; which is explained further by Rabbi Akiva Eger, *ad loc.,* to mean the woman or minor may be included in the seven but not in less than seven; since even six (as on Yom Kippur) are basic, only one such can be called on a Sabbath morning! On the other hand, the question came before Rabbi Meir of Eisenstadt—on Rosh Hodesh Nisan (1719), like this *D'var Torah*—and he, siding with the *Shulhan Arukh,* affirmed the theoretical legality of calling a minor or a woman for any of the Torah honors that Rosh Hodesh morning. (Resp. *Panim Me'irot,* Vol. II, No. 44).

12. *Tosafot* to *Rosh Hashanah* 33a, *s.v. ha,* and parallels.

13. *Beit HaB'hirah* to *Megillah* 23.

14. *P'rishah* to *Tur O.H.* 282.

15. *Sotah* 20a; *Shulhan Arukh* Y.D. 246:6. See also *Sefer Hasidim,* Mosad Kuk ed., No. 313.

16. *Agur,* No. 2, cited in *Shulhan Arukh O.H.* 47:14.

17. *Magen Avraham* to *Shulhan Arukh O.H.* 282:3.

18. *Bir'khei Yosef, ad loc.,* No. 7. In another context (*OH* 187), *Magen Avraham* reminds us of the Midrash (*Mekhilta* to Exodus 19,3) according to which the Torah was given to the women first *(ko tomar l'veit Ya'akov).*

19. See Note 45.

20. *T'shuvot Rashi,* ed. Elfenbein, No. 68. Similarly, *Or Zarua,* Vol. II, *P'sahim,* No. 256: "They may, just as they say the *b'rakhah* when they have an *aliyah,* were it not for *k'vod ha-tzibbur . . .*"

21. *Mahzor Vitri,* No. 359, end (ed. Hurwitz, p. 413); also *Siddur Rashi,* No. 267.

22. *Mahzor Vitri, ibid.; Hagahot Maimuni,* to *Yad, Tzizit* 3:9; Rashi to *R. H.* 33a and to *Sukkah* 42a; *Hagahot Asher,* to latter; *Or Zarua,* II, 266.
23. *Sefer Tashbatz,* No. 270.
24. *Bava Kamma* 87a.
25. See note 12.
26. *Yad, Tzizit* 3:9.
27. *Azulai,* for example, in *Yosef Ometz,* No. 81, reconsiders the position he took in *Bir'khei Yosef,* and, on the basis of Jacob of Marvege of *T'shuvot Min HaShamayim* (13th cent.), permits the *b'rakhah* on *lulav.*
28. *Maggid Mishneh* to *Yad, Sukkah* 6:13.
29. *RaN* to *R.H.* 33. See Hayyim HaLevi, *M'Kor Hayyim,* Vol. I, p. 39.
30. *Rosh Hashanah* 33a; *Tosafot s.v. ha.* See *Maharasha, ad loc.,* as to why *bal tosif* is not involved.
31. *Ravad* to *Sifra,* Ch. 2. See also *S'ridei Esh,* Vol. III, No. 104.
32. *RaN* to *Megillah* Ch. III (Ch. IV of Alfasi).
33. *Mishnah R.H.* 3:8 (29a).
34. *Tosafot* to *Kiddushin* 31a s.v. gadol.
35. *Y'vamot* 65b.
36. *Hiddushei RaN* to *Kiddushin* 41; *T'shuvot RaN,* No. 20; Azulai *Homat Anakh* to Lev. 12:2. See my *Birth Control in Jewish Law,* p. 55.
37. *Meshekh Hokhmah* to Gen. 9:1. Cf. Epstein, *Baruch SheAmar* p. 21.
38. *K'nesset HaG'dolah, O.H.* 55.
39. *Hagahot Ya'vetz* to *Meg.* 23. In *She'ilat Ya'avetz,* Vol. I, No. 79: "*Aliyot* are the 'easier' than *minyan.*"
40. *Eruvin* 96a.
41. *Tosafot ad loc.* The same deduction is made by Adret, *T'shuvot Rashba,* No. 123.
42. *ReMA* to *Shulḥan Arukh O.H.* 38:3. Interestingly, the Palestinian Aramaic paraphrase of the Torah, Targum Pseudo-Jonathan, subsumes *t'fillin* (and *tzizit*) for women as an instance of "a man's garment (should not be) worn by a woman" (Deut. 22:5), though the Talmud makes no mention of this exegesis.
43. *Megillah* 4a.
44. So also *Yad, Megillah* 1:1; and, especially *Or Zarua,* Vol. II, No. 368, who rejects the reading of *Tosefta Megillah* Ch. 2 upon which *Halakhot Gedolot* apparently bases its disagreement with Rashi (see *Tosafot* to *Arakhin* 3a s.v. *la' atuyei*). Hence, *Shulḥan Arukh O.H.* 689:2 cites *yesh om'rim* that women cannot discharge the obligation of men in the matter. *Ritva* to *Megillah* 4a also discounts the *Tosefta.*
45. *RaN* to *Megillah,* Ch. 2, end, *s.v. ha-kol.* L. Ginzberg, in *Perushim V'Hiddushim Birushalmi,* Vol. II, p. 176, Note 64, suggests that *k'vod hatzibbur* is not involved in public Megillah reading by a woman (because her *hiyyuv* is equal) where it would be at Torah reading. Yet, *Sefer Mitzvot Gadol,* of Moses of Coucy, says a woman cannot discharge men's obligations of Megillah because it is "like Torah reading," which leads Rabbi Eliyahu Mizraḥi, in his Commentary thereto, to introduce *k'vod hatzibbur* as the reason despite equal *hiyyuv.* The explanations dovetail, and a new understanding of *k'vod hatzibbur* is gained, through the viewpoint of Ritva (in his and Rashba's name) to *Megillah* 4a: Her equal *hiyyuv* means she may discharge the public's obliga-

tion by her Megillah reading; but, just as a woman may do the same with Grace after Meals for her illiterate husband, "a curse light on the man whose wife or children must say Grace for him" (*B'rakhot* 20b) or the *Hallel* for him (*Sukkah* 38a). Shame on him, say Rashi and Tosafot, for not having learned how to read it himself.

46. *Yerushalmi B'rakhot* VII, 3.

47. *B'rakhot* 21b and parallels.

48. *Kli Yakar* to Numbers 13:2.

49. *Sanhedrin* 74b.

50. *Gilyonei HaShas* to *Sanhedrin* 74b. (*Minhat Hinnukh* to No. 296, would not agree.) Also, *Margaliyot HaYam* to *Sanhedrin* 74b, No. 27: Since she has the *ḥiyyuv*, she is counted, as opposed to the case of public prayer.

51. *Mitwirkung von Frauen beim Gottesdienste*, in HUCA, vol. VIII-IX (p. 521).

52. *B'rakhot* 45b; *Arakhin* 3a.

53. *B'rakhot* 45b; *Rabbenu Yonah* and *Hame'iri*, *ad loc.* The applicability of this reason to family groups is really not clear from the Talmud, especially since the women's *zimmun* may be discharged by the men's "when they eat together"—*Responsa Rosh* IV, 16; *Shulḥan Arukh OH* 199:7. Mentioned often is the example of Rabbi Simḥah of Speyer (13th cent.), who permitted counting women to the minyan for *zimmun* (even to the "three," according to *Agur*, No. 249) and his ruling is accepted by *Mordecai* to *B'rakhot* (Nos. 158 and 173), though *Agur*, No. 240, says he has never seen nor heard this in practice. Rabbi Simḥah and Rabbenu Tam are cited to that effect, as are Rabbi Yehudah HaKohen and *Rosh*, by *Shiltei HaGibborim* to Alfasi, *B'rakhot* VII, beg., who adds that the majority of *pos'kim* differ. Rabbi Aaron HaLevi to *B'rakhot* 45 and *RaN* to *Megillah* Ch. 2, end, also permit counting women to the minyan of *zimmun*, as does *BaH* to *Tur OH* 689.

The Talmud's requirement of separate *zimmun* may mean separate from slaves to avoid *pritzuta*, but not separate from husbands, says *D'rishah* to *Tur*, *ad loc.* A series of halakhic texts by 13th-century Provencal authorities has just been published. Rabbi Meir Narbonne (d. 1263) in his *Sefer HaMe'orot* (citing *Sefer HaHashlamah* of Meshullam of Beziers, and being cited later by Manoah of Narbonne in *Sefer HaMenuhah*) makes it clear that *pritzuta*, and thus separate *zimmun*, does not apply to free men and women eating together. Nevertheless, commentaries such as *Elyah Rabbah* (R. Elijah Shapiro of Prague, d. 1712) to *L'vush* 199 say that regardless of theory, our custom is to separate.

54. *Bedek HaBayit* to *Tur*, *HO* 187. Cf. *Magen Avraham* thereto.

55. *B'rakhot* 49a; *Tosafot* to *B'rakhot* 20b and *Arakhin* 3a, *(s.v. m'zamm'not)*; *Or Zarua*, Vol. II, No. 368; *Leket Yosher*, *O.H.* p. 38 in the name of Isserlein. Cf. *Gan HaMelekh*, No. 75; and *Tzlakh*, *B'rakhot*, p. 95.

56. Note 50, above.

RABBI ISRAEL SILVERMAN deals in this teshuvah *(responsum)
with the question of the use of non-Jewish wine. Though the practice for centuries was to drink only wine produced by Jews, Silverman shows that under modern means of production, the reasons
for the prohibitions no longer apply. This is true because the wines
in our times are mechanically produced without the intervention
of human beings. Rabbi Silverman, however, urges that for ritual
purposes, Jewish wine be used and especially urges the use of Israeli wine.*

307

Are All Wines Kosher?

ISRAEL NISSAN SILVERMAN

Translated from the Hebrew by the Editors.

The Question. Many of my colleagues in the Rabbinical Assembly have asked whether it is permitted to drink the wine known as champagne. Although champagne bubbles when it is poured into a glass, and therefore is different from ordinary wine, it is produced from grapes and therefore is included in the category of *s'tam yeenam.* [wine made by gentiles falls into two categories: *ye'en nesekh*—wine used for offering libations to idols, and *s'tam yeenam*—wine of which it is not known whether it has been dedicated to an idol. (ed.)][1]

The Responsum.

Rabbi Moses Isserles (1525 or 1530–1572) was asked:[2] "In regard to the custom which has spread in the province of Moravia as well as in other provinces, namely, being lenient in drinking the wine of non-Jews [*s'tam yeenam*]: The authorities apparently do not object. Is there something which those who follow this custom can rely on?"

Rabbi Isserles answered:

> We have learned [in the Tractate *Baba Batra* 89b] . . . Regarding the deceptive methods employed by some unscrupulous merchants, that Rabban Yochanan ben Zakkai said: "Woe to me if I should speak of them, for knaves might thus learn them [the methods]. Woe to me if I do not speak, for knaves might say that the scholars are unacquainted with our practices." They asked the question: "Did he or did he not say it?" Rabbi Shmuel ben Rabbi Yitzkhok said: "He said it, relying on the verse: 'for the ways of the Lord are right, and the just walk in them, but the transgressors do stumble therein!' [Hosea 14:10]."

I share the sentiments of Rabbi Moses Isserles as I approach the task of finding a *heter* (leniency) for drinking non-Jewish wines currently produced in America—"Woe to me if I say it [leniency], woe to me if I do not say it."

Rabbi Moses Isserles, however, went on to state in his *teshuvah:* "I have seen that there is some good to find justification for their leniency in this matter." It is also incumbent upon us to find some justification.

First of all, in regard to *ye'en nesekh* (the wine of libation, i.e., wine specifically designated for ritual use in idolatrous worship), the *gaonim* and the majority of the later authorities have written in their response that non-Jews in our time are not experts on libations and their use.[3] Thus it is clear that the general category of *ye'en nesekh* does not exist in our time, especially in America. Therefore, all wines produced by non-Jews in America are classified not as *ye'en nesekh* but as *s'tam yeenam*, "non-Jewish wine." No one today denies that it is permitted to benefit from such wine *(mutar b'hana'ah)*,[4] but is it permitted to *drink* such wine as well?

In the Mishnah of *Avodah Zarah* (2:6) we read: "These things of the gentiles are forbidden [i.e., they may not be eaten], though it is not forbidden to [otherwise] benefit from them: their bread and their oil . . . stewed or pickled vegetables . . ." These prohibitions were made, according to Rashi and the *gemarah*, "because of marriage" (i.e., due to the prohibition against eating these foods, Jews and non-Jews would have no social contacts and thus would avoid intermarriage).

In the Mishnah preceding the one cited above, it is written: "These things of gentiles are prohibited, and it is also prohibited to have any benfit from them: wine . . ." According to Rashi, this prohibition is due to the possibility that "perhaps he used it [the wine] as a libation [in an idolatrous rite]." In our day, however, when non-Jews are not experts on libations, the reason for not drinking gentile wine is "because of marriage" (i.e., the fear of possible intermarriage resulting from social contact).[5]

It is interesting to note that since the time when the prohibitions against eating the four categories of food mentioned above were made, all of them except wine have become permissible.

Oil. Rabbi Yehudah Hanasi and his school permitted the consumption of non-Jewish oil because the prohibition had not been adopted by the majority of Jews, and we do not impose a decree upon the community unless the majority of the community can abide by it.[6]

Bread. In the time of Rabbi Yehudah, eating the bread of non-Jews was permitted. It is stated in the Jerusalem Talmud *(Avodah Zarah* 41d): "In a place where there is no Jewish bread, the bread of the non-Jews should have been prohibited. But they disregarded [the law] concerning this, and they made it [the bread of non-Jews] permitted because it was a necessity of life." There are those who believe that this leniency also resulted from the fact that the prohibition had not been accepted throughout the Jewish community.[7]

Foods cooked by non-Jews. The prohibition against eating foods cooked by non-Jews *(shelakot)* is very ancient, even preceding the prohibition against eating non-Jewish bread. Rabbi Yehudah Hanasi and his school did not permit *shelakot*.[8] The later Rabbis limited the prohibition by instituting two important rules. First, any food which can also be eaten raw (e.g., fruit) does not fall under the prohibition of "foods cooked by non-Jews," even when it is cooked. Second, any food which is not served on the table of kings is also permitted, since it is not served to guests, and the rule "because of marriage" is thus not applicable. In our own day, as we know, the custom of being lenient has spread to almost all Jewish homes in regard to the prohibition against "foods cooked by non-Jews," to a greater extent than the Rabbis permitted. This is especially true regarding cooked foods sold in cans or jars.

In regard to wine, there is also an obvious lenient tendency. At first it was prohibited to benefit in any way from non-Jewish wine. When it became obvious that non-Jews were no longer experts on libations, the authorities became lenient and permitted Jews to benefit from non-Jewish wines (though not to drink then). This was especially true in France, where Jews were very prominent in the production of wine for sale, and where it was customary for Jews to accept non-Jewish wine as payment for debts.[9]

In our time, because of the reasons which follow, it seems to me that we may also permit the consumption of non-Jewish wine which is produced in large factories.

1. In the production of wine in modern factories, the wine is made entirely by means of machines. (Because of the exigencies of competition, contemporary wine-producers are forced to utilize the most modern production techniques.) No human hand comes into contact with the product from the moment the grapes are placed in the crusher machine until the entire production process is completed and the wine resulting from it is placed in sealed containers under the supervision of federal tax inspectors.[10] The only exception is certain permissible handling of the wine with utensils which will be explained below.

During the production of wine today, experts occasionally remove some wine from the large containers in order to taste and examine it. This is always done with a utensil (i.e., the experts do not actually touch the wine; they take the wine with a ladle or some other utensil and they do not come into physical contact with the wine).

Rabbi Yaakov Castro (Egypt, 1525–1612), in his book *Erekh Lechem* (no. 124:7), writes:

> A Karaite does not make wine prohibited by his touching it. However, there is reason to prohibit such wine unless he [the Karaite] swears that a non-Jew had not touched it. An oath would be sufficent, for the Karaites are cautious about taking oaths, even though they are not concerned about non-Jews touching their wine. These are the words of the author of the *Kaftor veFerach* [Rabbi Estori Hafarchi]. In our lands I have seen that it is customary to drink [the wine of Karaites] even though the oath was not taken. Perhaps the reason for this is that the Ishmaelites amongst whom we live are not idolaters and we do not base a prohibition on a mere possibility. [i.e., the possibility that the wine of the Karaites had been touched by a non-Jew, and even if this were so, the non-Jew would not be an idolater (ed.)].

At the end of paragraph 127 Castro writes:

> There are those who say that in our time, when the non-Jews are not knowledgeable regarding libations, whenever they do touch wine it is not considered for purposes of making a libation, and therefore if the wine were touched with a utensil it would be permitted to drink [the wine].

Rabbi Raphael ben Eleazar Meldola (1754–1828), in his book *Mayim Rabbim* (pt. II, no. 28), writes:

> It is clearly apparent that the great scholars of the past have left us a wide open door making it possible to permit having benefit from wine touched by non-Jews in our day. Therefore, if the touching took place without the intention [of libation] and through the medium of some utensil, as in the matter before us, we descend one rung, and permit even the drinking of the wine, since the non-Jews in our days are not accustomed to make libations.

Rabbi Levi ibn Habib (ca. 1483–1545), in his responsum #41, permitted the drinking of wine which was touched by a non-Jew who had no intention of making a libation, relying on the view of Rabbi Shmuel b. Meir, the Rashbam (ca. 1080–1174; Rahsbam quotes his grandfather, Rashi, to the effect that the *gaonim* ruled that non-Jews in our own day

are not knowledgeable about libations). In the responsa of Rabbi Jacob
Weil (d. before 1456) it is written (no. 26): "For this reason I permitted
the drinking of wine where the non-Jewish worker put his stick into
the barrel of wine. It involved the touching of wine by a non-Jew by
means of something else without the intention of making a libation.
This was permitted by Rabbenu Tam [Rabbi Yaakov Tam, 1100–1171]
as well."

Rabbi Moses Isserles adds:

> Every place where there is no suspicion of idolatry, wine is not more strin-
> gent than intoxicating spirits of non-Jews about which we say in the sec-
> ond chapter of the Tractate *Avodah Zarah* 31b [see also *Tosaphot ad lo-
> cum.*, s.v. *v'tarveyhu mishum chatnut*] that it [i.e., the spirits] is prohibited
> because of "marriage." Nevertheless, we say that Rav Papa would take it
> outside the door of the store and drink it, and that Rav Ahai brought it to
> his house and drank it. Therefore the same law would apply to wine in our
> own time [i.e., drinking it should be permitted just as the drinking of spir-
> its was apparently permitted]. Even though the prohibition against wine is
> of greater force than the prohibition against other intoxicating beverages,
> since alcoholic beverages were not prohibited either in the Mishnah or in a
> *Beraita*, but the prohibition was instituted during the time of the *Amo-
> raim*, as was noted in the *Tosaphot* cited above. Nevertheless, we can say
> that this additional stringency against wine was true in their day when
> Jews were prohibited from deriving any benefit from *s'tam yeenam* even
> when the non-Jew only touched it, but in our day, since we are not prohib-
> ited from deriving benefit from wine [because the non-Jews are presumed
> not to be knowledgeable about libations], we are not more stringent con-
> cerning wine than concerning other substances which were prohibited be-
> cause of "their daughters."

There are workers employed in the production of wine who open
and close various taps in order to insure the flow of the wine from one
barrel to another. Regarding this kind of problem, the *Rama* wrote in
his glosses *(Yoreh Deah,* no. 124:24):

> It would be permitted [even for drinking] if he inserted a tap into the bar-
> rel or removed it without any intention [of making a libation]. In these
> times, non-Jews are not considered idolaters, and all of their touchings are
> considered to be "without intention." Therefore, if he touched the wine by
> means of a utensil, even though he knows it is wine, and even though he
> intentionally touches it, it is permitted to drink the wine since it is consid-

ered as "touching by means of a utensil without intention." However, it is
not advisable to publicize this among the ignorant.

Therefore, it is possible to allow the drinking of wine produced in
modern factories since no human being touches it, except in the permissible manner just explained.

2. In our own time there is still another consideration which permits
us to be lenient. We read in the Tractate *Avodah Zarah* (30a): "Wine
which is boiled does not come under the category of wine for libation."
The fact is that in the production of wine in our time, all wine can be
considered "boiled wine" since all wines go through the process of
pasteurization.

It is true that the Rabbi Louis Ginzberg, in his responsum concerning the permissibility of using grape juice for ritual purposes (where
wine is required), wrote:

> "In order that those who cavil should not say that he [the responder] has
> permitted boiled wine, about which there is controversy among the early
> authorities, I wish to say that grape juice is not considered "boiled wine"
> since it is not heated to the boiling point, and at a lower temperature [i.e.,
> below the boiling point] it is not considered "boiled wine.""

However, in the commentary *Be'er Hetev* to *Yoreh Deah* 123:3 it is
written: "It can be considered 'boiled wine' if the heating process di-
minishes the volume of the wine." I have it on excellent authority that
the pasterurization process does diminish the volume of the wine.
Therefore, according to this halakhic definition, pasteurized wine can
be considered "boiled wine" even when it does not reach the boiling
point. Therefore, from this point of view, it is possible to permit the
drinking of wine produced by non-Jews in America today.

3. In addition to these considerations, it is important to point out that
the non-Jews in our day—i.e., the Christians, and especially the Catholics—who use wine in their worship, use wines produced especially
for these purposes which are not sold on the open market. I have it on
the authority of a Catholic priest, who holds an important post in his
Church in the city of Boston, that it is prohibited for a Catholic to use
champagne for purposes of worship. Also prohibited are stronger spirits, such as cognac and brandy. Incidentally, it is interesting to point
out that Catholics use bread and oil in their worship, and in regard to
these substances our Sages long ago were lenient.

I wish to add three important points to this discussion:

1. In the Land of Israel today, the wine industry is very highly developed. The wines produced there win awards in all kinds of international competitions. Since the economic situation in the Holy Land is not of the best, it is a special mitzvah for every Jew, wherever he resides, to purchase the wines produced in our ancestral homeland, which are kosher without any question (Professor Ginzberg, of blessed memory, has pointed out that our Sages enacted many decrees for the purpose of improving the economic situation of the Land of Israel).

2. Especially when wine is required for the fulfillment of a mitzvah, such as the ceremonies of circumcision, weddings, kiddush, and havdalah, it is proper to use Jewish wine, and especially wine produced in Israel. Just as a Jew is commanded to enhance the fulfillment of the commandments of sukkah, lulav, etrog, and of festive Sabbath and Festival meals, it is proper that he enhance the fulfillment of the mitzvah through the use of Jewish wine when he fulfills the mitzvah of kiddush.

3. Anything that has been said in this responsum regarding non-Jewish wine is not applicable during Passover. I am convinced that the production of wine in America raises many questions involving leaven.[11] Therefore, during Passover, wine which has not been supervised by a competent rabbinic authority should not be used.

Notes

1. a. In the course of preparing this responsum, I visited several plants where wine and distilled spirits are produced. I also consulted several experts in the field and studied various published materials, including the relevant articles in the *Encyclopedia of Chemical Technology* and the *Encyclopaedia Britannica* (1947 ed.) as well as *The Wine Industry* and *Wine Growing and Wine Types*, two pamphlets published by the Wine Advisory Board. As a result, I believe I am well informed about the technical aspects of wine production in this country.

b. I have learned from specialists in the field that automatic machinery is not used in the production of wine in some places in Spain, France, Italy, and other countries, and that in some cases the workers still press the grapes with their feet, exactly as it was done hundreds of years ago. These practices raise questions which I cannot deal with here. Nevertheless, even in Europe and elsewhere some wine is produced through the same methods used in the United States, i.e., by means of automatic machinery—and wine so produced would have the same status as American wines.

c. One of my colleagues, who served in France with the U.S. Army during

World War II, has informed me that in many areas there are small churches or shrines in the vineyards. This also raises several questions. Therefore, this responsum is concerned *only* with wines that are produced through the use of automatic machinery in plants operated by large, well-known wine companies.

2. The *she'lot u-teshuvot* of Rabbi Moses Isserles, no. 124. This responsum was omitted in many editions. It appears in the Cracow edition, 1710.

3. In the Tractate *Avodah Zarah* 14b, it is written: "Rav Hisda said to Abimi: 'We have learned that the Tractate of *Avodah Zarah* of Abraham our Father contained four hundred chapters, and we have only five chapters, and we are not even positive what they are saying.'" This means that already in the days of Rab Hisda they recognized that idolatry was waning in the world. See also the *Tosaphot (Avodah Zarah* 57b, s.v. *La-afokey Midrav):* "The *Rashbam* and the *Rivan* explained in the name of Rashi that it is written in the responsa of the *Gaonim* that in these times there is no prohibition against deriving benefit from wine which was touched by a non-Jew since in these days they are not accustomed to making libations before idols, and they [i.e., the non-Jews] are considered as those who are not knowledgeable about idolatry and the cult connected with it, and they have the same status as newborn babes [i.e., they have no knowledge of the cultic practices of idol-worshippers], and we rely on this to take the wines of non-Jews as payment for their debts." Also in regard to libations, Rabbi Moses Isserles wrote *(Yoreh Deah,* no. 132): "However in our day, when the idolaters do not pour libations . . . " The same was written by the author of the book *Erekh Lechem:* "In our times the non-Jews do not know the nature of libations . . . " Also, the author of the book *Mayim Rabbim:* "The non-Jews of our time are not accustomed to make libations." And similarly, many more authorities.

4. The *Tosaphot* to *Avodah Zarah* 57b (s.v. *La-afokey Midrav,* at the end): "It is a question how do we permit having benefit from the wine of non-Jews, since there is a prohibition against their wine because of their daughters, and nowadays that reason still applies [i.e., though the suspicion of libation is gone, there is still the possibility of intermarriage]. It is possible to say that when they prohibited even deriving benefit from the wine of non-Jews more than they prohibited their bread and their wine, it was because there were non-Jews who still used wine for libations before idols. But since that is no longer applicable, because the non-Jews are not knowledgeable in the nature of libations, it is enough that their wine should be considered in the same category as their oil and their bread or their cooked vegetables, and therefore it would be prohibited from drinking, but not from having any benefit from it. 'But he who is stringent may he be blessed.'" See also what the Rama wrote in his glosses, *Yoreh Deah* 123:1: "In these days when the non-Jews are accustomed to pour libations before idols, their wine is only prohibited from drinking, but not from deriving benefit."

See also the book *Erekh Lechem* (Constantinople, 1718) by Joseph Castro, who wrote (no. 123a): "The Muslims are not idolaters, and therefore their wine is permitted to have benefit from it. There are those who permit wine [to have benefit] even when touched by Christians. There are those who are lenient in regard to all non-Jewish wine, and on the occasion of great loss we rely on those who are lenient. However, those stringent should be blessed."

5. In the Tractate *Avodah Zarah* 36b, we read: "They prohibited their bread and their oil because of their wine, and their wine [was prohibited] because of their daughters, and their daughters because of another thing [i.e., idolatry]." It is interesting that the prohibitions against bread and oil were lifted in the days of Rabbi Judah Hanasi. The *Rama,* of blessed memory, wrote that the prohibition against the wine of non-Jews is not more serious than the other "because of their daughters" prohibitions. In our time these prohibitions have dissolved. It is a fact that intermarriage is not *only* a direct result of the drinking of non-Jewish wine.

6. The Rebbe who is mentioned here is certainly the grandson of Rabbi Yehuda the Prince. See *Avodah Zarah* 35b.

7. *Sefer Ha-eshkol,* Pt. II, no. 49.

8. See n. 5 above.

9. See the *Machzor Vitri, Hilchot Ye'en Nesekh,* No. 115. See also Baron, *A Social and Religious History of the Jews,* Vol. 6, pp. 128 ff. (apparently there is a contradiction between the responsa of Rashi and the *Machzor Vitri* in regard to the acceptance of non-Jewish wine for the payment of debts to a Jew). Cf. *Tosaphot (Avodah Zarah* 57b s.v. *La-afokey Midrav).* See also Baron, *op. cit.,* vol. 4, p. 317, n. 14, regarding the role of French Jews in the wine industry.

10. There are merchants who purchase wine from factories in very large barrels, and they themselves bottle the wine under government supervision. Even in these instances, the hands of human beings do not touch the wine, except for experts and workers who contact the wine only by means of another object—as we have explained—and therefore they are all permitted.

11. In the production of wine, substances that speed up the process of fermentation are used, and also machines that fill the bottles with wine. These machines and substances are used during the year for all kinds of fermented spirits.

Glossary

AGGADAH. Jewish ideas and theology.

AGUNAH. A woman who is unable to obtain a divorce from her husband, either because his whereabouts are not known or because he refuses to grant her one.

AMORA. A post-Mishnaic rabbi.

ASHKENAZ[I]. The Jews of Eastern Europe and Germany, and their customs.

BERAITA (PL. *beraitot*). A Tanaitic statement not canonized in the Mishnah of Judah HaNasi.

BIMAH. The pulpit.

CHALITZAH. If a married man dies without progeny, his brother (*yabam*) must offer to marry his wife. The ceremony freeing the widow and the brother from this marriage is called *chalitzah*.

DERASH. The exegetical meaning of a text.

D'VAR TORAH. A sermon based on the Torah portion of the week.

GAONIM. The highest Jewish legal authorities in Babylonia between the sixth and eleventh centuries.

GEHINOM. The place reserved for sinners after death.

GET. A Jewish divorce.

317

HALACHAH. Jewish law.

HETER. A leniency.

HETER ISKA. A leniency providing Jews a method to lend money and collect interest from other Jews.

KABBALAH. The esoteric teachings of Judaism and Jewish mysticism.

KADDISH. The Aramaic prayer affirming faith in God, usually associated with the death of a relative.

KARAITES. The group involved in a movement begun in the first part of the eighth century, which negated the authority of the rabbis and the Talmud.

KOHEN (PL. *Kohanim*). Member of the priestly class descended from Aaron.

MASKIL. An adherent of the nineteenth-century European Enlightenment movement.

MINHAG. Jewish custom.

MINYAN. The required quorum for public prayer.

MOHEL. A person authorized to perform a ritual circumcision.

PESHAT. The literal meaning of a text.

PILPUL. A method of rabbinic argumentation involving the the use of fine distinctions and detailed analysis.

RASHI. Eleventh-century French scholar and commentator.

SANHEDRIN. The supreme governmental and religious authority in Israel during Roman times. Napoleon attempted to ressurrect this body in France during his religious reforms.

SEPHARAD[I]. Referring to Jews originally from Spain and Northern Africa, and their customs.

SEFIRA. The seven-week period intervening between Passover and the Feast of Weeks (Shavuot).

SHECHINAH. The mystical presence of God.

SHALIACH. A messenger.

SHOCHET. A person authorized to slaughter animals according to ritual law.

TAKKANAH. A rabbinical edict.

TALLIT. A prayer shawl.

TANNA. A rabbi of the period preceding the canonization of the Mishnah.

TERAIFOT. Non-kosher food.

TESHUVAH (PL. *Teshuvot*). A legal opinion offered by a rabbi in response to a specific problem.

TOSAFOT. The commentaries on the Talmud attributed to the school of the grandchildren of Rashi.

TOSEFTA. A collection of *baraitot*. *see* BERAITA.

TZITZIT. The fringes on the corners of a four-cornered garment.

Notes on Contributors

JACOB AGUS, a long-time member of the Committee on Jewish Law and Standards, is on the faculty of the Reconstructionist Rabbinical College and Temple University, serves as the Rabbi of Beth El Synagogue in Baltimore. Among his writings are *Guideposts in Modern Judaism* and *Modern Philosophies of Judaism*.

AARON H. BLUMENTHAL is a member of the Committee on Jewish Law and Standards and is the Rabbi Emeritus of the Emanuel Jewish Center in White Plains. He is the author of many responsa.

BOAZ COHEN was Professor of Talmud at the Jewish Theological Seminary until his death. He also served as Secretary and Chairman of the Committee on Jewish Law and Standards. His works include *Kunteres haTeshuvot* and *Law and Tradition in Judaism*.

DAVID M. FELDMAN, a member of the Rabbinical Assembly Committee on Jewish Law and Standards, is Rabbi of the Bay Ridge Jewish Center. He has published many works, including *Birth Control in Jewish Law*.

LOUIS FINKELSTEIN is Chancellor Emeritus of the Jewish Theological Seminary as well as the Solomon Schechter Professor in Theology and Joseph M. and Dorothy Levine Research Professor in Talmudic Ethics. Among his works are *The Pharisees* and *Akiba: Scholar, Saint and Martyr*.

LOUIS GINZBERG served for over half a century as Professor of Talmud and Ethics at the Jewish Theological Seminary. A book of essays,

321

Students Scholars and Saints, and the scholarly *Legends of the Jews* are among the best known of his works.

SIMON GREENBERG is Vice-Chancellor and Professor of Homiletics and Education at the Jewish Theological Seminary. He has published *Foundations of a Faith* and *Words of Poetry* among other books and articles.

ROBERT GORDIS is Meyer and Fannie Rappaport Professor in Philosophies of Religion and Professor of Bible at the Jewish Theological Seminary. He has been President of the Rabbinical Assembly and Rabbi of Temple Beth El in Rockaway Park, New York. His works include *The Root and the Branch, Judaism for the Modern Age,* and the forthcoming *Commentary on the Book of Job.*

WILL HERBERG was Graduate Professor of Judaic Studies and Social Philosophy at Drew University. His works include *Judaism and Modern Man* and *Protestant–Catholic–Jew.*

ABRAHAM JOSHUA HESCHEL was Ralph Simon Professor of Theology and Ethics at the Jewish Theological Seminary until his death. His works include *God in Search of Man* and *The Theology of Ancient Israel* among others.

MAX KADUSHIN has been a rabbi for many years and is Professor of Ethics and Rabbinic Thought at the Jewish Theological Seminary. His works include *Organic Thinking* and *Worship and Ethics.*

LOUIS JACOBS is the Rabbi of the New West End Synagogue in London, England. He has authored, among other works, *We Have Reason to Believe,* and *Principles of the Jewish Faith.*

MORDECAI M. KAPLAN has been on the faculty of the Jewish Theological Seminary for almost seventy years. He is the founder and first Rabbi of the Society for the Advancement of Judaism, the cornerstone of the Reconstructionist movement. His works include *Judaism as a Civilization* and *The Religion of Ethical Nationhood.*

ISAAC KLEIN has served for many years on the Committee on Jewish Law and Standards, and on the faculty of the Jewish Theological Seminary. His works include *Respona and Halakhic Studies,* and the forthcoming *Guide to Jewish Religious Practice.*

SEYMOUR SIEGEL is Ralph Simon Professor of Theology and Ethics at the Jewish Theological Seminary. He serves as Chairman of the Committee on Jewish Law and Standards of the Rabbinical Assembly, and is the editor of this volume.

PHILLIP SIGAL is the author of many responsa and a member of the Committee on Jewish Law and Standards.

ISRAEL SILVERMAN is the Rabbi of Beth Jacob Synagogue in Hamilton, Ontario, and a member of the Committee on Jewish Law and Standards. He is the author of many articles and responsa.

ERNST SIMON is Professor of Philosophy and History of Education at the Hebrew Universtiy in Jerusalem. He is the author of many works on scholarly themes.

Index